FIND IT FAST

FIND IT FAST

FOURTH EDITION

*How to Uncover
Expert Information
on Any Subject*

Robert I. Berkman

HarperPerennial

A Division of HarperCollinsPublishers

Copyright acknowledgments follow the index.

HarperCollins books may be purchased for educational, business, or sales promotional use. For information, please write: Special Markets Department, HarperCollins Publishers, Inc., 10 East 53rd Street, New York, NY 10022.

FOURTH EDITION

LIBRARY OF CONGRESS CATALOGING-IN-PUBLICATION DATA

Berkman, Robert I.
Find it fast : how to uncover expert information on any subject / Robert I. Berkman. — 4th ed.
    p. cm.
Includes index.
ISBN 0–06–273473–3
    1. Information retrieval. 2. Research. I. Title.
ZA3075.B47 1997   96-52526
025.5'24—dc21   CIP

97 98 99 00 01 ❖/RRD 10 9 8 7 6 5 4 3 2 1

To Sol, Pat,
Budd, and Don

Contents

PART I: UNLOCKING THE INFORMATION VAULT

Contents

PART II: EXPERTS ARE EVERYWHERE

Acknowledgments

I'd like to express my gratitude to the people who in one way or another had a big part in making this book come to pass.

Mary Walsh gave me encouragement at the most critical moments—without it, this book would not have been written. George Finnegan has been a true mentor. I'll always be thankful for the chance to work for him and receive a once-in-a-lifetime learning opportunity. Janet Goldstein, my editor at HarperCollins, believed enough in the book to give it a chance, and always gave me her support and great ideas.

I'm grateful to Nancy Brandwein, Ken Coughlin, and Lilli Warren, all of whom provided critical insights, suggestions, and critiques of the final manuscript.

I also want to thank Sandy Gollop for her assistance, knowledge, and kindness; my colleagues at PIN for their encouragement and interest in the book; Debbie Cohen for her hard work and sharp eye for detail; Ginny Fisher; Leigh Woods; and Pam and Jeff Goodman for so generously helping me out in the final stages. Trisha Karsay put in a lot of hours and top-notch work—her enthusiasm for the book meant a lot to me and is genuinely appreciated.

A special thank-you goes to everyone in the Norris family up in Cape Cod for providing me with such a beautiful and relaxing spot to think and write.

And finally, thanks to my parents and brothers for their love, support, and invaluable ideas.

Preface to the Fourth Edition of *Find It Fast*

What a difference a few years makes! The last time this book was updated, in 1994, the Internet discussion took up all of 3½ pages! Today, the entire space of this book could be filled discussing doing research on the Net. In fact, the Internet has become such a force that doing research is almost becoming synonymous with searching the Internet! In the space of those few short years, the Net has evolved from a fairly obscure computer network known only to a small percent of the population to a near mass phenomena world-wide. Research guides that today discuss using libraries and magazines are beginning to seem positively old-fashioned!

But while it is true that the Internet is, indeed, an incredible source of information on virtually any topic of human endeavor, contrary to what some may think, it is certainly *not* the last word for researchers. It remains one of many tools at your disposal, and like all tools, the key is to know *when* to use it, *how* to best use it, and when to use a *different* tool. Much of chapter 5 of this book is devoted expressly to examining research on the Net—what you can find, how to perform an effective search, and what are the drawbacks.

In the last edition, we also briefly mentioned the growing problem of an "infoglut"—the fact that there seems to be just "too much" information to deal with. A few years later, it's clear that the problem has gotten worse, not better. Today, in addition to regular mail, telephone messages, and print journals, you now also have to deal with voice mail, E-mail, and the 20,000-plus items that your Internet search engine just served up to you! Now that's information overload!

Now, of course, the same firms that helped create the infoglut are turning around and kindly creating new technological solutions to your information overload problems. Intelligent agents, Personalized Broadcast Networks, customized news services, off-site Web browsers, and a whole host of technological solutions to electronic information overload are being introduced. While these devices may indeed be of use in some situations, I'd advise being wary of technology as the solution. Belgian futurist Michel Bauwens has noted that the science fiction writer Tom Maddox has written that "any device we invent to filter information to come into circulation causes more information to come into circulation than it can filter." So, paradoxically, just as laying down highways around the country to handle traffic resulted in more cars on the road, making it easier to access data will likely just speed up its production! And it is unlikely in the foreseeable future that computers will be able to replace the subtleties of human judgment in determining what information is truly worth noting and reading.

Individuals, of course, aren't the only ones whose lives have been changed by the Internet. Libraries around the country and around the world are trying to reinvent themselves—figuring out how to remain true to their original mission of providing access to information to all, while still offering the latest technologies to an increasingly information-savvy clientele. Some are predicting the emergence of "virtual libraries"—libraries purged of most of their physical collections and holdings, which provide their patrons with online access and "just in time" delivery of vast cybercollections of electronic journals and books.

Another institution that finds itself enmeshed by the Net are publishers and newspaper companies. Several hundred newspapers and magazines have launched electronic versions on the

Internet, and the vast majority of them are free. Many of these publishers are caught, though, in something of a bind: They feel that they need to have a presence on the Web but have yet to figure out how to actually charge for their news and information, and make money!

Some analysts, in fact, are even predicting that soon publishers may not even be able to charge for information, since so much information is being made available free on the Net, and that the Internet's model of free access is becoming the dominant model. According to this theory, businesses, authors, publishers, and consultants that have in the past been able to charge for information will soon have to rely on other means to bring in revenue (e.g., consulting, training, software development, etc.) and that their information publishing activities will only be done to attract new customers for their other services. Perhaps author Stewart Brand's remark that "information wants to be free" will be realized by the Net.

Another trend that I think you can expect to see pick up steam is the antitechnology backlash, which was already starting around 1994 but is now growing faster. Many thoughtful authors and writers are taking a critical look at all the promises that information technology has made for society, and are finding those promises wanting. I've named what I feel to be some of the best of these books in the appendix.

Okay, enough about the Internet already! What else has been happening in the information and research world since this book was last published? Well, at that time, CD-ROMs were coming into their own, and while that technology has been eclipsed somewhat by the excitement over the Internet, searching CD-ROMs for free at your library still represents one of the most efficient and powerful ways to conduct research. The consumer online services—America Online, CompuServe, Prodigy, and Microsoft Network—are battling to stay relevant in the Internet age. All offer full access to the Internet and are integrating their services more tightly with the Net. (If this is confusing to you, chapter 5 will help you understand the differences between consumer online and the Internet, and how they intersect.)

Other than CompuServe though, which offers some very powerful databases, the other consumer online services' research-

oriented offerings are fairly lightweight. Serious researchers have traditionally turned to the professional online firms—companies like Dialog, Dow Jones, and Lexis/Nexis to conduct the most powerful and sophisticated database searching. But these services are also feeling pressure from the Internet. A typical search on one of these services might run around $25 to $50, but as the Internet's model of free, cheap and easy information becomes the norm, these companies are also rethinking their services. Dow Jones, for example, moved its entire "text library" of searchable magazines from its expensive Dow Jones News/Retrieval service to its *Wall Street Journal* interactive site and made it available for a very modest per-year subscription fee. Some have predicted that these firms may not be able to survive the new information world.

Well, as you can see, I did try to discuss something other than the Internet, but ended up discussing all these services within the context of the Net. This just goes to show you how all-encompassing and influential it has become. What about print sources, then? Where do they stand in the age of the Internet? While it is true that many print journals are now available on the Net, and that some are predicting the demise of print, if this were to ever occur, it is a very long way off. The vast majority of the world's knowledge still resides in hardcopy books, directories, and journals. Print also still retains certain advantages that computer technology has not been able to replicate: portability, ease of browsing, and the simple fact that is more pleasing to read ink on paper than glowing phosphorus on a computer screen. Just as the radio did not wipe out newspapers, and television did not eliminate radio, print will continue to coexist with the new media—at least for the foreseeable future.

Ultimately, as we move into an age where there seems to be an unlimited amount of data available at one's fingertips, it becomes even more important not just to know *where* to find data or how to access the Internet, but how to choose the *right* type of source and *understand* each medium's strengths and limitations. A new section at the end of this book called the Researcher's Road Map is designed to help you do just this. Ultimately, your goal is not just to collect raw data, but to turn collected data into information, which is data organized into a meaningful structure, and then to integrate that information into your own set of experi-

ences and what you know, thereby transforming that information into knowledge. That knowledge can then be applied by you to make better decisions in all areas of your life. And it is knowledge that is the inexhaustible critical resource everyone will need to be successful as we move into the twenty-first century.

Introduction

Taking Advantage of the Information Explosion

It may come as a surprise to you, but for virtually any subject, facts and information are "out there"—by the truckload. Whether it is moviemaking, the wine industry, real estate investments, or baseball historical statistics, information and expertise are available—at no or low cost.

Perhaps you're a market researcher digging up forecasts on the growth of the computer software industry, a college student studying the latest advances in genetic engineering, a writer who needs facts about a new form of dream research, an entrepreneur interested in starting a health food store, or an activist investigating the pornography industry. Whatever your particular situation, this book will provide the knowledge, information sources, and strategies you need in order to quickly find top-quality advice and answers. With this know-how, you'll be able to get the kind of information that's normally available only to a select few.

As everyone knows, we are living in the age of information. Every day, book and periodical publishers, government agencies, libraries, professional associations, conventions, private companies, research centers, and museums are adding to our store of

knowledge. Unfortunately, most of us have little idea how to find the specific information we need, when we need it.

In this book you'll discover where to go and what to look for in searching for information on any subject. First, *key resources,* including many little-known information gold mines, are identified and described, and for each of these you will be given a contact address and phone number or other specific advice for locating the source.

Second, you'll be given strategies on how to go beyond the written sources and phone information services to learn from the experts themselves. Most people would assume that experts don't bother to talk to a lay information seeker. But nothing could be further from the truth. This book will show you not only how to find experts—"the sources behind the sources"—but also how to get them to freely share their knowledge with you.

Finally, this book will help you learn how to conduct an information search from beginning to end. You'll discover what the various steps of an information-finding project are—all the way from defining your problem to receiving a final "expert review" of your finished project. This process is summarized in chapter 12, A Researcher's Road Map.

WHY THIS BOOK

Some years ago I found myself in a new position where I had to learn how to find information on many subjects—fast. I had just landed a job at McGraw-Hill Inc., where my duties were to research and write in-depth analyses and reports for businesses and government agencies on a wide range of topics—from cutting energy costs to selecting the best computer and dozens of other technical subjects. With each of these projects, I'd start off knowing absolutely nothing about the topic. But in the course of a few short weeks I needed to turn out an accurate and authoritative report.

To create these analyses, I needed to have top-quality information at my immediate disposal. So I did some digging and began talking with professional information specialists, investigating lit-

tle-used documents, and developing my own sources. I began to build a bank of information resources. Over the next few years, every time I'd find a valuable and easy-to-use information source, I'd add it to the bank. I also developed techniques for quickly finding experts and getting them to share their knowledge, which I'd also add to the bank.

My friends and family were intrigued when I described to them this process of finding information and quickly becoming knowledgeable on a subject. Their interest motivated me to create the course "You Can Be an Instant Expert," which I taught at the Learning Annex, an adult education program in New York City, for three years.

The people who took the class had varied backgrounds and reasons for being there. Many were businesspeople who wanted to sharpen their job skills and learn where to find the best information in their field. Some were writers who wanted to unearth new sources of expertise. College students took the class, too, hoping to add unexplored dimensions to their research and to learn to be more creative. Others took the class to learn how to dig up facts about a new field, in the hopes of starting their own business. And, confirming my own experience, students told me that they were amazed to discover that so much good information was available so easily and so cheaply. They were equally surprised at how available experts were, and how easy it could be to talk to them.

Sometimes I heard from people after they had taken the course. Here are some of their success stories: A detective novelist found background information about countries where she set her stories. A director of research at a national television network found the right demographic statistics to back up his report on TV viewing trends. A student found free consumer assistance and resolved a complaint with an automobile manufacturer. A man found inexpensive business advice to assist him in starting a consulting firm in a high-technology field. A woman found out where to apply for a grant to get funding for an art-related project. An international marketing executive discovered how to find free industry forecasts instead of paying hundreds of dollars for them.

You undoubtedly will have your own success stories to tell. Perhaps you'll find consumer-oriented information you need to

help you buy a home, manage your money, or raise your child. Or maybe you'll get important business information, aiding you in finding a new job, making investments, going public, or getting a loan. Some of you will have a need for obscure information that can be answered by offbeat sources—like the Association for Symbolic Logic or the Paint Research Institute!

HOW TO USE THIS BOOK

Here's a brief rundown on how this book works and what the different chapters will provide.

A preliminary section, "Getting Started," will help you define what information you're really after and organize your plan of attack. Part I identifies actual information sources and provides tips on how to best find and use each of them. It contains chapters covering the initial selection of information sources, including how to choose the right library for your needs and discover which sources to check once you get there; how to identify "super-sources" on your topic, ranging from associations to museums and much more; how to tap into the huge storehouse of knowledge and data available from the U.S. government—much of it for free; how to locate the best information sources related to business; and, finally, how to perform computer searches, whether or not you actually have your own computer.

Each chapter presents many specific sources, along with suggestions for further avenues to try. You may want to highlight those that sound most interesting to you and appropriate for your needs so that you can later locate them quickly. Or scan the "Quickfinder" feature, which begins each resource chapter and lists every information source included in those chapters.

Part II moves into the second component of the information search—talking to the experts. You'll find out how to locate the nine types of expert, and what the pros and cons are of each type; how to make contact with the experts; and then how to get them to open up and share their knowledge. You'll find out that experts *will* talk to you—but it helps to have some strategies to increase

their willingness to do so. We'll also examine ethics in finding information, the issue of information quality, and how to evaluate experts' information. Finally, you'll get advice on knowing how to tell when it's time to wind up your project and some tips on writing up your results if you choose to do so.

The book concludes with a Researcher's Road Map guide to choosing and understanding information sources, an appendix that lists additional resources, and a comprehensive index, which will be helpful in targeting specific sources, techniques, and topics.

Naturally, a book like this cannot include every potential information source, but I believe that I've provided some of the best. The sources selected for this book have been carefully culled from among many. Those included were specifically chosen as being most useful for people who are not professionals in finding information. This means that, to qualify for inclusion, each source had to be easy to obtain and easy to use. Unless otherwise noted, each source also is free, inexpensive, or available for use at a public institution such as a library. You'll note that the cost of individual documents described in the book is generally not provided, since prices change so quickly. However, unless otherwise noted, no document mentioned costs over about $40, and the great majority are *much less or free*—unless available for use in a library, through some other inexpensive outlet, or by a special technique described in the book. I'd greatly appreciate hearing from readers who want to suggest other sources and information-finding strategies worth including in future editions. Write to me c/o HarperCollins, 10 East 53rd Street, New York, NY 10022.

When you've finished reading this book, I'd suggest keeping it handy so that you can use it as a ready reference guide. This way, whenever you need a fact, some advice, or information, you can find out where to look to get the answers you need.

Getting Started

Before plunging into your project, take a few minutes to consider your endeavor. Try to define for yourself exactly what kind of information you need, and why. What are your *reasons* for wanting to find this information? What are your overall goals? Try to be as *specific* as possible, even though it may be difficult to do so at this early stage. The more you can narrow your scope and break your task into subprojects, the easier your search will be, and the more likely your project will be a success. For example, say your goal is to find information on how to travel overseas inexpensively. With a little reflection, you can break that topic into its major components: cutting costs on overseas transportation, lodging, meals, car rental, shopping, currency exchange, and so on. Now you have some specific and concrete subtopics to zero in on in your research. If during your research you discover that your subject was too broad to adequately handle within the strictures of your plan, you can decide whether to choose one or more of your subtopics instead. (If you are not familiar enough with your subject at the outset to identify subdivisions, you'll find that you'll discover them once you begin your research.)

The first step in the information-gathering process is to find the very best *published* information sources in your field (in print or in electronic form). Although some of your best finding will eventually come from talking to experts, you don't want to begin your

project by contacting them. It's much better to first read and learn about your subject, and *then* speak with the experts. This way, when you do eventually talk to the authorities in the field, you'll be knowledgeable enough to ask the right questions and get the most out of your conversation.

Before you actually start your search, you should come up with a method for recording the information you'll be receiving from your written and "people" sources. Your approach to note taking and organization is important, because it will affect the course of your entire project. If you need advice in this area, see chapter 10. If, however, you feel confident enough to jump right into the information search, continue on to the first chapter.

PART I

Unlocking the Information Vault

1

Libraries

Zeroing in on the Best Resources

(continued)

4

When most of us think of libraries, we think of books. But the library is a place where you can find an extraordinary variety of in-depth, timely information in nonbook formats ranging from fashion newsletters to company financial data to government research reports, and much more. You can even perform electronic information searches on CD-ROMs, free! But before you go to the library, you'll need to know how to match the right type of library to your specific needs, and how to get the most out of the library once you get there.

SELECTING A LIBRARY

There are three basic types of library: public libraries, college and university libraries, and special libraries (which include corporate libraries). Let's look at each.

Public Libraries

The best public libraries for information gatherers are *large*, usually main branches, because these are most likely to contain

an extensive reference collection. It's here in the reference section that you'll find some superb information-providing sources. (These sources will be identified and described later in this chapter.) If the only public library in your area is a very small one, you might want to look to one of the other types of libraries described in this section.

College and University Libraries

Academic libraries typically have more information sources than an average town's public library. Many are open to the public. The academic library's collection will normally reflect the majors and specialties of the particular institution.

TIP: How to Find an Academic Library
• Contact the Association of College and Research Libraries, American Library Association, 50 Huron Street, Chicago, IL 60611; 312–944–6780. At no charge, the association will help you find college and research libraries that specialize in your subject of interest.

Special Libraries

There are thousands of libraries around the country that specialize in a particular subject—astronomy, baseball, the environment, Asia, minorities, marketing, and countless other topics. Most of these libraries are open to the public, and even those that officially are not may still let you come in if you let the librarian know you are working on an important project. Working at one of these special subject libraries is like working in a gold mine where you are surrounded by resources that pertain to the specific subjects you need to find out about.

One particularly valuable type of special library is the *corporate library*. Corporate libraries contain a wealth of information on subjects related to a firm's special interests. Exxon's library, for example, has extensive information on energy, while CBS's library contains top-notch information on broadcasting. Unfortunately, many of these libraries allow access only to their company

employees. But don't despair—sometimes you can get around the official policy. If you've identified a company library you want to use, call up the librarian, introduce yourself, and politely explain what kind of information you are trying to find, and why. Let the librarian know your project is a serious and important one, and explain that you've heard that the library has the resources you need. Describe specifically what you'll want to do at the library and what kind of materials you'll want to examine.

Often—but not always—you'll find that the librarian will allow you to come in and work. Of course, you won't be able to take anything out of the library. And when you get to the library, you should work on your own and not use up the corporate librarian's time, which must be dedicated to serving the company's own employees.

If you happen to know someone who works at a company that has a library you want to use, you should be able to gain entrance by using that person as a reference.

TIPS: Identifying a Special Library
• Contact the Special Libraries Association, 1700 18th Street NW, Washington, DC 20009; 202–234–4700. Ask to speak with one of the "information specialists." These people will try to identify a special library in your area of interest. Another way to find a special library is to check a large library's reference department for one of these directories: *Subject Collections*, published by R. R. Bowker, or *Subject Directory of Special Libraries and Information Centers*, published by Gale Research. Both of these directories list thousands of special libraries.
• Once you've identified the right library for your needs, the next step is to find the best information-providing sources kept at the library you select. But don't forget that the library staff is itself a major resource not to be overlooked.

EASY STARTS: ALL-PURPOSE RESOURCES

Now we're ready to identify and describe some of the very best library information sources. We'll begin with a few basic—but

---

TIPS: Getting the Most Out of Any Library
• If you've located a library that has the information you want, but it is not nearby, you can usually get a certain amount of information and answers by writing or calling with your specific question. You'll find librarians to be very helpful people! Some libraries even take reference questions by E-mail!
• When you get to the library, remember to ask the reference librarian for assistance. That's what these people are there for! By enlisting their help, you can save yourself a lot of research time.
• If the library doesn't have a source you need, don't forget to ask for an interlibrary loan.
• Try calling your town library's reference department on the phone. At no charge, the library will try to find any fact you need. For example, you could ask, "What's the flying time from New York to Istanbul?" or "When was the clock invented?" Answering such questions by mail or phone is a public service that nearly every public library provides.

---

excellent—sources and then progress to some very valuable lesser-known ones. All of the sources described in this section are typically found in the reference department. Note that today many libraries have these sources available not only in print, but electronically on CD-ROM disks. Use of these electronic sources can *vastly* reduce your initial research time. The end of this chapter examines these electronic resources in detail. Let's start off simply:

✔ **Source: *New York Times Index***

An index to articles published in *The New York Times*. The user looks up key words, such as a subject or a person's name, and the index provides a brief summary of all pertinent articles published, giving the date of publication and page. Supplements are issued twice every month. You'll find this index in practically every library.

The New York Times is a newspaper of record with historical significance. Checking its index is a quick and easy way to begin an information search. Most likely, the librarian will provide you with the articles on microfilm. Sometimes the short summary of the article provided by the index itself will be all the information you need.

TIRANA (Albania). See also Albania, Ap 16

TIRES. See also Astronautics, Ap 20, My 6

Goodyear Tire & Rubber Co expects its US tire plants to run near capacity during 1985 (S), Ap 10,IV,4:5

Tires are again bearing labels indicating how well they wear in comparison to other tires; National Highway Traffic Safety Administration discontinued tread wear grading in 1983, holding tests were unreliable; US Appeals Court ordered practice resumed, acting on suit by Public Citizen and Center for Auto Safety; tires are also graded for traction and temperature resistance (M), My 4,I,52:1

Harvey E Heinbach (Merrill Lynch) comments on strong US sales of imported tires (S), My 12,III,1:1

Dunlop Holdings PLC says it has agreed to sell its United States tire operations to group including management for $118 million, plus repayment of $60 million in loans (S), My 16,IV,4:6

TISCH School of the Arts. See also Dancing, Ap 19

TISDALE, Wayman. See also Basketball, Je 19

TISHMAN, Peggy. See also Jewish Philanthropies, Federation of, Je 30

TISHMAN Realty & Construction Co. See also Building (Construction), Je 1. Disney, Walt, World (Lake Buena Vista, Fla), Ap 30

TISHMAN Speyer Properties. See also Ecumed, Ap 26

TITANIUM

Finland's state-owned chemicals company, Kemira Oy, says it will pay $100 million for American Cyanamid Company's titanium dioxide business, including manufacturing plant at Savannah, Ga (S), My 18,I,36:5

TITCHBOURNE, Julie Christofferson. See also Scientology, Church of, My 18

TITONE, Vito J (Judge). See also Courts, Ap 24, My 29

TITUS, Becky (Judge). See also Roads, Je 6

TLS Co

TLS Company names Larry G Stolte chief financial officer (S), Je 27,IV,2:4

TOBACCO. See also Smoking. Taxation, Je 2

Series of measures designed to reshape Japan's telecommunications, financial and tobacco industries and open them to foreign competition go into effect on April 1; new regulations outlined (M), Ap 1,IV,5:1

Scientists and doctors tell panel of New York State lawmakers that packages of chewing tobacco and snuff should contain labels warning that use of those products may cause oral cancer and other diseases; legislaiton to require such labeling has been introduced in both houses, and key lawmakers say they expect it to pass (M), My 2, II,4:3

Article by John Crudele in Market Place column discusses conflicting views concerning value of tobacco stocks; graph (M), My 2,IV,8:3

Article on Japan's attempt to open up tobacco market to foreign companies; various factors hindering United States and other foreign tobacco companies from establishing market in Japan discussed; illustration (M), My 13,IV,10:1

Editorial holding that it is possible that teen-agers might believe that chewing tobacco is safer than smoking it, notes that tobacco is just as addictive either way and there is strong link between smokeless products and oral cancer; holds New York should enact legislation requiring package warning on such products, Je 10,I,18:1

Panel of Government scientists, appointed by Surgeon Gen C Everett Koop, is preparing comprehensive report on whether snuff and chewing tobacco are health hazards, decision that is likely to influence whether warning labels should be required on such products (S), My 18,I,16:5

New York Assembly, 87-53, approves bill that would require packages of smokeless tobacco to contain warning label that use of product is dangerous to health (S), Je 27, II,4:2

TOBEY, Alton. See also Westchester County (NY), My 5

TOBIAS [...] Taxation, Je 28

TOLLESON, Richard L. See also Oscar Mayer Corp, My 17

TOLLMAN-Hundley Hotels. See also Hotels, A[...]

TOLLS. See also Bridges and Tunnels, Je 2. R[...] 24

TOMAHAWK (Missile). See also Eur, Ap 8

TOMB of the Unknown Soldier (Arlington Natio[...] Cemetery)

Article on soldiers who guard Tomb of Unkno[...] Arlington National Cemetery; they are drawn fr[...] US Army's Old Guard, elite ceremonial unit tha[...] at various events in nation's capital; Sgt Larry J[...] comments; photo (M), My 27,I,8:3

TOMKO, Jozef (Bishop). See also RC Ch, My 1[...]

TOMLINSON Junior High School (Fairfield, Conn[...] also Educ, Ap 9, My 17

TOMS, Gerald (Dr). See also Circuses, Ap 11[...]

TOMS River (NJ). See also Amusement Parks, J[...] Fires, Ap 21

TONAMO Transportation Co. See also Delivery[...] Je 13

TONELSON, Alan. See also Latin America, M[...]

TONG On (Gang). See also Shootings, My 2[...]

TONY Awards (Theater Awards). See also T[...] 25, My 3,4,8,13,19, Je 2,3,4,5. Theater—Big[...] Adventures of Huckleberry Finn (Play), Je[...]

TOOL & Engraving Co. See also Explosions, [...]

TOOLE, Ottis. See also Murders, Ap 18

TOOLS. See also Machine Tools and Dies. R[...]

TOON, Al. See also Football, My 1

TOON, Malcolm. See also Radio, Je 2

TOOTSIE Roll Industries. See also Cella's Conf[...] My 25

TOP Rank Inc. See also Boxing, Je 24

TOPPING, Audrey. See also Archeology, My 1[...]

TOPPING, David R. See also Gulf Corp, Je 4

TOPPS Chewing Gum Inc. See also Trading Ca[...]

TORADZE, Alexander. See also Music, Ap 14

TORAN, Sylvia. See also Music, Ap 28

TORBORG, Jeff. See also Baseball, My 4

TORELLI, Mario (Prof). See also Archeology, A[...]

TORES, Pablo Jr. See also Children, Ap 25

TORGAU (East Germany). See also World War[...]

TORIN Machine Division of Clevepak Corp

Workers at Torin Machine Division of Cleve[...] Torrington, Conn, weigh making bid to take o[...] which employs 90 people; Clevepak has put fa[...] sale, and state and local officials fear that if a[...] company buys division it may close (M), My [...]

TORNADOES

Four people die as tornadoes and thunderst[...] section of US from Illinois to Deep South; tw[...] winds strike Ohio, Indiana, Illinois, Tennessee[...] Georgia and Alabama (S), Ap 6,I,5:4

Photo of damage caused by tornado in Doug[...] Ap 7,I,22:3

Texas is struck again by several tornadoes, d[...] twister claims lives of three people in state; to[...] touch down in Nebraska and Oklahoma in fou[...] violent weather across Great Plains (S), Ap 23,[...]

Outburst of violent weather that has caused [...] batters parts of Texas again on April 29; rising[...] continues to threaten much of north Texas; at [...] tornadoes were reported over Texas during wee[...] April 27 and up to six inches of rain fell in sor[...] Ap 30,I,16:6

Tornadoes and heavy thunderstorms rip acro[...] Midwestern states (S), My 12,I,29:6

Photo of tornado aproaching Agra, Kansas; [...] and dozens of tornadoes struck Kansas, Misso[...] South Dakota over weekend, damaging build[...] downing trees (S), My 13,I,12:2

Tornadoes and high winds cut five-mile s[...]

✔ **Source: *Readers' Guide to Periodical Literature*
(H. W. Wilson Company)**

The *Readers' Guide* indexes articles published in about 240 popular magazines such as *Newsweek, Health, Ms., Sports Illustrated,* and *Popular Science.* Supplements are issued monthly. You can find this guide at nearly every library. As with the *New York Times Index,* the user looks up key words to find articles on subjects he or she is interested in.

These familiar green volumes provide a quick way of finding back issues of popular magazines that have published articles on your subject of interest. You may not always get "inside" information from articles published in these general-interest magazines, but they can still be good information sources. And because these periodicals are so popular, you can usually find back issues of many of them right in the library.

TIP: Use the *Readers' Guide* to Understand a Technical Subject
• Because the magazines indexed in the *Readers' Guide* are read mainly by the general public, any description of a technical matter will be clearly defined and explained. This makes the guide especially helpful if your subject is technical and you don't quite understand it yet. The term "genetic engineering," for example, would be explained clearly to readers in a magazine like *Newsweek,* but probably would not be in a publication like *Applied Genetic News.*

✔ **Source: *Business Periodicals Index* (H. W. Wilson Company)**

The *Business Periodicals Index* is an index to articles published in nearly 350 periodicals oriented toward business. Its scope is broad, ranging from advertising and marketing to real estate, computers, communications, finance, and insurance. Supplements are issued monthly. Almost all libraries have it.

The *Business Periodicals Index* is an extremely valuable index. Its name may mislead some people, because the guide actually indexes periodicals that contain information on topics beyond the scope of what most people consider simply "business." For example, it indexes articles from publications like the *Journal of Consumer Affairs, Human Resource Management, Telecommunications,* and *Automotive News.* "Trade" periodicals like these generally provide

more specialized and in-depth information than the popular magazines indexed in the *Readers' Guide*, but at the same time the articles are usually not overly technical or hard to read. This is a nice balance for the information seeker who is not technically oriented or an expert in the field but still wants more than a superficial examination of a subject. I once used this index to find some excellent information about the topic of office ergonomics—how to design and furnish healthy and safe work areas.

✔ **Source: *Subject Guide to Books in Print* (R. R. Bowker Company)**

SGBIP lists all new and old books hardbound, paperback, trade, text, adult, and juvenile that are currently in print, by subject. Virtually all libraries (and bookstores, for that matter) have it.

This is the standard guide for finding books in print on any subject. (Books "in print" are kept in stock by the publisher and can be ordered at a bookstore.) If you look under "Circus," for example, you'll find about twenty-five books; each entry includes the author's name, book title, date of publication, price, and publisher. There are accompanying volumes that list books by title and by author as well.

✔ **Source: *Forthcoming Books* (R. R. Bowker Company)**

This guide lists books that have just been released or are projected to be released within five months. Supplements are issued bimonthly. You'll find this guide in large libraries and most bookstores.

Forthcoming Books is an intriguing source, as it identifies what books are about to be published in a given field. This can be especially useful when you are digging up information on a timely issue and you want to find the very latest books. (Note, however, that because books take a long time to produce, they will probably not be the best source of information on events occurring in the last few months or even year.) This source is good to use in conjunction with the *Subject Guide to Books in Print*.

> **TIPS: Finding Out-of-Print Books**
> • Strand Bookstore in New York City stocks 2.5 million books, and a large percentage of these are out-of-print books. Contact the store to see if it has a book you seek: 828 Broadway, New York, NY 10003; 212–473–1452.
> • Book search companies and out-of-print specialty stores often advertise in *The New York Times Book Review* and other literary publications.

SPECIAL PERIODICAL INDEXES

✔ **Source: H. W. Wilson Subject Indexes**

The Wilson Subject Indexes are multivolume series that identify articles published within many major subject areas. There are different series for different fields (e.g., humanities, social science, science, art, business, education, agriculture, and law). To use these indexes, you consult the volumes devoted to your field of interest and look up specific subtopics. The index identifies which periodicals have published articles on the topic, and when. You'll find the Wilson indexes at medium-size and large libraries.

Two well-known indexes published by H. W. Wilson have already been described—the *Readers' Guide to Periodical Literature* and the *Business Periodicals Index*—but Wilson also indexes literature published in specific fields. For example, there is the *Education Index*, which I've used to locate articles published in education-oriented periodicals on the subject of personal-computer use in schools.

Not only will the articles that you locate be of great assistance, but so will the names of the authors of those articles and the experts cited in the pieces. These are people that you'll want to speak with later on to obtain answers to your own particular questions.

The trick in using these guides is to figure out which subject index to consult. What you need to do is determine into which subject area established by Wilson your topic falls. For example, if you wanted to find out about growing tomatoes, that would be a food science question, and you'd check the *Biological and Agricultural Index*. If your subject were meditation, that would fall under psychology, and so you'd look in the *Social Science Index*.

(As noted previously, I've found Wilson's *Business Periodicals Index* worth checking for almost any subject.)

Here are some samples of the major subtopics covered in the different Wilson indexes:

If Your Area of Interest Is	The Wilson Guide to Check Is
Fire, mineralogy, oceanology, plastics, transportation, and other applied scientific subjects	Applied Science and Technology Index
Architecture, art history, film, industrial design, landscape design, painting, photography	Art Index
Animal breeding, food science, nutrition, pesticides	Biological and Agricultural Index
Accounting, advertising, banking, economics, finance, investment, labor, management, marketing, public relations, specialized industries	Business Periodicals Index (see p. 11)
Curriculums, school administration and supervision, teaching methods	Education Index
Astronomy, physics, and broad scientific areas	General Science Index
Archaeology, classical studies, folklore, history, language and literature, literary and political criticism, performing arts, philosophy, religion, theology	Humanities Index
Legal information, all areas of jurisprudence	Index to Legal Periodicals
Anthropology, environmental science, psychology, sociology	Social Sciences Index

There are two other very useful specialized subject indexes, not published by Wilson, worth mentioning. The **Engineering Index** (published by Engineering Information Inc.) covers all aspects of engineering; and the **Public Affairs Information Service (PAIS) Bulletin** (published by Public Affairs Information Service Inc.) covers politics, legislation, international law, public policymaking, and related topics worldwide. You can find special subject indexes either at a large public library or at an appropriate special library (e.g., the *Index to Legal Periodicals* at a law library).

TIP: Start a Search Narrowly
• If you're gathering information on a topic that combines two subjects (*e.g.*, *marketing* done by *museums* or *new technologies* in *videocassettes*) identify the narrowest approach to take. To find information on marketing by museums, I might look under "Museums" in the *Business Periodicals Index*. But it would not be a good idea to use the *Business Periodicals Index* and look under "Marketing," since I'd find too much information, and maybe none of it related to museums. If you don't find enough information by taking the narrower path, then you can always try the broader approach.

TIP: Spotting Hot Periodicals
• Use the periodical indexes described above to identify publications that are worth examining in depth. Take a look at the opening pages, where the magazines and journals that the index scans are listed. Reading this listing is a good way to identify the hottest and most relevant periodicals in your field of interest. Say your subject is the paper industry—you might spot the magazine *Pulp and Paper*. Another way of identifying the best publications is to note whether most of the articles you find when using an index were published in the same magazine or magazines. If so, those publications are also worth looking at in more depth. If you identify such a "hot" publication, try to locate the most recent issues and peruse these for valuable articles not yet indexed, or consider talking to the editors of the publication.

MAGAZINE AND NEWSLETTER DIRECTORIES

✔ **Sources:** *Ulrich's International Periodicals Directory*
Gale Directory of Publications
Standard Periodical Directory
Oxbridge Directory of Newsletters

There are periodicals and newsletters covering thousands of different subjects. The directories above identify tens of thousands of magazines, newsletters, newspapers, journals, and other periodicals. The most comprehensive of these directories, but the most difficult to use, is *Ulrich's,* which lists 126,000 periodicals in 554 subject areas. Two easier indexes to use are the *Gale Directory* and the *Standard Periodical Directory.* Virtually all libraries have one or more of these directories.

These are all excellent resources for tracking down specific periodicals covering a particular subject. The way these guides work is simple: You look up your subject, and the guide lists the magazines or newsletters published within the field. Entries typically include the name of the periodical, the publisher, address, and circulation.

TIP: Newspaper Feature Editors
• One particularly valuable section in the *Gale Directory* is its "newspaper feature editors" listing. This is a compilation of the names and phone numbers of the editors of the most popular newspaper features (e.g., art, automobiles, fashion, movies, real estate, society, sports, and women) appearing in daily newspapers with a circulation of 50,000 or more. It's superb for identifying subject experts and regional publications.

There are loads of specialized publications being published around the United States. Even if your topic is extremely narrow, there may just be a periodical devoted to that subject alone. Let me give you a few examples. If you looked under "Folklore" in *Ulrich's*, you'd find *Folklore Center News*, and under "Motion Pictures" you'd see magazines like *Amateur Film Maker* and *Motion Picture Investor*, a newsletter that analyzes private and public values of movies and movie stock. Under the category "Nutrition and Dietetics" you'd find loads of publications, including *Jewish Vegetarian*, published by the International Jewish Vegetarian Society of London.

✔ **Source: *Magazines for Libraries* (R. R. Bowker Company)**
 Another directory of publications. This one covers fewer periodicals (about 6,500) but provides much more in-depth information on each one.

This is an excellent and highly recommended directory for researchers. Although it does not cover the most obscure publications, it provides a superb analysis and review of the coverage and usefulness for those it does include. The directory is actually designed to assist librarians in deciding which magazines to

BEVERAGES - BREWING

Michigan Beverage Journal
PUBLISHING CO.: Sponsor-Associated Beverage Pub., MBJ, Inc., 8750
Telegraph Rd., #104, Taylor, MI 48180 (313) 287-9140
PERSONNEL: Publ-Larry Stotz, Adv Dir-Ann Cook, Prom Dir-William Slone,
EDITORIAL DESCRIPTION: Covers merchandising, product information, news,
laws & regulations of beverage industry.
MISCELLANEOUS DATA: 1982 M 8 3/8 x 10 7/8 Sheeted Color-4 p bind (Last
updated in Aug. 88):
CIRCULATION (BPA):
  Total: 5,417
ADVERTISING: One Time   Annual   CPM: $201
  Full pg. b/w: $1,089 $973
  Full pg. 4/c: $1,942 $1,826
  1/3 pg. b/w: $457 $396

Michigan Beverage News
PUBLISHING CO.: Michigan Beverage News Inc., 27716 Franklin Rd.,
Southfield, MI 48034-2352 (313) 357-6397
PERSONNEL: Ed-Publ-David Brown, Adv Dir-Anne Platenik, Circ Mgr-Diane
Brown;
EDITORIAL DESCRIPTION: Reporting marketing, sales and other spirits,
wine and beer news.
MISCELLANEOUS DATA: 0026-2021 1939 BW $11.75 $.50/copy 10 1/4 x 14 1/4
Web 30pp Color-4 c stock (Last updated in Nov. 87)
CIRCULATION (ABC, 100% controlled):
  Total: 6,000
ADVERTISING: One Time   CPM: $259
  Full pg. b/w: $1,555
PRINTING CO.: Webco, Northville, MI

Mid-Continent Bottler
PUBLISHING CO.: Fan Publications, Inc., 10741 El Monte, Box 7406,
Overland Pk., KS 66207 (913) 341-0020
PERSONNEL: Ed-Publ-Floyd Sageser,
EDITORIAL DESCRIPTION: For and about soft drink bottlers in the mid-
continent area
MISCELLANEOUS DATA: BM $9 $1.50/copy 8 1/2 x 11 Sheeted 64pp. Color-4
(Last updated in July 88)
CIRCULATION (100% controlled):
  Total: 3,220
ADVERTISING: One Time   CPM: $281
  Full pg. b/w: $905
LIST RENTAL $35/M
PRINTING CO.: Joslens, 11000 Adams, Topeka, KS 66601

Modern Brewery Age
PUBLISHING CO.: Modern Brewery Age, 50 Day St., Box 5550, Norwalk, CT
06854 (203) 853-6015
PERSONNEL: Ed-Terri Finnegan, Publ-Mac Brighton;
EDITORIAL DESCRIPTION: Bimonthly magazine supplement.
MISCELLANEOUS DATA: 1933 W $65 $4/copy 8 1/4 x 11 Sheeted Color-4
(Last updated in Nov. 87)
CIRCULATION (BPA, 100% controlled):
  Total: 5,500
ADVERTISING: One Time   CPM: $254
  Full pg. b/w: $1,400

Nebraska Beverage Analyst
PUBLISHING CO.: Golden Bell Press, 2403 Champa St, Denver, CO 80205
(303) 296-1600
PERSONNEL: Ed-Mariette Bell, Publ-Allen Bell;
EDITORIAL DESCRIPTION: Complete price lists, new products, industry
news, legal notices and information for distilled spirits, beer &
wine
MISCELLANEOUS DATA: 1934 M $7 $1.50/copy 8 3/8 x 10 7/8 Offset 194pp.
Color (Last updated in Feb. 88)
CIRCULATION:
  Total: 4,500
ADVERTISING: One Time   CPM: $122
  Full pg. b/w: $550

New Brewer
PUBLISHING CO.: Institute for Fermentation, 734 Pearl, Boulder, CO
80302 (303) 447-0816
PERSONNEL: Ed-Virginia Thomas, Publ-Adv Dir-Charlie Papazian, Prom Dir-
Alan Dikty, Circ Mgr-Rob Cunov, Art Dir-David Bjorkman;
EDITORIAL DESCRIPTION: Technical Journal for micro-and Pub-Brewers.
MISCELLANEOUS DATA: 0741-0506 1983 BM $48 $8/copy 8 1/2 x 11 Sheetled
36pp. No Color c stock s bind (Last updated in Aug. 87)
CIRCULATION (100% controlled):
  Total: 800
  Subscript.:   600
ADVERTISING: One Time   CPM: $937
  Full pg. b/w: $750
LIST RENTAL
PRINTING CO.: D&K Printing, Boulder, CO 80302

New Jersey Beverage Journal
PUBLISHING CO.: Gem Publishers Inc., 2400 Morris Ave., Union, NJ 07083
(201) 964-5060
PERSONNEL: Ed-Publ-Harry Slone, Adv Dir-Max Slone, Circ Mgr-Angel
Wolters,
EDITORIAL DESCRIPTION: Business publication for alcohol beverage
industry (spirits, wines, b

  Full pg. 4/c: $1,570
  1/3 pg. b/w: $380
  1/3 pg. 4/c: $1,110
LIST RENTAL $60/M
PRINTING CO.: Ranno Printing Co., 20 10 Maple Ave.
NJ 07410

Observer
PUBLISHING CO.: Observer Corp., 226 N. 12th St., Ph
(215) 567-6221
PERSONNEL: Ed-Anthony West, Publ-James Curran,
EDITORIAL DESCRIPTION: The alcoholic beverage inc
For state operated liquor and distributors, restauran
etc
MISCELLANEOUS DATA: 1936 BW $12 10 x 16 Web (L
CIRCULATION:
  Total: 20,000
ADVERTISING: One Time   CPM: $85
  Full pg. b/w: $1,785

Ohio Beverage Journal
PUBLISHING CO.: Beverage Journal, 3 12th St., Wheeling,
232-7620
PERSONNEL: Ed-Publ-Adv Dir-Arnold Lazarus, Circ Mgr-Da
EDITORIAL DESCRIPTION: Edited for beverage alcohol reta
local & natl. industry news.
MISCELLANEOUS DATA: Former Title-Buckeye Beverage Jo
$1/copy 8 1/2 x 11 Sheetled 48pp. Color-4 s bind (Last upd
July 88)
CIRCULATION (100% controlled):
  Total: 7,200
ADVERTISING: One Time   CPM: $120
  Full pg. b/w: $870
PRINTING CO.: Boyd Press, 112 31st St., Wheeling, WV 26(

Oklahoma Beverage News
PUBLISHING CO.: Beverage News, Inc., Box 1677, Wichita
263-0107
PERSONNEL: Ed-Chas Walters, Jr.;
EDITORIAL DESCRIPTION: Carries complete news cove
beverage industry with emphasis on legal and econor
MISCELLANEOUS DATA: 1959 M $6 $1/copy 8 1/2 x 1
(Last updated in Aug. 87)
CIRCULATION (100% controlled):
  Total: 2,250
ADVERTISING: One Time   CPM:
  Full pg. b/w: $525
  Full pg. 4/c: $900

Patterson's California Beverage Journal
PUBLISHING CO.: Wolfer Printing Co., Inc., 1613 E. Gl
Glendale, CA 91206-2825 (213) 627-4996
PERSONNEL: Ed-Harry Bradley, Publ-Robert Good, Ad
Circ Mgr-Pearl Cooper;
EDITORIAL DESCRIPTION: Trade publication; covers alc
and pricing information.
MISCELLANEOUS DATA: Former Title-Patterson's Califor
Gazetteer, 1941 M $29.95 $5/copy 8 3/8 x 10 7/8 Web 4(
stock p bind (Last updated in Apr. 88)
CIRCULATION (100% controlled):
  Total: 10,145
ADVERTISING: One Time   CPM: $162
  Full pg. b/w: $1,645
PRINTING CO.: Wolfer Printing Co., 422 Wall St., Los Angele:

Practical Winery Vineyard
PUBLISHING CO.: Don Neel, 15 Grande Paseo, San Rafael, C
479-5819
PERSONNEL: Ed-Stan Hock, Publ-Don Neel, Circ Mgr-F. Ne
Cobb;
EDITORIAL DESCRIPTION: Information on equipment and
winemaking and grape growing, marketing.
MISCELLANEOUS DATA: 0739-8077 1980 BM $8 $3.95/c
56pp. 18% ads Color-2-4 c stock s bind (Last updated
CIRCULATION (100% controlled):
  Total: 2,500
  Newsstand: 200
  Subscript.:   2,125
  Internatl.:   175
ADVERTISING: One Time   CPM: $2
  Full pg. b/w: $605

Quarterly Review of Wines
PUBLISHING CO.: QRW Publishing, 24 Garfield Ave., Win
(617) 729-7132
PERSONNEL: Ed-Randy Sheahan, Publ-Prod Mgr-Richard
Lynch, Circ Mgr-Beth Hamilton, Art Dir-Lily Yamamoto;
EDITORIAL DESCRIPTION: For those interested in wines, rel
selected spirits & beers & gourmet foods. The nation's seco
consumer wine magazine-dedicated to bringing the world's
wine writers to our readers
MISCELLANEOUS DATA: 0740-1248 1978 Q $9.95 $2.95/cop
36pp. Color-2-4 c stock s bind (Last updated in Nov. 87)
CIRCULATION:

obtain, so it is also an excellent tool for researchers who want to know which publications are considered the best in the field and how their scope compares.

TIP: Identifying the Right Periodical

• If your topic is *very* obscure, look up subjects that are a little broader. For example, while working on an information-finding project on the topic of "rebuilding school buses," I could not find any publications covering just that narrow topic, but I did find a magazine called *School Transportation News*. It seemed logical that such a publication might, at one time or another, have written an article on rebuilding school buses, so I telephoned the magazine and asked for the editorial department. An editor was happy to check the files, and sure enough, the magazine had published three different articles on that topic during the previous two years; the editor mailed me copies. So, if you are having trouble finding a periodical on a very narrow topic, try looking up some broader subjects whose scope may encompass it. You can always try calling a publication to find out if it has published an article on a particular topic during the last year or two.

TIP: Locating Hard-to-Find Periodicals

• Once you identify the specialized magazine or newsletter you need, how do you obtain it? Because there are so many special-interest and obscure periodicals, it's unlikely that even the largest library will have all the ones you seek. What you need to do is, contact the publisher of the periodical you're interested in (the address and phone number are listed in the directory) and request a sample copy or two. Then you can decide whether you want to subscribe or interview the writers and editors for information or find a library that specializes in the subject and contact the librarian to find out if the library subscribes to it (see page 8 for tips on locating special libraries).

PEOPLE INFORMATION

✔ **Source: Marquis Who's Who Series**
The Who's Who volumes are the standard and most popular sources of biographical details on people of various accomplishments. The best-known of these books is *Who's Who in America,* which lists

facts on prominent Americans. There are scores of more specialized Who's Who volumes, such as *Who's Who in Finance and Industry, Who's Who in the East,* and *Who's Who of American Women.* Virtually all libraries have *Who's Who in America.* Larger and specialized libraries have the other volumes.

Who's Who in America, the most popular of the Who's Who series, lists various information about prominent Americans' place and date of birth, schools attended, degrees awarded, special accomplishments, and current address. A caution in using these books is that the information is often furnished by the biographees themselves, so accuracy will depend on their truthfulness.

Large libraries have a master Who's Who index titled *Index to Who's Who Books.* With this guide you can look up a name and find out which, if any, of the fifteen or so Who's Who books includes a listing.

✔ **Source: *Current Biography* (H. W. Wilson Company)**

This is a monthly magazine with articles about people prominent in the news in national and international affairs, the sciences, arts, labor, and industry. Obituaries are also included. At the end of each year, the articles are printed in a single volume, and an index at the back helps users find biographies published during the current year and a few years back. Medium-size and large libraries have the set.

Current Biography strives to be "brief, objective, and accurate, with well-documented articles." It may be more reliable than Who's Who, since its editors consult many sources of biographical data, rather than rely solely on the biographers' own accounts.

✔ **Source: *Biography Index* (H. W. Wilson Company)**

Biography Index scans more than 2,700 periodicals, many books, and various biographical sources like obituaries, diaries, and memoirs to identify and index sources of information on prominent people. You can find *Biography Index* in large libraries.

Checking *Biography Index* is a fast way to find articles and other sources of information on all sorts of people from comedian Robert Klein to Buonarroti, Michelangelo.

✔ **Source: *Biography and Genealogy Master Index*
(Gale Research)**

Biography and Genealogy Master Index is an index to biographical directories, providing information on more than 8.8 million current and historical figures. Five hundred sixty-five publications are indexed, including the various Who's Who volumes. Large libraries have this guide.

This source will tell you whether there is a directory or publication that lists biographical information on a historical or well-known figure. For example, if you looked up Bob Dylan, you'd find that biographical sketches could be found in *Baker's Biographical Dictionary of Musicians*, *Biography Index*, *The New Oxford Companion to Music*, *Who's Who in the World*, and elsewhere. Once you've located a directory, try to find a library that has it. (You might call the Special Libraries Association to help you identify a likely library.) Then write or call the library to find out if the person you need information on is listed in the directory.

TIP: Finding Celebrities
• *The Address Book: How to Reach Anyone Who's Anyone* (Facts on File) is a fun book that informs readers where they can reach over 3,500 prominent persons. I used it recently to try to find out where I could contact the singer Carly Simon, just to find out if she would be holding another concert. You can find it at many bookstores.

✔ **Source: *National Directory of Addresses and Telephone Numbers* (Omnigraphics, Inc.)**

A listing of about 136,000 addresses and phone numbers of various institutions such as government agencies, corporations, associations, retailers, hotels, restaurants, banks, colleges, magazines, TV and radio stations and more.

This is a handy and useful source for finding addresses and phone numbers of all sorts of popular organizations. It is not as comprehensive as directories devoted to a single type of institution, but it is still a useful research tool, because it is inexpensive and can be found in many bookstores.

TIP: A Fax Directory
• Another useful directory published by Gale Research is its *National Fax Directory,* which lists the fax numbers of over 170,000 organizations and businesses.

✔ **Source: *New York Times Obituaries Index***

An index to all the obituaries published in *The New York Times* from 1858 to 1978. Most libraries have it.

Obituaries published in the *Times* are a good source of information about well-known people. Usually the obituary will identify organizations and individuals that the person was affiliated with—these are fruitful leads for digging up more information.

(If you seek biographical information on someone who died after 1978, you can find obituary articles published in the *Times* by checking the regular *New York Times Index.* Look under "Deaths" in the volume covering those issues published the year the person died.)

TIP: Check Periodical Indexes
• Other good library sources of biographical information on well-known individuals are the Wilson Subject Indexes (see page 13). Figure out which of these guides would most likely index periodicals covering the profession in which the person was active. For example, if you want to find information on someone who was well-known in the electronics industry, look up his or her name in the *General Science Index.*

BUSINESS AND INDUSTRY INFORMATION

Libraries can be particularly valuable to people seeking business information. Specialized periodical indexes, industry directories, and special business guides can provide you with important facts about companies and industries. (Many more business information sources, not found in libraries, are identified in chapter 4.)

The following is a selection of some leading and most broadly useful business library sources.

✔ **Source:** *Wall Street Journal Index*

> An index to articles published in the *Wall Street Journal* and *Barron's.*
> There are two parts: a subject index and a company name index.
> Supplements are issued monthly. You'll find the *Wall Street Journal
> Index* in nearly all libraries.

This is one of the quickest and best ways to search for authoritative information on a particular industry, company, or business topic. Articles published in the *Wall Street Journal* are generally not too technical, yet they are in-depth and probing enough to provide very valuable information. Most libraries keep back issues of the *Journal* on microfilm, so you can often read the articles you find right at the library. Like the *New York Times Index,* the *Wall Street Journal Index* is itself a source of facts and information, because each entry typically contains a one- or two-line summary of the indexed article. (You can also read *The Wall Street Journal* on the Web at http./www.wsj.com but it is a fee-based, not free, site.)

✔ **Source:** *Funk & Scott Index* **(Information Access Co., Inc.)**

> The *Funk & Scott Index* (or *"F&S"*) is a leading guide to published
> articles about industries and about company activities and develop-
> ments. *F&S* indexes articles published in leading business periodi-
> cals, such as *Barron's* and the *Wall Street Journal,* as well as more
> specialized industry publications like *Iron Age* and *Aviation Week.*
> Most large libraries and almost all business libraries have this index.
> *F&S* issues weekly and monthly supplements.

The *F&S Index* is an extremely *fast* and *helpful* tool for digging up information on specific industries and companies. This includes information on corporate acquisitions and mergers, new products, technology developments, forecasts, company analyses, and social and political factors affecting business. To find information about a particular *industry,* you can turn to the front of the book to find the industry's **SIC** code (**SIC** = Standard Industrial Classification, the accepted method of categorizing industry types using assigned reference numbers) and then check the appropriate section of the volume to find citations of articles that discuss a given issue within that industry.

This index is conveniently organized so that you can also look up the name of a particular firm and find references to relevant articles, with a brief description of each article's scope.

GAS
(*see* **Industrial Gases, Natural Gas**)

GASOLINE
Motor gasoline stocks in week ended Nov. 1 totaled 215,796,000 barrels; motor gasoline production totaled 42,532,000 barrels. 11/6-48;6

Motor gasoline stocks in week ended Nov. 8 totaled 215,821,000 barrels; motor gasoline production totaled 43,568,000 barrels. 11/14-53;3

Motor gasoline stocks for week ended Nov. 15 totaled 213,460 barrels; motor gasoline production totaled 45,913,-000 barrels. 11/20-51;3

Motor gasoline stocks in week ended Nov. 22 totaled 214,403,000 barrels; motor gasoline production totaled 45,038,000 barrels. 11/27-38;6

Energy futures prices plunged Nov. 27, with heating oil and gasoline contracts falling by as much as the permissible daily limit amid concern that the past few months' rally may be faltering. (Futures Markets) 11/29-20;3

GASOLINE STATIONS
(*see* **Service Stations**)

GEKAS, GEORGE
Can staggered filing of returns break up the processing logjam?; Rep. Gekas' bill would let returns claiming refunds be filed early, but would make returns--and taxes owed--due at the later of April 15 or the end of the filer's birth month. (Tax Report) 11/20-1;5

GENEALOGY
Beatrice Bayley Inc. mails postcards offering for $29.85 a 'Family Heritage Book' that promises to trace a family's genealogy; but many buyers have discovered that book contains not their lineage but simply a list of people with the same last names; complaints have led to investigations by the U.S. Postal Inspector and Wisconsin and Pennsylvania state officials. 11/4-27;3

GENERAL ACCOUNTING OFFICE
The SEC, responding to criticism from the General Accounting Office, proposed closing certain loopholes in its program for finding lost or stolen securities; proposal would force 19,000 brokerage firms and banks nationwide to become more active in the program. 11/22-6;4

GENERAL AGREEMENT ON TARIFFS & TRADE
The General Agreement on Tariffs & Trade finds the slowdown in trade is more serious than it expected; GATT estimated that the growth in trade for 1985 will be 2% to 3%, well below the forecasts of other analysts. 11/15-35;2

U.S. trade officials, impatient with opposition from India, Brazil, Egypt, Yugoslavia and Argentina, are prepared to call a vote in an effort to force the beginning of a new round of global trade negotiations under the General Agreement on Tariffs and Trade. 11/20-35;2

U.S. hopes for a new round of global trade talks are expected to get a boost in the upcoming meeting of the General Agreement on Tariffs & Trade; the talks sought by the U.S. are likely to be the most difficult and longest ever. 11/25-32;1

The Mexican government will begin negotiations to enter the General Agreement on Tariffs and Trade, closing another chapter in the country's longstanding debate over external economic policy. 11/26-35;4

Trade officials from 90 countries agreed unanimously to launch a new round of global trade talks next September; at the end of a four-day meeting, delegates

GHANA—Foreign Relations
Justice Department said a cousin of leader has secretly pleaded no contest to c on the U.S.; he was sent back to Ghana about 10 Ghanians 'of interest to the U.S.'

GIFTS
(*see also* **Illegal Payments**)

New Form 8283 for deducting non-cash c valued at more than $500 should be ava offices by the end of November. (Tax Report

Alexander Calder's widow received 1,2 from her husband's estate and valued them the $949,750 accepted by the IRS for es reflected 60% discount from retail value; b discounts of 18% to 25%, valued gifts at $2. billed Mrs. Calder for $459,419 more in Report) 11/20-1;5

When Judge Shirley Kram called lawye the pending litigation between Hanson Tr Corp., they were expecting a decision on fight; but judge wanted to know whether she a complimentary copy of a book written by represents Hanson. (Shop Talk) 11/21-33;3

Colleges find gifts such as racehorses a bet; property donations can cost dearly, be lots that slide into the sea. 11/25-1;4

GINNIE MAE
(*see* **Government National Mortgage Ass**

GIOVANNINI, ALFIO
Yugo Yearning: Editorial page article by nini on how Yugoslavia's latest car import, affect East-West trade. 11/20-30;4

GLICK, ALLEN
A government witness described how application to the Teamsters Central States led him into a partnership with organized Glick's testimony provided substance to a Senate subcommitteee in the late 1970s tha fund had served for decades as 'the mob's ba

GOING PRIVATE
Beatrice Cos. accepted Kohlberg Kr offer of $50 a share, or $6.2 billion, to after Kohlberg Kravis threatened to with buyout pact ever is set after board spurne a share, or $5.9 billion, from Dart Group 11/15-2;2

GOLD
New methods enable miners to step gold; the more developed process, heap le boost annual U.S. production to 2.3 milli year; second, less-developed technolgy, is thiobacillus ferrooxidans, which eats away s unreachable by cyanide solutions. 11/1-33;1

The U.S. dollar fell against most major fc cies after the release of several U.S. economic were more discouraging than the market hac on the Comex, gold fell to $324.70 an ounce.

Foreign-exchange traders are now convin jor nations are serious about lowering the banks' determination was underscored Nov reportedly intervened and old on the Comex

---

TIP: Finding Leading Industry Periodicals
• The front of the book lists all the periodicals indexed in *F&S*, which cover industries ranging from rubber to fertilizer. Since these periodicals have been selected by *F&S* for indexing, it's a good bet that they are leading trade publications. The description of each includes the title, frequency of publication, subscription price, and single-issue price. (Some are expensive, but many are moderately priced or even free.)

Note: Predicasts also publishes two companion international directories: *F&S Index Europe* identifies published information on companies operating in Western and Eastern Europe, and *F&S Index International* covers business activity in Canada, Latin America, Africa, Middle East, and Asia. Another popular volume from the same publisher is *Predicasts Forecasts*, which lists published forecasts for hundreds of different products, industries, and topics (for example, the estimated growth in the number of hospital beds through the 1990s and the increase in personal computers).

✔ **Source: *Standard & Poor's Register of Corporations, Directors and Executives***

Standard & Poor's Register, or the "S&P," is a leading industry directory of company information. The register consists of three volumes. Volume 1, *Corporations,* is a straight alphabetical listing of approximately 55,000 corporations, giving their addresses, phone numbers, names and titles of key officers and directors, subsidiaries, numbers of employees, and certain financial data like gross sales. Volume 2, *Directors and Executives,* is a listing of about 400,000 officers, directors, trustees, partners, and so on. The information provided about them includes date and place of birth, college attended, professional affiliations, and place of residence. Volume 3 is a set of indexes. You'll find the *S&P* volumes in large general libraries and in business libraries.

S&P is a very highly regarded source of information about companies. It and the Dun & Bradstreet volumes described below are considered leading industry directories.

Purch Agt—Edward Stone
Product Mgr—Fred Delp
Traffic Mgr—Evert Jackson
Mktg & Prod Mgr—Clarence Bowman
Qual Con Mgr—Robert W. Stratton
Accts—Hill, Barth & King, Salem, Ohio
Primary Bank—Farmers National Bank of Canfield
Sales $5.50Mil   Employees: 110
   *Also   DIRECTORS —Other Directors Are:
John Tonti
PRODUCTS: Tool & die, metal stamping, assembly special machines
S.I.C. 3544; 3469; 3559

QUAKER OATS CO.
321 N. Clark St., Quaker Tower, Chicago, Ill. 60610
Tel. 312-222-7111

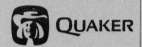

*Chrm & Chief Exec Officer—William D. Smithburg
*Pres & Chief Oper Officer—Frank J. Morgan
Exec V-P (Pres. Grocery Specialties Div)—Philip A. Marineau
Exec V-P (Diversified Grocery Products)—Douglas W. Mills
*Exec V-P (Intl Grocery Products)—Paul E. Price
Exec V-P (Pres-Fisher-Price Div)—R. Bruce Sampsell
Sr V-P (Human Resources)—Lawrence M. Bayton
Sr V-P (Fin)—Michael J. Callahan
*Sr V-P (Law) & Secy—Luther C. McKinney
Sr V-P (U. S. Grocery Products Serv)—David R. Nogle
V-P & Assoc Gen Cor Coun—John H. Calhoun
V-P (Tax)—Leland R. Chalmers
V-P (Dir-Latin America)—James F. Doyle
V-P & Gen Cor Coun—R. Thomas Howell, Jr.
V-P (Bus Devel & Cor Plan)—Terry G. Westbrook
V-P (Pres-Quaker Oats of Canada)—Jon K. Grant
V-P & Treas—Richard D. Jaquith
V-P (Dir-Europe)—Jose A. Rodriguez
V-P (Cor Affairs)—Deborah E. Kelly
V-P (Cor Adm Serv)—Richard E. Koznika
V-P (New Areas)—William C. Trotter
V-P (Govt Rel)—Thomas F. Roeser
V-P (Inf Sys)—Ronald T. Brzezinski
V-P & Cont—Raymond C. Eggleston
V-P (Pres Pet Foods)—George J. Yapp
V-P (Cor Programs)—W. Thomas Phillips
V-P (Pres-Food Service Div)—Russell L. Jones
Accts—Arthur Andersen & Co., Chicago, Ill.
Sales $4.42Bil   Employees: 30,000
Stock Exchange(s): NYS, BST, PAC, MID, TOR, PSE
   *Also   DIRECTORS —Other Directors Are:
Richard D. Harrison   Weston R. Christopherson
William J. Kennedy, III   Vernon R. Loucks, Jr.
Thomas C. MacAvoy   Donald E. Meads
G. G. Michelson (Mrs.)   Walter J. Salmon
William L. Weiss
PRODUCTS: Foods, pet foods & toys
S.I.C. 2032; 2038; 2041; 2043; 2045; 2047; 2051; 2052; 2099; 3942; 3944; 5411; 5621; 5945

QUAKER SALES CORP.
Cooper Ave., Johnstown, Pa. 15907
Tel. 814-536-7541

*Pres—Elvin W. Overdorff, Jr.
*V-P—Calvin Q. Overdorff
*Secy & Treas—Donald Overdorff
Accts—Martin, Waltman & Kotzan, Inc., Johnstown, Pa.
Primary Bank—Johnstown Bank & Trust Co.
Primary Law Firm—Kaminsky, Kelly, Wharton & Thomas
Sales Range: $5—8Mil   Employees: 100
   *Also DIRECTORS
BUSINESS: Road & paving contractors & supplies
S.I.C. 1611; 5083

QUAKER STATE CORP.-SOUTHEAST REGION
(Subs. Quaker State Corporation)
5500 S. Cobb Dr., Smyrna, Ga. 30080
Tel. 404-799-7212

*Chrm & Chief Exec Officer—Jack W. Corn
*Pres & Chief Oper Officer—Homer M. Ellenburg
*Exec V-P (Admin) & Secy—Maurice G. Erwin
V-P (Coml Sales)—Ennis Mobley
V-P (Sales)—Robert E. Hardesty
V-P (Purch)—Patricia Woodall
Treas—K. Joe Sutton
*Asst Treas—Conrad A. Conrad
Compt—William H. Fields, Jr.
Accts—Coopers & Lybrand, Pittsburgh, Pa.
Primary Bank—National Bank of Georgia
Primary Law Firm—Smith, Eubanks & Smith, P.C.
Sales $53.60Mil   Employees: 250
   *Also   DIRECTORS —Other Directors Are:
W. B. Cook
Quentin E. Wood

QUAKER STATE CORPORATION
255 Elm St., Oil City, Pa. 16301
Tel. 814-676-7676

*Chrm—Quentin E. Wood
*Pres & Chief Exec Officer—Jack W. Corn
*Vice-Chrm—Roger A. Markle
Exec V-P—James D. Berry, III
*Exec V-P—Walter B. Cook
*V-P, Secy & Coun—Gerald W. Callahan
*V-P (Fin) & Chief Fin Officer—Conrad A. Conrad
/-P (Research)—Embert H. DeLong
*V-P (Distr)—Homer M. Ellenburg
*V-P (Mktg)—William C. Helsley
V-P & Treas—R. Scott Keefer
V-P (Sales)—William E. Marshall
V-P & Cont—John R. Sedlacko
V-P (Mktg)—Earl V. Swift
Public Rel Mgr—Benton H. Faulkner
Purch Mgr—William E. Kingsley
Mktg Dir (Motor Oil)—Richard L. Pennington
Accts—Coopers & Lybrand
Revenue: $847.95Mil   Employees: 4,400
Stock Exchange(s): NYS, BST, MID, PSE
   *Also   DIRECTORS —Other Directors Are:
Lee R. Forker   Thomas A. Gardner
H. Bryce Jordan   W. Craig McClelland
Kenton E. McElhattan   William J. McFate
Delbert J. McQuaide
PRODUCTS: Lubricants, fuels, other automotive aftermarket products, quick lube serv. centers; ins., truck & auto lights; coal
S.I.C. 5172; 2992; 5013

QUAKER STATE MINIT-LUBE, INC.
(Subs. Quaker State Corporation)
1385 W. 2200 S., Salt Lake City, Utah 84119
Tel. 801-972-6667

*Chrm—Roger A. Markle
*Vice-Chrm—John P. Pearson
*Pres & Chief Oper Officer—Jeffrey J. O'Neill
Exec V-P & Cor Coun—David E. Neff
Exec V-P (Mktg)—Paul G. Remund
V-P & Cont—Kirk A. Umphrey
*V-P (Hallmark Ins)—Wanda M. Hall
V-P & Asst Coun—Kerry A. Scovill
V-P (Oper)—Kay D. Olsen
*Secy & Treas—George D. Morgan
Accts—Coopers & Lybrand, Salt Lake City, Utah
Primary Bank—Key Bank
Primary Law Firm—Jones, Waldo, Holbrook & McDonough
Sales $21Mil   Employees: 1,500
   *Also   DIRECTORS —Other Directors Are:
Jack W. Corn   Quentin E. Wood
PRODUCTS: Franchisor & operator of fast lube service centers
S.I.C. 5141; 5172; 5812

QUALCORP, INC.
(Affil. Penn Central Federal Systems Co.)
Shelter Rock Rd., Danbury, Conn. 06810
Tel. 203-796-5000

Pres—W. Derek Buckley
Sr V-P (Sys)—Joseph A. Savarese
Sr V-P (Serv)—Allen R. Schwartz
V-P (Admin)—Phyllis F. Zappala
Chief Fin Officer—D. Joseph Gersuk
Accts—Deloitte Haskins & Sells, New York, N. Y.
Sales $50Mil   Employees: 700
PRODUCTS: Quality assurance service & equip.
S.I.C. 3829; 3825

QUALHEIM, INC.
1225 16th St., Box 368, Racine, Wis. 53401
Tel. 414-634-6671

*Chrm & Pres—Ellen A. Qualheim
*V-P (Mktg)—Robert F. Karis
Secy & Treas—Julane Nelson
Accts—Robert G. Berkley, Racine, Wis.
Primary Bank—M&I Bank of Racine
Primary Law Firm—Reinhart, Boerner, Van Deuren, Norris & Rieselbach
Sales $1Mil   Employees: 20
   *Also DIRECTORS
PRODUCTS: Electric coml. vegetable cutters, coml. can & bottle crushers, glass washers
S.I.C. 3556; 3565; 2589

QUALI-TECH MACHINE & ENGINEERING CO.
330 Bond St., Elk Grove Village, Ill. 60007
Tel. 312-439-1311

*Chrm & Pres—Paul Carson, Jr.
*V-P—Barbara L. Carson

Herbert Birtes
BUSINESS: Construction, metal work, oil field serv
S.I.C. 1629; 1389; 1791; 1799; 3441; 3448; 3449

QUALITAD SALES CORP.
Quality Lane, Rutland, Vt. 05701
Tel. 802-773-9141

*Chrm & Pres—Daniel Bernhardt
*V-P—A. Bernhardt
Sales Range: $2—5Mil   Employees: 50
   *Also DIRECTORS
PRODUCTS: Plastic trays & containers
S.I.C. 3089

QUALITEX, INC.
19 Industrial Lane, Providence, R. I. 02919
Tel. 401-751-5727

*V-P & Treas—Mauro Primo
*V-P (Mfg)—David E. Monti
*V-P (Sales)—Nancy Monti
*Secy—Jonathan Cole
*Purch Agt—Joe Riccitelli
Accts—Laventhol & Horwath, Providence, R. I.
Primary Bank—Hospital Trust National Bank
Primary Law Firm—Edwards & Angell
Sales Range: $10—30Mil   Employees: 80
   *Also DIRECTORS
PRODUCTS: Extruded rubber thread
S.I.C. 3069; 2241

QUALITONE
(Div. Biscayne Holdings, Inc.)
4931 W. 35th St., Minneapolis, Minn. 55416
Tel. 612-927-7161

Pres—Lane Burger
Exec V-P—Max Harada
V-P (Mktg & Sales)—Joel Wernick
V-P (Fin)—James Anderson
Per Dir—Cleo DeBina
Purch Agt—Thomas McGregor
Sr Engr—Katsumi Tanaka
Mktg Mgr—David Wessell
Audiology—Dawn Galloway
Employees: 170
PRODUCTS: Hearing aids & audiometers
S.I.C. 3842; 3825

QUALITONE INDUSTRIES, INC.
696 Locust St., Mount Vernon, N. Y. 10552
Tel. 914-668-1135

Pres—Robert Karns
Gen Mgr—David Cutler
Sales Range: $2—5Mil   Employees: 10
PRODUCTS: Phonograph needles
S.I.C. 3679

QUALITROL CORP.
(Subs. Danaher Corporation)
1385 Fairport Rd., Fairport, N. Y. 14450
Tel. 716-586-1515

*Pres—John R. Bosher, Jr.
V-P (Mktg & Sales)—Daniel F. McNulty
*Treas—P. W. Allender
*Secy—M. T. Lynch
Cont—David E. Winterton
Accts—Arthur Andersen & Co., New York, N. Y.
Primary Bank—National Westminster Bank USA
Primary Law Firm—Skadden, Arps, Slate, Meagher & Flom
Sales $10Mil   Employees: 150
   *Also   DIRECTORS —Other Directors Are
Mitchell P. Rales   Steven M. Rales
PRODUCTS: Liquid level gauges controls, thermometers, high temperature alarms, pressure relief devices, press electrical switches
S.I.C. 3824; 3492; 3613; 3643

QUALITY ALUMINUM CASTING CO.
1242 Lincoln Ave., Waukesha, Wis. 53186
Tel. 414-542-0731

*Chrm—Gregory E. Pauly, New Holstein, Wis.
*Pres & Chief Exec Officer—C. C. McMullen
*V-P (Qual Con & Tech Support)—P. C. Gottgetreu
V-P (Mfg)—John Nebeo
V-P—Paul Thompson
Treas—David J. Rutkowski
Purch Mgr—G. F. Fahl
Mgr Ind Rel—Robert Swanson
Accts—Arthur Young, Milwaukee, Wis.
Primary Bank—M&I Marshall & Ilsley Bank
Sales: $11.50Mil   Employees: 200
   *Also   DIRECTORS —Other Directors Are
J. W. Blakey   James Butler
Gilbert A. Harter   Jeff Pauly
Theodore Pauly
PRODUCTS: Aluminum alloy castings, lost foam molded, permanent molded, cold-set molded, & machined
S.I.C. 3365; 3363

QUALITY ARCHITECTURAL PRODUCTS, INC.
16804 S. Gridley Pl., Box 549, Cerritos, Ca
Tel. 213-402-7884

*Chrm & Pres—Warren R. Olson
*V-P (Fin, Data Proc & Cr) & Treas—John A.
*Secy—Virginia L. Olson
Purch Agt—Dave
Engr M

✔ **Source: Dun & Bradstreet *Million Dollar Directory***

The D&B *Million Dollar Directory* is composed of five volumes of information on over 160,000 companies with a net worth in excess of $500,000, with 250 or more employees or with $25 million or more in sales volume. The directory provides an alphabetical listing of company names, subsidiary relationships, headquarters, addresses, phone numbers, officers, numbers of employees, stock exchange numbers, SIC numbers, and annual sales. A cross-reference volume enables users to look up companies by geographical location or SIC code. Most large libraries and business libraries have Dun & Bradstreet.

This well-known directory is especially helpful for finding information on smaller firms, because it includes companies that are worth only $500,000. The *Million Dollar Directory* is one of the most popular of Dun & Bradstreet's industry directories.

D&B's other business guides include a directory of international firms, a directory of biographical data about principal officers and directors of 12,000 leading companies, a directory of ranking of company size within industrial categories and states, and a directory that traces the structure and ownership of multinational corporations.

✔ **Source: Ward's Business Directory (Gale Research)**

Ward's Directory is a five-volume set that provides information on 142,000 U.S. public and private companies. Volumes 1–3 list companies alphabetically; volume 4 is organized geographically by state; and volume 5 classifies businesses by their 4-digit SIC code, and then ranks them by sales. Data provided include name, address, city, SIC code, sales, number of employees, name of chief executive, year founded, and type of firm (e.g., private, public, subsidiary, or division).

Ward's is a very interesting and useful directory. Unlike other popular company directories, *Ward's* provides various *rankings* in its listings. For example, *Ward's* lists the largest pharmaceutical firms, and ranks firms geographically and by other categories. *Ward's* also claims that more than 90 percent of the firms in its directory are privately held—data on these companies are harder to find than for public firms.

✔ **Source:** *Hoover's Handbook of American Business* **(Hoover's)**

Hoover's Handbook provides one-page profiles of 500 major enterprises in the U.S., arranged alphabetically. For each listing, the directory provides an overview, history, names of top executives, address, phone, fax, major divisions and subsidiaries, rankings, names of competitors, stock price history, and other data.

A relatively new entry to the company directory field, Hoover's has made quite a name for itself by being the first to offer a company directory at a bargain price. While the preceding competitors' books cover many more firms, they cost well into the mid-hundreds of dollars, but you can get your own copy of the *Hoover's Handbook* for just $39.95 at many bookstores. Note that Hoover's also publishes a World Business edition as well, which covers international firms, and a Guide to Private Companies.

✔ **Source: Moody's** *Manuals* **(Dun & Bradstreet)**

Moody's *Manuals* provide a great deal of background and detail on specific companies. Typical information provided includes company history, structure, capital, lines of businesses and products, properties, subsidiaries, names of officers and directors, income statement, balance sheet, financial and operating data, and various stock charts and tables.

Much of the information provided in Moody's comes from documents that public companies are required to file by the Securities and Exchange Commission (SEC). The *Manuals* are a particularly good source for tracing the history of a large company.

✔ **Source:** *Business Rankings* **(Gale Research)**

A collection of 3,800 citations of ranked lists of companies, for various categories. Also included is a salary list for over 150 occupations.

This directory helps answer the question "who's number one" in a certain field. It is actually a compilation of information that the Brooklyn Public Library scans in its daily duties, gleaned from scores of reference sources.

✔ **Source: *Thomas Register of American Manufacturers***

Thomas Register tells you who manufactures what product, and where the manufacturer is located. There are three sets of volumes. One set consists of sixteen volumes and is organized alphabetically by product. It lists manufacturers' names and addresses. A companion two-volume set lists 145,000 U.S. companies in alphabetical order, providing addresses, phone numbers, asset ratings, and other information. These two volumes also include a trademark index at the back. A third set of volumes provides more than 10,000 pages of actual catalog data from about 1,800 companies. Most libraries keep a set of *Thomas Register.*

Thomas Register is a very useful resource. Volume 1 of the first set starts with a listing of abacus manufacturers, and the last volume ends with a listing of manufacturers of Zonolite (a form of insulation). If you look up radiation detectors, you'll find about twenty-five manufacturers—about the same number of firms that manufacture poultry netting. Although *Thomas Register* does not list every manufacturer of a product, it is still an extraordinarily comprehensive directory. *Thomas Register* is also available for searching on the web: http://www.thomasregister.com

---

TIP: To find more obscure manufacturers, check trade magazines that publish an annual buyers' guide. These are special issues devoted to listing manufacturers and suppliers.

✔ **Source: *Gale's U.S. Industry Profiles/Gale's Encyclopedia of American Industries* (Gale Research)**

The *Encyclopedia of American Industries* is split into two volumes: manufacturing industries and service/nonmanufacturing industries. Both volumes cover approximately 1,000 industries. The book provides an industry snapshot, organization and structure, background and development, current conditions, industry leaders, workforce, international issues, R&D, and industry information sources. The other guide is shorter and covers 100 of the most significant industries in the U.S.

These two directories from Gale make a nice substitute to the popular *U.S. Industrial Outlook*, which was discontinued in 1995 by the Department of Commerce and replaced by the *U.S. Global Trade Outlook*, which is more international in focus but provides fewer details on as many industries.

> **TIP:** Gale Research is probably the leading publisher of business, statistical, and all-purpose directories in the U.S. Get a catalog of all of its offerings by calling 800–877–GALE.

✔ **Source: *The Wall Street Transcript* (Richard A. Holman)**

The Wall Street Transcript is a verbatim transcript of roundtable discussions conducted by the publication's editors with CEOs and industry leaders. It is published weekly and covers industries ranging from aerospace to waste management.

This source can be a bit difficult to wade through, and its indexing system is cumbersome, but it is unusual and intriguing. It provides actual transcripts of conversations of business leaders on developments within their industry, covering topics such as major strategic thrusts of leading companies, technology developments, and other factors influencing the industry.

✔ **Source: *Organization Charts* (Gale Research)**

Contains organization charts for over 200 businesses and organizations around the United States. Also provides detailed listings of department and division names and, where available, identification of subsidiary and parent companies.

A unique source for researching a corporation's structure and organization. According to the publisher, the data were compiled from public sources and then verified with the specific companies.

> **TIP:** Another interesting business source that may come in handy is *Companies and Their Brands* (and *International Companies and Their Brands*), published by Gale Research. It identifies which companies are behind which trade names (e.g., Band-Aid is the trade name of Johnson & Johnson's adhesive bandages).

SUBSIDIARIES AND DIVISIONS DIRECTORIES

One of the most difficult tasks of business researchers is discovering linkages between corporate parents and their subsidiaries and divisions. The following sources will help identify connections.

✔ **Source: *America's Corporate Families* (Dun & Bradstreet)**

A description of 11,000 U.S. parent companies and their 60,000 subsidiaries and divisions. Includes any firm worth more than $500,000, conducting business from two or more locations, and having a controlling interest in one or more subsidiaries.

This is a very useful tool for finding out the subsidiaries and divisions a corporation operates and for finding names of division vice presidents and managers. Each listing provides names, addresses, sales, and the industry of each division and subsidiary listed. Volume 2 in this set is titled *International Affiliates*, which provides data about companies with foreign parents and U.S. subsidiaries. These directories are designed to be rather easy to use.

✔ **Source: *Who Owns Whom* (Dun & Bradstreet)**

Lists connections among companies. Parent firms are listed in alphabetical order.

Not as easy to use as *America's Corporate Families*, but it may still be worth checking to dig up hard-to-find information. Separate directories cover North America; Australia and the Far East; United Kingdom and the Republic of Ireland; and Continental Europe.

✔ **Source: *Directory of Corporate Affiliations* (National Register Publishing)**

Lists data on 3,700 U.S. parent companies and 44,200 divisions, subsidiaries, and affiliates and 12,650 outside the United States.

An easier directory to use than *Who Owns Whom*, but not as simple to use as *America's Corporate Families*.

INTERNATIONAL BUSINESS DIRECTORIES

Today's business world is global, and researchers can no longer confine themselves to finding facts on firms and industries that operate within the boundaries of the United States. The following is a selected listing of some of the most useful directories of information on companies in other parts of the world. If you have trouble finding any of these at your local public library, try visiting a nearby university's business school library.

✔ **Source: *Major Companies of Europe* (Graham & Trotman, London)**

A three-volume set that provides facts about companies in Western Europe and the United Kingdom. Information provided includes company name, address, names of top executives, trade names, company activities, subsidiaries, sales, profit, and number of employees.

This is a straightforward directory, broken down into three volumes. Volume 1 contains information on 3,000 firms located in the European Community (EC); volume 2 lists data on 1,300 British firms; and volume 3 lists information about 1,400 firms located in Western Europe that are not part of the EC.

✔ **Source: *Japan Company Handbook* (Toyo Keizai Inc.)**

Provides financial information on all Japanese companies listed in the first and second sections of the Tokyo, Osaka, and Nagoya stock exchanges. Approximately 2,000 firms are covered.

This directory is considered the leading sourcebook for finding out about Japanese companies. It is filled with loads of useful data, including company descriptions, profit and loss statements, breakdown of sales by categories, methods for raising funds, in-depth financial statements, balance sheets, company outlooks, stock price graphs, and more. Amazingly, with so much data provided for each firm, the handbook is still very easy to use and read and is accompanied by clear explanatory material.

✔ **Source: *Principal International Businesses: The World Marketing Directory* (Dun & Bradstreet)**

Lists data on 50,000 firms in 143 countries around the world. Companies are selected for inclusion based on their size and prominence. This directory provides names, addresses, sales, year founded, names of top executives, number of employees, and type of industry.

This is a very useful source if you need to get some basic information on any major company located anywhere around the world. The directory makes it easy to find firms by providing both an alphabetical and industry index.

The authors, Ruth A. Pagell and Michael Halperin, are both well-known experts in the business information world.

TIP: If you need to find facts on a lesser-known company or one that is in a smaller country, I'd suggest visiting a good university business school's library and simply sit and browse for a while at the business directory reference section. There you will likely find a variety of directories that cover firms operating in *just one specific country.* (By the way, you'll also likely find there many *state directories* as well—compilations of data about firms operating within an individual state. These are often published by Chambers of Commerce or state economic development offices.)

"INSIDER" DIRECTORIES

✔ **Source: *Directories in Print* (Gale Research)**

This directory describes over 15,500 different types of specialized directories, covering subjects such as banking, agriculture, law, government, science, engineering, education, information science, biography, arts and entertainment, public affairs, health, religion, hobbies, and sports. You can find this guide, published annually, at most large public libraries.

This excellent source unearths an amazingly diverse range of specialized directories. (A directory is any kind of reference book that tells readers where they can find sources of information within a specific field.) Here are some samples of the directories indexed in this "ultimate" directory: *Special Libraries of Israel,*

★7622★
AMERICAN COUNCIL ON CONSUMER INTERESTS—
MEMBERSHIP LIST
American Council on Consumer Interests
Stanley Hall, Room 240
University of Missouri
Columbia, MO 65211   Phone: (314)882-3817
Number of listings: 2,000. **Frequency:** Biennial, odd years.
Price: Available to members only.

★7623★
AMERICAN GROUP PSYCHOTHERAPY ASSOCIATION—
MEMBERSHIP DIRECTORY
American Group Psychotherapy Association
25 E. 21st Street, 6th Floor
New York, NY 10010   Phone: (212)477-2677
Covers: 3,500 physicians, psychologists, clinical social
workers, psychiatric nurses, and other mental health
professionals interested in treatment of emotional problems by
group methods. **Entries include:** Name, office or home
address, highest degree held, affiliate society of which a
member. **Arrangement:** Alphabetical. **Indexes:** Geographical.
Pages (approx.): 160. **Frequency:** Reported as biennial;
previous edition 1984; latest edition summer 1987. **Price:**
$25.00. **Other formats:** Cheshire labels, $65.00 per thousand;
pressure-sensitive labels, $75.00 per thousand.

American Humane Agency Directory See **Directory of**
Animal Care and Control Agencies (7747)

★7624★
AMERICAN SOCIETY OF ACCESS PROFESSIONALS—
MEMBERSHIP DIRECTORY [Freedom of information]
American Society of Access Professionals
2001 S Street, N. W., Suite 630
Washington, DC 20009   Phone: (202)462-8888
Covers: Over 300 individuals concerned with the methods,
procedures, and techniques of administering statutes
pertaining to the availability of records or information contained
therein, including freedom of information, privacy protection,
open meetings, and fair credit reporting laws. **Entries include:**
Name, address, phone, affiliation. **Arrangement:** Alphabetical.
Indexes: Geographical. **Pages (approx.):** 35. **Frequency:**
Annual, winter. **Editor:** Clifford M. Brownstein. **Price:** Available
to members only.

American Society of Association Executives—
Convention & Exposition Managers Section Directory
See **Who's Who in Association Management (8281)**

American Society of Association Executives—Directory
See **Who's Who in Association Management (8281)**

★7625★
AMERICAN SOCIETY OF JOURNALISTS AND
AUTHORS—DIRECTORY
American Society of Journalists and Authors
1501 Broadway, Suite 1907
New York, NY 10036   Phone: (212)997-0947
Covers: Over 750 member freelance nonfiction writers.
Entries include: Writer's name, home and office addresses
and phone numbers, specialties, areas of expertise; name,
address, and phone of agent; memberships; books; periodicals
to which contributed; awards; employment history.
Arrangement: Alphabetical. **Indexes:** Subject specialty, type
of material written, geographical. **Pages (approx.):** 90.
Frequency: Biennial, October/November of even years.
Former title(s): Society of Magazine Writers - Directory of
Professional Writers (1975); American Society of Journalists

and Authors - Directory of Professional Writers. **Price:** $50.0
Other formats: Mailing labels.

★7626★
AMERICA'S HIDDEN PHILANTHROPIC WEALTH:
TOMORROW'S POTENTIAL FOUNDATION GIANTS
Taft Group
5130 MacArthur Boulevard, N.W.
Washington, DC 20016   Phone: (202)966-708
Covers: 300 small family foundations with the potential t
become billion dollar philanthropies. Published in four loos
leaf editions covering 75 foundations each. **Entries inclu**
Foundation name, location, analysis of wealth, philanthro
interests, study of the conditions leading to expansion
future giving interests, biography, giving history, ir
relationship information. **Indexes:** Individuals are alphab
foundations are geographical; grants are by cat
Frequency: Annual; suspended indefinitely. **Price:**
each edition, postpaid; $197.00 per set.

★7627★
AMERICA'S NEWEST FOUNDATIONS: THE
SOURCEBOOK ON RECENTLY CREATED
PHILANTHROPIES
Taft Group
5130 MacArthur Boulevard, N. W.
Washington, DC 20016   Phone: (202)966-
Covers: Over 500 foundations created since 1980 that prov
grants to charitable organizations. **Entries include:** Foundat
name, address, phone, name and title of contact, curre
charitable and geographic preference, previous recipient an
grant types, assets. **Arrangement:** Alphabetical. **Indexes:**
Personal name, type of grant, giving interest, recipient location.
Frequency: Annual, February. **Editor:** Ben Lord. **Price:** $89.95.
Other information: Former publisher, Public Service Materials
Center.

★7628★
ANIMAL ORGANIZATIONS & SERVICES DIRECTORY
Animal Stories
16787 Beach Boulevard
Huntington Beach, CA 92647
Covers: Over 400 national and state organizations involv
animal protection and welfare; also lists veterinary and m
organizations such as clinics, pet insurance comp
zoological societies, pet transporting and other service
fancier clubs, consultants, and publishers of magazine:
newsletters concerned with animals. **Entries include:** Nar
organization, address, phone, branch offices, year establis
key personnel, membership information, objectives, descrip
of materials available by mail. **Arrangement:** Classified by ty
of organization or service. **Indexes:** Alphabetical. **Pag**
(approx.): 230. **Frequency:** Biennial, fall of odd years. **Edito**
Kathleen A. Reece. **Advertising accepted.** Circulation 5,00(
Price: $16.95, plus $1.50 shipping.

Annotated Directory of Exemplary Family Based
Programs See **Annotated Directory of Selected**
Family-Based Service Programs (7629)

★7629★
ANNOTATED DIRECTORY OF SELECTED FAMILY-
BASED SERVICE PROGRAMS
National Resource Center on Family Based Services
Oakdale Hall, Room N240
University of Iowa
Iowa City, IA 52319   Phone: (319)335-4
Covers: 275 social service programs nationwide dealing
family-centered services and operating out of public a
voluntary agencies. **Entries include:** Name, address, pho

Computer Software Applications in Oceanography, Bicycle Resource Guide, Major Companies of Europe, American Indian Painters, Index of Stolen Art, and *Free Things for Teachers.* A detailed subject index is provided at the back of the book, so all you need to do is look up the topic of your choice, and *Directories in Print* refers you to a particular directory, giving you its name, publisher and address, phone number, specialties, and other details.

TIP: Getting the Directory You Want
• Many of the directories listed in this guide are cheap or moderately priced, but certain ones are expensive and are best used at a library. To find a library that has a directory you need, contact the Special Libraries Association (see page 8) and find out which libraries specialize in your topic of interest. Then, just call or write the library to see if it has the guide. If it does, you can then ask the librarian there to look up what you need.
• For example, let's say you need information on whether a particular food is kosher. Checking the guide, you'll locate a directory called *Kosher Directory: Directory of Kosher Products and Services.* To get this directory, you could write to the address listed and purchase it, or you could contact the Special Libraries Association to find a library devoted to Jewish studies. Such a library may have this directory, and you could ask the librarian there to look up the food and supply you with the answer.

✔ **Source: *World Directory of Environmental Organizations* (California Institute of Public Affairs)**

Covering more than 2,600 organizations in over 200 countries, this directory provides detailed descriptions and contact information for key national governmental and nongovernmental organizations. In addition to the listings, this directory has a number of extra features, including a timeline, glossary, "who's doing what" analysis, description of U.N. programs, and more. The book is a cooperative project of The California Institute of Public Affairs, the Sierra Club, and the International Union for Conservation of Nature and Natural Resources.

This source can be helpful to anyone researching environmental issues and needs a place to start looking for data. Other places to find good environmental reference sources would be *Directories*

in Print, The Encyclopedia of Associations, and *Research Centers Directory.* Also, the publisher of these three guidebooks (Gale Research, Detroit, MI) lists several environmental reference directories in its catalog.

✔ **Source: *Research Centers Directory* (Gale Research)**

An annual directory of 13,400 university, government, and other nonprofit research organizations. Major subjects span agriculture, business, education, government, law, math, social sciences, and humanities. You'll find this guide in university and other academically oriented libraries.

The *Research Centers Directory* provides a wealth of information on who's conducting research on what subjects around the country. You'll find an incredible diversity of studies being conducted. Some examples of the research organizations listed in this directory: the Alcohol Research Group, the National Bureau of Economic Research, the International Copper Research Association, the Birth Defects Institute, the Center for Russian and East European Studies. . . you get the idea.

I once used this guide when I was researching the topic of "rebuilding rather than replacing automobiles." By checking the directory, I found a research institute associated with a university in Detroit that was conducting a study on just that topic.

The directory is easy to use. You just look up your subject, and the directory refers you to a particular research center. It provides the center's name, a contact person, the address, the phone number, a description of the activities conducted, and the organization's publications.

✔ **Source: *Foundation Directory* (Foundation Center)**

The *Foundation Directory,* published by the Foundation Center, is a guide that can help you find the right foundation to apply to in order to obtain funding and grants. Many libraries have it.

This guide is only one of many directories and publications published by the Foundation Center. The Foundation Center maintains information on over 27,000 active foundations and supports a national network of 170 library reference collections made

available for free public use. The biggest collections are located in New York City, Washington, DC, Cleveland, and San Francisco. These libraries provide important reference tools, such as sample application forms and the annual reports, tax information, and publications of foundations.

The center publishes a variety of helpful information sources, including specialized directories that tell you where to get grants for projects that cover subjects like public health, the aged, minorities, museums, and so on. For more information on the Foundation Center's publications and to locate a foundation library collection near you, contact The Foundation Center, 79 Fifth Avenue, New York, NY 10003; 212–620–4230.

TIP: *Research Centers Directory* is a good source for finding "think tanks"—institutions such as the Cato Institute, the Heritage Foundation, the Brookings Institution, and other centers that study public policy–related issues and publish their findings in reports or articles. Think tanks are mainly listed in the section of the directory named "government and public affairs." You can also link to home page of many think tanks on the World Wide Web.

✔ **Source: *National Directory of Nonprofit Organizations* (Taft Group)**

Data on over 260,000 nonprofit organizations. Directory provides addresses, phone numbers, annual income, IRS status, and activities.

Included in this interesting directory are organizations such as hospitals, museums, conservation organizations, alumni organizations, and many other types of nonprofits.

✔ **Source: Congressional Information Service Indexes**

Check university or large public libraries for any of the following comprehensive statistical directories published by the Congressional Information Service: *American Statistics Index,* for sources of government statistics; *Index to International Statistics,* for sources of foreign statistics; *Statistical Reference Index,* for sources of U.S. nongovernment statistics.

Together these guides index more than 1,600 sources of statistical information.

ment grants, and foundations. Staff: 2 research professionals, 8 supporting professionals, 2 technicians, 1 other.

Research Activities and Fields: tress effects on natural ecosystems, integrated pest management, acid rain, solar energy, and behavioral, agricultural, community, and population ecology. Maintains 16 quarter-acre animal enclosures, aviaries, and a database on precipitation chemistry. Offers field ecology courses.

Publications and Services: Research results published in scientific journals. Provides graduate and undergraduate training.

★983★
MIAMI UNIVERSITY
INSECT COLLECTION
Department of Zoology   Phone: (513) 529-5454
Oxford, OH 45056   Founded: 1910
Dr. D.L. Deonier, Curator

Governance: Integral unit of Department of Zoology at Miami University. Supported by parent institution. Staff: 2 research professionals, 2-5 supporting professionals, 1 technician, 1 other.

Research Activities and Fields: Systematics, behavior, and ecology of aquatic insects, primarily Diptera, Ephydridae, and Chironomidae. Maintains an extensive collection of shore flies and rearing facilities for aquatic insects.

Publications and Services: Research results published in professional journals and published symposia. Maintains a library on entomology; Marian Winner, librarian.

★984★
MIAMI UNIVERSITY
INSTITUTE OF ENVIRONMENTAL SCIENCES
Oxford, OH 45056   Phone: (513) 529-5811
Gene E. Willeke, Director   Founded: 1969

Governance: Integral unit of Miami University. Supported by parent institution, U.S. government, and local governmental agencies. Staff: 3 research professionals, 1 supporting professional, 1 other.

Research Activities and Fields: Environmental sciences, including studies on river restoration techniques, hazardous and toxic substances, acid precipitation, environmental history, ecological dynamics, conservation, land use planning, water quality, community environmental planning, and energy. Produces environmental media, especially tape and slide programs. Offers a master's degree in environmental sciences.

Publications and Services: Research results published in scientific and technical journals and project reports. Maintains a library.

★985★
MIAMI UNIVERSITY
~~RT A. HEFNER ZOOLOGY MUSEUM~~

✔ **Source: The Yellow Pages**

Don't forget this familiar resource. You can use the Yellow Pages to find manufacturers, dealers, and all types of service firms. It is a great and underestimated source of information! Large libraries have the Yellow Pages of most of the bigger cities, and you can use these listings to supplement what you get out of *Thomas Register* (see page 28). The Manhattan Yellow Pages alone constitute an immense source of information on products and services. (Large libraries usually have the white pages of the major cities, too.)

TIP: Locating International Phone Directories
• Most large libraries contain a selection of white and Yellow Pages from major cities around the world. But if you don't see the region you want, you can call US West Direct and ask for their very valuable free paperback guidebook called *The Directory Source*. In addition to listing and describing a wide range of useful business directories, it is also a comprehensive guide to ordering phone books—both white and Yellow Pages—from countries spanning the globe. To get a copy, write to The Directory Source, US West Direct, c/o PDC, 13100 E. 39th Ave., Unit U, Denver, CO 80239–3527; 800–422–8793, ext. 150.

CD-ROMS IN LIBRARIES

One of the most powerful and valuable offerings at today's public and academic libraries are computer terminals equipped with CD-ROM disks and drives. CD-ROMs look similar to audio CDs and, like them, contain codes created by lasers. The key difference between the two, though, is that the CDs you use in your stereo play music, while the CD-ROM databases in a library contain and "play" information. The storage capacity of a CD-ROM is enormous: about 550 MB, or the equivalent of about 250,000 pages!

The information that you may find in a CD-ROM disk varies enormously. For example, there are CD-ROMs today that contain abstracts of articles published in hundreds of popular newspapers and magazines; the full text of articles from business and trade periodicals, excerpts from U.S. government reports, scholarly literature in psychology, company financial filings, and so on.

The nice thing about library CD-ROMs is not only are they free, but you don't need to be a computer expert to use them. They are

designed to be fairly simple to search and, to a large degree, self-explanatory.

Still, they can be a bit tricky, since there are several different vendors of CD-ROMs, and each one has its own unique procedures and methods for conducting a search. For this reason, it's quite important that before you do a search, you either ask a librarian for some assistance (believe me, the 5 or 10 minutes you take to do it can save you hours of frustration!), or at least look for some explanatory handouts that the library often puts together and makes available for users. Sure, you can still sit down and "wing it" and you'll probably be lucky and find a lot of what you want—but if you want to do it really well, then take a few minutes to prepare.

Typically, to search any library CD-ROM database you'd follow these basic steps (simplified here for clarity):

- **Choose the appropriate database**
  When you sit down at a CD-ROM terminal, the computer screen typically displays the title of the CD-ROM database currently "ready" to be searched or a menu of CD-ROMs on a network that you can choose from. You may be able to hit a key to read a description of the various databases available. Or there may be print literature next to the terminal that describes each of them. In any case, the first step is to make sure that you've selected a CD-ROM that is relevant to your information search.

- **Decide on a search method**
  You may be given a choice as to the *kind* of search you can perform. Typically, this includes either choosing an option to "browse" an already created list of subject terms, or to enter your own "key words" to try and match items contained in the database. (A fuller discussion of "keyword" database searching can be found in chapter 5.)

- **Search the database**
  If you choose to browse subject terms, you then scan through an alphabetical list of already created index terms and "mark" one or more terms that seem most relevant. If you choose to enter key words, you simply type in the word or words. In either case, the system then checks the database and informs you how many items

(e.g., article abstracts, report titles, or whatever else the particular CD-ROM contains) were matched to your search.

- **View results**
  After you find out how many items matched your search, you then normally can "view" a display listing those items. So, for example, say you were searching a newspaper abstract database for articles on the country of Borneo, and the system located twelve items. You could then view those abstracts, one at a time. Normally, you can also print out those items on an attached printer.

If you need additional background on databases and computer searching, take a look at chapter 5, which deals with this subject in detail.

TIP: Don't Get CD-ROM Database Terminals Confused with a Library's "Online Catalog."
• While both workstations may appear alike, an online catalog contains only information on the *holdings* of the particular library you're working at. A full CD-ROM workstation, however, contains disks that include bibliographies, abstracts, or the full text of articles and/or reports from many sources, not necessarily just those found in that library.

Systems Available

What kind of CD-ROMs are available at libraries, and how do they differ? Although today there are several major vendors of CD-ROM systems that you might encounter, only a few are truly widespread, and we'll examine those here:

InfoTrak

InfoTrak is the brand name of a series of CD-ROMs produced by a firm called Information Access Company of Foster City, California. That firm pioneered the placement of consumer-oriented CD-ROMs in public libraries with the introduction of its computerized indexing systems in 1986. Today, you may find any or all of these specific InfoTrak products at a public or academic library:

- **Academic Index**
  Indexes approximately 400 scholarly and general-interest journals, including substantial abstracts for most titles. Also provides 6 months coverage of *The New York Times*.

- **Business Index**
  Abstracts 700–850 journals, plus *The Wall Street Journal, The New York Times, The Asian Wall Street Journal,* and *The Financial Times of Canada.*

- **General Periodicals Index**
  Indexes and abstracts 1,100 business and general-interest periodicals, as well as *The New York Times, The Wall Street Journal,* and the *Christian Science Monitor.*

- **Government Publications Index**
  An index to the monthly catalog of the Government Printing Office.

- **Health Index**
  An index to over 160 core publications on health, fitness, nutrition, and medicine.

- **Health Reference Center**
  Provides the full text of 150 titles on health, fitness, nutrition, and medical issues. Includes 100 consumer-oriented magazines and 500 medical educational pamphlets.

- **Investext**
  Indexing and the full text of company and industry research reports prepared by over 60 leading Wall Street firms, as well as regional and international brokerage and financial firms.

- **LegalTrac**
  An index to over 800 legal publications. Sources include all major law reviews, 7 legal newspapers, law specialty publications, and bar association journals.

- **Magazine Index Plus**
  Indexes 400 general-interest magazines most frequently found in public libraries, plus the current two months of *The New York Times* and *The Wall Street Journal.*

- **Magazine ASAP Plus**
  Provides the full text of articles found in 100 titles selected from Magazine Index Plus.

- **National Newspaper Index**
  Indexes 5 national newspapers combined in one source. Covers indexing of *The New York Times, The Wall Street Journal, Christian Science Monitor, Washington Post,* and *Los Angeles Times.*

  ### University Microfilms
  University Microfilms Inc., or UMI (Ann Arbor, MI), with its "ProQuest" system is another major provider of CD-ROMs in libraries. Here is a list of some of its most popular databases:

- **ABI/INFORM**
  Provides 150 word abstracts from articles published in major leading business periodicals.

- **Business Dateline**
  Provides the full text of articles from 350 regional business journals.

- **Newspaper Abstracts**
  Provides indexing (and brief abstracts) for 8 major national newspapers: *The New York Times, The Atlanta Constitution, The Boston Globe, Chicago Tribune, Christian Science Monitor, Los Angeles Times, The Wall Street Journal, The Washington Post* and *USA Today.*

- **Newspapers Fulltext**
  This database provides the full text of *American Banker, Atlanta Constitution* and *Atlanta Journal, Christian Science Monitor, The New York Times, San Francisco Chronicle, USA Today, The Wall Street Journal,* and *The Washington Post.*

- ***New York Times* Ondisc**
  Provides the full text of articles printed in *The New York Times.* Updated monthly.

- **Periodical Abstracts**
  Abstracts hundreds of popular magazine articles.

InfoTrak and ProQuest are not the only CD-ROM systems you may encounter in a library. Other major vendors include H. W. Wilson and SilverPlatter.

H. W. Wilson
Earlier in this chapter we described some of the special subject index print directories published by H. W. Wilson. That firm also makes

much of its indexing available on CD-ROM. Here are some of their most popular offerings:

- **Applied Science and Technology Index**
  Over 650,000 citations from 400 English-language trade and industry publications, covering topics from aeronautics to waste treatment.

- **Biological and Agricultural Index**
  Indexes to articles, symposia, conference papers, and more from 225 periodicals covering biological and agricultural issues.

- **Business Periodicals Index**
  Indexes to articles from about 400 periodicals covering all areas of business.

- **Humanities Index**
  Provides indexes to about 400 publications covering the humanities, with topics spanning art and archaeology to religion and philosophy. International coverage.

- **Index to Legal Periodicals**
  Citations to articles in 670 legal periodicals, covering all English-speaking countries.

- **Reader's Guide to Periodical Literature**
  An index to articles appearing in 240 of the most popular publications, plus *The New York Times*. Corresponds to the familiar green hardcopy volumes.

- **Social Science Index**
  Provides citations to articles in about 400 English-language periodicals on topics from anthropology to women's studies.

Another major provider of CD-ROMs in libraries is a firm called SilverPlatter. Its titles include EconLit for economic literature, PsychLit for psychological abstracts, and Disclosure, which is a database of company filings with the SEC.

Some other popular CD-ROMs include Books in Print Plus, Business Dateline (local and regional publications), Historical Abstracts, ERIC (educational literature), NewsBank (recent newspaper articles), PAIS (public affairs related information), Periodical Abstracts, Philosopher's Index, and the Religion Index. A wide range of government information is also available on CD-ROM.

Some of the major titles here include the U.S. Bureau of the Census, U.S. County Statistics, U.S. Government Periodicals Index, the National Trade Data Bank, County Business Patterns, Marcive, and the National Economic, Social, and Environmental Data Bank (NESE).

Finally, you may also encounter a system in the library called FirstSearch, which actually is not a CD-ROM at all, but an actual online search system from an outfit called OCLC that is becoming popular in libraries. (In an online search, you are linked via a telephone line to a remote computer where you search databases stored there; CD-ROMs, remember, are just discs inserted in the computer or computer network located where you are searching.) FirstSearch provides a wide range of popular information databases and allows for advanced and sophisticated searching. Because FirstSearch charges libraries for usage, you may not be permitted to use FirstSearch at academic libraries unless you are affiliated with the institution, or you may have to pay a fee.

Note that CD-ROMs differ not only in the subjects they cover, but also in their *level* of coverage, i.e., whether they offer you only citations, abstracts, or the full text. Citation databases only provide the most basic bibliographic data (e.g., title, author, date, name of source, page number), so you can track down the original source yourself. Abstracts give you a short summary of the original piece, which may run as short as a few lines or as much

---

TIP: Finding a Library with the CD-ROMs You Need
• How do you know whether the library nearest you is going to have the CD-ROM that you want? You can, of course, call the library ahead of time and ask, but if it does not, you don't have to give up. The trick then would be to find a college or university library that specializes in or at least strongly emphasizes the particular broad field you are researching, and then to contact that library. You can always call a reference librarian and ask him or her to do a quick CD-ROM search for you, and if they are not too busy, most will oblige. (There are several reference directories and special issues of popular magazines that can help you find out what schools are strong in what areas. One of the most popular is the yearly *U.S. News and World Report* college ranking issue.)

as a couple of paragraphs. This may or may not be enough information to satisfy you. Finally, full-text databases provide the complete text of the original item. In those cases, you normally then have no need to obtain the original item.

The newest type of CD-ROM, though still not widely available, offer not just full text but "full image." This means that instead of just getting page after page of straight text, you can actually view and print out duplicates of how the original article looked in the original publication. That means you get all the nice graphics, headlines, charts, graphs, etc., which are normally deleted in almost all regular full text CD-ROMs. The best known of these full image CD-ROMs is one called "Business Periodicals on Disc," a product of UMI. The only catch in using this system (other than finding a library that has it) is that it takes an extra step to conduct a search (first you need to find the citation to an article, then you get a corresponding code number to load an image), and secondly, you will almost certainly be charged a fee to make printouts. The fee is normally pretty low, though—probably 10 to 20 cents per page on a laser printer.

Search Tips

Although, as mentioned earlier, it is not all that difficult to search a library CD-ROM, it's still true that conducting a *good* search is something of both an art and a science. If you are inexperienced in performing searches, you may be disappointed in your results. If you're not sure what you are doing, your search may turn up irrelevant results, too many, or none at all. Here are a few basic tips and techniques you can follow to help your CD-ROM searches go smoothly and efficiently.

• Always make sure that the CD-ROM you are searching contains the type of information you are seeking! While it seems obvious that you wouldn't pick up a book titled *Consumer's Guide to Healthy Living* if you were researching facts on the furniture industry, it's easy to mistake one CD-ROM for another, since they don't as prominently display their contents in as familiar a fashion. Note the name of the specific CD-ROM you are searching, and if you have the opportunity, read (in print or on screen) a description of the database.

- Find out how far back in time the CD-ROM's coverage extends. CD-ROM database "backfiles" vary widely: Some go back five years, while others include data for only one year. Obviously, if you are searching for reports on an incident that occurred three years ago in a CD-ROM whose backfile is only one year, you're not going to find much!

- Find out how timely the CD-ROM is, and determine whether it is timely enough for your purposes. A CD-ROM's timeliness is usually measured by its "update frequency." Most vendors update their products on a monthly basis; however, some update theirs more or less frequently.

    Update frequency is not as straightforward as it sounds and can be misleading. For example, say you were searching a newspaper article database in late June, and the CD-ROM vendor claimed a monthly update frequency. What would be the *most recent* date of an article that you would expect to be able find in that database?

    The answer depends on many factors. Let's look at a worst case—but not at all atypical—scenario. Say that the vendor updates its file at the beginning of every month. That means that the last update sent to the library would have been in early June. Clearly, then, you're not going to find any articles published during June. But just because the library received an update in June doesn't mean that that disk necessarily will contain articles through the end of May. There is a "lag-time" that database vendors work with, which reflects the time it takes them to get data from the original sources keyed into the CD-ROM. So a disk received at a library in early June may still not have articles from, say, the last two weeks of May.

    Adding potential further delays is the fact that sometimes a workstation hasn't even been loaded with the latest version of a CD-ROM. This can occur for a number of reasons, such as the library not receiving it on time, or simply that the librarians have been too busy to getting around to loading it. I have had several experiences of sitting down at a CD-ROM terminal to discover that it had been two months or more since an updated disk was installed.

    The lesson here is simply this: Find out the date of the last reload of the CD-ROM, and take that into account accordingly. Often the reload date is displayed on the initial screen display when you first "open" the CD-ROM. If you don't find it there, you might ask a nearby librarian if he or she knows. If you still can't get an answer, you can "test" the CD-ROM by searching for occurrences of articles on some recent event.

Since CD-ROM timeliness is inherently limited, what do you do if you need the *very latest* information on a subject? Don't rely on CD-ROMs! You'll need to supplement your research with more timely sources: either by going "online" and searching databases updated on a weekly or daily basis (see chapter 5 for more on this) or by doing your research the old-fashioned way—by poring through the most recent print copies of the newspapers, journals, etc., that are relevant to your research!

- Plan your search "strategy." While there's nothing wrong with "playing" around on a CD-ROM system and experimenting with different key words and search terms, a little foresight and planning is likely to pay off with superior results. Take a few moments and, with a pen and pad, write a couple of sentences that best describe what you are searching for. Isolate the most critical ("key") words in those sentences and use them to create your search. If you need help doing this, ask a nearby librarian for assistance. Most have become something of an expert at database searching, and one of their main jobs is to help people like you use these systems efficiently. Librarians are very helpful people, and you are paying for them, so use their services!

- Practice, practice, practice. The more you do CD-ROM searching, the better you'll get. These amazing devices are free, so search to your heart's content and improve your skills!

- What if the library you use doesn't have any CD-ROMs? Well, then they're behind the times! Your best bet then is to find the *largest* library in your area, as the bigger ones usually have the most electronic resources. If there is a college or university library nearby, it will almost certainly have several CD-ROMs available for searching.

- Finally, when in the library, it's always useful to walk around and browse the open shelves where the library keeps the very latest issues of the journals and magazines it receives. Doing this allows you to quickly scan the names and front covers of a wide range of periodicals; one or more that you may have never heard of may catch your attention as relevant to your research. Another reason why browsing the open shelves is important is that they contain the very latest issues, and those may have not yet been keyed or scanned into electronic databases and CD-ROMs. So the timeliest information then, surprisingly, is often found in print, and not digital form.

2

Selected Supersources

The Cream of the Crop

The resources described in this chapter are the cream of the information-source crop. They range from museums to the federal government to bookstores to other storehouses of information, but they all have a few things in common. Each contains information on an enormous scope of subjects. Each can easily be tapped for answers and advice. And each provides answers for no charge or dirt cheap.

✔ Source: Associations

Perhaps the single best resource discussed in this book, associations offer a bountiful harvest of information. They are staffed by knowledgeable and helpful people whose job is to provide information about their field to those who need it.

There are thousands of associations, one for nearly every conceivable purpose and field of interest: the Chocolate Manufacturers Association of the U.S.A., the International Barbed Wire Collectors Association, the Laughter Therapy Association, the American Association for Career Education, the Committee to Abolish Legal Sized Files, the Tin Research Institute, even the Flying Funeral Directors of America—for funeral directors who

own and operate their own planes. And naturally there is the Star Trek Welcommittee—an association whose reason for being is to answer fans' questions about the Star Trek TV series.

Associations have helped me out more times than I can remember. A couple of occasions stand out: One time I needed to find out the "average life of a flag." Well, naturally a group called the North American Vexillological (a fancy word for the study of flags!) Association had the answer. (Flag life depends on the material and height flown.) Another time, a city agency was seeking advice on how to stop the local water pipes from leaking. To the rescue with an answer was the American Water Works Association, of Denver, Colorado.

Associations can also be a quick source of industry statistics and news. For example, if you want to find out how the sales of potatoes were last year, you need only inquire of the Potato Association of America or, if you prefer, the National Potato Promotion Board.

How to Find:

To find the name of an association that deals with your area of interest, call or write to the American Society of Association Executives (an association of associations!) at 1575 I Street, NW, Washington, DC 20005; 202–626–2723, and it will help identify the right one for you. Or look up your subject in the priceless *Encyclopedia of Associations,* published by Gale. Nearly all libraries have it. (Gale publishes companion volumes on international organizations, as well as local and regional associations.) You can also search the association's Web site of its members at: http://www.asaenet.org

Often, the *Encyclopedia of Associations* lists more than one association that sounds promising. In such cases, try contacting the largest one first, as it will most likely have the most resources to help you. To compare the size of different associations, examine the published data on the size of the association's staff and the number of members. Many libraries often contain the companion volumes to the *Encyclopedia of Associations: International Associations* and *State and Regional Associations.*

annual; (3) IFTF Perspectives (newsletter), irregular; also publishes papers and research reports.

★5851★   WORLD FUTURE SOCIETY (WFS)
4916 St. Elmo Ave.   Phone: (301) 656-8274
Bethesda, MD 20814   Edward S. Cornish, Pres.
Founded: 1966. Members: 30,000. Staff: 20. Local Groups: 80. Individuals interested in forecasts and ideas about the future. Formed "to contribute to a reasoned awareness of the future and the importance of its study, without advocating particular ideologies or engaging in political activities; to advance responsible and serious investigation of the future and to promote development of methods for the study of the future; to facilitate communication among groups and individuals interested in studying or planning for the future." Is developing services for professional forecasters and planners, including a register, special studies sections, and professional activities. Offers chapter activities in various U.S. cities as well as in Toronto, ON, Canada and London, England; sponsors book service; maintains library; offers specialized education service. Publications: (1) Future Survey, monthly; (2) The Futurist, bimonthly; (3) Futures Research Quarterly; also publishes books and Resource Catalog. Convention/Meeting: biennial - 1985 Aug. 8-9, Washington, DC.

★5852★   WORLD FUTURES STUDIES FEDERATION (WFSF)
2424 Maile Way, Office 720
University of Hawaii   Phone: (808) 948-6601
Honolulu, HI 96822   James A. Dator, Sec.Gen.
Founded: 1973. Members: 521. Institutions, scholars, policymakers, and individuals involved in futures studies. Promotes futures studies and innovative interdisciplinary analyses. Serves as a forum for the exchange of information and opinions through national and international research projects. Conducts regional colloquia and seminars. Maintains extensive collection of correspondence, monographs, serials, audiovisual materials, and books on social, political, economic, and environmental futures-related topics. Publications: (1) Newsletter, quarterly; (2) World Conference Proceedings, biennial; also publishes seminar papers. Convention/Meeting: biennial - next 1986.

★5853★   AMERICAN SOCIETY OF GAS ENGINEERS (ASGE)
P.O. Box 936   Phone: (312) 532-5707
Tinley Park, IL 60477   Charles R. Kendall, Exec.Dir.
Founded: 1954. Members: 600. Local Groups: 10. Professional society of engineers in the field of gas appliances and equipment. Publications: (1) Digest, quarterly; (2) Membership Directory, annual. Formerly: (1975) Gas Appliance Engineers Society. Convention/Meeting: annual technical conference.

INSTITUTE OF GAS TECHNOLOGY
See Index

★5854★   AMERICAN GENETIC ASSOCIATION (Genetics) (AGA)

Urbana, IL.

★5857★   NATIO
(NCGR)
2855 Telegraph A
Berkeley, CA 9470
Founded: 1980. S
and professional o
conservation and
resource conserva
information, tech
diversity of gene
microorganisms re
the problems, issu
use of genetic res
continues, the U.S
quality of life du
pharmaceutical a
including the produ
to initiate statewic
publish newsletter
Committees: Advi
Resources; Dougl
Programs: Californ

TOMATO GENETIC
See Index

★5858★   U.S. AP
P.O. Box 15426
San Francisco, CA
Founded: 1972. S
the encouragemen
documentation sta
distinctive genetic
and cell samples
nitrogen. Offers
18,000 volume l
Review. Publicat
Register, quarterly

GEOCHEMISTRY
See Geoscience

★5859★   AMERIC
156 Fifth Ave., Sui
New York, NY 100.
Founded: 1852.
educators, and oth
research in geogra
sponsored research

> **TIP:** Sometimes associations produce reports and studies that are of inter-est to researchers. However, these can be expensive to purchase, and you may only need a single statistic or data from just a portion of the study. Try contacting either the association's library or, if the association pub-lishes a magazine, the publication's editor. Sometimes the staffers at those departments won't mind finding the report and reading you the significant information you need. (Staff in marketing or publications-ordering depart-ments may only agree to sell you the entire study.)

✔ Source: Conventions

Every day, hundreds of conventions and professional confer-ences are held around the country—the National Accounting Expo, the American Academy of Sports Physicians, the Bee-keepers Convention, and the Nuclear Power Expo, to name a few. Conventions are especially good sources of information on fast-changing subjects, like computer technology. The seminars and talks presented at these conventions reflect the state of the art in a profession or field. Often brand-new products are displayed and groundbreaking research is presented.

How to Find:

Consult the *Directory of Conventions* (Successful Meetings, New York City) found at large libraries. Or check an "upcoming events" column in a relevant trade publication. (I recently found the con-vention I needed on computer printers by consulting a popular com-puter magazine's "events to watch" column.) Another way to find a convention on your subject is to find an association. Nearly all asso-ciations hold conventions.

Typically, two major activities take place at such conventions: technical presentations by authorities in the field and product exhibits by vendors who set up booths to try and sell their wares to the conference attendees. Although it is often inexpensive or free to visit the exhibition hall, it may run into the hundreds of dollars to sign up for the technical information sessions. However, there *is* a way you can tap into the information presented there *without* actually attending.

Here is the secret to tapping into convention information. If you find one that interests you, write and request a free "prelimi-nary program." These programs typically describe the technical

seminars to be held at the convention and provide the names and affiliations of the speakers or panelists. These speakers are *excellent* people to speak with to obtain information.

Here's an example of how I utilized this strategy. Once I had to research the subject of asbestos removal from school building insulation. I discovered that a convention of school administrators was being held the following month in Texas. Although I could not attend the convention, I wrote away for the preliminary program. Inside the program, I spotted a description of a planned technical session on asbestos removal. The description included the name of the speaker and the name of his school district. It was then an easy matter to contact that person to set up an information interview. I was then able to obtain his expertise and information for free instead of paying hundreds of dollars to hear him speak.

It's worth noting that programs from *past* conventions as well as for upcoming ones are often available.

Another way to obtain convention information without actually attending is to request a "conference proceedings," a transcript of the technical sessions published after the conference is over. Conference proceedings vary in cost and occasionally are expensive. Sometimes tape recordings of the technical sessions are available, too.

If you are interested in actually attending a conference in your area, call your city's convention and visitors bureau or the Chamber of Commerce. They should be able to provide you with a list of upcoming conventions.

✔ Source: Scientific Honor Society (Sigma Xi)

If you have a scientific question for which you need to get a quick answer, the Media Research Service of the Scientific Honor Society may be able to help you. The service can handle just about any scientific inquiry—from toxic wastes to cancer treatments. They've even answered the question as to whether it really is ever hot enough to fry an egg on the sidewalk! (It *is* possible—depending not only on the temperature but the construction of the sidewalk.) Although the center is designed to serve journalists, the staff will help other researchers as well.

How to Find:

Contact the Scientific Honor Society at P.O. Box 13975, Research Triangle, NC 27709; 800–223–1730.

✔ **Source: New York Public Library**

The New York Public Library is a tremendous source of all kinds of information. The library's **mid-Manhattan branch** is especially rich in information and regularly answers reference inquiries from around the country. Its collections include the fields of art, business, education, history, literature and language, and science. In addition, it contains an extensive picture collection. Other specialties of the New York Public Library include the Schomburg Center for Research in Black Culture, the Early Childhood Resource and Information Center, and the Job Information Center. There is also the **Performing Arts Research Center,** which answers written or phone inquiries regarding music, dance, and theater at no charge. (Because the New York Public Library handles so many requests, you may have to be patient if you telephone and get a busy signal.)

How to Find:

Contact the mid-Manhattan branch at 455 Fifth Avenue, New York, NY 10016; 212–340–0849. Contact the Performing Arts Research Center at the New York Public Library, 40 Lincoln Plaza, New York, NY 10023; free reference numbers are as follows: dance, 212–870–1657; music, 212–870–1650; theater, 212–870–1639. For other questions contact the library's public relations office at 8 West 40th Street, New York, NY 10018; 212–221–7676.

Pages 55 through 66 list some of the best and most widely used government information sources. Be sure to read through chapter 3 for details on many more resources available from various federal agencies.

✔ **Source: Library of Congress**

The U.S. Library of Congress in Washington, DC, is the largest library in the world. Its collection includes 20 million volumes and pamphlets, over a million technical reports, 3.5 million maps, 34 million manuscripts, and 8.5 million photographs, negatives, prints, and slides. The library is also known for its collection of rare books and foreign publications. It sometimes can be tricky to

use the Library of Congress's vast resources—not only because there is so much information available, but also because the Library's policy discourages phone reference usage by the public when materials are available on a more local level. However, it will assist users when it can help in researching topics unique to the Library. Some of these areas include copyright, legislative research, and international law.

One division that may be of help is the library's Telephone Reference Service. If the librarian has time, he or she will try to locate any obscure facts or information you have been unable to find elsewhere, and may be located at the Library of Congress.

How to Find:

You can contact the library's Telephone Reference Service at the Correspondence Section of the Library of Congress, Washington, DC 20540; 202–707–5522. On the Web: http://www.loc.gov

Another excellent resource is the Library of Congress's photoduplication service. The service will search the library's books, technical reports, maps, manuscripts, and photographic materials to find what you need, and send you photocopies. Turnaround time can run to 4 to 6 weeks, but you can't beat the price—you pay only for photocopying, copyright fees, and postage ($10 minimum charge).

How to Find:

Contact the Library of Congress, Photoduplication Service, Washington, DC 20540; 202–707–5640.

A very useful and interesting publication series of the Library of Congress is its *LC Science Tracer Bullets*. These are twelve- to sixteen-page pamphlets covering popular science-oriented topics that identify key information sources, such as introductory textbooks, general books, conference proceedings, government publications, journals, articles, technical books, associations, and more. Subjects have included *Japanese Technology, Inventions and Inventors; The History of Technology;* and *Fiber Optics.*

How to Find:

Contact the Library of Congress, Science Reference Section, Science and Technology Division, 10 First Street SE, Washington, DC 20540; 202–707–5522.

Finally, there is the Library of Congress's Performing Arts Library. The Library will try to answer, at no cost, any question regarding the performing arts—dance, music, theater, motion pictures, broadcasting, puppetry, circus, costuming, stage sets, and arts management and administration.

How to Find:

Contact the Performing Arts Reading Room, 101 Independence Ave. SE, Madison Building, Washington, DC 20566; 202–707–5507.

You can keep up with some of the Library of Congress's publishing activities by obtaining a catalog called *New from CDS*, which is the Library of Congress's Cataloging Distribution Service.

How to Find:

Contact the Library of Congress, Cataloging Distribution Service, Washington, DC 20541; 202–707–6100.

TIP: England's equivalent to the Library of Congress is the British Library, with millions of documents ranging from books and maps to worldwide conference proceedings to sheet music from around the globe. The time span of coverage ranges from the first items printed with movable type before 1501 to the present. Much of this invaluable material is available online or through an intercountry lending system. This is truly one of the world's great depositories of information.

Contact the British Library Document Supply Centre, Boston Spa, Wetherby, West Yorkshire, LS23 7BQ, United Kingdom. Phone: 44–1–937–546049; fax: 44–1–937–546333.

✔ **Source: Government Printing Office (GPO)**

The U.S. government is the largest publisher in the world. A mind-boggling amount of information pours out of Washington, DC, daily. Tens of thousands of books, pamphlets, and magazines are published each year by federal departments and agencies. Topics span nearly all areas of human endeavor from starting a business to finding a mortgage to getting rid of acne. Documents are typically concise and very readable, and they are specifically aimed at the general, nontechnical public. They are prepared by experts in the various federal departments and agencies whose job

is to keep the public informed. Best of all, the information is free or dirt cheap. The only caution in using these documents is to check the issue dates. Although many documents are timely and up to date, sometimes older ones are offered, too.

There are a number of ways to dig out the publications on your subject of interest. One way is to contact a specific department directly. The following chapter lists many of the information specialties of the departments and provides addresses and phone numbers.

A typical approach to finding government documents available from the GPO is through consulting *The Monthly Catalog of U.S. Government Publications*. Use the subject index in the back of each volume to identify published literature on your topic of interest. Each listing provides helpful information, such as the office that issued the document, the price, and ordering instructions. You can obtain monthly catalogs directly from the Superintendent of Documents or at a medium-size or large library.

A simpler and quicker way to find publications directly available from the GPO is to order its *Subject Bibliography Index*. The index is a listing of 240 major subject categories for which specific catalogs of bibliographies have been created. The index represents over 15,000 different pamphlets, booklets, guides, and periodicals. You circle which bibliography you'd like to get and send in the form, and the information is then sent to you, along with price information.

How to Find:

Contact the Superintendent of Documents, U.S. Government Printing Office, Washington, DC 20402; 202–512–1800. The GPO takes MasterCard or Visa telephone orders and checks payable to Superintendent of Documents, Government Printing Office. To order a catalog, write to the Superintendent of Documents, Box 371954, Pittsburgh, PA 15250–7954.

✔ Source: National Technical Information Service (NTIS)

The National Technical Information Service (NTIS) provides access to the results of both U.S. and foreign government-sponsored research and development (R&D) and engineering activities.

A

Accidents and Accident Prevention / 229

Accounting and Auditing / 42

Adolescence
Children and Youth / 35

Adult Education / 214

Aeronautics
Aircraft, Airports, and Airways / 13
Aviation Information and Training Materials / 18
Civil Aeronautics Board Publications / 186
Federal Aviation Regulations / 12

Africa / 284

Aging / 39

Agricultural Research, Statistics, and Economic Reports / 162

Agriculture
Agricultural Research, Statistics, and Economic Reports / 162
Agriculture Yearbooks (Department of) / 31
Census of Agriculture / 277
Farms and Farming / 161

Agriculture Yearbooks (Department of) / 31

Air Force Manuals / 182

Air Pollution / 46

Aircraft, Airports, and Airways / 13

Airman's Information Manual / 14

Airplanes
Aircraft, Airports, and Airways / 13
Federal Aviation Regulations / 12

Alcohol, Tobacco, and Firearms / 246

Alcoholism / 175

American Revolution / 144

Annual Reports / 118

Anthropology and Archeology / 205

Archeology
Anthropology and Archeology / 205

Architecture
Architecture / 215
Census of Construction / 157
The Home / 41

Armed Forces / 131

Armies
Army Technical and Field Manuals / 158
United States Army Corps of Engineers / 261

Arms Control
Disarmament and Arms Control / 127

Army Corps of Engineers (U.S.) / 261

Army Technical and Field Manuals / 158

Art and Artists / 107

Artists
Ar............. / 107

Astrophysics
Astronomy and Astrophysics / 115

Atomic Energy and Nuclear Power / 200

Atomic Power
Atomic Energy and Nuclear Power / 200

Auditing
Accounting and Auditing / 42
General Accounting Office Publications / 250

Audiovisual Materials
Motion Pictures, Films, and Audiovisual Information / 73

Automobiles
Motor Vehicles / 49

Aviation Information and Training Materials / 18

Awards
Grants and Awards / 258

B

Background Notes / 93

Banks and Banking / 128

Birds / 177

Birth Control
Family Planning / 292

Board of Tax Appeals and Tax Court Reports / 67

Budget of the United States Government and Economic Report of the President / 204

Building Science Series / 138

Building Trades
Construction Industry / 216

Bureau of Land Management Publications / 256

Bureau of Reclamation Publications / 249

Business
Business and Business Management / 4
Census of Business / 152
Federal Trade Commission Decisions and Publications / 100
Small Business / 307

C

Camping
Recreational and Outdoor Activities / 17

Canada / 278

Cancer
Diseases in Humans / 8
Smoking / 15

Canning, Freezing, and Storage of Foods / 5

Cardiovascular System
Diseases in Humans / 8

Care and Disorders of ...

Census of Manufactures ,

Census of Mineral Industrie.

Census of Population and Ho

Census of Population and Hou.
Statistics / 311

Census of Population and Housi
Tracts / 312

Census of Transportation / 149

Charts
Posters, Charts, Picture Sets,
cals / 57

Child Abuse and Neglect / 30

Child Welfare
Child Abuse and Neglect / 3
Children and Youth / 35

Children
Child Abuse and Neglect / 30
Children and Youth / 35
Courts and Correctional
tions / 91
Day Care / 92
Elementary Education / 196
Juvenile Delinquency / 74

China / 299

Circulatory System
Diseases in Humans / 8

Citizenship
Immigration, Naturalization, an
ship / 69

Civil Aeronautics Board
tions / 186

Civil and Structural Engineeri

Civil Defense
Disaster Preparedness and
fense / 241

Civil Rights and Equal Opportu

Civil Service
Office of Personnel Manageme

Civil War / 192

Classification
Procurement, Supply Catalc
Classification / 129

Coast Guard Publications (U.S.

Coins and Medals / 198

Collective Bargaining
Labor-Management Relations

College Debate Topic / 176

Commerce
Business and Business Manage
Foreign Trade and Tariff / 1
Interstate Commerce Comm.
sions and Reports / 187
Small Business / 307

Comptroller General
General Accounting Office ,

Computers and Data Processi

Congress / 201

.... **Budget Off**

This includes more than 60,000 summaries of U.S. and foreign government-sponsored R&D and engineering activities annually, complete technical reports, and access to software and databases produced by federal agencies.

A collection of more than a million technical reports on completed government research is made available. NTIS is the central source for the public sale of U.S. government-sponsored research and development and engineering reports, as well as foreign technical reports. Dozens of technical areas are covered, including aeronautics, biological sciences, energy, materials, and medicine. A couple of sample research reports: "General Aviation Aircraft Noise Problem: Some Suggested Solutions" and "World Trade in Fruits and Vegetables: Projections for an Enlarged European

---

TIPS: Government Depository Libraries and Bookstores
• There are 1,400 designated libraries around the United States that are legally required to store government documents and provide the public with free access. Ask the Government Printing Office to send you a free "Government Depository Library" directory, which tells where these libraries are located, what kinds of documents they store, and how to use them.
• You can also ask for a listing of GPO bookstores, which are government bookstores located in most major cities. These carry the most popular of the government's published materials.

Community." Many reports are gathered from sources around the world. Some are expensive, but others are very moderately priced. Here is a sample of some of the different ways you can tap into this information:

- NTIS publishes weekly newsletters that abstract its research summaries. These newsletters can be expensive, however.
- NTIS makes available "Published Searches"—already completed computer searches of abstracts of technical reports in over 3,000 subject areas gathered from both NTIS sources as well as 23 other international sources. Searches usually yield 100 to 200 individual summaries for each topic.
- NTIS's Center for the Utilization of Federal Technology (CUFT) keeps U.S. industry aware of government R&D and

engineering efforts that have special potential or are at a breakthrough stage. Publications include *Federal Technology Catalog*, containing more than 1,000 summaries of government technologies and resources in 23 subject fields, with full telephone or other contact sources for further information.

- A superb guide is the *Directory of Federal Technology Resources*, which guides readers to hundreds of federal agencies, laboratories, and engineering centers willing to share their expertise, equipment and sometimes even their facilities.

- Many NTIS databases (a database is a collection of information on one particular subject, like energy or agriculture—see chapter 5) are available online (through computers) from popular commercial database vendors. See chapter 5 for more information on how to tap into these databases. One of the most useful and interesting ones for researchers is on the Web and is called World News Connection, which provides full-text translations of important articles from newspapers and magazines and other sources from around the world. These are produced by the Foreign Broadcast Information Service (FBIS), a division of the Central Intelligence Agency. You can link to World News Connection on the Web at http://wnc.fedworld.gov

How to Find:

Contact the National Technical Information Service, Springfield, VA 22161; 703–487–4650. For a complete description of all of NTIS's print sources and computer databases, ask for the latest edition of the free publication *NTIS Catalog of Products and Services.* Another catalog, titled *CD-ROMs & Optical Disks,* lists the agency's CD-ROM products.

✔ **Source: Bureau of the Census**

Do you want to know which neighborhoods have the highest concentration of elderly people? How many men in Latin America own TV sets? Which sections of Wyoming are the wealthiest?

The U.S. Bureau of the Census can supply you with figures on these and countless other data-oriented questions. Major areas covered include agriculture, business, construction, foreign nations, foreign trade, geography, governments, housing, manu-

facturing, mineral industries, people, retail trade, service industries, and transportation.

You can obtain a listing of the names of subject data experts at
the bureau and their phone numbers by ordering an especially
useful and free pamphlet, "Telephone Contacts for Data Users."
This publication will tell you, for example, who the expert is for
statistics on religion or for foreign-owned U.S. firms.

How to Find:

Contact the User Training Branch, Data User Services Division,
Bureau of the Census, Washington, DC 20233; 301–457–4608. Or
call the Public Information Office at 301–763–4040.

Another excellent source is the *Census Catalog & Guide*. This is
a clear and comprehensive 400-page book that lists and describes
census products, services, and programs, and provides complete
ordering information. A useful subject index and table of contents
identify sources on topics including agriculture, business, foreign
trade, population, transportation, and much more. Remember
much of the Bureau of the Census's products and services are free
or inexpensive. An excerpt from the 1989 catalog's list of sources
for statistics within the federal government is on page 66.

How to Find:

Available from the Superintendent of Documents, U.S. Government
Printing Office, Washington, DC 20402; 202–512–1800. Stock number 003–024–07009–0.

Finally, you should know that during the last few years the
Bureau of the Census has been making quite an effort to trans-
form much of its print data into low-priced electronic databases
and the Internet. Two excellent guides to these resources are a
booklet called *Census, CD-ROM and You*, which lists and
describes Census products on CD-ROM, and *CENDATA: The
Census Bureau Online*, a nontechnical manual that describes
where one can find Census data online, what kind is available, and
how to best use it. Contact the Data User Services division phone
number, listed above. The biggest drive has been to put Census
information up on the World Wide Web, virtually all at no cost to
the user. You can link to the Bureau's home page at http://www.
census.gov

TIP: Using census information can be a fairly complex and technical matter, and can be confusing for people who are not used to working with all of the data series, tables, etc. published by the Bureau. If you think you may have a need to go very deep into census data, I highly recommend a book called *Understanding the Census,* by Michael R. Lavin, and published in 1996 by Epoch/Oryx.

✔ **Source: *Statistical Abstract of the United States***

The bible for statistics of all types is the *Statistical Abstract of the United States,* published annually. The kinds of statistical data you can find in this guide are extremely diverse—the number of eye operations performed, murder victims by weapons used, consumer price indexes, new business failure rates, retail sales of men's fragrances, pottery imports, railroad accidents, consumption of ice cream, and much more.

This book is the standard summary of statistics on the social, political, and economic organization of the United States. Major sections include population; vital statistics; immigration and naturalization; health and nutrition; education; law enforcement; courts and prisons; geography and environment; parks and recreation; elections; state and local government finances and employment; federal government finances and employment; national defense; veterans' affairs; social insurance and human services; labor force, employment, and earnings; income expenditure and wealth; banking, finance, and insurance; business enterprise; communications; energy; science; transportation; agriculture; forests and forest products; fisheries; mining, and mineral products; construction and housing; manufacturers; and comparative international statistics.

How to Find:

You can order this guide from the Superintendent of Documents, Box 371954, Pittsburgh, PA 15250–7954; 202–512–1800. Or you can find a copy at GPO bookstores and at nearly all libraries. You can also find at least some summary material from the *Statistical Abstract* on the Web by linking to http://www.census.gov:80/stat_abstract

✔ Source: United States General Accounting Office (GAO)

The United States GAO is an independent, nonpolitical agency that serves as the investigative agency for Congress and carries out investigations and makes recommendations. The GAO publishes findings in reports and testimony transcripts that are available to the public for free. These reports cover fields such as education, health, housing, justice, defense, technology, and more. Past reports have included "Air Pollution: Uncertainty Exists in Radon Measurements," "Hazardous Wastes: Contractors Should Be Accountable for Environmental Performance," "Failed Thrifts: The Resolution Trust Corporation's Working Capital Needs," "Medical Device Recalls: An Overview and Analysis, 1983–1988," "In-Home Services for the Elderly," and "Non-Traditional Organized Crime."

How to Find:

Requests for copies of GAO reports and testimony are available from the U.S. General Accounting Office, Box 6015, Gaithersburg, MD 20884–6015; 202–512–6000.

✔ Source: State Government

Your state government can be an excellent resource for a variety of topics. Subject expertise varies from state to state, but typically you can find information on most of these topics:

Aeronautics	Consumer affairs
Aging	Criminal justice
Agriculture	Disabled
Air resources	Disaster preparedness
Alcoholism	Drug abuse
Archives	Economic opportunity
Arts	Education
Banking	Energy
Child labor	Environment
Child welfare	Fish and game
Civil rights	Food
Commerce	Handicapped
Community affairs	Hazardous materials

Health	Parks and recreation
Highways	Taxation
Housing	Tourism
Labor	Transportation
Land	Veterinary medicine
Mental health	Water resources
Natural resources	Women
Occupational safety	

How to Find:

Consult a library copy of the *State Executive Directory,* published by Carroll Publishing Company. This guide provides a detailed listing of the various offices in each state and a listing of state personnel names, titles, and phone numbers. A subject index makes it easy to locate who in your state can be of assistance to you. (This directory also lists state historic preservation offices and legislative reference numbers.) You'll find the directory at large libraries. Or check the name of the state in your phone book to find the division you need (in many cities, government listings are separated into a special blue-pages section). You can also find state related information on the Web by linking to the National Association of State Information Resource Executives' "StateSearch" site, which is a topical clearinghouse to state government on the Net. Link to http://www.state.ky.us/nasire/NASIREhome.html

✔ **Source: College and University Faculty Experts**

College and university faculty members can provide information on topics ranging from architecture to international relations as well as other subjects taught at academic institutions. A computer database established in 1993 at the State University of New York (SUNY) in Stony Brook is a network of college public information

---

TIP: Consumer and Legal Advice
• Your state attorney general's office can answer many questions about your legal rights as a citizen of your state. Typical questions handled by this office relate to subjects like tenant–landlord disputes, buying a car, mail-order fraud, investment fraud, and so forth. The expertise of this office varies from state to state. Check the blue pages in the phone book under "State Government" to locate the address and phone of your state's attorney general.

Assistant Secretary for Public Affairs,* U.S.
Dept. of Health and Human Services,
Room 647-D, Humphrey Building, 200
Independence Avenue, S.W.,
Washington, D.C. 20201 Information:
202/245-1850. Locator: 202/245-6296

Administrator for Health Resources and
Services, U.S. Dept. of Health and
Human Services, 5600 Fishers Lane,
Park Lawn Building 14-05, Rockville,
MD 20857. Information: 301/443-2216.
Publications: 301/443-2086

Alcohol, Drug Abuse, and Mental Health
Administration, U.S. Dept. of Health
and Human Services, 5600 Fishers Lane,
Rm. 12C15, Rockville, MD 20857.
Information/Publications: 301/443-3783.
Alcohol: 301/443-4733. Drug Abuse:
301/443-6245. Mental Health: 301/443-
4536 or 3600. Substance Abuse
Prevention: 301/443-0373

Centers for Disease Control, U.S. Dept. of
Health and Human Services, 1600
Clifton Road, N.E., Atlanta, GA 30329.
Information: 404/639-3311. Public
Affairs: 404/639-3286

Food and Drug Administration, U.S. Dept. of
Health and Human Services, 5600
Fishers Lane, Rockville, MD 20857.
Information: 301/443-2404. Publications:
301/443-3170

Health Care Financing Administration, U.S.
Dept. of Health and Human Services,
330 Independence Avenue, S.W.,
Washington, D.C. 20201. Public Affairs:
202/245-6113. Publications: 301/597-
2618

Health Resources and Services Administration
U.S. Dept. of Health and Human
Services, 5600 Fishers Lane, Rockville,
MD 20857. Public Affairs: 301/443-2086

Indian Health Service, Office of Tribal Affairs,
U.S. Dept. of Health and Human
Services, 5600 Fishers Lane, Room 6A-
07, Rockville, MD 20857. Director's
Office: 301/443-1083.

National Center for Health Statistics, U.S.
Dept. of Health and Human Services,
3700 East-West Highway, Hyattsville,
MD 20782. Information: 301/436-8500

National Institutes of Health, U.S. Dept. of
Health and Human Services, 9000
Rockville Pike, Bethesda, MD 20892.
Information/Publications: 301/496-4000

Office of the Surgeon General, Office of
Communications, 725 H, U.S. Dept. of
Health and Human Services, 200
Independence Avenue, S.W.,
Washington, D.C. 20201. Information:
202/245-6867

Public Health Service,* Office of Public
Affairs, Office of the Assistant
Secretary, U.S. Dept. of Health and
Human Services, 200 Independence
Avenue, S.W., Washington, D.C. 20201.
Public Affairs: 202/245-6867

Social Security Administration, U.S. Dept. of
Health and Human Services, Office of

Research and Statistics and International
Policy, Room 912, Universal North
Building, Publications: Room 209, 4301
Connecticut Avenue, N.W.,
Washington, D.C. 20008. Information/
Publications: 202/282-7138

Housing

Assistant Secretary for Community Planning/
Development, U.S. Dept. of Housing
and Urban Development, 451 7th Street,
S.W., Washington, D.C. 20410.
Information: 202/755-6270

Assistant Secretary for Housing, U.S. Dept. of
Housing and Urban Development, 451
7th Street, S.W., Washington, D.C.
20410. Information: 202/755-6600

Immigration

Immigration and Naturalization Service, U.S.
Department of Justice, 425 I Street,
N.W., Washington, D.C. 20536. Office
of Information: 202/633-4316. Statistics
Office: 202/633-3053

Income and Taxation

Internal Revenue Service, Statistics of Income
Division, U.S. Dept. of Treasury, 1111
Constitution Avenue, N.W.,
Washington, D.C. 20224. Information/
Publications: 202/376-0216

Office of the Secretary, Public Affairs Office,
U.S. Dept. of the Treasury, Room 1500,
15th Street and Pennsylvania N.W.,
Washington, D.C. 20220. Information:
202/566-2041

Office of Tax Analysis, U.S. Dept. of the
Treasury, Room 4217, 15th Street and
Pennsylvania Avenue, N.W.,
Washington, D.C. 20220. Information:
202/566-5374. Publications: 202/566-
5282

International

United Nations, D.C. 2 1628, Statistical Office,
United Nations, New York, NY 10017.
Information: 212/754-4562

Labor and Employment

Bureau of Labor Statistics,* U.S. Dept. of
Labor, Washington, D.C. 20212.
Information/Publications: 202/523-1221.
Locator: 202/523-6666. Latest BLS data:
202/523-9658. CPI detail: 202/523-1239.
PPI detail: 202/523-1765

Employment and Training Administration,
Office of Public Affairs, U.S. Dept. of
Labor, 200 Constitution Avenue, N.W.,
Room S2322, Washington, D.C. 20210.
Information/Publications: 202/523-6871

Miscellaneous

Commission on Civil Rights, 1121 Vermont
Avenue, N.W., Washington, D.C. 20425.
Locator: 202/376-8177

Executive Office of the President, Office of
Management and Budget, Washington,
D.C. 20503. Information: 202/395-3000.

Public Affairs: 202/395-3080.
Publications: 202/395-7332

National Archives and Records
Administration, 7th and Pennsylvania
Avenue, N.W., Washington, D.C. 20408.
Information/Locator: 202/523-3218

National Technical Information Service, U.S.
Dept. of Commerce, 5285 Port Royal
Road, Springfield, VA 22161.
Information/Orders: 703/487-4650

Science and Technology

National Oceanic and Atmospheric
Administration, Office of Public Affairs,
U.S. Dept. of Commerce, Room 6013,
14th and Constitution Avenue, N.W.,
Washington, D.C. 20230. Information/
Publications: 202/377-8090

Energy Information Administration,* Nationa
Energy Information Center, EI-20, U.S
Dept. of Energy, 1000 Independence
Avenue, S.W., Washington, D.C. 2058
General Information: 202/586-8800

Bureau of Mines, U.S. Dept. of the Interior,
4900 LaSalle Road, Avondale, MD
20782. Information: 301/436-7966

Office of Public Information, Bureau of Mines,
U.S. Dept. of the Interior, 2401 E
Street, N.W., Washington, D.C. 20241.
Information: 202/634-1004

U.S. Geological Survey, Public Affairs Office
U.S. Dept. of the Interior, 503 Nationa
Center, Reston, VA 22092. Information/
Publications: 703/648-6892

National Science Foundation, Office of
Legislative and Public Affairs, 1800 G
Street, N.W., Washington, D.C. 20550.
Information: 202/357-9498

Transportation

Federal Highway Administration, Office of
Public Affairs, U.S. Dept. of
Transportation, 400 7th Street, S.W.,
Room 4210, Washington, D.C. 20590.
Information/Publications: 202/366-0660

Materials and Transportation Bureau,
Information Services Division (BMT-
11), Office of Operations/Enforcemen
U.S. Dept. of Transportation, 400 7th
Street, S.W., Washington, D.C. 20590
Information: 202/426-2301

National Highway Traffic Safety
Administration, Office of Public Affair
U.S. Dept. of Transportation, 400 7th
Street, S.W., Washington, D.C. 20590.
Information: 202/366-9550

Urban Mass Transportation Administration,
Public Affairs Office, U.S. Dept. of
Transportation, 400 7th Street, S.W.,
Room 9328, Washington, D.C. 20590.
Information: 202/366-4040

Veterans

Veterans Administration, 810 Vermont
Avenue, N.W., Washington, D.C. 20420.
Information: 202/233-2563

Census Catalog & Guide, "Federal Government Statistical Sources"

officers located at over 300 campuses around the country. It was established to serve as a clearinghouse of over 300,000 faculty.

Journalists and other researchers can contact ProfNet to pose a question for the faculty experts. For example, not too long ago, a reporter from *The New York Times* used the network to try to locate an expert on computers and children. Another recent use was by a *Boston Globe* staffer who was looking for someone on the forefront of research in electric vehicles. ProfNet is free, so you should be sensitive to making queries as straightforward as possible, and not overusing this service.

How to Find:

You can call ProfNet toll-free at 800–PROF–NET. It is also available on the Internet at http://www.vyne.com/profnet

---

TIP: If you are trying to find information that is maintained at a college or university, get a copy of *The Sourcebook of College & University Records,* which profiles how to obtain data from over 3,800 colleges and universities. The book is published by BRB Publications of Tempe, AZ; 800–929–3811.

✔ Source: Doctoral Dissertations

An unusual but potentially very valuable source of information is published and unpublished doctoral dissertations. These may provide you with information unavailable elsewhere.

How to Find:

You can locate dissertations on your subject by contacting University Microfilms International in Ann Arbor, Michigan. Through a computerized system called Datrix II, this firm can search more than 500,000 dissertations to find one that covers your subject of interest. If any are located, a copy can be sent to you directly. A modest fee is charged for the service. University Microfilms can also send you a subject index of its dissertations. Contact them at 300 North Zeeb Road, Ann Arbor, MI 48106; 800–521–0600.

✔ Source: Museums

There are museums for loads of topics—antiques, whaling, theater, and much more—and many museums have libraries that

take written and telephone inquiries on subjects in their specialty areas. For example, the Museum of Radio and Television in New York City, which has a holding of over 40,000 radio and television programs and advertising broadcasts, will tackle any information query relating to a broadcasting matter. Questions it has handled include who produced *The Ed Sullivan Show* and when did the *I Love Lucy* show premiere. You can contact the Museum at 25 West 52nd Street, New York, NY 10019; 212–621–6600. The staff takes research questions by fax at 212–621–6632. And the museum is open to the public. (P.S. Marlo Lewis coproduced *The Ed Sullivan Show* along with Ed Sullivan himself in the 1950s. *I Love Lucy* premiered October 15, 1951, on CBS.)

TIP: You can obtain transcripts of many news, documentary, and public policy broadcasts from Journal Graphics. The firm provides transcripts from *60 Minutes, 48 Hours, Nova, Frontline, Adam Smith's Money World, Oprah Winfrey, Nightline,* and many other broadcasts. Transcripts are modestly priced, and rush service is available. For more information, or to obtain a catalog of transcripts by topic, contact Journal Graphics, 1535 Grant Street, Denver, CO 80203; 303–831–9000. To find an actual video of a broadcast (and not just a written transcript), contact Vanderbilt University's Television Archives, which contains over 23,000 evening news broadcasts and 8,000 other news-oriented videos. Call 615–322–2927, or search its index on the Web at http://tvnews.vanderbilt.edu

---

How to Find:

To find a museum that matches your subject of interest, take a look at the *Official Museum Directory,* which lists 7,000 institutions. These include art, history, nature, and science museums, as well as more specialized museums—museums of agriculture, antiques, architecture, audiovisual materials and film, the circus, clocks and watches, electricity, fire fighting, forestry, furniture, guns, hobbies, industry, logging and lumber, mining, money and numismatics, musical instruments, philately, religion, scouting, sports, technology, theater, toys and dolls, transportation, typography, whaling, and woodcarving.

The directory provides the museum's name, address, phone number, officers, collections, research fields, facilities, activities, and publications. It's published by the R. R. Bowker Co., New Providence, New Jersey, and can be found at many libraries.

One museum with extensive resources on a number of different subjects is the Smithsonian Institution in Washington, DC. Its specialties include art, history, air and space, zoology, horticulture, and marine life. You can pose a question on any of these or related topics, and the museum will try to answer it. The service is free. Write to the Smithsonian Institution, Washington, DC 20560.

✔ **Source: Specialized Bookstores**

The Yellow Pages of some of the larger cities group bookstores into specific subject areas. For example, if you get hold of a copy of New York City's Yellow Pages (check any large library), you'll see bookstores devoted solely to art and sculpture, astrology, automobiles, China, cooking, health and nutrition, the occult, philosophy, religion, science fiction, theater, travel, and women. Remember, too, that the people who work at these bookstores are good sources of information themselves.

✔ **Source: Private Companies**

One last "everything" source to keep in mind: private companies. Sometimes firms publish free pamphlets and guides related to their industry or products. For example, Prudential-Bache offices offer free advice on money management; Evenflo (Ravenna, Ohio), a maker of products for babies, provides free information and advice to expectant mothers about exercise, nutrition, and child care; and Delsey Luggage (Jessup, Maryland) provides tips on proper packing. Try to identify large firms that sell a product or service related to your subject. You may then want to call the public affairs department of these firms to inquire whether any free materials are available.

Also, individuals who work at companies can naturally be excellent persons to interview on their subjects of expertise. See chapters 6–8 on finding and interviewing experts for more information.

✔ **Source: Advertisements**

Granted, it's an offbeat idea, but one worth considering—especially if other sources don't pan out. Place an advertisement and

describe as specifically as possible what kind of information you're looking for and why. (You sometimes see such ads as "author's queries" in popular book review sections.) You may be pleasantly surprised at the response you receive—people do like to help! A friend of mine placed an ad in a large city newspaper requesting input from collectors of "snow dome" paperweights, and she received about fifty responses!

If you've found a trade publication covering your subject, try placing the ad there so that you can reach a specific audience. Otherwise, a daily newspaper is fine, and the bigger the better.

Ads can be an especially good way to find out if anyone has information on a particular person or to find users of a product or customers of a firm.

And if you're hooked to the Internet, you can post your request to a relevant electronic discussion group, which may prove to be even more fruitful—and free! (See chapter 5 for more details.)

3

The U.S. Government

Mining for Information Nuggets

QUICKFINDER: THE U.S.
GOVERNMENT DEPARTMENTS

The U.S. government is a gold mine of information. Although many government publications and services have been eliminated during the last few years, an awesome amount of advice, data, and information is still available. The expertise is all there for the taking—if you know how to find what you need.

Because the government is so huge, it is impossible to describe in a single chapter (or book, for that matter) anywhere near the full amount of information available. However, to give you a feel for what's available, this chapter lists some of the most popular and helpful information sources and provides you with a head start on digging out information from each of the thirteen U.S. *departments* (Department of Justice, Department of Transportation, and so on) and a select number of the government's smaller independent *agencies* (Federal Communications Commission, Environmental Protection Agency, and so on). For each one, an address, main phone number, public affairs phone number, and Web site are provided. Then, to alert you to specific subjects that the department or agency covers and information sources available, the following two descriptive listings are provided:

Scope Includes

This is a sample of some of the subjects that are covered within the department or agency. Because each department and agency may deal with hundreds or thousands of different areas, only a sample of those judged to be of greatest appeal to the largest number of readers are included.

Rich Resources

Under this heading you will find specific offices and divisions within a department or agency that have been identified as sources of the very best and most useful information. An address and phone number are provided for each one.

For information on	Check
Agriculture	Department of Agriculture
Air travel/flight	National Aeronautics and Space Administration
Arts and literature	National Foundation on the Arts/ National Endowment for the Arts
Astronomy	National Aeronautics and Space Administration
Broadcasting	Federal Communications Commission
Business	Small Business Administration; see also chapter 4, "Business Information"
Consumer information	General Services Administration; Consumer Product Safety Commission; Department of Health and Human Services; Federal Trade Commission
Crime	Department of Justice
Education	Department of Education
Energy	Department of Energy
Engineering	Department of Commerce/ National Bureau of Standards
Environment	Environmental Protection Agency; Department of Commerce/National Oceanic and Atmospheric Administration
Food and nutrition	Department of Agriculture

Foreign affairs	Department of State
Health and medicine	Department of Health and Human Services
Housing and real estate	Department of Housing and Urban Development
Humanities	National Endowment for the Humanities
International affairs	Department of State; Department of Defense
Labor and employment	Department of Labor
Minority concerns	Department of Commerce; Department of Education; Department of the Interior; Department of Housing and Urban Development
Natural disasters	Federal Emergency Management Agency
Natural resources	Department of the Interior
Taxes	Department of Justice
Transportation	Department of Transportation
Travel	Department of State

TIP: Guides to Government Information
• If you want to get a much fuller understanding of the structure and offices of the federal government, I'd recommend you check out some of the special publications described at the end of this chapter. These are specifically designed to provide detailed listings of government offices and to examine their organizational structure.

AFTER YOU LOCATE AN AGENCY

What do you do if you find a department or agency that covers a subject you are interested in? There are several ways to track down the information you need, but the key is to zero in on as specific an individual or subagency as possible in making contact. Your first choice would be to contact a "rich resource" office—a source that has *already been identified for you* as providing excellent information. If you don't find a relevant resource listed there, you can try calling the public affairs/information number of the

department or agency and pose your question. However, although you should be able to obtain information on publications available, it's hard to zero in on an expert by placing a call to a department's or agency's main public information number. You may be more successful if you take a more "targeted" route first.

Finally, you can dig out more specialized subdivisions and offices by examining one of the guides to government information described at the end of this chapter. These locator sources will help you find out if there is a division, bureau, or office that has the specific answers you seek.

TIP: Government Phone Information

• Because personnel and departments in Washington often change, it's very possible that some of the phone numbers listed below will be outdated by the time you read this. If you dial a number that is no longer accurate, simply call 202–555–1212 and ask the operator to give you the "locator" telephone number for the specific department you are trying to reach.

DEPARTMENTS

✔ **Department of Agriculture**

14th Street and Independence Avenue SW
Washington, DC 20250
Main number: 202–720–8732
Public affairs: 202–720–4623
Web site: http://web.fie.com/fedix/usda.html

Scope Includes

Animal and Plant Health
Consumer Affairs
Family Nutrition
Food Safety and Inspection
Human Nutrition
Veterinary Medicine

Rich Resources

The USDA's Cooperative State Research Education and Extension Service can provide you with information that links research, science, and technology to the needs of the people, where they live and work. There are more than 3,100 county offices located around the country.

Contact: USDA Extension Service, Washington, DC 20250; 202–720–4423 (to find a local office). Or check your phone book's government blue-page listing under "Agriculture."

The USDA's Food and Nutrition Information Center can provide you with information or educational materials on human nutrition and food. The center lends books and audiovisual materials to specified borrowers, makes photocopies of journal articles, and provides comprehensive reference services such as computer searches.

Contact: Food and Nutrition Information Center, National Agricultural Library, 10301 Baltimore Blvd., U.S. Department of Agriculture, Beltsville, MD 20705; 301–504–5755. Reference Desk: 301–504–5479.

The Human Nutrition Information Service will answer your questions about the nutrient composition of food—calories, fat content, vitamins and minerals, food consumption and dietary levels of the population.

Contact: Human Nutrition Information Service, U.S. Department of Agriculture, Hyattsville, MD 20782; 301–734–8457.

The Home Economics and Human Nutrition unit publishes information on managing a household, providing nutritious meals, managing resources such as money and energy, planning and caring for clothing, improving personal and community relationships, and providing an attractive, safe, and healthy home environment.

Contact: Home Economics and Human Nutrition, Extension Service, U.S. Department of Agriculture, Food Surveys Research Group, USDA ARS BHNRC FSRG, Room 6C63, Unit 83, Hyattsville, MD; 301–734–8457 (see above, Human Nutrition).

The National Agricultural Library is a great information source. Its specialties include botany, poultry, forestry, veterinary medicine, chemistry, plant pathology, livestock, zoology, and general agriculture topics. The library provides reference service by mail or phone. You can request the "Bibliography Series," which lists topics on which bibliographic citations are available—"Indoor Gardening," "Pesticide Safety," "The U.S. Poultry Industry," and so on.

Contact: The National Agricultural Library, U.S. Department of Agriculture, 10301 Baltimore Blvd., Beltsville, MD 20705; 301–504–5755.

✔ ## Department of Commerce

14th Street and Constitution Avenue NW
Washington, DC 20230
Main number: 202–482–2000
Public affairs: 202–482–3263
Free reference: 202–482–2161
Web site: http://www.doc.gov

Scope Includes

Business Outlook Analyses
Economic and Demographic Statistics
Engineering Standards
Imports and Exports
Minority-Owned Business
Patents and Trademarks
Technology
Travel
Weather and Atmosphere

Rich Resources

The Department of Commerce is filled with sources of information about business. Chapter 4, which is devoted to business information, discusses some of the best of these. Here are other offices of the department that provide helpful materials and assistance:

The Minority Business Development Agency provides business management and technical assistance for members of minorities. Personal counseling is available, sometimes for free. The main office will give you a regional location near you.

Contact: Minority Business Development Agency, U.S. Department of Commerce, Washington, DC 20230; 202–482–1936.

The National Computer Systems Laboratory publishes free and inexpensive newsletters that examine computing issues that range from security to networks to buying software. It has a limited capacity for answering technical questions, however.

Contact: National Computer Systems Laboratory, 225-A31 Technology Building, National Bureau of Standards, Gaithersburg, MD 20899; 301–975–3587.

You can order a free guide listing the names of over 150 subject experts in the Department of Commerce. Areas of expertise include, for example, aerospace, biotechnology, economic affairs, environmental research, industry surveys, materials research, patents and trademarks, telecommunication, and much more. Order the list from the departments' FlashFax service below.

Contact: Department of Commerce, 202–501–1191 (enter document number 1060).

The National Institute of Standards and Technology is devoted to the science of measurement and develops standards. It has a staff of experts in areas such as manufacturing engineering, chemical engineering, electronics, and electrical engineering. Also covered are radiation, building technology, applied mathematics, chemical physics, analytic chemistry, and computer science and technology. A good publication to get is "Co-operative Research Opportunities at NIST," which includes a directory that identifies the bureau's experts and gives their phone numbers.

Contact: U.S. Department of Commerce, National Institute of Standards and Technology, Research Information Center, Gaithersburg, MD 20899; 301–975–3052.

The National Oceanic and Atmospheric Administration will try to answer your questions about climate, earth and ocean sciences, the environment, and marine life. It will also refer you to other agencies and to published information.

Contact: NOAA Central Library, 1315 East-West Highway, Silver Spring, MD 20910; 301–713–2600.

✔ **Department of Defense**
The Pentagon
Washington, DC 20301
Main number: 703–545–6700
Press/Public affairs: 703–697–5131
Web site: http://www.dtic.mil/defenselink

Scope Includes

Atomic Energy
Foreign Country Security
Mapping
Military History
Nuclear Operations and Technology
Tactical Warfare

Rich Resources

The Department of Defense publishes about 150 "foreign area studies," which are in-depth studies of a particular country's social, economic, political, and military organization and are revised every three to five years. These are clothbound books, usually a few hundred pages long and very detailed. They are designed for the nonspecialist. Prices are very reasonable.

Contact: Superintendent of Documents, Box 371954, Pittsburgh, PA 15250–7954; 202–783–3238.

The U.S. Army Military History Institute answers thousands of inquiries per year on military history. The institute has an extensive collection of unofficial documents, such as personal papers. You can call or write with your question.

Contact: Historical Reference Branch, U.S. Army Military History Institute, Carlisle Barracks, PA 17013–5008; 717–245–3611.

✔ **Department of Education**
400 Maryland Avenue SW
Washington, DC 20202
Main office: 202–401–2000
Public affairs: 202–401–1576
Web site: http://www.ed.gov

Scope Includes

Adult Education
Bilingual Education
Civil Rights
Educational Statistics
Elementary and Secondary Education
Handicapped
Higher Education
Libraries
Special Education

Rich Resources

The Office of Educational Research and Improvement (OERI), Education Information Branch, disseminates statistics and other data related to education in the United States and other nations. OERI conducts studies and publishes reports regarding all kinds of educational data. Past publications include "The Condition of Education," "Hispanic Students in American High Schools," and "Faculty Salaries."

Contact: OERI, U.S. Department of Education, 555 New Jersey Avenue, Washington, DC 20208; 800–424–1616.

Education Resource Information Center (ERIC) provides users with ready access to literature dealing with education through abstracting journals, computer searches, document reproductions, and other means. There are sixteen subject-specialized clearinghouses: adult, career, and vocational; counseling and personnel; educational management; elementary and early childhood; handicapped and gifted children; higher education; information resources; junior colleges; languages and linguistics; reading and communication skills; rural education and small schools; science, mathematics, and environmental; social studies/social science; teacher education; tests, measurement, and evaluation; urban education. These clearinghouses answer more than 100,000 written and telephone inquiries per year.

Contact: ERIC, U.S. Department of Education, 555 New Jersey Avenue, Washington, DC 20208; 202–219–2289 or 800–424–1616.

✔ Department of Energy

Forrestal Building
1000 Independence Avenue SW
Washington, DC 20585
Main number: 202–586–5000
Public information: 202–586–6827
Web site: http://www.em.doe.gov
DOE Reports Bibliographic Database Web site:
http://www.doe.gov/html/dra/dra.html

Scope Includes

Coal Liquids, Gas, Shale, Oil
Conservation
Energy Emergencies
Fusion Energy
Inventions
Nuclear Energy
Nuclear Physics
Radioactive Waste

Rich Resources

DOE's Office of Scientific and Technical Information has information on nearly any energy-related topic. The scientists on the staff may be able to help you with a question, or even run a free computer search on the "EDB"—Energy Data Base—the world's largest database on energy.

Contact: Office of Scientific and Technical Information, Box 62, Oak Ridge, TN 37831; 423–576–1301.

The Energy Information Administration (EIA) provides energy information and referral assistance to the public. The best publication to ask for is "The Energy Information Directory," which is a list of government offices and experts. Topics in its subject index include appliances, buildings, coal, dams, diesel fuel, fusion power, ocean energy, safety, solar energy, and vehicles. The directory refers the user to a specific government office, describes the function of that office, and provides the name of a contact person. The publication is free and published semiannually. The EIA also publishes a free newsletter.

Contact: National Energy Information Center, Energy Information Administration, U.S. Department of Energy, EI–231 Forrestal Building, Washington, DC 20585; 202–586–8800.

The Energy Efficiency and Renewable Energy Clearinghouse is an information clearinghouse on energy conservation and renewable energy (e.g., solar, wind, and ocean). The service will answer questions or refer you to an expert. Various free pamphlets and books are available.

Contact: Energy Efficiency and Renewable Energy Clearinghouse, Box 3048, Merrifield, VA 22116; 800–363–3732.

✔ **Department of Health and Human Services**
200 Independence Avenue SW
Washington, DC 20201
Main number: 202–690–7000
Public affairs: 202–690–7850
Locator service: 202–619–0257
Web site: http://os.dhhs.gov/

Scope Includes

The department's Public Health Service division has key offices devoted to the following medical and health-related subjects:

AIDS
Alcohol Abuse
Diseases
Drug Abuse
Drug Research
Family Planning
Food Safety
Minority Health
Occupational Safety
Smoking
Statistical Data
Toxic Substances
Veterinary Medicine

The department's National Institutes of Health (NIH) include:

National Cancer Institute
National Eye Institute
National Heart, Lung, and Blood Institute
National Institute of Arthritis and Musculoskeletal and Skin
  Diseases
National Institute of Child Health and Human Development
National Institute of Diabetes and Digestive and Kidney
  Diseases
National Institute of Dental Research
National Institute of Environmental Health Sciences
National Institute of Neurological and Communicative
  Disorders and Stroke

NIH has its own Web site: http://nih.gov/
In the Office of Human Development Services, you can find these offices:

Administration on Aging
Administration for Children, Youth, and Families
Administration on Developmental Disabilities
Administration for Native Americans
President's Committee on Mental Retardation

Other major divisions of HHS include:

Family Support Administration
Health Care Financing Administration
Social Security Administration

Rich Resources

The Office of Disease Prevention and Health Promotion's (ODPHP) National Health Information Center provides information on virtually all health-oriented questions ranging from weight control to rare disorders. Up-to-date expertise and literature are available on most health problems, including alcoholism, allergies, arthritis, birth defects, cancer, child diseases, dental problems, depression, drug addiction, genetic diseases, high blood pressure, poisoning, and sexually transmitted diseases.

Contact: Telephone the Information Center at its toll-free number: 800–

336–4797. To request information in writing: Box 1133, Washington, DC 20013–1133.

The National Center for Health Statistics provides expert advice and statistical data relating to health matters, including illness, disabilities, and hospital and health care utilization and financing. You can call to talk to an expert or write to receive a publication—many are free. This center can also help you track down vital statistics: records on births, deaths, marriages, and divorce. You will be provided with the vital statistics office to contact in the proper state.

Contact: National Center for Health Statistics, U.S. Department of Health and Human Services, 6525 Belcrest Road, Hyattsville, MD 20782; 301–436–8500.

The department maintains clearinghouses of information on special health concerns, including:

Aging

Contact: Office of Program Development, Administration on Aging, U.S. Department of Health and Human Services, 330 Independence Avenue SW, Room 4661 Cohen Building, Washington, DC 20201; 202–619–0011.

Family Planning

Contact: National Clearinghouse for Family Planning Information, Office of Family Planning, U.S. Department of Health and Human Services, Box 30436, Bethesda, MD 20814.

Mental Health

Contact: National Institute of Mental Health, Public Inquiry Branch, 5600 Fishers Lane, Room 7C02, Rockville, MD 20857; 301–443–4513.

The National Institute for Occupational Safety and Health (NIOSH) publishes a variety of free reports and publications. You can talk to a staff expert who specializes in a particular hazard (e.g., asbestos, formaldehyde).

Contact: NIOSH Publications, 4676 Columbia Parkway, Cincinnati, OH 45226; 513–533–8326.

The National Library of Medicine is the world's largest medical library, with over 4 million items. Specialties include the health sciences and, to a lesser degree, chemistry, physics, botany, and zoology. The library will assist you by checking its resources or by referring you to another organization.

Contact: U.S. Department of Health and Human Services, National Institutes of Health, National Library of Medicine, Bethesda, MD 20894; 301–496–6308. Reference Desk: 800–272–4787.

A free catalog of the department's publications is available from the editorial operation branch of the communication division. Call 301–496–4143.

The U.S. Office of Consumer Affairs, located in HHS, will try to tell you who can help you with a consumer complaint.

Contact: U.S. Office of Consumer Affairs, HHS 1009 Premier Building, Washington, DC 20201; 202–727–7000.

✔ Department of Housing and Urban Development

451 7th Street SW
Washington, DC 20410
Main number: 202–708–1422
Public affairs: 202–708–0980
Web site: http://www.hud.gov

Scope Includes

Block Grants
Elderly Housing
Energy Conservation
Fair Housing
Indian/Public Housing
Urban Studies

Rich Resources

HUD's Library and Information Services will answer housing-related questions or will refer people with housing questions to the correct department.

Contact: HUD Library and Information Services, U.S. Department of Housing and Urban Development, Room 8141, 451 7th Street SW, Washington, DC 20410; 202–708–2370.

HUD User is a service that will try to locate research reports sponsored by the department and help you get them. Many of these reports are inexpensive.

Contact: HUD User, Box 6091, Rockville, MD 20850; 301–251–5154 or 800–245–2691.

The Housing Information and Statistics Division can provide various housing statistics free, as well as answer inquiries. Topics on which statistics are generated include mortgages, neighborhoods, construction, and prices.

Contact: Statistical and Actuarial Staff, U.S. Department of Housing and Urban Development, 451 7th Street SW, Washington, DC 20410; 202–755–7510.

Finally, the Department of Housing and Urban Development has a hotline for discrimination complaints: 800–669–9777.

✔ **Department of the Interior**
18th and C Streets NW
Washington, DC 20240
Main number: 202–208–3100
Communications: 202–208–6416
Web site: http://www.doi.gov

Scope Includes
Archaeology
Fish and Wildlife
Geology
Mapping
Minerals
Native Americans
Natural Resources
Water

Rich Resources

Do you want to know how to place reservations to go to Yosemite? When the Cherry Blossom Festival is being held? The best time to visit Shenandoah National Park to see the peak foliage? The National Park Service's public inquiries office answers such questions and provides information on national parks. Written or telephone inquiries are accepted.

Contact: National Park Service, Public Inquiries Office, Box 37127, Washington, DC 20013–7127; 202–208–4747.

The Department of the Interior's Natural Resource Library will try to answer phone or mail inquiries on matters related to natural resources, including conservation, public lands, Native Americans, the environment, and fish and wildlife. The library also publishes bibliographies on areas of current interest ranging from the survival of the Florida panther to pollution problems in wildlife areas.

Contact: Natural Resources Library, U.S. Department of the Interior, 18th and C Streets NW, Washington, DC 20240; 202–208–5815.

The Bureau of Indian Affairs will help you obtain information about Native Americans, their culture, and their relationship with the federal government.

Contact: Bureau of Indian Affairs, Public Affairs Office, U.S. Department of the Interior, MS 1340, 18th and C Streets NW, Washington, DC 20245; 202–208–5116. For inquiries, call 202–219–4150.

✔ **Department of Justice**

10th Street and Constitution Avenue NW
Washington, DC 20530
Main number: 202–514–2000
Public affairs: 202–514–2007
Web site: http://www.usdoj.gov

Scope Includes

Antitrust
Civil Rights
Drug Enforcement

Immigration
Justice Statistics
Juvenile Justice
Prisons

Rich Resources

A special division of the Bureau's National Institute of Justice is its National Criminal Justice Reference Service (NCJRS). NCJRS provides the latest criminal justice findings via databases, reference and referral sources, publications, audiovisual materials, and more. Membership in NCJRS is free.

Contact: National Institute of Justice, NCJRS, Box 6000, Department F, Rockville, MD 20849–6000; 800–851–3420 (in Washington, DC: 301–251–5500).

A relatively new program from the department is the Justice Statistics Clearinghouse. Among the services offered by the clearinghouse are responding to statistical requests (e.g., how many burglaries occurred in the past year), providing information about JSC services, suggesting referrals to other sources, and conducting custom literature searches of the NCJRS database.

TIP: If your research requires investigation of federal courts, you should get hold of a book called *The Sourcebook of Federal Courts,* which provides contact information and search advice for each of the 295 U.S. District, 184 U.S. Bankruptcy, and 13 Federal Records Center courts. The 672-page directory is reasonably priced and can be ordered from BRB Publications, 4653 S. Lakeshore Drive, Tempe, AZ 85282; 800–929–3811.

Contact: Telephone the Justice Statistics Clearinghouse at its toll-free number: 800–732–3277 (in Washington, DC: 301–251–5500).

The bureau also publishes its free *Bureau of Justice Statistics Bulletin.* The bulletin identifies key individuals within the department and their area of expertise, and lists various free studies and reports.

Contact: Bureau of Justice Statistics, U.S. Department of Justice, Box 6000, 633 Indiana Avenue NW, Washington, DC 20521; 800–732–3277 (in Washington, DC: 301–251–5500).

The FBI's "Uniform Crime Reports" is a reliable set of criminal statistics used in law enforcement operations and management. It covers such areas as crime trends in the United States by state, city, and county; number of types of crime; statistics on officers; and so forth. The division will answer inquiries from the public on these statistics. It also publishes the annual *Crime in the United States*, available from the U.S. Government Printing Office.

Contact: Uniform Crime Reports, Federal Bureau of Investigation, Washington, DC 20535; 202–324–5015.

✔ **Department of Labor**

200 Constitution Avenue NW
Washington, DC 20210
Main number: 202–219–6666
Public affairs: 202–219–7316
Web site: http://www.dol.gov

Scope Includes

Employment Training
Labor–Management Relations
Labor Statistics
Occupational Safety and Health
Pension and Welfare Benefits
Productivity and Technology
Veterans' Employment
Women

Rich Resources

The Bureau of Labor Statistics publishes statistical data on employment, prices, wages, living conditions, and productivity. Other specialties include state economic statistics, industry statistics, consumer expenditures, economic growth projections, and occupational outlooks. A special free directory, "Telephone Contacts for Data Users," identifies the bureau's experts and specialties. Also available free is a periodical titled *Bureau of Labor Statistics News*.

Department of Justice Telephone Contacts

Contact: U.S. Department of Labor, Bureau of Labor Statistics, Inquiries and Correspondence Branch, Washington, DC 20212; 202–606–5900. On the Web: http://stats.bls.gov/blshome.html

The Occupational Safety and Health Administration will answer general inquiries regarding health and safety in the workplace. It also publishes various pamphlets and materials. A helpful guide is "All about OSHA," which lists its regional offices.

Contact: OSHA Publications, OSHA Publications Distribution Office, U.S. Department of Labor, 200 Constitution Ave. NW, Room N–3101, Washington, DC 20210; 202–219–8151.

✔ **Department of State**
   2201 C Street NW
   Washington, DC 20520
   Main number: 202–647–4000
   Public affairs: 202–647–6575
   Web site: http://www.state.gov/index.html

Scope Includes

   African Affairs
   Arms Control
   Canadian and European Affairs
   East Asian and Pacific Affairs
   Human Rights
   Inter-American Affairs
   International Environmental Affairs
   International Narcotics
   Near Eastern and South Asian Affairs
   Nuclear and Space Arms Negotiations
   Passport Inquiries
   Prisoners of War/Missing in Action
   Refugees
   Visa Inquiries

Rich Resources

The department publishes short "background note" booklets that contain information on about 170 countries' social, economic, political, and military organization. These booklets are designed for the nonspecialist. They are inexpensive and provide both a cultural and historical overview.

Contact: Superintendent of Documents, Box 371954, Pittsburgh, PA 15250–7954; 202–512–1800.

The State Department publishes many free short periodicals, too. To get a list of what is available, order the document "Selected State Department Publications."

Contact: Public Information Service, Room 6808, U.S. Department of State, Washington, DC 20520; 202–647–6575.

An especially useful publication, reasonably priced, is the "Diplomatic List," a listing of foreign diplomatic representatives in Washington, DC, and their addresses.

Contact: Superintendent of Documents, Box 371954, Pittsburgh, PA 15250–7954; 202–512–1800.

The State Department publishes "Foreign Consular Offices in the U.S.," which lists country consulates, their addresses, phone numbers, and personnel. You can obtain help on questions you have about a particular country by contacting its consulate. The British consulate, for example, reports that it receives questions such as: Where is the county of Middlesex, England, located? How can I trace my relatives? How can I find information about what the British law says regarding divorce? How can I get information on the fashion industry in your country?

Contact: Superintendent of Documents, U.S. Government Printing Office, Washington, DC 20402. Or check the white pages of a major city phone book to find the consulate you seek.

✔ **Department of Transportation**

400 7th Street SW
Washington, DC 20590
Main number: 202–366–4000
Public affairs: 202–366–4570
Web site: http://www.dot.gov

Scope Includes

Automobile Safety
Aviation Safety
Aviation Standards
Boating
Hazardous Materials Transportation
Highway Safety
Mass Transit
National Highway Traffic Safety Administration
Railroad Safety
Shipbuilding
Vehicle Accident Statistics
Vehicle Crashworthiness

Rich Resources

The department's library will try to answer your questions related to transportation. Topics it covers include accident prevention, automobile safety, boating information, bus technology, driver education, energy, environmental research, highway research, mass transit, pollution, railroad information, traffic safety, and transportation for the handicapped.

Contact: U.S. Department of Transportation Library, Room 2200, SVC–122.20, 400 7th Street SW, Washington, DC 20590; 202–366–0746.

A separate branch of the library can assist you with reference inquiries.

Contact: U.S. Department of Transportation Library, FOB–10A, SVC–122.40, 800 Independence Avenue SW, Room 931, Washington, DC 20591; 202–267–3115.

✔ **Department of the Treasury**

15th Street and Pennsylvania Avenue NW
Washington, DC 20220
Main number: 202–622–2000
Public affairs: 202–622–2960
Web site: http://www.ustreas.gov/treasury/homepage.html

Scope Includes

Coin and Medal Production
Currency Production
Currency Research and Development
Customs
Savings Bonds
Secret Service Protection
Taxpayer Assistance
Tax Return Investigation

Rich Resources

The U.S. Customs Service publishes various free leaflets and newsletters. For example, "Customs Hints—Know Before You Go" explains customs privileges for returning U.S. residents and lists prohibited and restricted imports. Other publications cover importing pets and wildlife, cars, and alcoholic beverages.

Contact: U.S. Customs Service, 1301 Constitution Avenue NW, Room 3338, Washington, DC 20229; 202–927–1644.

You can contact experts from the U.S. Customs Service, who can answer questions about import rules and regulations for scores of different commodities.

Contact: U.S. Customs Service, Department of the Treasury, 6 World Trade Center, Room 425, New York, NY 10048; 212–466–4547.

If you have questions about your taxes, you'll likely find the answer you need in the Internal Revenue Service's publication number 910. Inside you'll find out about all of the services and publications available to help you prepare a tax return.

Contact: Telephone IRS Information at its toll-free number: 800–829–1040.

SELECTED ADMINISTRATIVE AGENCIES

✔ **Consumer Product Safety Commission**
Washington, DC 20207
Main number: 800–638–2772
Public affairs: 301–504–0580
Web site: http://www.cpsc.gov

Scope Includes

Fire and thermal burn hazards, product safety assessment, mechanical hazards, injury information, electrical shock hazards, safety packaging, chemical hazards.

Rich Resources

The Consumer Product Safety Commission publishes a number of free pamphlets and reports on product safety, mostly devoted to specific products, such as wood stoves or toys. It also has a toll-free number that you can call if you have a complaint about a hazardous product or if you want to report an injury resulting from a consumer product.

Contact: Consumer Product Safety Commission, Washington, DC 20207; 800–638–2772.

✔ **Environmental Protection Agency**
401 M Street SW
Washington, DC 20460
Main number: 202–260–2090
Public affairs: 202–260–7963
Web site: http://www.epa.gov

Scope Includes

Air and radiation, pesticides and toxic substances, acid deposition, environmental monitoring and quality assurance, solid waste and emergency response, water, noise control.

Rich Resources

The EPA supports a staff of experts who specialize in subjects such as air quality, drinking water, noise, radiation, and toxic substances. A $15 headquarters telephone directory will identify

exactly the person you need. In this directory you can look up the name and telephone number of the Director of the Office of Solid Waste, the Director of Acid Deposition, and so on.

Contact: Superintendent of Documents, Box 371954, Pittsburgh, PA 15250–7954; 202–512–2250.

✔ **Federal Communications Commission**
1919 M Street NW
Washington, DC 20554
Main number: 202–632–7000
Public affairs: 202–632–7000
Web site: http://fcc.gov

Scope Includes

Cable television, broadcast stations, radio regulation.

Rich Resources

The FCC publishes some helpful documents, among them "The Information Seekers Guide," issued by the Consumer Assistance and Small Business Division. That division provides personal assistance and publishes free bulletins regarding communication issues (including cable television and other broadcasting matters).

Contact: Federal Communications Division, Consumer Assistance Branch, 1919 M Street NW, Washington, DC 20554; 202–418–0190.

The FCC Library is a good source of information on various telecommunications issues.

Contact: FCC Library, 1919 M Street NW, Washington, DC 20554; 202–418–0450.

✔ **Federal Emergency Management Agency**
Federal Center Plaza
500 C Street SW
Washington, DC 20472
Main number: 202–418–0200
Public affairs: 202–418–0200
Web site: http://www.fema.gov

Scope Includes

Arson information, flood insurance, fire education, fire statistics, nuclear attack protection, radioactive hazards, earthquake research.

Rich Resources

FEMA publishes a catalog of free publications covering various issues related to emergency preparedness. Subjects range from shelter design to earthquakes, winter storm safety tips, and so forth.

Contact: FEMA, 500 C Street SW, Washington, DC 20472; 202–646–3484 or 800–480–2520 to order publications.

✔ **Federal Trade Commission**
Pennsylvania Avenue and 6th Street NW
Washington, DC 20580
Main number: 202–326–2000
Public affairs: 202–326–2180
Web site: http:// www.ftc.gov

Scope Includes

Advertising practices, competition and antitrust matters, consumer protection, financial statistics.

Rich Resources

The Federal Trade Commission (FTC) can provide information and advice regarding consumer problems and complaints, especially in areas such as deceptive advertising and unordered merchandise.

Contact: FTC, Correspondence Branch, Room 692, Pennsylvania Avenue and 6th Street NW, Washington, DC 20580; 202–326–3768.

✔ **General Services Administration**
7th and D Streets SW
Washington, DC 20407
Main number: 202–708–5082
Public affairs: 202–501–0705
Web site: http://www.gsa.gov

Scope Includes

Consumer information, government audits and investigations, fraud hotline, federal property, purchasing of equipment and supplies, information management, public buildings management.

Rich Resources

The GSA's Consumer Information Center publishes an extremely useful free quarterly catalog that describes more than 100 free and inexpensive consumer pamphlets and guides available from the government.

These pamphlets are very practical and helpful. "Ideas into Dollars," for example, provides advice on patenting, financing, and marketing a new invention or product. It lists various sources of assistance, such as universities, government offices, inventors, and associations. "Occupational Outlook Quarterly" provides descriptions of new occupations, salary figures, job trends, and a lot of helpful advice.

Contact: Consumer Information Center, Box 100, Pueblo, CO 81009.

The *Consumer Resource Handbook* describes how and where to go to get help in resolving complaints and problems with companies. The handbook provides a complaint contact person at more than 1,000 well-known companies and gives advice on how to get help from a wide variety of sources, such as third-party resolution organizations, Better Business Bureaus, media programs, municipal consumer offices, licensing boards, and federal agencies. The handbook is free.

Contact: Consumer Information Center, Pueblo, CO 81009; 719–948–3334 or 800–664–4435.

The Washington headquarters of the Consumer Information Center may be able to help you further.

Contact: Consumer Information Center, General Services Administration, 18th and F Streets NW, Room G–142, Washington, DC 20405; 202–501–1794.

HEALTH

FDA Consumer. Interesting articles for consumers based on recent developments in the regulation of foods, drugs, and cosmetics by the Food and Drug Administration. **Annual subscription—10 issues.** (FDA) **252W. $12.00.**

Fitness Fundamentals. A "must" for anyone starting to exercise. Discusses how to set up a program and monitor your progress. 7 pp. (1987. PCPFS) **129W. $1.00.**

How to Take Weight Off Without Getting Ripped Off. Discusses weight reduction and products, fad diets, and other diet aids; and provides tips on a sensible weight loss program. 4 pp. (1985. FDA) **529W. Free.**

Indoor Tanning. How tanning devices work, and why they can be as hazardous to your health as tanning outdoors. 4 pp. (1988. FTC) **422W. 50¢.**

Quackery—The Billion Dollar "Miracle" Business. How to protect yourself from health fraud. Discusses how bogus remedies for cancer, arthritis, and the "battle of the bulge" can hurt you much more than help. 4 pp. (1985. FDA) **530W. Free.**

Who Donates Better Blood For You Than You? Discusses the advantages of donating blood to yourself before undergoing planned surgery. 3 pp. (1988. FDA) **531W. Free.**

Drugs & Health Aids

Anabolic Steroids: Losing at Winning. Discusses the dangerous side-effects and reactions of these popular muscle-building drugs. 5 pp. (1988. FDA) **532W. Free.**

Comparing Contraceptives. Discusses effectiveness and possible side effects of nine types of birth control with a comparison chart and statistics on use. 8 pp. (1985. FDA) **533W. Free.**

A Doctor's Advice on Self-Care. There are more over-the-counter drugs available now than ever before which can cure, prevent and diagnose illnesses. The U.S. Commissioner of Food and Drugs tells how to use them safely and effectively. 7 pp. (1989. FDA) **534W. Free.**

Do-It-Yourself Medical Testing. Medical self-tests are available today for everything from eyesight to pregnancy to high blood pressure. Explains how some tests are used, how they work, and their accuracy. 7 pp. (1986. FD...

Food and Drug Interactions. How some commonly used drugs affect nutritional needs. How some foods affect drug actions; and how to avoid ill effects. 4 pp. (1988. FDA) **549W. Free.**

Myths and Facts of Generic Drugs. What they are and how they may save you money. Also corrects some common misconceptions about generic prescriptions. 3 pp. (1988. FDA) **536W. Free.**

Some Things You Should Know About Prescription Drugs. Even prescription drugs can be dangerous. Here's tips for safe use. 4 pp. (1983. FDA) **537W. Free.**

X-Ray Record Card. Wallet-sized card for recording X-ray examinations. (1980. FDA) **538W. Free.**

Medical Problems

AIDS. How AIDS is spread, how to prevent it, and what to do if you think you've been infected. 2 pp. (1988. FDA) **539W. Free.**

Breast Exams: What You Should Know. Eighty percent of breast lumps are not cancer. How to check for lumps, how doctors examine them, and treatments available. 17 pp. (1986. NIH) **540W. Free.**

Chew Or Snuff is Real Bad Stuff. Poster/booklet for teenagers describing dangers from smokeless tobacco including cancer, gum disease, stained teeth, and more. (1988. NIH) **542W. Free.**

Clearing the Air: A Guide to Quitting Smoking. No-nonsense tips on kicking the habit. 32 pp. (1985. NIH) **543W. Free.**

The Colon. While this part of the body is not generally discussed, it performs important functions and is the site of many problems, such as colitis, diverticulitis, and cancer. 6 pp. (1985. FDA) **544W. Free.**

Dizziness. Explains the various causes, diagnostic tests, and treatments for people suffering from dizzy spells. 27 pp. (1986. NIH) **130W. $1.00.**

Facing Surgery? Why Not Get a Second Opinion? Answers these and other questions of the prospective patient. Includes a toll-f... ...b... for locating specialists. 5 ...

✔ National Aeronautics and Space Administration

300 East Street SW
Washington, DC 20546
Main number: 202–358–0000
Public affairs: 202–358–1750
Web site: http://www.nasa.gov/
Center for Aerospace Information Technical Report Server:
http://www.sti.nasa.gov/RECONselect.html

Scope Includes

Aeronautics and space technology, life sciences, astrophysics, earth sciences, solar system exploration, space shuttle payload, Mars observer program, microgravity science, upper atmosphere research, solar flares.

Rich Resources

NASA's Industrial Application Centers are designed to provide assistance in solving technical problems or meeting information needs. The centers offer online computer retrieval to 2 million technical reports in the NASA database and to more than fifty times that many reports and articles in 250 other computer databases. Topics covered include aerospace, energy, engineering, chemicals, food technology, textile technology, metallurgy, medicine, electronics, surface coatings, oceanography, and more. The centers operate on a cost-recovery basis.

Contact: To find the center closest to you, write or phone NASA, Technology Utilization Office, 800 Elkridge Landing Road, Linthicum Heights, MD 21090; 410–859–5300.

Do you want to know how work is progressing toward development of a plane that can fly to Japan in two hours? Curious about the atmosphere on Venus? The NASA headquarters library will try to answer questions you have on flight and space. It can also send you documents from its collection or tell you where to obtain them.

Contact: NASA Headquarters Library, 300 East Street SW, Washington, DC 20546; 202–358–0168.

You can obtain an overview and a full description of several useful reports and information services available from NASA by

getting a very valuable catalog called *NASA STI Products and Services at a Glance.*

Contact: NASA Access Help Desk, NASA Center for Aerospace Information, Box 8757, Baltimore, MD 21240; 301–621–0390. E-mail help is available at help@sti.nasa.gov

NASA also makes its inventions available to the public for licensing. For more details, see page 140.

✔ **National Archives and Records Administration**
NARA, Washington DC 20408
Main number: 202–501–5400
Public affairs: 202–501–5525
Web site: http://www.nara.gov/

Scope Includes

Naturalization records, census data, military records, land records, passenger lists, passport applications, selected vital statistics.

Rich Resources

One popular use (among many others) of the National Archives is researching genealogy records. Although major projects need to be performed in person in Washington, DC, a reference services department will answer phone questions about holdings and furnish copies of documents for a modest fee. A useful bibliography is the *Archives' Select List of Publications.*

Contact: Reference Services Branch, National Archives and Records Administration, Washington DC 20408; 202–501–5400.

✔ **National Endowment for the Arts and the Humanities**
Arts: 1100 Pennsylvania Avenue NW
Washington, DC 20506
Main number: 202–682–5400
Public affairs: 202–682–5400
Web site: http://gopher.tmn.com:70/Artswire/Govarts/NEA

Humanities: 1100 Pennsylvania Avenue NW, Room 406
Washington, DC 20506
Main number: 202–606–8438
Public affairs: 202–606–8438

Scope Includes

Literature, museums, folk arts, visual arts, dance arts, music arts, theater arts and musical theater, opera, media arts (film, radio, TV), history, language, and so on.

Rich Resources

Program specialists at the National Endowment for the Arts may be able to help you with questions on design arts, expansion arts, folk arts, interarts, literature, media arts, museums, and visual arts.

Contact: National Endowment for the Arts, Old Post Office Building, Nancy Hanks Center, 1100 Pennsylvania Avenue, Washington, DC 20506; 202–682–5400.

The Division of Research Programs of the National Endowment for the Humanities will refer you to a division that can help you track down an answer to a humanities-related question, including inquiries related to history, philosophy, languages, linguistics, literature, archaeology, jurisprudence, the arts, ethics, and comparative religion. You can call the division directly or send for a booklet that will help you identify the expert you need.

Contact: Division of Research Programs, Room 318, National Endowment for the Humanities, 1100 Pennsylvania Avenue NW, Washington, DC 20506; 202–606–8200.

✔ **National Science Foundation**
1800 G Street NW, Room 527
Washington, DC 20550
Main number: 703–306–1234
Public affairs: 703–306–1234
Website: http://www.nsf.gov

Scope Includes

Atmospheric/astronomical and earth-ocean sciences, mathematical and physical sciences, arctic and antarctic research, anthropology, engineering, biology, genetic biology, chemistry, computer science, earthquakes, economics, ethics in science, meteorology, galactic and extragalactic astronomy, geography, geology, history and philosophy of science, nutri-

tion, linguistics, marine chemistry, metallurgy, minority research, nuclear physics, science and technology to aid the handicapped, small-business research and development, sociology.

Rich Resources

The National Science Foundation funds research in all fields of science and engineering, except for clinical research, by issuing grants and contracts. If you'd like information on how to apply for a grant, you can obtain the publication "Grants for Scientific and Engineering Research," which describes the guidelines for preparation of proposals, proposal processing and evaluation, and all other steps related to applying for NSF grants.

Contact: Public Affairs, National Science Foundation, Washington, DC 20550; 202–357–9498.

✔ **National Transportation Safety Board**
490 L'Enfant Plaza East
Washington, DC 20594
Main number: 202–382–6600
Public affairs: 202–382–6600
Web site: http://www.ntsb.gov

Scope Includes

Accident investigations involving aviation, railroads, highways, and hazardous materials.

Rich Resources

The National Transportation Safety Board (NTSB) conducts independent accident investigations and formulates safety improvement recommendations. The public can find out about these investigations by obtaining the board's "Accident Briefs" and "Accident Reports," which identify the circumstances and probable cause of the accident investigated. The reports are reasonably priced. To find out more, send for the board's publication "NTSB Documents and Information."

Contact: National Transportation Safety Board, Public Inquiries Section, 490 L'Enfant Plaza East, Washington, DC 20594; 202–382–6735.

NTSB's Safety Studies and Analysis Division will provide you with data regarding air accidents. For example, you can ask how many accidents occurred that involved a particular type of aircraft, or airline, during a specific year. There is no cost for the information.

Contact: National Transportation Safety Board, Safety Studies and Analysis Division, 490 L'Enfant Plaza East, Washington, DC 20594; 202–382–6536.

✔ **Small Business Administration**
409 Third Street SW
Washington, DC 20416
Main number: 202–606–4000
Public affairs: 202–205–6744
Toll-free help: 800–827–5722
Web site: http://www.sba.gov

Scope Includes

Women's businesses, veteran affairs, disaster assistance, financial assistance, management assistance, minority small businesses, statistical data, export advice.

Rich Resources

See chapter 4, "Business Information," for a description of the various kinds of business help available.

✔ **U.S. International Trade Commission**
500 E Street SW
Washington, DC 20436
Main number: 202–205–2000
Public affairs: 202–205–1819

Scope Includes

Agriculture, fisheries and forests, textiles, leather products and apparel, energy and chemicals, machinery and equipment, minerals and metals, instruments and precision manufacturers, automotive statistics.

Rich Resources

For a description of ITC's research reports, see chapter 4, "Business Information."

GUIDES TO GOVERNMENT INFORMATION

There are a number of excellent resources available to help you track down the precise bureau, division, or even person that can provide you with the information you need. These guides are published by both the government itself and commercial publishers. Here's the best of the bunch:

✔ Source: *United States Government Manual*

This comprehensive guide to the agencies and offices that make up the federal government is published by the office of the Federal Register, United States General Services Administration. All the departments are broken down into their various bureaus and offices, and key personnel within those offices are identified. The guide also includes information on quasi-governmental organizations like the Smithsonian Institution and multilateral organizations such as the Pan American Health Organization. Regional offices and Federal Information Centers—a specialized source of help described below—are also identified. Many libraries have this reasonably priced book, or you can order it from the Superintendent of Documents, Box 371954, Pittsburgh, PA 15250–7954; 202–512–1800.

✔ Source: Federal Information Centers (FIC)

These are clearinghouses set up by the United States for citizens who want to obtain information about the federal government. People who have questions about a government program or agency, but are unsure about which office can help, may call or write to their nearest center. The FIC will either answer the question or locate an expert who can. Local numbers are listed in the *United States Government Manual* or check the "blue pages" governmental section of a nearby large city phone directory.

✔ Source: Internal Telephone Directories

The internal telephone directories of the federal departments are superb "insider's guides" to finding the person in the govern-

ment who can help you. These directories provide the names, titles, and phone numbers of the individuals who work in specific divisions. Departments that make their directories available for the public's use include Defense, Energy, Health and Human Services, Labor, State, and Transportation. The directories are reasonably priced. To order, contact the Superintendent of Documents, Box 371954, Pittsburgh, PA 15250–7954; 202–512–1800.

TIP: The Freedom of Information Act of 1966 requires federal agencies to provide the public with any identifiable records on request, unless the information falls into a special exempted category, such as classified national defense secrets or internal personnel data. If your request for some information is denied, you may seek assistance from the Freedom of Information Clearinghouse, Box 19367, Washington, DC 20036;

✔ **Source: *Washington Information Directory***

Published by Congressional Quarterly, this is an excellent guide to information resources in Washington, DC. The directory breaks down the various departments and agencies into their particular divisions, and it provides a one-paragraph description of the division's specialties and scope. A contact person and phone number for each division are also provided. This directory identifies sources of information within *not only federal agencies but*

TIP: I've found this guide—and Washington sources in general—especially helpful for answering consumer-oriented questions. For example, once I had to find out whether a certain energy-saving device really worked as claimed. The product was a device that fit on top of a furnace's flue, and the vendor claimed it recirculated the hot air and thereby cut heating bills. I figured that the U.S. Department of Energy might have some kind of expert who could handle a question like this. The *Washington Information Directory* listed a Department of Energy division called Building Technologies, whose purpose is to keep up to date on technologies that may reduce building energy costs. Upon contacting the division, I discovered that, sure enough, there was a technical person in the division who was able to help. (Final verdict on the device: It *can* save some energy on older, inefficient furnaces, but not very much on newer ones.)

STATE

	Office Phone	Home Phone
		21
Southern Africa Division (AA/S) Mary S Seasword 4635..........	647-7163	362-7259
OFFICE OF ANALYSIS FOR INTER-AMERICAN REPUBLICS (INR/IAA)		
Director John W DeWitt 7358........	647-2229	861-8314
Middle America-Caribbean Division (INR/IAA/MAC) Chief		
David Smith 7637........	647-4466	243-4278
South American Division (INR/IAA/SA) Chief		
James Buchanan 7534........	647-2251	971-6450
OFFICE OF ANALYSIS FOR EAST ASIA AND THE PACIFIC (INR/EAP)		
Director John J Taylor 8840........	647-1338	241-3792
Deputy Director Louis G Sarris 8840........	647-1179	951-0064
China Division (INR/EAP/CH) (Vacant)........	647-1343	
Northeast Asia Division (INR/EAP/NA) Chief		
Murray D Zinoman 8840........	647-2100	768-5370
Southeast Asia and Pacific Division (INR/EAP/SEA) Chief		
Allen Kitchens 8647	647-2061	536-9310
OFFICE OF ANALYSIS FOR NEAR EAST AND SOUTH ASIA (INR/NESA)		
Director George S Harris 4643........	647-8397	229-7175
Deputy Director Ronald D Lorton 4636........	647-2757	
North Africa and Arabian Peninsula Division		
(NESA/NAP) Chief (Vacant)	647-8403	

Internal Telephone Directory: Department of Transportation

FEDERAL AVIATION ADMINISTRATION

	Exch.	Ext.

AIRWORTHINESS, OFFICE OF—Continued

	Exch.	Ext.
Technical Advisor Robert Allen rm 336B	426	8161
Policy and Procedures Branch John McGrath Manager rm 335C	426	8192
Technical Analysis Branch A C Caviness rm 337A	426	8200
Aircraft Manufacturing Division Sandy DeLucia Manager rm 333B	426	8361

AVIATION MEDICINE, OFFICE OF

	Exch.	Ext.
Federal Air Surgeon Frank H Austin Jr MD rm 300E	426	3535
Secretary Louise C Dille rm 300E	426	3535
Deputy Federal Air Surgeon Jon L Jordan MD rm 300E	426	3537
Secretary Monica Russell rm 300E	426	3537
Chief Psychiatrist Barton Pakull MD rm 327	472	5866
Aeromedical Standards Division William H Hark MD Manager rm 322	426	3802
Occupational Health Division Donald M Watkin MD Manager rm 327	426	3767
Computer Systems Analyst Carol A Thomas rm 329	426	3783
Industrial Hygiene Robert N Thompson PhD rm 327	426	3769
Biomedical and Behavioral Sciences Division Evan W Pickrel PhD Manager (Acting) rm 325	426	3433
Program Scientist—Accident Investigation Andrew F Horne MD rm 325	426	3434
Program Scientist—Human Resources Evan W. Pickrel PhD rm 325	426	3435
Program Scientist—Human Performance Alan H Diehl PhD rm 325	426	3433
Program Scientist—Protection & Survival William T Shepherd PhD rm 325	426	3436
Program Operations Division Virginia Meadows Manager rm 300E	426	3536
Administrative Officer Annette Lyles rm 321A	426	8326
Management Programs Leonard C Ryan rm 321B	426	8318
Program Evaluation Charles O Ensor rm 321D	426	8318

CIVIL AVIATION SECURITY, OFFICE OF

Internal Telephone Directory: Department of State

also virtually any important organization—private or public—that operates out of Washington, DC. These organizations deal with topics that range from health to the environment, labor, minorities, and much more. A subject index at the back of the book makes it easy to track down the particular information source that can best help you. The directory also lists the current top-level government personnel, such as members of the cabinet, Senate, and House of Representatives. You'll find the *Washington Information Directory* in many libraries.

✔ **Source: *Federal Executive Directory***

Published by Carroll Publishing Company in Washington, DC, this is another excellent guide to the federal government. Unlike the *Washington Information Directory*, it does not provide descriptive material on each agency and does not include a description of nongovernment organizations in Washington. However, it does provide a very detailed listing of federal personnel—their names, titles, and phone numbers. Using this guide enables you to zero in on the specific person who specializes in your subject of interest. A very handy subject index is provided at the back. This directory is available at most large libraries.

There are other guides and directories that pinpoint who's who in the government. For example, a series of "yellow books" published by Leadership Directories, Inc. of New York, NY, identifies names, titles, postitions, and career information for leaders in the federal, state, and municipal branches of government, as well as in Congress, the judiciary, and other institutions.

GOVERNMENT INFORMATION ONLINE

The U.S. federal government, over the past few years, has been making an effort to turn at least some of its massive information holdings into electronic databases. The following are the best sources for pinpointing which of these sources may cover a topic of interest to you.

10804	Administrative Compliance Br	David T Read	301-443-3650
10805	Regulatory Affairs Div	Albert Rothschild	301-443-3640
10806	Deputy Director	Vacant	301-443-3640
10807	Product Information Coordination Staff	Ann Myers	301-443-4320
10808	Files and Reporting Sec	Ann Myers	301-443-4320
10809	Documents and Records Sec	Paul Chapman	301-443-5896

10810 **Drug Research and Review**

10811 *5600 Fishers Lane, Rockville, MD 20857*

10812	**Director**	Dr. Robert Temple	301-443-4330
10813	Program Management Dep Dir	Richard A Terselic	301-443-4330
10814	Medical Affairs Dep Dir	Paula Botstein (A)	301-443-4330
10815	Pharmacology Asst Dir	Dr. Vera C Glocklin	301-443-4330
10816	Chemistry Assistant Director	Dr .Charles Kumkumian	301-443-4330
10817	DRUG BIOLOGY DIV	Dr. Elwood O Titus	245-1118
10818	Deputy Director	Dr. Sidney Ellis	245-1118
10819	Technical and Animal Services Staff	Daniel Walker	472-5746
10820	Drug Bioanalysis Br	Dr. Joseph F Reilly	245-1400
10821	Drug Pharmacology Br	Elwood Titus (A)	245-1118
10822	Drug Toxicology Br	Dr. Tibor Balazs	245-1356
10823	Antimicrobial Drugs Br	Dr. Joseph H Graham	245-1034
10824	CARDIO-RENAL DRUG PRODUCTS DIV	Dr. Raymond J Lipicky (A)	301-443-4730
10825	Deputy Director	Stewart J Ehrreich	301-443-4730
10826	Project Management Staff	Natalia Morgenstern	301-443-4730
10827	NEUROPHARMACOLOGICAL DRUG PRODUCTS DIV	Dr. Paul D Leber	301-443-4020
10828	Project Management Staff	John S Purvis	301-443-3800
10829	Drug Abuse Staff	Edward C Tocus	301-443-3504
10830	ONCOLOGY AND RADIOPHARMACEUTICAL DRUG PRODUCTS DIV	Dr. John F Palmer	301-443-4250
10831	Deputy Director	Robert A Jerrusi	301-443-4250
10832	Project Management Staff	Robert G Scully	301-443-4250
10833	SURGICAL- DENTAL DRUG PRODUCTS DIV	Dr. Patricia Russell	301-443-3560
10834	Deputy Director	Philip G Walters	301-443-3560
10835	Project Management Staff	Gary H Boyer	301-443-3560
10836	Administrative Officer	Sandra Howard	301-443-2806

10837 **Center for Food Safety and Applied Nutrition**

10838 *200 C Street, SW, Washington, DC 20204*

10839	**Director**	Dr. Sanford A Miller	245-8850
10840	Deputy Director	Richard J Ronk	245-1057
10841	Scientific Advisor	Dr. William Horwitz	245-1057
10842	PROGRAM OPERATIONS DIV	Edward A Steele	245-2140
10843	Field Programs Br	Shane Carter	755-1606
10845	Center Programs Br	Dr. Ray L Russo	245-1564
10846	INFORMATION RESOURCES MGT DIV	Charles Exley	485-0010
10847	Administrative Ofcr	Thomas J Walsh	485-0009
10848	Automation Br	Dr. James Tucker	485-0018
10849	Computer Systems Br	George A Brindza	245-1233

10876
10877 PC
10878
10879
10880 C
10881 NUT
10882 Dep
10883 Med
10884 Staf
10885 Reg
10886 Con
10887 Nut
10888 D
10889 Co
10890 N
10891 C
10892 E
10893 Mi
10894
10895
10896 E
10897 10
10898 F
10899 L
10900 109
10901 M
10902 Mi
10903 109
10904 Vi
10905 109
10906 Foc
10907 D
10908 F
10909 10
10910 F
10911 D
10912
10913 Fi
10914 C
10915 R
10916 Cc
10917 Cc
10918 Re
10919
10920
10921
10922 Fc
10923
10924
10925
10926 P
10927 D
10928 A
10929 A
10930 C

✔ **Source: FedWorld**

There are scores of federal government agency databases, and you can connect to over 100 of them by linking up with FedWorld, a one-stop electronic gateway, created by the National Technical Information Service (NTIS). Among the services available:

- National Agricultural Library
- Computer Security Bulletin Board
- Energy Information and Data
- FDA Information and Policies
- Department of Labor Information and Files
- Human Nutrition Information Service
- Health and AIDS Information and Reports
- Pollution Prevention
- Total Quality Management
- FCC Daily Digest, Statistics, Reports
- EPA Office of Research and Development
- Space Environment Information Service

While FedWorld is not free, it's quite inexpensive. It costs $35 per year to subscribe, which entitles you to four hours of online time. After that, the hourly charge ranges from $3 to $12, depending on the time of day.

TIP: It's important to remember that, while the NTIS gateway provides an extremely useful link-up to all kinds of federal agency data, it does not connect to *every* such service. For example, one not accessible through the NTIS gateway is the Environmental Protection Agency's Online Library System. This free system contains bibliographic citations to a wide variety of environmental information. (For information on signing up, call 919–541–1370.)

FedWorld also offers its own files. For example, the Patent Licensing Bulletin Board allows for full-text searching of public inventions. An abstract describes the invention, and a complete copy of the patent application can be ordered from NTIS.

How to connect: To connect to FedWorld, you can link to the Web site listed below. If you are not linked to the Internet, set your communications

software to dial 703–321–8020. Set parity to "none," data bits to 8, and stop bit to 1. Terminal emulation should be set to ANSI or VT–100. If you have questions, you can call Bob Bunge at 703–487–4608.

NEW: BEST OF THE
GOVERNMENT ON THE WEB

The following is a list of some of the most broadly useful federal government sites on the Web, organized into key categories. Some of these have already been mentioned in this chapter, or in other places in this book.

For more information on searching the Web, see chapter 5. For the best overall federal Web site locator, you can link to the Federal Web Locator at the Villanova Center for Information Law and Policy: http://www.law.vill.edu

Major Clearinghouses of Information

- FedWorld: http://www.fedworld.gov
- US Business Advisor: http://www.business.gov
- GPO Access: http://www.access.gpo.gov
- Thomas: http://thomas.loc.gov
- Federal News Service: http://www.fednews.com
- GPO Monthly Catalog (citations to government publications): http://www.access.gpo.gov/su_docs
- Bureau of the Census: http://www.census.gov
- Trade/Exporting/Business: Stat-USA: http://www.stat-usa.gov
- Federal Register: http://www.access.gpo.gov/su_docs/aces/dcff001.html#fr

Pointers

- http://www.law.vill.edu/Fed-Agency/fedwebloc.html
- http://www.lib.umich.edu/libhome/Documents.center/govweb.html

The following sites are not all actually derived from the federal government, but provide a variety of other related political and governmental information.

International

- Foreign Government Resources on the Web: http://www.lib. umich.edu/libhome/Documents.Center/foreign.html
- U.S. Bureau of the Census International Database: http://www. census.gov/ftp/pub/ipc/www.idbnew.html
- Directory of Science and Technology Organizations in Japan: http://www.netaxs:com/-aengel/JapanSciTechDirectory/

State Government

- Council of State Governments: http://www.csg.org/
- State and Local Government Information on the Net: http://www.piperinfo.com/piper/state/states.html
- StateSearch: http://www.state.ky.us/nasire/NASIREhome.html

Miscellaneous

- The Activists Oasis: http://www.matisse.net/politics
- Congressional Member Ratings and Voting Records: http:// www.vote-smart.org
- Guide to U.S. Congress—CapWeb: http://policy.net/capweb/ congress.htm
- Senate Web Site: http://www.senate.gov
- Find a congressperson by zip code: http://www.stardot.com/ zipper

For more information on searching government information on the Internet, I highly recommend getting a book called *Electronic Democracy*, written by Graeme Browning and published by Pemberton Press of Wilton, CT. That book lists most of the above sites as well as hundreds more, and provides general tips and strategies for searching government information on the Web.

4

Business Information

A Sampling of Sources

QUICKFINDER: BUSINESS INFORMATION

(continued)

(continued)

Many information searches involve the need to find business data of some sort. This chapter identifies some of the most popular and most available sources of quick information on six popular business topics: industries, companies, economic statistics, investments, starting a new business, and international business.

If you need to find business information, you should not only read about the specific business sources described in this chapter, but also note the broader information sources identified earlier in this book that include business within their scope (*Subject Guide to Books in Print*, periodical directories, trade associations, and so on). In addition, you should read about those business information sources found in the library, covered in chapter 1.

INDUSTRY INFORMATION

Do you want to find out all about the jewelry industry? Need to dig up some business growth projections on the restaurant business? Here are the places to turn to for information about industries:

First See:

- The following indexes to find articles on industry news and trends:
    The Wall Street Journal Index, p. 22
    Funk & Scott Index, p. 22
    Business Periodicals Index, p. 11
- Trade associations for free advice and information, p. 50
- Convention information for up-to-the-minute developments in an industry, p. 53

✔ Source: Brokerage Houses

Let's say you need to find out the latest developments in the hotel industry, or discover what the experts think the chances are of a takeover of a television network. An excellent place to go is a brokerage house. Talking to stock analysts is one of the very best ways to obtain inside information about industries and about companies within an industry. Often, you'll see these analysts quoted in newspapers like *The Wall Street Journal*, giving an expert opinion about some industry development.

> **TIP:** Security analysts are very busy and often tough to reach on the phone. You might try asking to speak with the analyst's "associate" instead. Also, I've found that analysts located in the South or on the West Coast have more time and are more available to chat than those in the Northeast.

How do you find these analysts? The bible is probably a guide called *Nelson's Directory of Investment Research*, which provides the names, phone numbers, and areas of expertise of 4,500 security analysts whose expertise ranges from aerospace to waste disposal. The book is quite expensive, however, so try to locate it in a university business library or a corporate library. Or consider contacting the publisher and asking the editor to look up the name of the analysts for the industry you are interested in.

How to Find:

Contact W. R. Nelson & Company, 1 Gateway Plaza, Port Chester, NY 10573; 914–937–8400.

Another way to track down brokerage analysts is simply to call a very large brokerage firm like Merrill Lynch and ask to speak to an analyst who follows your industry of interest. (See chapters 6–10 for advice on interviewing experts for information.)

✔ Source: International Trade Administration

A superb and free source of information on specific industries can be found on the staff of the U.S. Department of Commerce's International Trade Administration. The ITA has 350 analysts who provide free information on industries such as automobiles, aerospace, capital goods, construction, electronics, services, textiles, and basic industries. The experts will give you up-to-date statistics, information on major U.S. and international markets, and more.

How to Find:

To find the expert you need, contact the U.S. Department of Commerce, International Trade Administration, Herbert C. Hoover Building, 14th and Constitution Ave. NW, Room 4805, Washington, DC 20230; 202–482–2000. The ITA will send you a photocopied list of their industry analysts from the *ITA Directory of Services and Employers* for seven cents per page. You can also order the entire directory of industry analysts and their phone numbers by calling ITA's publications department at 202–482–5494.

✔ Source: International Trade Commission

The International Trade Commission publishes free reports that cover various industries. Past reports include the monthly report on the steel industry, the world market for fresh-cut roses, generic pharmaceuticals from Canada, an annual report on selected economic indicators for rum, and studies of natural-bristle paint brushes from the People's Republic of China and cellular mobile telephones from Japan. These are the kinds of reports that, if prepared by a private research firm, could cost well into the hundreds or thousands of dollars.

How to Find:

Contact the International Trade Commission, Attention: Publications, 500 E Street SW, Washington, DC 20436; 202–205–1806. Ask for "Selected Publications of the United States International Trade Commission."

INDUSTRY	CONTACT	PHONE 377-	ROOM	CLUSTER	INDUSTRY
A					
Abrasive Products	Presbury Graylin	5157	H4055	BI	Cement (Major Proj
Accounting	McAdam Milton B	0346	H4320	SERV	Ceramics
ADP Support (For Dir Invest in US)	Simon, Leslie S	3867	H2204	TIA	Ceramics (Advancer
ADP Support for Aerospace	Westover Harlon	2038	H3015	AERO	Cereals
Advertising	Nelson Theodore	4581	H1122	SERV	Chemicals
Aerospace Financing Issues	Rand, Elizabeth	8228	H6881	AERO	Chemicals (Liaison
Aerospace Industry Analysis	Kingsbury, Gene	0678	H6733	AERO	Chemicals (Major
Aerospace Industry Analysis	Myers, Randolph Jr	0678	H6733	AERO	Chemicals & Allie
Aerospace Industry Data	Kingsbury, Gene	0678	H6733	AERO	Chinaware
Aerospace Industry Data	Myers, Randolph Jr	0678	H6733	AERO	Chloralkali
Aerospace Information & Analysis	Myers, Randolph Jr	0678	H6733	AERO	Coal Exports
Aerospace Market Development	Cohen, Richard E	8228	H6885	AERO	Coal Exports
Aerospace Market Promo	Sarsfield, Claudette	2835	H1012	AERO	Coal Exports
Aerospace Market Promo	Bevans, Samuel	2835	H1012	AERO	Cobalt
Aerospace Market Support	Bowie, David C	8228	H6883	AERO	Cocoa Products
Aerospace Marketing Assistance	Bowie, David C	8228	H6883	AERO	Coffee Products
Aerospace Military	Jackson, Jeff	8228	H6881	AERO	Coloring Extracts
Aerospace Policy & Analysis	Bath, Sally H	8228	H6887	AERO	Commercial Light
Aerospace Trade Issues	Jackson, Jeff	8228	H6733	AERO	Commercial/Indus
Aerospace Trade POLICY	Rand Elizabeth	8228	H6881	AERO	Commonline/Stan
Aerospace Trade Promo	Grafeld, George	3353	H1014	AERO	Components & Ec
Agribusiness (Major Proj)	Bell, Richard	1246	H2013	CGIC	Computer Progran
Agricultural Chemicals	Maxey, Francis P	0128	H4029A	BI	Computer Service
Air Conditioning Eqpmt	Shaw, Eugene	3494	H2100	CGIC	Computer Service
Air, Gas Compressors	McDonald, Edward	0680	H2128	CGIC	Computer Eqpmt
Air, Gas Compressors (Trade Promo)	Zanetakos, George	0552	H2126	CGIC	Computer Eqpmt
Air Pollution Control Eqpmt	Jonkers, Loretta	0564	H2811	CGIC	Computer Eqpmt
Aircraft & Aircraft Engines	Driscoll, George	8228	H6883	AERO	Computer & Busir
Aircraft & Aircraft Engines	Grafeld, George	3353	H1014	AERO	Computers (Trade
Aircraft Auxiliary Equipment	Driscoll, George	8228	H6883	AERO	Computers (Trade
Aircraft Equip	Grafeld, George	3353	H1014	AERO	Computers (Trade
Aircraft Parts	Driscoll, George	8228	H6883	AERO	Computers & Bu
Aircraft Parts/Aux Eqpmt	Grafeld, George	3353	H1014	AERO	Confectionery Pr
Airlines	Elliott, Frederick T	5071	H1122	SERV	Construction, Dr
Airports, Ports, Harbors (Major Proj)	Piggot, Deboorne	3352	H1012	CGIC	Construction Ma
Alum Sheet, Plate/Foil	Cammarota, David	0575	H4059	BI	Construction Ma
Alum Forgings. Electro	Cammarota, David	0575	H4059	BI	Construction Ma
Aluminum Extrud Alum Rolling	Cammarota, David	0575	H4059	BI	Consumer Electro
Ammunitions Ex Small Arms. Nec (Trade Promo)	Cummings. Charles	5361	H2126	CGIC	Consumer Goods
Ammunitions Ex Small Arms Nec	Nordlie, Rolf	0305	H2124	CGIC	Contract Machin
Analytical Instrument (Export Promo)	Gwaltney, G.P	3090	H1108	S&E	Converted Paper
Analytical Instruments	Donnelly, Margaret	5466	H1104	S&E	Conveyors/Conve
Asbestos Prod (Part)	Manion, James J	5157	H4055	BI	Conveyors/Conve
Audio Visual Equipment	Beckham, Reginald	0311	H4040	AACG	Copper Brass Wi
Auto Ind Affairs Parts/Supplies	Jerschkowsky, Oleg	1419	H1003	AACG	Copper
Auto Ind Affairs Parts/Supplies	Reck, Robert O	1419	H1003	AACG	Copper Products
Auto Ind Affairs Supplies	Allison, Loretta M	1419	H1003	AACG	Cosmetics
Auto Ind Affairs Parts/Suppliers	Springmann, Michael J	1419	H1003	AACG	Costume Jewel
Auto Ind Affairs Parts Suppliers	Deborah Semb	1418	H1003	AACG	Current-Carryir
Auto Ind Affairs Parts Suppliers	Heather Jones	1418	H1003	AACG	Cutlery
Auto Industry Affairs	Warner Albert T	0669	H4039	AACG	
Automobile Dealers	Kostecka, Andrew	0342	H4316	SERV	

The Federal Trade Commission issues reports concerning industries as well; these are related to its activities in protecting consumers from deceptive advertising and marketing.

How to Find:

Contact the Federal Trade Commission, Public Reference, Room 130, Washington, DC 20580; 202–326–2222.

✔ **Source: Congressional Committee Hearings**

Before final action is taken on a proposed piece of legislation, the Congress holds hearings. As part of these hearings, Congress often obtains testimony from various industry experts and notable persons. Transcripts of these hearings are ultimately created, and they are available to the public.

The following sample of standing committees and subcommittees in the House of Representatives should give you a feel for the scope of subject areas and industries that these hearings may cover.

- *Agriculture:* Subcommittees include cotton, rice, and sugar; forests, family farms, and energy; livestock, dairy, and poultry; tobacco and peanuts; and wheat, soybeans, and feed grains.
- *Energy and Commerce:* Subcommittees include commerce, transportation, and tourism; energy conservation and power; fossil and synthetic fuels; health and the environment; and telecommunications, consumer protection, and finance.
- *Public Works and Transportation:* Subcommittees include aviation; public buildings and grounds; and surface transportation.
- *Veterans Affairs:* Subcommittees include hospitals and health care; housing; and memorial affairs.
- *Select Committees:* These include aging; children, youth, and families; hunger; and narcotics abuse and control.

How to Find:

Here's how to track down transcripts of past hearings as well as find out what's currently happening in Congress. First, to find out if there are any *current* bills pending in the House or Senate on your subject of interest, call **Washington Legislative Information** at 202–225–1772. The person at that number will be able to tell you if there is such a bill and which committee is sponsoring it. The office can pro-

vide information as timely as one-day old and as far back as 1979. The office will also perform free keyword searches on its own database to locate legislative information and provide printouts from its legislative database for twenty cents per page ($5 minimum charge). To get the best results from this office you should try to be as specific as possible in your request; rather than asking for anything on "child care," narrow the topic down further to prevent being swamped with data. You can call the committee and ask to speak with an aide to the congressperson sponsoring the bill. He or she will be able to give you more details on the bill and tell you how to obtain copies of transcript hearings.

TIPS: Locating a Committee

• For a list of all the House's standing and select committees, contact the Office of the Clerk, House of Representatives, Room H, The Capitol, Washington, DC 20515; 202–225–7000. For Senate committees, contact the Office of the Secretary of the Senate, The Capitol, Room S–208, Washington, DC 20510; 202–224–2115.

• To find transcripts of past hearings, get hold of the Congressional Information Service's *CIS Index* or its *Index to Congressional Committee Hearings.* Both index hearings held prior to 1970, and the *CIS Index* also lists other committee reports and documents. These sources can be found in university or large public libraries. The actual transcripts themselves may be kept on microfilm at the library.

✔ **Source:** *United States Global Trade Outlook 1995–2000*

The Department of Commerce has long published the *United States Industrial Outlook,* which provides projections on the economic outlook for over 350 manufacturing and service industries. However, due to budget constraints, it has replaced this guide with this *Global Trade Outlook* book, which covers fewer industries and provides less details on those industries covered. For detailed industry information, you might wish to examine one of the Gale Research publications described in chapter 1: *Gale's Encyclopedia of American Industries and Gale's U.S. Industry Profiles: The Leading 100.*

How to Find:

Order it from the Superintendent of Documents, PO Box 371954, Pittsburgh, PA 15250–7954; 202–512–1800 or check a library for a copy.

✔ **Source: Market Research Studies**

How can you find out what studies have been privately conducted on, say, the cheese market, or the drug packaging industry? Check out a free publication, *The Information Catalog*, published by FIND/SVP. This catalog is published bimonthly and lists dozens of industry, market, and company studies. One problem, however, is that most of these studies are *very* expensive, ranging from hundreds of dollars to a couple of thousand. But you can use the "information interview" techniques outlined in chapters 6–10 to try to speak with the reports' authors.

TIP: Often, excerpts of these research reports are published in relevant trade publications. See page 18 for advice on identifying publications in your field of interest. Alternatively, you might identify a relevant trade association and check to see if their library will make a copy available. Some market research providers also make some of the aggregate or top-level data from their studies available for free on their Web site. If you have the name of a market research firm that you want to check but not its Web site, use one of the search engines to try to find it (see chapter 5) or try guessing the site by entering the firm's name. For example, to see if the market research firm Dataquest had any of its findings up on the Web, you might try entering http://www.dataquest.com (and you'd get to that company's home page).

How to Find:

Contact FIND/SVP, 625 Avenue of the Americas, New York, NY 10011; 212–645–4500. On the Web link to http://www.findsvp.com

When reading a study that purports to measure the size of a market, or forecast an industry's or product's growth, it's wise to be a bit skeptical. Here are some guidelines for analyzing these types of reports.

• **Where did the data come from?** A seemingly obvious question, but Portia Isaacson, Ph.D., chairman of DREAM IT, Boulder, Colorado, says published market numbers are derived from all manner of sources: complex and statistically valid measurement studies, informal questionnaires, someone's educated guess, or even "a remark overheard at a trade show." You need to pin down

the provider of the data to explain specifically where the data came from.

• **How were the data collected?** Was it via personal interviews, phone calls, mail surveys, or a combination? If you can, it is desirable to get a copy of the actual questionnaire and examine it closely.

• **Who provided the data?** Isaacson notes that data that are "demand driven"—derived from users rather than manufacturers—are the most reliable. Reliability of data obtained from distributors or dealers sits between the two.

• **Does the study provide text?** Raw data alone are not enough. You need to be able to find out what the assumptions, reasoning, and logic were behind those numbers. Then you can determine for yourself whether the numbers derived from those assumptions are legitimate.

• **Can you speak with the researcher?** This is important to get your specific questions answered.

• **Does the firm have experience and credibility?** Is the specific subject of the report a field where the firm has credibility? If not, be sure to find out the analysts' and other principals' competencies in this field. Recent MBAs, says Isaacson, may someday be experts but not right away. Sometimes you can find out a firm's track record by obtaining copies of their previous market reports and checking to see how accurate they were.

If the study is a forecast, it should try and take into account the various social, economic, and political events that may affect the phenomena being measured. Be wary of forecasts whose projections increase or decrease in a strict linear manner, because these calculations will not be taking into account real-world events that alter neat progressions.

How Is the Report Marketed? Beware of published data that appear more "sensational." In those cases, the need to market and sell the information can take precedence over the truth. Also be careful of slickly packaged market studies that scream of exploding markets and industries without providing convincing evi-

dence. Some firms tend to be extremely optimistic in their projections, because a soaring new market will mean more buyers of their reports and consulting services. Similarly, beware of very positive projections where the issuer has something to gain. For example, city Chamber of Commerce studies nearly always show growth and positive trends for their region.

Experts in this field advise users of market studies not to rely on a single study, but to try to find as many studies as possible and compare the findings. Plot low and high points, and look for consensus. When in doubt, go with the most conservative numbers and assume that even those numbers may be optimistic. Even more to the point, never use published market data alone as the basis for making a major decision. Instead, get input from many different sources—talking to vendors, attending trade shows, talking to customers, and doing your own research.

Keep in mind, too, that for very fast moving industries—e.g., high technology, healthcare, finance, and so on—some reports (just like books) may go out of date very quickly and be too tied to conventional ways of defining the market and competition to be able to provide much of an edge.

COMPANY INFORMATION

If you're trying to get information on a particular company, there are several avenues to try, ranging from the company itself to the U.S. government.

First See:

The following indexes, to dig up published articles about a company:

- *Wall Street Journal Index,* p. 22
- *Funk & Scott Index,* p. 22
- *Business Periodicals Index,* p. 11

These directories to find financial data and information on company officers:

- *Standard & Poor's Register,* p. 24
- Dun & Bradstreet *Million Dollar Directory,* p. 26

12 CONSUMER DURABLES

The Market for Rugs & Carpeting
Manufacturer & retailer profiles.

Their homes are their castles, and consumers are spending more than ever to furnish and decorate them. In this study—one of three available from FIND/SVP on segments of the home furnishings market—the market for residential rugs and carpeting is analyzed. Sales by type of rug, domestics versus imports, and by style are included. Competitor profiles of leading rug and carpeting manufacturers and retailers are provided.
AA210 June, 1989 119 pages $695

The Market for Lifestyle & Ready-to-Assemble Furniture
"Nesting" fuels growth for emerging market.

Typified by furniture sold in stores like Conran's and Pottery Barn, lifestyle and ready-to-assemble furniture represents a growing share of the overall residential furniture market. Baby boomers setting up new homes are the main force behind this dynamic, emerging market.

The study by FIND/SVP—one in a series of three on important segments of the home furnishings market—analyzes sales and growth for the category. It examines the role of offshore sourcing in the industry and profiles major retailers and manufacturers such as IKEA, Armstrong World, Bush, and Rospatch.
AA211 January, 1989 131 pages $695

The Market for Home Textiles
Stable, long-term growth; player profiles.

In the past three years, designers and manufacturers have turned home textiles—tablecloths, curtains, towels and linens—into upscale fashion, as trendy and appealing as apparel. Home textiles will increasingly become consumers' primary means of updating their homes without buying entire new rooms of expensive furniture—fueling the market and insuring stable, long-term growth.

The FIND/SVP study—one in a series of three studies on segments of the home furnishings market—examines the market for all types of home textiles, including sheets/pillowcases, towels, bedspreads/comforters, blankets, table linens, kitchen linens and curtains/drapery. Sales and growth, import data, and the growing trend toward designer fashions are included. Forecasts by segment and profiles of leading competitors are provided.
AA212 May, 1989 140 pages. $695
AA213 Order any two reports & save $140 . . . . $1,250
AA214 Order all three reports & save $285 . . . . $1,800

The Tabletop Market
Latest developments in this $3+ billion market.

The Packaged Facts study explores in depth the three major tabletop categories—dinnerware; glassware; and flatware. Products are analyzed according to type, style, pricing, distribution and import vs. domestic. Overall sales and growth are highlighted, and pinpointed are the significant growth factors. Sales statistics are given for the past five years, and projected to 1993. Also covered are advertising and promotion and the competition.
LA140 April, 1988 420 pages $1,250

Personal Care Appliances
New products spur sales in $1.5 billion market.

The comprehensive report from FIND/SVP examines forces shaping the $1.5 billion personal care appliance business. The study analyzes three segments in depth: cosmetic appliances, grooming appliances and health aids. Producs covered include hair dryers, electric curlers, electric shavers, lighted mirrors, electric toothbrushes and digital scales. Consumer demographics are addressed. Major marketers are profiled.
AA187 July, 1988 c. 200 pages $995

The Greeting Card Market
Projections to 1995 for $4 billion retail market.

The Packaged Facts study analyzes the $4 billion retail market for greeting cards and pinpoints trends propelling the market into the 1990s. Discussion covers the continued growth of "alternative" cards, the increased emphasis on alternative line segmentation and marketer exploitation of new market niches.

The report offers sales projections to 1995. Current sales are broken out by type of card, distribution outlet, holiday and season. The competitive situation, involving leaders as well as the dozens of smaller players, is examined in detail. New product trends, advertising/promotion, the situtation at retail and consumer usage are also highlighted.
LA163 June, 1989 125+ pages $1,150

The Lawn & Garden Market
3 major components of the $14 billion market.

The comprehensive Packaged Facts study covers three major components of the $8 billion lawn and garden market: tools and equipment; supplies; and professional lawn care services. For each segment, it details the products involved, growth factors, projected sales, market composition, leading marketers, the competitive situation, new product development, advertising, promotion, distribution channels, retail outlets and consumer usage—both of specific products and of gardening in general.
LA138 March, 1988 270 pages . . . . $1,3\[5\]

1988-1989 National Gardening Survey
Consumer trends & sales; 15 major segments.

This in-depth study by the National Gardening Association in arrangement with the Gallup Organization, provides marketing information and analysis and sales in 15 key areas: lawn care, flower gardening, houseplants, landscaping, ornamentals, vegetable gardening and more. The report includes consumer profiles, market size data, five-year market trends and a 1988-1989 Sales Index. New to this year is purchase trend information on more than 120 specific types of lawn and garden products. Also included are cross-tabulation of all data.
NG04 July, 1989 370 pages $350

Large Kitchen Appliances
1989 international market; prospects to 1992.

This report from Euromonitor Publications covers the markets for large kitchen appliances in France, Italy, U.K., U.S. and West Germany in detail and provides summary coverage for other major international markets. Retail sales trends are examined for the 1983-1988 period. In-depth market studies—including market sizes, the latest brand shares and major company profiles—are offered for the five countries. Product categories include: laundry appliances; refrigeration equipment; cooking appliances (freestanding and built-in cookers, microwave ovens) and dishwashers. Forecasts are provided to 1992.
EP136 1989 225 pages . . . . $2,3\[9\]

Small Kitchen Appliances
International analysis: 1982-1988 & 1992 forecast.

The Euromonitor Publications report analyzes dynamics driving the market for drinks makers, food processors, deep-fat fryers, kettles, toasters and electric carving knives in the following countries: U.S., U.K., France, Italy and West Germany. Trends in retail sales and manufacturers' brand shares, sales breakdown by subsector, retail distribution trends, advertising expenditures, demographics and purchasing patterns are analyzed for the 1982-1988 period. Forecasts are available to 1992.
EP106 1989 130 pages $2,395

FIND/SVP, 625 Avenue of the Americas, New York, NY 10011

FIND/SVP catalog

Strategies for finding information on large companies and corporations are somewhat different than for small firms. Let's look at both cases.

Large Firms

A good place to start digging out information is the company itself. Call the public affairs or public relations office and ask for a copy of the company's *annual report*, issued by any publicly held corporation. The annual report will give you a very broad overview of the company's goals and operations, including an

---

TIP: If you do not know how to read financial tables, send for Merrill Lynch's excellent free publication "How to Read a Financial Report." Contact Merrill Lynch, Market Communications, Box 9019, Princeton, NJ 08543; 800–MERRILL. Another superb guide, which concentrates on how to analyze business rations, is Dun & Bradstreet's *Understanding Financial Statements: A Guide for Non-Financial Professionals.* Contact Dun & Bradstreet, One Diamond Hill Road, Murray Hill, NJ 07974; 800–234–3867.

---

opening letter from the chief executive, results of continuing operations, market segment information, new product plans, subsidiary activities, research and development activities for future programs, information on the highest officers, an evaluation of performance over the last year, and a detailed financial statement. Getting the annual report is a good first step, but the financial tables are difficult to understand for most people.

If the firm is not publicly held and does not issue an annual report, it may produce a "company fact book" that serves a similar purpose. You can ask for it from the public affairs or public relations office.

Another source of information on large firms is the government. Here's where to go:

✔ **Source: Securities and Exchange Commission**

The SEC keeps information on corporations with publicly traded stock. All publicly held corporations and investment companies

> **TIP:** You can request a free copy of an annual report from thousands of U.S. public companies by contacting a firm called Bay Tact. Call them at 800–654–6825 to make your request. If you want to order a glossy annual report from a non-U.S. firm, contact Ark Information, a division of Disclosure Inc., at 212–397–6232.

must file certain documents with the SEC, which are then made available to the public at no charge.

The following types of document are among those available from the SEC:

- *Annual Report:* See page 128 for a description.
- *Prospectus:* This is the basic business and financial information on the issuer. Investors use it to help appraise the merits of the offering.
- *10K Report:* This important document identifies the company's principal products and services, tells where properties are located, describes any legal proceedings pending, identifies owners of 10 percent or more of the stock, provides data on the background and salaries of the officers, and gives extensive financial information.
- *8Q Report:* This is a quarterly report that provides more timely data than the 10K.
- *8K Report:* The 8K Report must be filed within fifteen days of certain specified significant developments; these include filing for bankruptcy, a major acquisition, or a change in control.

> **TIP:** A company called the Washington Service Bureau has established a library of SEC filings and documents. The firm can send you the materials you need for 40 cents per page. The Washington Service Bureau can also obtain other federal documents for you, such as FCC rulings, Supreme Court opinions, and patent searches, at varying rates. Contact them at 655 15th Street NW, Washington, DC 20005; 202–508–0600. Another firm that offers the same service is called Disclosure. Their toll-free number is 800–638–8241. Disclosure offers two excellent free brochures: "A Guide to SEC Corporate Filings" and "Contents of SEC Filings." Disclosure also produces CD-ROMs containing data filed with the SEC by over 11,000 public companies. Many larger libraries (especially business-oriented ones) offer these.

How to Find:

You can obtain the documents you need by visiting or writing the SEC offices. Public reference rooms are maintained in New York, Chicago, and the Washington, DC, headquarters. During normal business hours, individuals are permitted to review and photocopy all public findings. Or you can ask for request forms; contact SEC Public Reference Branch, Stop 1–2, 450 5th Street NW, Washington, DC 20549; 202–942–8088. The SEC charges 22 cents per page to photocopy and sends you any requested reports. Turnaround time is three to four weeks.

The SEC has the capability to perform computer searching of certain files. A free booklet, "A User's Guide to the Facilities of the Public Reference Room," explains all the information and services available and how to make the best use of them.

TIP: Brokerage houses, discussed previously with regard to finding information on industries, can also provide information about large companies that operate in industries they follow. See page 119 for more details.

Small Companies

Finding information on small companies is harder, but there are still some avenues worth trying.

✔ Chambers of Commerce

Local Chambers of Commerce keep certain information on companies operating within their town or city: for example, the number of years a firm has been conducting business and whether any problems have been reported, such as customer complaints.

✔ Better Business Bureaus

BBBs keep reports on the performance records of companies based on their files and investigations. To find a local BBB office, check your phone book's white pages. (Also note that the Council of Better Business Bureaus, 4200 Wilson Boulevard, Suite 800, Arlington, VA 22203, or 703–276–0100, publishes inexpensive consumer advisory materials, such as "Tips on Buying a Home Computer" and "Tips on Car Repair.")

12

Quick Reference Chart to Contents of SEC Filings

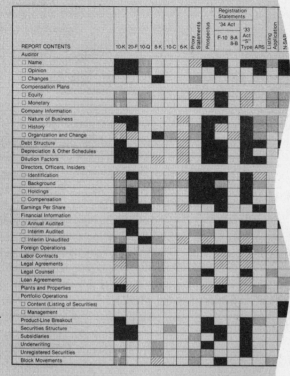

REPORT CONTENTS	10-K	20-F	10-Q	8-K	10-C	6-K	Proxy Statements	Prospectus	'34 Act F-10 8-A 8-B	'33 Act "S" Type	ARS	Listing Application	N.SAR
Auditor													
□ Name													
□ Opinion													
□ Changes													
Compensation Plans													
□ Equity													
□ Monetary													
Company Information													
□ Nature of Business													
□ History													
□ Organization and Change													
Debt Structure													
Depreciation & Other Schedules													
Dilution Factors													
Directors, Officers, Insiders													
□ Identification													
□ Background													
□ Holdings													
□ Compensation													
Earnings Per Share													
Financial Information													
□ Annual Audited													
□ Interim Audited													
□ Interim Unaudited													
Foreign Operations													
Labor Contracts													
Legal Agreements													
Legal Counsel													
Loan Agreements													
Plants and Properties													
Portfolio Operations													
□ Content (Listing of Securities)													
□ Management													
Product-Line Breakout													
Securities Structure													
Subsidiaries													
Underwriting													
Unregistered Securities													
Block Movements													

Legend

■ always included

▨ frequently included

▨ special circumstances

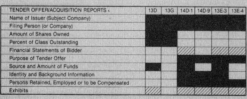

TENDER OFFER/ACQUISITION REPORTS	13D	13G	14D-1	14D-9	13E-3	13E-4
Name of Issuer (Subject Company)						
Filing Person (or Company)						
Amount of Shares Owned						
Percent of Class Outstanding						
Financial Statements of Bidder						
Purpose of Tender Offer						
Source and Amount of Funds						
Identity and Background Information						
Persons Retained, Employed or to be Compensated						
Exhibits						

✔ Local Government

According to Washington Researcher's *How to Find Information About Companies*, City Hall may have certain records on file that you could find useful. For example, the county or city clerk could tell you the buyer and seller and description of a parcel of land; the tax assessor could tell you the property value and tax; the planning department may be able to provide you with information on building permits, environmental impact statements, and other data; and the building department could give you information on permit records and the building itself, such as its size and type of construction.

If you need assistance in searching local government records, you should request a catalog from a publisher called BRB. That firm has produced six inexpensive volumes providing sources and strategies for searching public records. These include: *County Court Records*, *Public Record Providers*, *Asset/Lien Searching*, and more. Contact BRB Publications, 1200 Lincoln, #306, Denver, CO 80203; 800–929–3811.

✔ Source: Local Media

Editors of local business journals and business editors of the local dailies can be excellent sources of information on firms operating within their community. These people are generally very easy to speak with and don't mind spending a few minutes telling you what they know.

Detective Work. You may need to do some detective work to unearth the information you need. Here are some hints on how to do the digging:

- Call the company itself. You might be surprised how much help you receive.

TIP: If you need to find information on a nonprofit organization—a charity, religious organization, professional association, and so on—you are legally permitted to examine a copy of that organization's tax return (form 990). Contact the IRS at Freedom of Information Reading Room, Internal Revenue Service, U.S. Department of the Treasury, Box 388, Ben Franklin Station, Washington, DC 20044; 202–622–5000.

- Talk to customers. To find customers, send for company literature, which often provides names, or just call the company and ask for references. Once you've contacted the customers, ask them if they know of others who are also customers; this way you'll get to speak to people who were not directly named by the company. Another way to find customers is to post a request on a relevant Internet discussion group.
- Talk to competitors. Check the Yellow Pages to find them.
- Talk to businesses that operate in the same building or are nearby neighbors.
- Talk to suppliers.
- Talk to employees.

Digging up information on companies is a recognized discipline called "Competitive Intelligence." See page 250 for ethical guidelines and considerations when undertaking this type of research.

ECONOMIC STATISTICS

Statistics are a typical component of many business information searches. Here are some good places to check.

First See:

- *Statistical Abstract of the United States,* p. 63
- U.S. Bureau of the Census, p. 61

✔ Source: Bureau of Economic Analysis

This bureau within the Department of Commerce measures and analyzes U.S. economic activity and provides information on issues such as economic growth, inflation, regional development, and the nation's role in the world economy. An excellent periodical issued by the bureau is the *Survey of Current Business,* which provides estimates and analyses of U.S. economic activity and includes a review of current economic developments and quarterly national income and product account tables. The bureau also publishes various economic papers, such as "Selected Data on

U.S. Direct Investment Abroad 1950–1976" and "New Foreign Securities Offered in the United States 1952–1964."

How to Find:

Contact the Bureau of Economic Analysis, U.S. Department of Commerce, 1441 L St. NW, Washington, DC 20230; 202–606–9900. A helpful document is "A User's Guide to BEA Information."

TIP: Economic Statistics by Computer
• If you have a computer, you can obtain economic statistics inexpensively by tapping into the Department of Commerce's database "The Economic Bulletin Board."

✔ Source: Bureau of Labor Statistics

The Department of Labor publishes statistical data on employment, prices, wages, living conditions, and productivity. Other specialties include state economic statistics, industry statistics, consumer expenditures, economic growth projections, and occupational outlooks. The BLS publishes a special directory called "Telephone Contacts for Data Users," which identifies the bureau's experts and specialists with their phone numbers. A periodical titled *Bureau of Labor Statistics News* is free.

How to Find:

Contact the U.S. Department of Labor, Bureau of Labor Statistics, Division of Information Services, 2 Massachusetts Avenue NE, Washington, DC 20212; 202–606–5902.

✔ Source: Federal Reserve Board Publications

The Federal Reserve Board publishes statistical data on banking and monetary interest rates, subjects like flow of funds and savings, business conditions, wages, prices, and productivity.

How to Find:

Contact the publications service of the Board of Governors of the Federal Reserve System, Washington, DC 20551; 202–452–3245. Ask for the guide "Federal Reserve Board Publications."

134

✔ **Source: Bureau of the Census**

The Census Bureau makes available data about employment, unemployment, housing starts, wholesale and retail trade, manufacturers' shipments, inventories and orders, and exports and imports, as well as other business and economic statistics.

Two helpful guides published by the Bureau are designed specifically to assist businesspersons who want to understand various economic reports and series. *Introduction to the Economic Censuses* is a short pamphlet that identifies the different economic censuses and advises businesses how to use data appropriately; *Census ABCs* explains more broadly how the census collects its data, and how to choose the right type of data depending on a business' particular needs.

How to Find:
Contact the Bureau of the Census, Customer Services Division, Washington, DC 20233; 301–763–4100.

One particularly useful series is "County Business Patterns." These are employment and payroll statistics in each county in the United States, broken down by SIC code. For each SIC classification, information is provided on number of people employed, payroll figures, and other data. (Be careful in using this source— sometimes the information is old.)

How to Find:
Contact the Superintendent of Documents, Box 371954, Pittsburgh, PA 15250–7954; 202–512–1800. For more details on census information sources, see page 61.

✔ **Source: IRS Statistics of Income Division**

This division can provide you with various financial statistics drawn from past tax returns. Statistics are broken down into various filing categories—corporation income tax returns, industry statistics, investment tax credit statistics, estate tax returns, foreign income and taxes, partnership returns, the underground economy, and so forth. The statistics are published in the *Statistics of Income Bulletin,* which includes both statistics and summaries that explain and interpret the data. Many statistics are not published in the bulletin but are available if you write to the division directly.

How to Find:

The bulletin is available from the U.S. Government Printing Office. To contact the division itself, write Internal Revenue Service, Statistics of Income Division, 500 North Capitol Street NW, Washington, DC 20224; 202–874–0700.

✔ **Source: United Nations**

Annual publications issued by the United Nations are a good source of facts and statistics on international business. Samples include "Agricultural Trends in Europe," "International Trade Statistics: Concepts and Definitions," "Statistics of World Trade in Steel," and "World Economic Survey." Some U.N. publications are expensive, but many are reasonably priced.

How to Find:

Contact United Nations Publications, Room DC2–0853, United Nations, New York, NY 10017; 212–963–8325/8302.

INVESTMENT INFORMATION

Here are a few places you can go to get some readily available and inexpensive help on learning the basics about investments.

✔ **Source: Standard & Poor's *The Outlook* (McGraw-Hill)**

This is a leading source designed to provide some general investment-type information for nonexperts. *The Outlook* is a weekly bulletin that analyzes and projects business and market trends. It analyzes changes in the stock market, discusses firms currently in the limelight, and evaluates the worthiness of buying or selling particular stocks. The graphics are pleasing, and it is overall very easy to use and read. It can be found in most large public libraries or in nearly all business libraries.

✔ **Source: New York Stock Exchange (NYSE)**

The NYSE publishes a very inexpensive "Investor's Investment Kit." The kit consists of four guides that provide a detailed

description of how the market and various investments work, definitions of accounting and financial terms, and descriptions of the advantages and disadvantages of various types of investments. The four guides are "Glossary," "Understanding Stocks and Bonds," "Getting Help When You Invest," and "Understanding Financial Statements."

How to Find:

Contact the New York Stock Exchange, Inc., Publications Division, 11 Wall Street, New York, NY 10005; 212–656–2089.

✔ **Source: National Association of Securities Dealers**

This is the self-regulating organization of the securities industry. Its members represent virtually all the broker-dealers in the nation doing a securities business with the public. The association publishes two free useful guides: "Guide to Information and Services," which lists various specialists within the association, and the "NASDAQ Fact Book," which provides various data and summaries of stock prices and volume of the NASDAQ (National Association of Securities Dealers Automated Quotation System) securities. The association can also help you if you have a complaint against a broker or are looking for market statistics.

How to Find:

Contact the National Association of Securities Dealers Inc., 1735 K Street NW, Washington, DC 20006; 202–728–6900.

Finally, the **Securities and Exchange Commission** publishes free advice on investing. Their booklet is titled "What Every Investor Should Know." Call 202–942–4040 for more details.

HELP IN RUNNING OR STARTING A BUSINESS

One of the most sought-after types of business information is that which will assist in operating a current business or in the start-up of a new one. Here are some of the best places to turn for help.

✔ Source: Small Business Administration

Among the services and resources offered by the SBA are business loans; assisting small high-technology firms; special programs for veterans, minority, and women-owned small businesses; encouraging international trade by educational, outreach, and trade programs; assistance in procuring federal contracts; counseling and training in developing new business; and other programs.

Various books and pamphlets to help people in business are published by the SBA. Materials include general advisory publications that would be of interest to all beginning businesspersons, like "Going into Business," "Business Plan for Home-Based Businesses," "Researching Your Market," and "Outwitting Bad-Check Passers," as well as publications about starting a business in one particular field, such as "Starting Out in Cosmetology." The booklets are all free or very inexpensive.

Unfortunately, the SBA's services and publications have been drastically cut back from what they once were. However, the agency can still provide useful materials and services.

How to Find:

A useful free brochure outlining the various programs available is titled *Your Business and the SBA*. Write Office of Public Communications, Small Business Administration, 409 Third Street SW, Washington, DC 20416. For a free catalog of publications, contact SBA Publications, Box 15434, Fort Worth, TX 76119. You can also call a toll-free "answer desk" at 800–827–5722, but the advice given over this hotline is so simple that it is virtually useless.

✔ Source: National Technical Information Service

You can obtain a very useful publication that lists more than 180 federal and 500 state business assistance programs. This directory provides information on finding funding, obtaining mailing lists of prospects, how to find free management consulting, and more. It's called *The Directory of Federal & State Business Assistance*.

How to Find:

Write the National Technical Information Service, 5285 Port Royal Road, U.S. Department of Commerce, Springfield, VA 22161; 703–487–4650.

✔ Source: NTIS Center for Utilization of Federal Technology

You can locate government inventions with specific commercial value, obtain relevant technical information, and then negotiate a license by contacting the National Technical Information Service's Center for the Utilization of Federal Technology (CUFT). Inventions have been developed at various federal laboratories associated with NASA, the U.S. Army, the Department of Energy, and other government agencies. Those that have been made available free to the public to develop and market have included a low-cost humidity sensor, a Braille reading system, a book-retrieving device for use by handicapped people in libraries, and thousands of other devices and ideas.

The CUFT also publishes the *Directory of Federal Laboratory and Technology Resources*, which is a guide to more than 800 government sources of state-of-the-art research and development expertise, laboratory facilities, and technology information centers. These federal agencies and laboratories are willing to share expertise, equipment, and sometimes even their facilities. Technologies covered include environmental science, medicine and health, transportation, engineering, and computer technology. You look up your subject of interest in the directory, and it refers you to the resources available.

How to Find:

Contact the National Technical Information Service, Center for the Utilization of Federal Technology, U.S. Department of Commerce, Box 1423, Springfield, VA 22151; 703–487–4838. To find out about NASA's inventions and apply for licenses, subscribe to a free publication called *NASA Tech Briefs,* available from Associated Business Publications Inc., 317 Madison Avenue, Suite 921, New York, NY 10017; 212–490–3999. NASA will provide you with back-up data on any of its inventions that you express an interest in developing commercially.

✔ Source: Wisconsin Innovation Service Center

If you already have an idea for an invention, but aren't sure how good it is or how it stacks up against the competition, here's a place to turn for help. The Wisconsin Innovation Service Center, which is associated with the University of Wisconsin, will provide

you with a comprehensive and *confidential* evaluation at a relatively low cost. You submit your idea, and the center consults with university and private experts to form an evaluation. You are sent the full evaluation report, which includes the center's verdict on a variety of criteria, such as legality, safety, environmental impact, profitability, and competition. The report tells you the center's conclusions on your idea's strong points and provides an overall evaluation of its chances for success in the commercial market.

How to Find:

Contact the Program Manager, WISC, 402 McCutchan Hall, University of Wisconsin, Whitewater, WI 53190; 414–472–1365.

✔ Source: Patent and Trademark Office

If you want to find out whether your idea for a new product has already been registered for a patent, or find out about the use of a trademark, contact the U.S. Patent Office. The office registers and grants patents and trademarks, and it provides information on them to the public. You can obtain an index of patents and order printed copies of patents for $3 each. There are also many depository libraries around the United States where you can go and inspect copies of patents.

How to Find:

Contact the Patent and Trademark Office, Washington, DC 20231; 800–786–9199 (General Information).

TIP: You can find out about patent depository libraries located nearer to you; request a copy of "Basic Facts about Patents," available from the office. You can also search a free database of patent filings on IBM's Patent Server on the Web. Link to: http://patent.womplex.ibm.com

---

✔ Source: Mailing List Brokers

Here's a good way of finding the type of person or organization who might be most interested in buying your product or using your service. Mailing list brokers can provide you with thousands of names and addresses of people in specific professions (say, rab-

bis or biologists) and types of business and organizations (pet shops, funeral homes, and so on). You can order the names and addresses on pressure-sensitive labels, so you can stick them on envelopes and mail your promotional flyer or other information. Prices for the names are less than what you may think—typically running about $45 to $100 per thousand labels.

How to Find:

Look in the Yellow Pages under "Mailing Lists" to find a firm.

TIP: Free Tax Advice
• Free tax-planning booklets are available from most local offices of "Big 6" accounting firms, such as Peat Marwick, Ernst & Young, and Price Waterhouse.

✔ **Source: *Deciding to Go Public***

A free 140-page booklet *Deciding to Go Public: Understanding the Process and Alternatives* is offered by the national accounting firm Ernst & Young. Among the subjects discussed in the book are the benefits and drawbacks of going public, selecting an underwriter, use of an accountant, and alternatives to going public.

How to Find:

Contact Herbert S. Braun at Ernst & Young, 2000 National City Center, Cleveland, OH 44114 or 216–861–5000, or call a local branch office.

TIP: Marketing Information
• The previously mentioned "County Business Patterns" (page 135), published by the Bureau of the Census, can be used as a marketing tool to find out what kinds of establishments exist in a particular region of the country. For example, according to the Census Bureau, an East Coast department store chain considered opening a new store in an established shopping mall when store planners used census data to find the numbers and types of retail outlet in the area. From this information, they established business growth in the area and potential sales in the new store.

TIP: Consumer Demographic and Opinion Sources

Here are four handy sources for finding out about characteristics, opinions, and other data on potential customers.

• *Population Reference Bureau* is a private, scientific, and educational organization established to gather, interpret, and disseminate facts and implications of population trends. It covers almost all areas in the field, such as income statistics, the elderly in America, the world labor market, international demographics, and much more. Most of the Bureau's reports and publications are very inexpensive. Contact Population Reference Bureau, 777 14th Street, Washington, DC 20005; 202– 483–1100.

• *The Roper Center for Public Opinion Research,* located at the University of Connecticut in Storrs, has a database of over 7,000 "opinions" of the public on subjects ranging from views on AIDS to supermarket buying habits. You can find out answers to questions such as how many people own home computers or whether consumers are willing to pay more for a brand name. (This source is more expensive than others listed in this book; it costs about $50 for the center to do a typical search.) Contact the Roper Center at 203–486–4440.

• *The Insider's Guide to Demographic Know-How* (American Demographics, Ithaca, New York) provides a "do-it-yourself" approach to analyzing demographic data (e.g., analyzing characteristics of certain targeted populations by key variables such as sex, age, and income) and lists 600 federal, state, local, and private sources of demographic information.

• *Almanac of Consumer Markets,* an invaluable sourcebook also published by American Demographics, is a compilation of data on consumer demographics and behaviors for hundreds of cross-categories: age, income, marital status, race, education, labor force, health, expenditures, and more. The book isn't an inexpensive purchase but could well be worth it if you need this kind of data. American Demographics has a toll-free phone number: 800–828–1133. The company also has an excellent Web site, filled with a wide range of useful business, demographic, marketing, and survey-related information. Link to http://www.demographics.com

✔ **Source: *Small Business Sourcebook* (Gale Research)**

An extremely comprehensive yet easy-to-use directory for finding all sorts of sources of information and assistance for the small business. The book not only identifies where to find general business help but also includes special sections covering 250 specific types of small business and where to find advice and assistance. Some of those industries include antique shops, art

Cheese/Wine/Gourmet Food Shop

Start-up Information

★2681★
"Cheese and Wine Shop" in *Small Businesses That Grow and Grow and Grow (pp. 206-207)*
Betterway Publications, Inc.
White Hall, VA 22987   Phone: (804)823-5661

Woy, Patricia A. 1984. $7.95 (paper). A chapter about establishing a cheese and wine shop.

★2682★
Gourmet Wine and Cheese Shop Start-up Manual
American Entrepreneurs Association (AEA)
2311 Pontius Ave.
Los Angeles, CA 90064   Phone: (800)421-2300

$59.50 ($54.50 for AEA members). Contains step-by-step instructions on how to start a cheese, wine, and gourmet food store. Includes information on profits and costs, location, market potential, financing, advertising and promotion, customers, and related data. Toll-free/Additional Phone Number: 800-352-7449 (in California).

Primary Associations

★2683★
American Cheese Society (ACS)
Main St.
P.O. Box 97
Ashfield, MA 01330   Phone: (201)236-2990

Purpose: To provide a network for members who seek solutions to problems regarding cheesemaking processes or related regulations. Activities include cheese tastings, gourmet cooking demonstrations, and cheese making demonstrations. **Membership:** Primarily small-scale cheese producers; also includes retailers and wholesalers.

★2684★
International Dairy-Deli Association (IDDA)
313 Price Pl., Suite 202
P.O. Box 5528
Madison, WI 53705   Phone: (608)238-7908

Purpose: Promotes professional development and the exchange of information and ideas among members. Bestows awards for outstanding achievement. Holds annual seminar and exposition. **Membership:** Companies and organizations engaged in the production, processing, packaging, marketing, promotion, and/or selling of cheese, bakery, or delicatessen-related products. **Publications:** 1) *Dairy-Deli Digest* (monthly); 2) *Dairy-Deli Wrap-Up* (quarterly); 3) *Who's Who in Deli*Dairy*Bakery* (semiannual); 4) *Annual Seminar Proceedings*. Also publishes research reports and produces educational slide-tape programs.

★2685★
National Association for the Specialty Food Trade (NASFT)
215 Park Ave., S., Suite 1606
New York, NY 10003   Phone: (212)505-177

Purpose: To promote the specialty food industry. Sponsors competitions; bestows awards. Holds annual trade show. **Membership:** Manufacturers, processors, importers, and brokers of specialty and gourmet foods. **Publications:** 1) *NASFT Showcase* (semimonthly); 2) *RD Trends* (bimonthly).

Other Organizations of Interest

★2686★
International Federation of Wine and Spirits (IFWS)
103 Blvd. Haussmann
F-75008 Paris, France   Phone: 1 265

Purpose: To protect the industry at all levels of comm **Membership:** Industrialists and wholesalers of wine, spirits, br and liqueurs. **Publications:** 1) *Bulletin* (5/year); 2) *Newsletter* (5/:

★2687★
National Association of Specialty Food and Confection Broker (NASFCB)
Burgess, Bradstreet, and Associates
14229 Bessemer St.
Van Nuys, CA 91401   Phone: (818)997-056

Membership: Professional food brokers who supply department stores, gourmet shops, grocery chains, health food trades, and other companies with quality products for retail purposes. **Publications:** 1) *Newsletter* (quarterly); 2) *Directory of Members* (annual).

Educational Programs

★2688★
International Dairy-Deli Association (IDDA)
313 Price Pl., Suite 202
P.O. Box 5528
Madison, WI 53705   Phone: (608)238-79

Provides slide-tape programs on merchandising, sales, empl. motivation and training, customer satisfaction, and research in cheese and deli industry. Offers home-study courses, cosponsore the Cornell University Food Industry Management Program.

Reference Works

★2689★
The Cheese Handbook: A Guide to the World's Best Cheeses
Dover Publications, Inc.
31 E. Second St.
Mineola, NY 11501   Phone: (516)294-7000

Layton, T. A. Revised edition, 1973. $3.50 (paper).

galleries, bed and breakfasts, bookstores, gourmet food stores, consumer electronic stores, day-care centers, ice cream shops, magazine publishing, pet shops, pizzerias, software publishing, and videocassette stores. Overall, the guide is an excellent place to begin digging out information on starting a new business.

How to Find:

Check large libraries and university business school libraries, or contact Gale Research Company directly at 800–877–4253. The book is expensive, however.

REACHING FOREIGN MARKETS

If you want to know how to reach foreign markets for your product, the government can be a great place to turn for assistance.

✔ Source: Export Promotion Service

The mission of the U.S. International Trade Administration's Export Promotion Service is to 1) increase awareness and provide counseling to U.S. businesses to initiate and increase export activities; 2) provide information on overseas trade opportunities; 3) offer guidance on the use of market identification, market assessment, and contact information; and 4) provide related statistics, regulations, and other data.

The following programs and services are all available for a modest cost:

- Market sector analyses for 173 countries
- Access to a National Trade Databank—a comprehensive source of information and statistics on international trade
- Comparison Shopping Services to locate agents/distributors in host countries, D&B-type credit evaluations of agents, and competitive assessments of a product's market potential

How to Find:

Contact the U.S. Department of Commerce, Export Promotion Services, Room 2810, Washington, DC 20230; 202–482–6220 or 202–482–2867.

✔ Source: Flash Fax Service

A number of U.S. agencies have recently begun a "Fax on Demand" information service. This is a system that uses voice mail technology and presents callers with a menu of items that can be selected via a touch tone phone. After making selections, the caller taps in his or her fax number before hanging up. The system then automatically faxes the desired materials, often in a matter of just a few minutes. One of the biggest users of this technology is the U.S. Department of Commerce. The following is a listing of offices currently offering free reports and documents on international markets via its "Flash Fax" service. Users may request up to five documents per call.

- Eastern Europe Business Information Center: 202–482–5745
- Office of the Pacific Basin: 202–482–3875
- Business Information Service for the Newly Independent States: 202–482–3145

    (BISNIS also offers a wide range of useful documents and publications on how to do business in the ex-Soviet Union—Commonwealth of Independent States, or CIS. For more information contact BISNIS at 14th and Constitution Ave. NW, Room H–7413, Washington, DC 20230; 202–482–4655. Or link to its Web page at http://www.iep.doc.gov/bisnis/bisnis/html)

- Offices of Africa, Near East, and South Asia: 202–482–1064
- Office of Mexico: 202–482–4464

Among the types of information available are export financing sources, investment opportunities, upcoming trade shows, permits and customs, statistics and demographics, country profiles, investment opportunities, and publications.

✔ Source: Eastern Europe Business Information Center (EEBIC)

Recently established by the U.S. Department of Commerce, the EEBIC is designed to be a "first-stop"-type clearinghouse for companies interested in doing business in Eastern Europe.

One of the specialties of the EEBIC is assisting businesses in analyzing a country's overall climate for doing business. For example, the center will advise whether a country's phone systems

are workable. Also available is the Eastern Europe Looks for Partners service, whereby Eastern European firms send in requests for U.S. partners, and the "Bulletin," a monthly newsletter profiling countries, industry sectors, and trade opportunities.

How to Find:

Contact the EEBIC at Room 6043, U.S. Department of Commerce, 14th and Constitution Avenue NW, Washington, DC 20230; 202–482–2645.

✔ **Source: *Overseas Business Report***

Another good, moderately priced publication put out by the Department of Commerce's International Trade Administration is its *Overseas Business Report*. Each issue covers a different country and provides detailed information on trade and investment conditions and marketing opportunities. Information is provided on trade patterns, industry trends, natural resources, population, trade regulations, market prospects, and more.

How to Find:

Contact the Superintendent of Documents, U.S. Government Printing Office, Box 371954, Pittsburgh, PA 15250–7954; 202–512–1800.

✔ **Source: Export Counseling Center**

If you've decided you'd like to give selling overseas a try, you can obtain free help from the International Trade Administration's Export Counseling Center, a "one-stop shopping" location set up by the government to assist exporters. The center publishes a variety of helpful publications, such as "How to Get the Most from Overseas Exhibitions," "A Guide to Financing Exports," and a regular bulletin, which is a weekly publication on export opportunities for U.S. firms. The bulletin includes direct sales leads from overseas buyers, foreign government bid invitations, notification of foreign buyer visits to the United States, and more. Lots of other help is available, too, including a mailing list of foreign business contacts agents, distributors, retailers, wholesalers, manufacturers, and exporters for virtually any industry in 116 countries.

How to Find:

Contact the Trade Information Center, U.S. Department of Commerce, International Trade Administration, USSCS, HCHB–7424, Washington, DC 20230; 800–872–8723. A particularly useful guide to ask for is called "Export Programs: A Business Directory of U.S. Government Resources."

✔ **Source: Country Desk Officers**

Other good sources of help in finding out about foreign markets are the International Trade Administration's Country Desk Officers—about 200 government staff members who are true experts on a particular country's economic and commercial situation. These officers may also have some expertise in a country's political situation, because they keep in touch with the U.S. State Department's desk officers.

How to Find:

To find the expert you need, contact the U.S. Department of Commerce, International Trade Administration, Washington, DC 20230; 202–482–2867. The ITA will send you a photocopied list of their Country Desk Offices from the *ITA Directory of Services and Employees* for seven cents per page.

✔ **Source: Country Consulates and Embassies**

Finally, you can obtain help on questions you have about a particular market in a country by contacting its consulate office. Check the white pages of a major city phone book to find the consulate you seek. Or you can try the country's embassy in Washington, DC. The State Department publishes a "Diplomatic List," which gives the names and addresses of embassy personnel.

How to Find:

You can obtain this list from the Superintendent of Documents, Box 371954, Pittsburgh, PA 15250–7954; 212–512–1800.

The United Nations also publishes a list called "UN Services and Embassies." This is a listing of the addresses and phone numbers of consulate and embassy locations. Finally, a Web site called

The Electronic Embassy provides links to dozens of embassy Web sites around the globe. Link to http://www.embassy.org

How to Find:

Contact the U.N. Public Inquiries Unit, Department of Public Information, United Nations, Room 6A57, New York, NY 10013; 212–963–1234.

✔ **Source: *Exporters Guide to Federal Resources for Small Business***

This handbook is an exception to the generally poor quality of recent publications being issued by the now pared-down Small Business Administration. This is a very useful and well-organized guide that identifies key contact points throughout the federal government designated to help small businesses reach markets in other countries. The book describes the various programs and services, provides full contact names and phone numbers, and includes an appendix that lists further sources of information. It is very inexpensive.

How to Find:

Contact Department 36-XK, Superintendent of Documents, Box 371954, Pittsburgh, PA 15250–7954; 212–512–1800. The stock number is 045–000–00250–1.

INTERNATIONAL INFORMATION SOURCES

As discussed earlier, because today we live in a global marketplace, it is critical to be aware not only of sources of information about U.S. businesses and industries, but of foreign ones as well. The following is a selection of some of the most useful and timely sources.

✔ **Source: *International Business Information: How to Find It, How to Use It***

An excellent and comprehensive guide to finding international company information, marketing data, and economic reports.

COUNTRY	DESK OFFICER	AREA	PHONE 377-	ROOM	CABLE CODE	COUNTRY
A						
Afghanistan	Stan Bilinski	ANESA/OSA	2954	2029B	4530	Germany (West)
Albania	James Ellis	EUR/EE	2645	3419	4232	Ghana
Algeria	Jeffrey Johnson	ANESA/ONE	4652	2039	4520	Greece
Angola	Simon Bensimon	ANESA/OA	0357	3317	4510	Grenada
Argentina	Mark Siegelman	WH/OSA/BRP	5427	3021	4332	Guadeloupe
ASEAN	George Paine	EAP/OPB/SA	3875	2332	4430	Guatemala
Australia	Tony Costanzo/					Guinea
	Gary Bouck	EAP/OPB	3646	2010	4430	Guinea-Bissau
Austria	Philip Combs	EUR/WE/NE	2434	3411	4212	Guyana
B						**H**
Bahamas	Libby Roper	WH/CB	2527	3029A	4322	Haiti
Bahrain	Claude Clement	ANESA/ONE	5545	2039	4520	Honduras
Bangladesh	Christine Coady	ANESA/OSA	2954	2029B	4530	Hong Kong
Barbados	Vacant	WH/CB	2527	3029A	4322	Hungary
Belgium	Boyce Fitzpatrick	EUR/WE/NE	2920	3415	4212	
Belize	Robert Dormitzer	WH/CB	2527	3029A	4322	**I**
Benin	James Robb	ANESA/OA	4564	3317	4510	
Bermuda	Libby Roper	WH/CB	2527	3029A	4322	Iceland
Bhutan	Richard Harding/					India
	Christine Coady/					
	Renee Hancher	ANESA/OSA	2954	2029B	4530	
Bolivia	Roger Turner	WH/OSA/AD	4302	3314	4331	Indonesia
Botswana	Reginald Biddle	ANEAS/OA	5148	3317	4510	
Brazil	Robert Bateman/					Iran
	Roger Turner/					Iraq
	Patricia Hanigan	WH/OSA/BRP	3871	3017	4332	Ireland
Brunei	Gary Bouck	EAP/PB/SA	3875	2310	4430	Israel
Bulgaria	James Ellis	EUR/EE	2645	3419	4232	Italy
Burkina Faso	John Crown	ANESA/OA	4564	3317	4510	Ivory Coast
Burma	Kyaw Win	EAP/PB/SA	5334	3820	4430	
Burundi	Simon Bensimon	ANESA/OA	0357	3318	4510	**J**
						Jamaica
						Japan
C						Jordan
Cambodia	JeNelle Matheson	EAP/PRC&HK	4681	2323	4420	
Cameroon	Philip Michelini	ANESA/OA	0357	3317	4510	**K**
Canada	Joseph Payne/					Kampuchea
	Kenneth Fernandez/					Kenya
	Caratina Alston	WH/OC	0849	3643	4310	Korea
Cape Verde	Renee Hancher	ANESA/OA	4564	3317	4510	Kuwait
Caymans	Libby Roper	WH/CB	2527	3029A	4322	
Central African Rep.	Philip Michelini	ANESA/OA	0357	3317	4510	
Chad	Fred Stokelin	ANESA/OA	4564	3317	4510	**L**
Chile	Herbert Lindow	WH/OSA/BRP	4302	3027	4332	Laos
Colombia	Richard Muenzer	WH/OSA/AD	4302	3027	4331	Lebanon
Comoros	Fred Stokelin	ANESA/OA	4564	3317	4510	Lesotho
Congo	Philip Michelini	ANESA/OA	0357	3317	4510	Liberia
Costa Rica	Fred Tower	WH/CB	2527	3029A	4322	Libya
Cuba	Ted Johnson	WH/CB	2527	3029A	4322	Luxembourg
Cyprus	Ann Corro	EUR/WE/SE	3945	3044	4220	
Czechoslovakia	James Ellis	EUR/EE	2645	3419	4232	

Country Desk Officers

Appendices include a glossary, a comparison chart of accounting standards in 48 countries, sample balance sheets, and more. The authors, Ruth A. Pagell and Michael Halperin, are well-known experts in the information industry.

How to Find:

Check the business section of an academic library or contact the publisher, Oryx Press, in Phoenix, AZ, at (602) 265–2651.

✔ **Source: *Japan–U.S. Trade and Technology: A Primer***

This book is designed to offer business researchers resources for finding leads on information on Japan. Among the resources listed in this directory are U.S. government agencies, research and academic organizations, publications, online databases, trade associations, consultants, translators, and more. The author, Mindy Kotler, is one of the leading experts on finding Japanese business information.

How to Find:

Contact: Japan Information Access Project, 2000 P. Street NW, Suite 620, Washington, DC 20036; 202–822–6040. Check the Web site for many more resources: http://www.nmjc.org/jap

✔ **Source: *Japan's High Technology***

This $45 directory lists descriptive data for over 500 of "the best" English-language sources of information on Japanese science, technology, and related business topics. Among the types of sources listed: conference reports, industry reports, online databases, patent literature, directories, periodicals, translation guides, and more.

How to Find:

Contact Oryx, 4041 North Central at Indian School, Phoenix, AZ 85012; 602–265–2651.

✔ **Source: Association for Asian Studies**

The Association for Asian Studies is a scholarly, nonpolitical, nonprofit professional association that facilitates contact and

exchange of information among scholars, students, businesspersons, journalists, and others for an increased understanding of Asia. It publishes a directory titled *Directory of Japan Specialists and Japanese Studies Institutions in the United States and Canada*, which provides information on nearly 1,500 Japan specialists, along with their research interests, areas of specialization, academic affiliations, and more.

How to Find:

Contact Association for Asian Studies, One Lane Hall, University of Michigan, Ann Arbor, MI 48109; 313–764–1817.

✔ Source: The Office of Japan, Department of Commerce

This office assists U.S. firms needing information about Japan. A key service that the office may be able to provide is a list of contact names. Building contacts is critical for doing business in Japan.

How to Find:

Contact Deputy Assistant Secretary Marjory Searing, Department of Commerce, International Trade Administration, Office of Japan, 14th Street and Constitution Avenue NW, Room H–2318, Washington, DC 20230; 202–482–4527.

✔ Source: *China Trade Directory*

Published by the Embassy of the People's Republic of China, this directory is a 50-page white paper that provides basic facts about China, an overview of foreign trade statistics and events, a description and analysis of China's foreign trade system, export and import licensing, tariffs, business practices and customs, and documentation. A chart lists China's major imports and exports, by country. At the end of the directory, there is a listing of key government offices with names of officials, titles, and contact information. The directory is free.

How to Find:

Contact Guang Ming Song, Commercial Attaché, Embassy of the People's Republic of China, 2300 Connecticut Avenue NW, Washington, DC 20008; 202–625–3380.

✔ Source: Single Internal Market: 1992 Information Service

The U.S. Department of Commerce is making a major effort to provide advice and assistance to businesses about the single European market. This special office will provide, for free, copies of the single internal market regulations, background information on the European Community, and assistance regarding specific opportunities or potential problems.

How to Find:

Contact the U.S. Department of Commerce, Office of European Community Affairs, Room 3036, 14th Street and Constitution Avenue NW, Washington, DC 20230; 202–482–5276. (Also see the desk officers described on page 147 for information about doing business in specific countries.)

✔ Source: *Latecomer's Guide to the New Europe*

A nice, inexpensive 95-page pamphlet designed for firms interested in expanding their market into Europe, but needing some basic advice. Easy to read, but filled with valuable information on developing a marketing strategy for the European Community.

How to Find:

Contact the American Management Association, Publications Division, 1601 Broadway, New York, NY 10020; 212–903–8270.

TIP: If you need to gather facts, statistics, and analyses of European countries and markets, request a catalog from a United Kingdom firm called Euromonitor. This company produces some of the most comprehensive and detailed reference directories on European business issues. Note, though, that most are quite expensive, so your best bet may be looking for these guides in a university business library and/or one whose scope includes international trade. You can reach the firm at Euromonitor, 87–88 Turnmill Street, London EC1M 5QU, UK. Phone (from the U.S.): 44–71–251–8024.

✔ Source: NAFTA and Doing Business in Mexico

One of the best places to turn for information on NAFTA and trade with Mexico are Chambers of Commerce. The following two can be of assistance:

- **American Chamber of Commerce of Mexico.** Among its publications are *Business Mexico, Directory of American Company Operations in Mexico, Maquiladora Handbook, Maquiladora Newsletter, Mexican Export Manual,* and *Mexican Import Manual.*

  How to Find:
  Contact the American Chamber of Commerce of Mexico, Lucerna 78, Co. Juarez, 06600 Mexico City, Mexico; phone, 011–525–705–0995; fax, 011–525–705–3908.

- **U.S. Mexico Chamber of Commerce.** Promotes private sector trade, conducts seminars, and publishes a newsletter, bulletin, and various booklets.

  How to Find:
  Contact the U.S. Mexico Chamber of Commerce, 1211 Connecticut Avenue NW, Suite 510, Washington, DC 20036; 202–296–5198.

BUSINESS SUPERSOURCES

The following sources are so comprehensive that they do not fit into any of the previous business information categories; each can provide many different types of business information statistics, industry or company data, and more.

✔ **Source: *The Dow Jones–Irwin Business and Investment Almanac***

This almanac, published yearly, is a comprehensive source of business and investment information. Each edition typically includes the following information: a month-by-month business review of the past year; industry surveys—financial data, trends, and projections; financial statement ratios by industry; general business and economic indicators—GNP, corporate profits, CPI, national income, and largest company data—rankings, assets, net income, stockholder equity, and employees; top growth companies; capital sources for start-up companies and small businesses; bonds and money market investment data; tax shelters;

investment in gold, diamonds, and collectibles—what to look for, terms to know; investing in real estate; online business databases; and a directory of other business sources.

The almanac is especially abundant in stock information—returns on stocks, bonds, and bills; major market averages; and guides to SEC filings, mutual funds, investment, and financial terms.

How to Find:

You can find this book in many bookstores. Or you can contact the publisher: Dow Jones–Irwin, 1333 Burr Ridge Parkway, Burr Ridge, IL 60521; 800–634–3966. (Dow Jones has a free catalog that describes many other business books, too. One interesting-sounding one is *The Dow Jones–Irwin Guide to Using The Wall Street Journal*.)

✔ Source: UNIPUB

An excellent source for finding a variety of publications from international organizations is through a publisher called UNIPUB: a distributor for the United Nations, the European Communities, the Food & Agriculture Organization (FAO), the World Bank, International Monetary Fund (IMF), General Agreement on Tariffs and Trade (GATT), the official British government publisher HMSO, Organization for Economic Cooperation and Development (OECD), the International Labor Organization (ILO), and other well-known international and non–U.S. based institutions.

How to Find:

Contact UNIPUB, 4611-F Assembly Drive, Lanham, MD 20706–4391; 800–274–4888.

✔ Source: Brooklyn, New York Business Library

Whether you need industry statistics, company financial data, or stock information, or have an inquiry on virtually any other business-related subject, the Brooklyn, New York Business Library may be able to help you. It's one of the leading, if not *the* leading, business library in the country. It takes phone inquiries and tries to answer any financial, economic, or industry-oriented question that can be answered with a fact or referral.

How to Find:

Call the library's reference desk at 718–722–3333.

✔ Source: State Government

Lots of buried business-related information is available from state governments. The best department to contact is the state's department of commerce, department of economic development, or a similar-sounding bureau. Just as an example, here is what I uncovered by contacting the Arizona Department of Commerce:

Arizona's business and trade division of its department of commerce publishes a number of free guides packed with business-related information. For example, it collects state export statistics and publishes an international trade directory that lists companies in Arizona that do exporting, and it publishes a guide to establishing a business in Arizona—licenses required, regulations, and so forth. The office prepares an economic profile of the state that gives data on areas like population, labor, and financing programs. Special research reports are issued, too. Past subjects have included a review of high-tech companies in Arizona and a study of the aerospace industry and its suppliers. The directory of high-tech companies listed the firms' names, addresses, current products, SIC codes, numbers of employees, and other data. All of these are made available free to the public.

Another division of the Arizona Department of Commerce is devoted to "policy and research." That division publishes a book, *Arizona's Changing Economy: Trends and Projections*, that lists data on trends in land, population, and different manufacturing and service economies.

Other departments that looked promising were the Arizona Department of Economic Security, for free employment and job search information; the Department of Revenue, for licensing information; and the Department of Tourism, for information on expenditures made by out-of-state visitors.

How to Find:

Check your phone book for a listing, or consult the *State Executive Directory* in a library (p. 65). Or you can simply call directory assistance in your state's capital.

✔ Source: Electronic Databases

Be sure to read the information in chapter 5 about electronic databases and Internet searching. As explained in detail in that

chapter, a database is simply a collection of related information, and "online" databases are those made available over a computer. Here's a tiny sample of the kind of business information you can tap into by using this technology:

- Summaries of articles from top business and management journals
- Company directory listings from Dun & Bradstreet
- Indexes to articles from economic journals and books
- Text of the *Harvard Business Review*
- The full text of *The Wall Street Journal*
- Summaries of published industry forecasts and historical data
- Late-breaking financial news on U.S. public corporations from Standard & Poor's
- Management summaries from Arthur D. Little's market research reports
- Detailed financial report listings from the SEC
- A nationwide electronic Yellow Pages, with over 9 million listings
- Descriptions of sources of financial and marketing data in major industries worldwide
- Highlights of business and management topics from business journals and proceedings
- Information on product introductions, market shares, strategic planning
- Trade opportunity information based on purchase requests by the international market for U.S. goods and services

Again, this list doesn't even scratch the surface. For much more information on the subject, see chapter 5.

Although there are thousands of databases in existence and the proper selection of a database is not always a simple task, I have a few specific "favorites." The following is a list of professionally oriented databases I use most often and have had the most success with when performing business research on the Dialog system (see chapter 5 for more information):

When looking for	Try these databases
Precise information or statistics about industries, products, market shares	Predicasts (PTS) Promt; Trade & Industry Database
Management techniques, general business trends, and developments	ABI Inform

Inside look at operations and executives of smaller, private firms	Business Dateline
Expert analysts' views on companies' outlooks, strengths, and weaknesses	Investext
Basic data on companies (e.g., size, number of employees, and sales)	D & B Market Identifiers
Fast breaking "insider" type news and analysis from industry experts	Newsletter Database, Information Express

BEST OF BUSINESS SOURCES ON THE WEB

Business-related information is all over the Internet. Much of it is still free, though some sites will charge you—if not for initial levels of service, then for more "premium" levels. Chapter 5 of this book is devoted specifically to doing research on the Internet.

It is impossible, of course, to list all of the useful business information sources. Not even an enormous book devoted to that topic could do that subject justice. The best way to find the kind of business information you need is to do a targeted keyword search on one of the Internet search engines, as described in chapter 5.

Here, though, I will provide a very selective list of my very favorite business-related sites on the Web. It's certainly not comprehensive, but it should provide you with a flavor of what's out there, as well as direct you to some truly valuable resources.

BUSINESS NEWS

✔ **Source: Bloomberg Personal**

Bloomberg is well known in the business community for its timely news and financial services. Its well-designed and data-packed "Bloomberg Personal" site makes a good deal of its information available at no charge.

Web Address: http://www.bloomberg.com

Company Directories and Profiles

✔ **Source: Hoover's**

Hoover's has done extremely well on the Internet. It made a name for itself in the late 1980s by offering affordable print business directories, and it has gone on to publish many more inexpensive business books. Hoover's makes a lot of its information available for free, but you will have to pay to get some of its more extensive and detailed data. (If you are a member of America Online, though, much of this information is available to AOL members for free.)

Web Address: http://www.hoovers.com

Public Company Financial Filings

✔ **Source: EDGAR**

Possibly the most popular of all business sites is the EDGAR site, which contains the financial data from public companies who have filed with the SEC. This includes data from annual reports, 10K reports, prospectuses, quarterly reports, and more.

Web Address: http://www.sec.gov/edgarhp.htm/

Market Research Reports

✔ **Source: NTDB**

The National Trade Data Bank (NTDB) is an enormous database of government-produced trade-related information, covering everything from imports statistics to economic trend data. Among its offerings are free access to over 18,000 market research reports analyzing trends and competition in scores of industries and for hundreds of products.

Web Address: http://www.sta-usa.gov

✔ **Source: FIND/SVP**

Although you can't actually obtain the full text of high-priced market research reports from FIND/SVP, its site does let you per-

form a search of titles for hundreds of reports, and so it can be a useful tool for simply locating the existence of a market research study. In addition, for many of the reports, you can view a table of contents for free, which alone can provide you with some knowledge about the market.

Web Address: http://www.findsvp.com

FIND/SVP has also launched an intriguing new service named "FINDOUT," which lets users submit reference-oriented questions in several subject categories and then receive personalized answers within two business days from the firm's staff of professional researchers.

Web Address: http://www.findout.com

COMPANY NEWS, FINANCIALS, AND STOCK QUOTES

✔ **Source: Quote.Com**

Quote.Com provides access to a wide range of business wires (e.g., PR Newswire, Businesswire), company directories like Standard & Poor's, stock quotes, and more.

Web Address: http://www.quote.com

✔ **Source: Company Link**

Well-designed site offers useful and credible information on 45,000 U.S. firms. Includes basic directory data, press releases, stock prices, and SEC data at no charge. More extensive information is available on a subscription basis.

Web Address: http://www.companylink.com

BUSINESS REFERENCE/SIC CODES

✔ **Source: OSHA**

For many business research projects, it's important to find out the correct SIC (standard industrial code) for the industry one is researching. Many directories and business data bibliographies

are organized by SIC codes, and it can make research much more efficient. You can search OSHA's free database of SIC codes to find the right one.

Web Address: http://www.osha.gov/oshstats/sicser.html

✔ **Source: Small Business Assistance**

The National Small Business Development Center Research Network provides a wide range of information and assistance to smaller businesses, entrepreneurs, and so on.

Web Address: http://www.smallbiz.suny.edu

INTERNATIONAL TRADE

✔ **Source: U.S. Global Trade Outlook**

The U.S. Department of Commerce's replacement for the U.S. industrial outlook provides information on emerging international markets, international trade, industry overviews, and a great deal of statistical data.

Web Address: http://www.clark.net/pub/lschank/web/ecostats.html

HIGH TECHNOLOGY INDUSTRY

✔ **Source: C/Net**

There are a staggering number of sites on the Web that relate in one way or another to high technology, computers, and the Internet. One that stands out, though, for high quality, broad-based journalistic-type coverage of the entire scene is C/Net.

Web Address: http://www.cnet.com

CLEARINGHOUSES AND POINTERS

Because there are so many sources of information on the Net, some of the most useful sites are those that attempt to gather and organize them. Here are three of my favorite business clearinghouse sites:

✔ **Source: Business Sources on the Net, Sheila Webber**

Pointers to economic statistics, company profiles and financial statements, country information, news, and more. There are many business pointer sites. This one stands out as superior.

Web Address: http://www.dis.strath.ac.uk/business/

✔ **Source: A Business Researcher's Interests**

Provides links to business directories, media sites, marketing related resources, and much more.

Web Address: http://www.brint.com

✔ **Source: A Business Compass (ABC)**

ABC selectively describes and links to key business sites on the Web. For each site listed, ABC describes its content, special features, and valuable pages.

Web Address: http://www.abcompass.com

ANNUAL REPORTS

✔ **Source: Public Register's Annual Report Service**

You can search through more than 3,200 public companies by company name or industry on the Web site, then request the annual reports via E-mail.

Web Address: http://www.prars.com/index.html

INTERNATIONAL SITES

Finally, here are some sites that can assist you in locating statistical, demographic, and economic information on countries around the world.

- CIA World Fact Book: http://www.odci.gov/cia/publications
- US Bureau of Census International Database: (demographic, economic, social data for all countries): http://www.census.gov/ftp/pub/ipc/www/idbnew.html

---

TIP: Two Last Potential Sources
Two other places you might look for all types of business information are universities and banks.
• State university business schools often publish data and studies and make them available to the public.
• Some large banks publish results of their own research, too. For example, the Valley National Bank of Arizona publishes the *Arizona Statistical Review,* which provides statistics on construction, employment, housing, income, manufacturing, real estate, retail trade, taxes, tourism, and other areas.

- I-Trade provides a wide range of free and fee-based information services for firms wishing to do business internationally): http://www.i-trade.com
- The Electronic Embassy: http://www.embassy.org

Keep in mind that hard, focused business data is still better found on the professional online services like Dialog, rather than the Web. Still, an increasing amount of very useful and intriguing business information is migrating quickly to the Web as well.

The subject of business information is a book in itself. In fact, an excellent one is *Business Information Sources,* by Lorna Daniells, published by the University of California Press. If it's business information you need, this is the place to turn to find out where to get it. If you're actually looking to build a business library, check out another top-notch book called *The Basic Business Library,* edited by Bernard S. Schlessinger and published by Oryx in 1995.

5

The Internet

QUICK PREVIEW

- The Internet is a huge network of computer networks begun by the Defense Department in the 1960s, that has grown by leaps and bounds since that time.
- You can connect to the Internet through a consumer online service like America Online or via an independent Internet service provider. You will need special software called a "browser" to effectively search the net. Netscape and Explorer are two popular browsers.
- People do many things on the Internet, including sending E-mail, participating in discussion groups, browsing the World Wide Web, and doing research.
- Although there is a lot of hype about the Internet, there truly is an enormous amount of information on the Net, covering virtually any topic imaginable.

(continued)

Note: This chapter includes several Web site addresses. I have been somewhat circumspect in listing those addresses, since they change so quickly and are likely to become obsolete. If you find that one of the Web addresses provided in this chapter (or anywhere else in this book) does not work, I would recommend that you use one of the search engines (described in this chapter) and do a search for the name of the site described. The search engine will hopefully direct you to the most recent mentions of that site, and its accompanying address.

- Some of the best research resources on the Internet include government-related information, health and medical issues, searchable telephone directories, library catalogs, business-related data, and news/media sources.
- Researchers can also find searchable databases on the Internet, which provide fast access to hundreds of magazines, newspapers, research studies, company profiles, and more.
- The best way to perform precision research on the Internet is to use a "search engine" which can search millions of web sites and discussion groups in seconds. Leading search engines include AltaVista, UltraSeek, Excite, HotBot, and Yahoo, which is actually a massive hierarchal index.
- Performing good searches takes practice, and depends on matters like selecting the best key words, understanding how a particular search engines works, and understanding a few basics about using "Boolean" operators like "and," "or," and "not."
- A fast-growing type of Internet service is the customized news retrieval service, which is a type of software that asks you to specify precisely the subjects you are interested in, and then searches and retrieves for you automatically just those items that match your profile. The most advanced of these are called "intelligent agents" which are supposed to be able to figure out what types of information are most likely of interest to you based on "watching" your information selection decisions and actions.
- Electronic discussion groups are one of the most valuable and fruitful sources of information on the net. There are thousands of such groups covering an enormous range of topics. By joining a group, or just "listening in," you can find experts, get your questions answered, and become an instant expert yourself.
- Research on the Net is hardly a panacea. Among the major pitfalls are determining reliability and quality of the information you've located, sorting the gems from all the junk, distractions, slow speed of retrievals, loss of context, overemphasis on speed and style, and a lack of historical perspective. Another problem is using the Web when it would be more appropriate or effective to use a CD-ROM, or just a standard print source.

(continued)

- The Internet is not the only place to perform online research. The professional online services—Dialog, Nexis, Dow Jones and others—still provide the most comprehensive and powerful set of searchable information available. They can be expensive though, and may take some time to learn to search well. The consumer online services are less useful for serious researchers, but of the batch, CompuServe offers the most in-depth databases.

Until a few years ago, any discussion of doing "online" research would be considered a rather esoteric topic. It might be of interest to a few select groups: librarians, professional researchers, scientists, some market researchers, and maybe a few computer-savvy students and businesspeople. But beginning around 1994, as use of the World Wide Web portion of the Internet exploded, more and more ordinary people with a home computer and a modem began discovering the enormous amounts of information on the Internet and began regularly searching for facts, data, and advice on the Net. And so, by early 1996 or so, online research had gone from a relatively arcane function to nearly a mass phenomenon.

This chapter will provide a basic introduction to doing research on the Net. Although this book is not designed to be an overall introduction to the Internet (we recommend books for this in the appendix), we will very quickly look at some basic definitions and answer some beginning questions.

AN INTERNET Q&A

What is the Internet?

The Internet can be viewed as a huge network of computers. For example, just as your office may have some of its computers linked together in an internal network where people send E-mail back and forth, the Internet can be likened to a giant global equivalent, linking millions of computers. Technically speaking, the Internet doesn't really link individual computers, but links already existing networks; therefore, it is more accurate to think of the Internet as a "network of networks."

How did the Internet come to be?

The Internet has its roots in a Defense Department project that began in the 1960s. The DOD wanted to create a computer network that would be less vulnerable to going down during a military attack. It created a system, then, called ARPANET, whose architecture and data transmission protocol (called "packet switching") was designed so that even if one portion of the network was destroyed, the rest of the network could continue to operate. (Kind of like the new Christmas lights that still work even when one bulb blows!) Once this network got up and running, government agencies other than the Defense Department were also permitted to use it to exchange scientific and technical information. That membership then began growing in the 1970s to include universities and research institutions, and then by the early 1980s, some libraries began participating as well. Still, all the information exchange on the Internet was of a scientific, scholarly basis: Commercial use was prohibited, and there were few ordinary people participating.

But by the late 1980s, more and more people began discovering the value of the Internet by their exposure to it in libraries and universities. The Internet then began to grow rapidly, and by the early 1990s, coinciding with the growth of home computers, it had grown so fast that it had become a mass phenomena. *Time* magazine even put the Internet on its cover. . . and here we are today!

What is the difference between the Internet and all those other online services I hear about, like America Online, CompuServe, and so forth?

Those services—America Online, CompuServe, Prodigy, Microsoft Network and other smaller ones—are privately operated online networks, which are usually called "consumer online services." They are geared to a popular audience and offer their users a wide range of activities, such as news, games, chat rooms, business information, travel information, reference, and so forth. They also charge a fee to join—typically $9.95 a month for 5 hours of use. However, they are *not* the same thing as the Internet, which is more akin to a self-operating entity with no centralized administration or authority. Now, what sometimes seems confusing is that these consumer online services also offer *access* to the Internet—like an "onramp" to the Internet. But they are not the same thing as the Internet. Adding to the confusion is that most of these consumer online services are now making themselves *accessible on the Internet.* In other words, instead of having your modem dial a special phone number to connect to these services, you can actually join and sign up by linking to their Web sites. In this case, the Internet is being used as an onramp to the consumer online services!

As you can probably tell, although there remains a real distinction between consumer online services and the Internet, the edges are getting fuzzier. As of this writing only America Online was holding out from integrating its service into the Internet, as it worked to maintain its strategy to remain a more distinct identity.

How do I get onto the Internet?

You can connect to the Internet by first signing up with one of these consumer online services, or you can connect to the Internet directly by signing up with a specialized Internet Service Provider (ISP). There are both national ISPs—including AT&T—as well as smaller local and regional ones. Most charge about $15–$20 per month for unlimited use. You can find out about ISPs by checking your phone book or browsing a recent popular newsstand computer magazine. If you can access the Internet on another computer, you can find a comprehensive listing of ISPs around the country by linking to http://www.thelist.com

What do people do on the Internet?

People do a lot of things. By far the most popular thing that people use the Internet for is to send and receive E-mail. You can send and retrieve messages to anyone else on the Internet or to whoever has an E-mail address on one of the consumer online services. One of the appeals of E-mail is that it is typically a whole lot cheaper than making long distance phone calls. Another advantage is that it can be done anytime—day or night—and the other person doesn't need to be "there" on the other end when you do send it.

In addition to E-mail, people on the Internet join special interest discussion groups, browse Web pages for fun, do research and find information (that's what this chapter is going to concentrate on), play virtual reality type games, and a lot more.

What is "gopher," "Telnet," and "ftp"?

These terms describe some of the traditional functions and information access methods on the Internet. Gopher describes a system for browsing menus of hierarchically organized information; Telnet means to connect to another computer on the Internet as if it were locally accessible; and ftp is a function to download information from a remote computer on the Internet.

Although you may eventually use some of these functions, these days, the great majority of activity takes place on the World Wide Web portion of the Internet, which has largely replaced these other functions as a means of accessing information.

What is the World Wide Web?

The World Wide Web, or "Web," is technically just one "part" or aspect of the Internet, but it has grown so quickly and become so popular that to a large degree it has become almost synonymous with the Internet (though that is technically incorrect). The Web consists of interconnected documents and sites on the Internet that you can link to, which not only provide text but also have graphics, sound, color, and other multimedia elements. In addition, Web sites allow you to instantly "surf" to other Web sites by a technology called "hypertext," which lets you just point and click on a highlighted Net address on the page in front of you to take you to that Web site instantly.

What is a Web site? A URL address? And a home page?

A Web site is a specific "place" on the Internet—like an address. Each Web site has its own address, and on the Internet that address is called a "URL" (for Uniform Resource Locator). Web addresses on the Net start with the prefix "http://" and are followed by a series of letters that signify the particular address. For example, the URL for the New York Public Library is http://www.nypl.org. The last three letters in the URL generally signify what type of organization is behind the Web site: "com" signifies a commercial, for-profit site; "org" is a public or nonprofit institution; "gov" refers to a governmental entity; and "edu" is an educational institution, like a university. Home page is the term used to designate the very first Web page that a user sees when he or she links to a Web site. Sometimes the phrase "home page" is used to designate a personal Web site.

What is a "browser"?

A browser is the name of a type of software that you need to be able to use the World Wide Web. There are a few different browsers on the market, but the one that is by far the most popular is Netscape. A competing browser sold by Microsoft is called Explorer. You can normally get browsers for free from your Internet Service Provider.

What is a keyword search? What is a Boolean search?

Much of what's available on the Internet can be located by the use of "keyword searching." To simplify, this means you enter a word or words that describe what you are looking for ("Smashing Pumpkins," "glaucoma," "postmodernism," etc.) in order to zero in on sites that contain what you want. A Boolean search allows you to combine multiple keywords by using three simple words: AND, OR, and NOT. So, for example, if you were looking for information on the topic of arthritis in children, you would enter "arthritis AND children," which would narrow your search to just those sites that contain BOTH those words. And, similarly, if you were looking for information on, say, coffee or tea, you would enter "coffee OR tea." Things are actually a bit more involved than this, and the precise way you need to enter the terms depends on the particular "search engine" you use, which is described later in this chapter.

WHY USE THE INTERNET FOR RESEARCH?

Okay, now that you've got a few basics down about the Internet, let's talk a little bit about what's really out there for you, and why you would want to bother doing research on the Internet.

Although there is an enormous amount of hype about the Internet, it is also true that there really and truly is an enormous amount of information on the Net, too! It's not *all* hype! It is nearly impossible to accurately describe the kind of information that's available on the Internet, because it would nearly be akin to answering the question of "what kind of information exists in the world today." I know that sounds ridiculous, but it's nearly true. If you can think of a topic—no matter how weird, arcane, or off-beat—there is very likely to be at least some information somewhere on the Internet. From A to Z, or from Aardvarks to Zorba the Greek, whatever your interest, hobby, or research project, you're almost certain to come up with something! And if your topic is something more widely known or popular—say, from Astronomy to Zoos—your dilemma won't be how to find information, but how to winnow out the hundreds or thousands of sites you do locate!

So the first reason why it does make sense to use the Internet to do research is simply because of the vast resources and amount of information on the Internet. Now before we go any further, I do want to make the point that, of course, not *everything* is on the Internet! In fact, only a very tiny percentage of all the world's knowledge is in any kind of electronic form. But even a small percentage of the world's knowledge is still a lot! And that number is growing rapidly.

The other reason why it's useful to do research on the Internet is that it can be (though isn't always!) fast and convenient. With a few taps of your keys on your computer, you can call up a research report on Antarctica, or an anarchist organization or an excerpt from a speech given at the latest American Medical Association conference, a map and photograph of Yellowstone Park, and so on and so forth! Instead of being a couch potato, you can be a Web potato and sit in front of your screen and bring the world to you.

Later on in this chapter I am going to talk about the drawbacks

and disadvantages of doing research on the Internet vis-à-vis other sources. But for now, let's talk some more about what some of the positive aspects are. And there are many!

For one thing, the Internet is an enormous source of government information. Most of the U.S. federal departments have been working very hard to get much of their valuable reports, newsletters, briefings, and other documentation up on the Net. (See chapter 3 for more on information from the government.) Whether it's the latest census data, State Department cautions, NOAA weather alerts, or market research reports from the Department of Commerce, you can access much of this for free off the Net!

Another area where the Internet really shines for researchers is in the health and medical area. Because this is an area where people naturally have so much interest, and is something where transmitting knowledge is so vital, accessing health and medical information has become one of the fastest growing uses of the Internet. Whether it's a common ailment, or a very rare disease, you are likely to find names of experts, reports, and, sometimes even more importantly, names of other people who have had similar experiences or are in a similar situation. We'll talk more about this point later in this chapter under "Electronic Discussion and Newsgroups."

Businesspersons can also find a wealth of information on the Net. While serious in-depth business research is still best conducted on professional online services such as Dialog, Nexis, and Dow Jones (discussed later in this chapter), a good deal of very useful business research can be conducted on the Net as well. One of the most useful business sources you can find on the Web are company home pages, which sometimes contain financial information, recent press releases, and job postings. However, you can even sometimes find other valuable business data, including organizational charts, market share reports, and various primary data sources and survey results from market research firms like Dataquest.

NEWS ON THE NET

Finally, one of the fastest growing portions of the Internet is the number of media sources on the Web. Hundreds of newspapers

and magazines have set up a Web site, where they offer either an Internet equivalent to their existing print publication, a separate Web publication to complement their print journals, or in some cases, an entirely new Internet publication that exists without any print counterpart.

These publications are too numerous to list, and span all topic areas. Just as a sampling of a few of the most well-known ones, there's the *Atlantic* magazine, the *Boston Globe, The Economist, The New York Times, Time, Utne Reader,* and *The Wall Street Journal.* Note that many of these publications do not charge for their Internet versions, though some do levy a small fee. Many only require you to register. One of the hottest Internet publications has got to be *HotWired* (http://www.hotwired.com), the electronic edition of the popular high technology newsstand magazine *Wired.*

There are a couple of Web sites that are devoted to listing, describing, and providing links to hundreds and hundreds of Internet-based media. Here are the names and Web addresses of my favorites:

- **Editor & Publisher.** Offers ongoing and authoritative coverage of emerging electronic newspapers.
  http://www.mediainfo.com

- **AJR/Newslink.** Free hyperlinks to hundreds of online newspapers, as well as magazines and journals.
  http://www.newslink.org

- **The Electronic NewsStand.** Free excerpts from the latest issue from hundreds of popular magazines.
  http://www.enews.com

- **WWW Virtual Newsstand.** A collection of links to media sites on the Web.
  http://www.edoc.com/ejournal/

- **MediaFinder.** A searchable directory of thousands of magazines, newsletters, directories, and catalogs.
  http://www.mediafinder.com.

- **dNET.** Browse several thousand directories by category or alphabetically by title. For a fee, you can also search the

full text of some of the directories themselves.
http://www.d-net.com

- **Amazon.Com.** A huge selection of all types of books, which can be ordered directly from the Web site. You can search on all sorts of parameters, including subject, author, title, and keywords on this very nicely designed online megaware-house.
  http://www.amazon.com

One of the most popular and slick sites for reporting the daily news has been none other than CNN (http://www.cnn.com). Interestingly, the Web has opened up the ability for nontraditional news providers to offer their own news online as well. These include:

- **AT&T's Lead Story.** An innovative site that identifies what its editors feel is the most noteworthy business story of the day and provides links to various online newspapers and news organizations. This lets users link to and read a wide range of articles on the same topic, but from many organizations.
  http://www.lead story.com

- **Microsoft's MSN News.** Primarily repackages and jazzes up wire service copy from the Reuters news agency, but increasingly appears to be developing its own content. Microsoft's most noteworthy media offering is political commentator and ex-*New Republic* editor Michael Kinsley's *Slate* online magazine (http://www.slate.com), which is supposed to combine the traditional editorial quality and approach of print journalism with the interactive possibilities of the Net. As of this writing, the jury is still out as to whether *Slate* will succeed in this mission. Note, too, that many traditional journalism organizations are watching Microsoft warily and are not unconcerned about what impact this 1,000-pound gorilla will have on the traditional media.
  http:///www.msn.com

- **C/Net Computer News.** Both flashy and substantive, this is one of the leaders in providing up-to-the-minute com-

puter and high tech news. In addition to breaking news, C/Net also offers features, reviews, and much more.
http://www.cnet.com

What else is on the Web? Hmmm, it might almost be easier to answer the question, what *isn't* on the Web—though not quite! There are entire books filled simply with Web site names and addresses, and even those massive tomes don't even scratch the surface of the kind of information you can find there. Just a caution: In general, we've been rather careful about listing Web sites in this chapter. Because the Internet changes so quickly, Web site addresses come, go, move, and change extremely rapidly. That's why magazines and Net listings themselves are better sources than books for finding the hottest sites. Still, for what they're worth then, just to give you the faintest whiff of what you can find on the Net, here are a few specific research-oriented sites that have stood the test of time. (On the Internet, that means they've been around for a whole year or two!)

- **CIA World Factbook.** A comprehensive statistical and demographic directory covering 264 countries around the world.
  http://www.odic.gov/cia/publications

- **New York Public Library.** No, you can't actually read or download all the books and magazines in this great repository of knowledge (. . . at least yet!), but you can search much of the library's holdings and get a lot of useful advice on doing research, as well as find at least some substantive information.
  http://www.nypl.org

- **Library of Congress.** Even bigger than the New York Public Library is the U.S. Library of Congress. The Library of Congress has been making a major effort the past several years to make much of its enormous collection accessible over the Net. It has grouped its resources into all sorts of reference-oriented categories, and you're likely to find what you need by browsing these sections.
  http://www.loc.gov

- **Phone Directories.** One of the fastest growing reference areas of the Web are searchable national telephone directories, which contain phone numbers for millions of residences and businesses. Some even provide E-mail directories, and a select few offer special features such as an actual street and region map of the location you're looking up. Here are the names and addresses of some of the leaders:

  - **Switchboard.Com:**
    http://www.switchboard.com

  - **Four11:**
    http://www.four11.com

  - **InfoSpace:**
    http://www.infospace.com

  - **BigBook:**
    http://www.bigbook.com

- **Thomas Register.** If you want to know who manufactures what product, check out Thomas Register online. It identifies over 100,000 brand names listed in 52,000 product and service categories.
  http://www.thomasregister.com

- **National Trade Data Bank.** A massive collection of world trade data produced by the U.S. Department of Commerce.
  http://www.stat-use.gov/ben.html

- **Hoover's Online.** A nicely designed Web site that offers free links to over 1,000 corporate Web presences and provides some basic directory data on major U.S. and international firms.
  http://www.hoovers.com

- **EDGAR.** One of the most popular, if not *the* most popular, site for business researchers, EDGAR provides free online access to the SEC filings of thousands of public companies in the U.S. This includes things like prospectuses, annual reports, 10K reports, 10Q reports, and so on.
  http://www.sec.gov/edgarhp.htm

- **Pathfinder.** A huge media site created by Time Warner. Offers selections of articles from major magazines such as *Fortune*, a searchable database of companies, and a wide range of business and consumer data and features. There may be a subscription fee to use this service. http://www.pathfinder.com

DATABASES ON THE WEB

So far we've been discussing specific *sites* on the Web, now let's switch gears just a bit and talk about *databases* on the Web. The terminology here can be a bit confusing, so let's see if we can get a few of the terms and definitions straight. An online database is a searchable collection of related information: For example, there might be a database of management articles from the business press, or of alternative-energy government reports, or of patent filings, animal diseases, chemical properties, and so on and so forth. Databases have traditionally been made available on the professional online services like Dialog, Nexis, and Dow Jones. However, as the Web has soared in popularity, some of these databases have migrated onto the Web, and there have also been new databases created that are searchable only on the Web.

Many of these databases are free to search, but many of the largest and most powerful ones are *not* free and charge some kind of monthly fee for access. However, they are generally a lot less expensive than the traditional databases from the professional services. I've listed a few of the more useful and popular of these below.

Keep in mind that the distinction between searchable databases and plain old Web sites isn't always completely clear cut. For example, a Web site devoted to, say, vegetarian cooking might put together a keyword searchable database of hundreds of recipes. So is it a database or a Web site? It's both, and you can see that these labels can become blurry and therefore increasingly unhelpful. But for now, there remains some distinction, and so it is worth noting.

Here are some of the larger searchable databases on the Web. Unlike most sites on the Web, all of the below charge a fee.

- **Profound.** Profound offers a searchable database of in-depth business news, market research reports from research firms like Frost & Sullivan, country studies, company backgrounders, stock quotes, and more. It is a very powerful system, more akin to a professional online service than a typical Web-based one; however, it is priced competitively for what you do get. Profound can be an excellent choice for the serious business researcher who doesn't mind paying for high-quality, timely information, but doesn't have an unlimited budget.
  http://www.profound.com

- **The Electric Library.** The Electric Library provides the full text of 150 newspaper and 900 magazines, as well as transcripts from National Public Radio and various other items such as maps, photos, and reference tools. It utilizes a natural-language search engine. A duplicate of this database is made available on the Prodigy online service, but there it is called "Homework Helper."
  http://www.elibary.com

- **IAC InSite.** IAC stands for Information Access Company, and this firm has for several years been one of the leading providers of top-quality popular and business databases. IAC has established a Web site to make these powerful databases available to a mass audience, and they represent some of the very best information available through the Net. However, searching these files is not cheap, and may be more suitable for organizations than individual consumers. You can take a look at the site yourself.
  http://www.iac-insite.com

- **FirstSearch.** The Web version of the FirstSearch discussed in chapter 1 searches the same databases, but offers more colors and graphics, additional navigational buttons, and hotlinks to bibliographic records and various Internet resources.
  http://www.ref.oclc.org

- **nLIGHTn.** This online service not only searches Internet sites but also other commercial databases, newswires, ref-

erence materials, and more. It attempts to let the user search all in one place, virtually all of the world's electronic information.
http://www.nlightn.com

THE SEARCH ENGINES

Sure it's fun to browse and surf the Net, but when you want to pinpoint some precise piece of data or information source, you don't want to spend hours rummaging around and hoping you'll find what you need. That's where the search engines come in—these powerful pieces of software can search literally millions of Web pages in only seconds to uncover just the data you need. And best of all, they are all free. You just type in the Web address and you'll be linked to them automatically and for no charge.

Search Engines

There are dozens of search engines. The biggies are:

- **AltaVista.**
  http://www.altavista.digital.com

- **Yahoo.**
  http://www.yahoo.com

- **Lycos.**
  http://www.lycos.com

- **HotBot.**
  http://www.hotbot.com

- **InfoSeek.**
  http://www.infoseek.com

- **OpenText.**
  http://www.opentext.com

- **Excite.**
  http://www.excite.com

Though each search engine has its own particular rules and procedures for conducting searches, all have a couple things in common. One is that the way they work is that you enter a word, words, or a phrase, and the engine will search Web sites and return a list of "hits," which are sites that contain the word, words, or phrases you entered. Those hits generally contain the title of the Web page and the first line or so from it, so you can read them and see which ones look to be the most relevant. You click on those and are then linked to those pages.

It can get complicated to try and use all these search engines, and it is really unnecessary to know how to use them all. So, I am are just going to give you my best search tips for my two favorite Internet search sites: AltaVista and Yahoo.

AltaVista:
http://www.altavista.digital.com

AltaVista, a product of the Digital Equipment Corporation (DEC), was introduced in early 1996 and has proven to be one of the most powerful, fast, and flexible of the search engines. It indexes tens of millions of Web pages and, importantly, allows you to perform advanced and sophisticated searches, so you can better pinpoint precisely what you need on the Net. Page 181 shows a sample list of hits on the "AltaVista" search engine that we ran to look for on the subject of nanotechnology.

The best way to get good at using a search engine is trial and error and practice, but here, in a nutshell, is my recommendation and tips for using AltaVista.

1. You might consider adding it to your "bookmarks," so it is the first page that comes up on your screen when you connect to the Internet.
2. Click on the "advanced searching" box in the upper right.
3. Now you have some choices in how to enter your search statement:
   - If it's a single word (e.g., spaghetti), just enter it and then hit submit.
   - If it's a phrase (e.g., chicken pot pie) then enter it all in quotes: "chicken pot pie."

 **Search**

AltaVista Search
OnSite Knowledge | Advanced | Simple | Private eXtensions Products | Help

Search [the Web] **and Display the Results** [in Standard Form]

[nanotechnology] [**Submit**]

Tip: To use all these apples: +apple pie tart cookie torte muffin

Word count: nanotechnology:15920

Documents 1-10 of about 5000 matching the query, best matches first.

Notes for Authors: Journals. 5.17. Nanotechnology
NANOTECHNOLOGY. Frequency: 4 issues per year. Subject coverage. Papers are expected to be original experimental or theoretical research or to be an...
http://www.ioppublishing.com/Journals/NFA/nfas517.html - size 3K - 14 Feb 96

CALL FOR SUBMISSIONS 1995 Feynman Prize in Nanotechnology
Date: Sat, 8 Apr 1995 11:57:15 -0700 X-Sender: foresigh@jobe.portal.com To: (Foresight members) From: foresight@cup.portal.com (Foresight Institute)...
http://mems.isi.edu/archives/Announcements/feynman_award.html - size 4K - 25 Jul 95

Brad Hein's Nanotechnology Page
Nanotechnology. I have a preliminary version of what this site will look like in the next few weeks at http://www.public.iastate.edu/...
http://www.public.iastate.edu/~bhein/nanotechnology.html - size 15K - 27 Apr 96

Molecular Nanotechnology
Molecular Nanotechnology (NT) Summary Of Concept. Products designed & built to molecular specifications. Such products could incorporate highly advanced...
http://www.ece.cmu.edu/afs/ece/usr/jka/html/NT.html - size 5K - 30 Mar 95

Small is Beautiful: a collection of nanotechnology links
The purpose of this page is to help facilitate access to information on the emerging science of nanotechnology. Molecular model of a hypothetical...
http://www.nas.nasa.gov/NAS/Education/nanotech/nanotech.html - size 6K - 20 May 96

Nanotechnology
Nanotechnology: Myth or Miracle? Molecular Engineering may sound like science fiction but is based on reasoning from hard science. The question is not...
http://alpha.genebee.msu.su/nanotech/ntmiracle.html - size 4K - 4 Jan 95

HotWired: Intelligent Agent -"Senate Interest in Nanotechnology: New Tech
Reprinted with permission from Foresight Update 14 (foresight@cup.portal.com): On June 26, 1992, the U.S. Senate Committee on Commerce, Science, and...
http://www.foresight.org/Hotwired.all.files/Nano/url15-1.html - size 28K - 20 Jun 96

Nanotechnology Wealth
Home] [Subscribe] [References] Nanotechnology Wealth... Super Materials! Smart Materials! Super Materials! Nano-constructed materials are to manufactured..
http://planet-hawaii.com/nanozine/NANOMATS.HTM - size 4K - 22 May 96

HotWired: Intelligent Agent -"VP Gore on Nanotechnology"
Reprinted with permission from Foresight Update 15 (foresight@cup.portal.com): Only days before he became a candidate for vice president, Senator Al Gore..
http://www.foresight.org/Hotwired.all.files/Nano/url15.html - size 25K - 20 Jun 96

HotWired: Intelligent Agent - "Unbounding the Future: The Nanotechnology
Unbounding the Future: The Nanotechnology Revolution by K. Eric Drexler and Chris Peterson with Gayle Pergamit (William Morrow, 1991, US$10 paperback). A..
http://www.foresight.org/Hotwired.all.files/Nano/url7.html - size 2K - 20 Jun 96

p. 1 2 3 4 5 6 7 8 9 10 11 12 13 14 15 16 17 18 19 20 [Next]

Sample AltaVista Search

181

- If you have two or more words or concepts that you want to be associated with each other, use an "and" to require that *all* appear in the same Web page, or "near" to specify that they have an even closer relationship. The "near" operator requires that the words you enter not only appear in the same Web page, but are separated by no more than 10 words. So, for example, if you wanted to know about Thai restaurants in Boston you would enter either:

  "Thai Restaurants" and Boston
  or "Thai Restaurants" near Boston.

  In most of my searches, I prefer the "near" operator to the "and" to make the search more precise.
- If you want to automatically search for the plural, gerund, and other suffixes of a word, you can use an asterisk to specify that. So, for example, if you were doing a search on kissing, you could enter the word kiss* and the search engine would automatically search for kiss, kissed, kissing, kisses, and even kisser.
- If you want to search for *either* of two concepts, you use "or" to instruct the search engine. So, for example, if you wanted to search for Web sites that contained *either* the word euthanasia or the phrase doctor-assisted suicide, you would enter: euthanasia or "doctor assisted suicide."
- And if you wanted to make sure that the concept or words you were searching were a major focus of the Web site, and not just some passing reference, you can require that the search engine only return to you a list of hits where those words appear in the main title of the Web page, and not just somewhere in the body. So, for example, if you were searching for articles on arthritis, you could enter: title: arthritis to make it more likely that arthritis will be a primary focus of the articles and Web sites you get back.

Try to avoid creating long, complicated search statements. If you do need to do so, though, use parenthesis to clarify for AltaVista how to interpret your search statement. For example, if you were searching for information on the occurrences of arthritis or diabetes in children living in China, you might be tempted to enter a search like this:

arthritis OR diabetes AND children AND China

The only problem with this is that the computer could read that statement in more than one way. For instance, it might think that you are asking it to find all articles that mention

arthritis OR

diabetes AND children AND China

That would mean an acceptable article—one that meets your criteria—is one that mentions arthritis OR diabetes, children, and China. But you don't want just any article that mentions arthritis—you'll be overloaded with results. What you need to do is to add parenthesis to ensure that the system reads your statement just the way you want it to be read:

(arthritis OR diabetes) AND children AND China

Parentheses group terms together and instruct the computer to act on those terms *first* and then go on to the next set, thereby avoiding any ambiguousness.

Note that not all search engines support parenthesis like AltaVista does, which is another reason I prefer this one to the others. There are a few more tricks of the trade, but the above should get you going on searching AltaVista.

Yahoo: http://www.yahoo.com

The other search engine that I personally like to use is the well-known Yahoo site. Actually, Yahoo isn't really an automated search engine at all, but a massive hierarchical index to much of the Web, created by humans. This is an important distinction for a couple of reasons. When people create an index, they can apply human judgment to decide what categories of information to create, and in which categories to place all those sites. So, although when you search Yahoo you are actually searching a much smaller set of sites than AltaVista, it is a more "filtered" set, and in many ways, it is easier to find relevant information. In AltaVista, you have to hope that the keywords that you entered are actually going to be the ones that appear on a Web site, in order for the search engine to make a match. If you get really good at doing keyword searches,

you'll eventually have a lot of success. But this takes time, and even when you are really proficient at doing keyword searches, it is still an imperfect art. But searching a human-created index is much more straightforward and less prone to error.

So, AltaVista and Yahoo actually complement each other nicely, and I often search them both when doing research. Now, as mentioned earlier, things can get a bit muddled and complicated on the Web (just a bit, right?), and one confusing aspect of Yahoo is that not only does it let you search its hierarchical index, but *also* integrate AltaVista's own search engine! So when you link to Yahoo's page, you have the choice of not only doing a Yahoo search of its categories and sites, but an AltaVista search of the Web, too. However, on Yahoo, you can only do a very basic AltaVista search, and not apply those advanced tips and strategies outlined above. So I would recommend sticking to the AltaVista site when you want to search AltaVista! (And no, AltaVista doesn't yet have an option to search Yahoo on its page—at least yet!)

Note that there is also a special category of search engines called "meta" search engines, which actually automatically search several other search engines simultaneously. These are best to use when you are searching for *very* obscure data and want to be sure you search every possible site. They are not recommended for ordinary searches since they work slower, and since they can only work at a lowest common denominator for each search engine. The two leading meta search engines are SavvySearch (http://www.wagner.cs.colostate.edu~dreiling) and MetaCrawler (http://www.metacrawler.com). A different type of meta search engine called isleuth doesn't actually search the other engines but is a collection of about 1,500 searchable databases from all over the Web gathered in one site for easy searching (http://www.isleuth.com).

What's nice about the Web is that you can keep practicing and it doesn't cost you anything (other than your monthly Internet fee). So keep working at it until you feel comfortable. But remember, if you are not an accomplished searcher, you can't assume that just because your search did not turn up anything that there isn't anything out there. You may just not have used the right keywords. Keyword searching is something of an art, and it takes practice to get good at it!

Business and Economy:Companies:Scientific:Nanotechnology

[   ] Search Options

⦿ Search all of Yahoo ○ Search only in **Nanotechnology**

- **Instruments** *(6)*

- Carl Zeiss - active in electron microscopy, fluorescence ccrrelation spectroscopy, histology, and scanning probe microscopy.
- Molecular Manufacturing Enterprises Incorporated - help accelerate advancements in the field of molecular nanotechnology.
- Munich Institute of Nanotechnology - provides microscopy, micro materials analysis and surface characterization services for high technology problem solving.
- Nanotec Scientific Research
- Nanothinc - providing information about nanotechnology and the related enabling technologies, which include supramolecular chemistry, protein engineering, molecular design and modelling software, STM/AFM/etc. (nanoscopy) and even progress in the top->down approach (which includes nanolithography and micromachines).

 Free for You! - **Click Now to Order.**
Trial Issue of the #1 Guide to the Best of the Web.

Copyright © 1994-96 Yahoo! All Rights Reserved.

Sample Yahoo Search

WEB SEARCH TIPS

As we have said, performing good searches is both a science and an art, and it takes practice to get good. One of the biggest problems novice and even pretty good searchers on the Net have is difficulty in coming up with good keyword searches, which will directly determine the outcome and success of your search. If you're not an accomplished searcher, it's easy to end up with literally thousands of results, which will seem impossible to use—or else you may retrieve no results at all, when in fact the information you want *is* out there, but just wasn't retrievable with the keywords that you entered.

Remember, the words that you choose to describe what you're looking for may or may not be the exact same words that are in the sites you want. For instance, say you're looking for information on global warming, and you enter that phrase. Well, maybe an important site doesn't use that phrase, but does mention the "greenhouse effect." You need to be aware of likely synonyms, and use them when necessary. It's a good idea to take a couple minutes out to plan your search ahead of time, thinking through issues like this.

In the meantime, before you get to be a pro, keep the following tips in mind to make your searches smoother. These tips are excerpted from a speech given by expert searcher, librarian, and author Hope Tillman of Babson College, from a presentation she gave at a "Computers in Libraries" conference:

- Pick the right Internet search engine. Some search only Web pages, others search discussion groups (see below), while others search gopher, Telnet, and ftp sites, which Tillman said, still sometimes have information unavailable over the Web. For example, Tillman noted that it's still necessary to use Telnet to access most library catalogs.
- Be sure to read the instructions of the search engine. Each one has its own protocols and special features.
- Even if you've just read a search engine's instructions a couple weeks ago, read them again. The Web engines, Tillman says, keep "reinventing" themselves, and so you need to keep

checking to see if they've added new features or made changes to existing ones.

- Keep your searches simple. Tillman says that in her experience, the most successful Internet searches are the simplest.
- Don't get sidetracked by interesting sites that are not relevant to your research project at hand. Instead, she advised bookmarking them, so you won't feel that it's lost forever, and you can continue with your research.
- Use more than one search engine.
- Don't forget to use the "find" command in your own Web browser for locating terms and concepts you are looking for in Web pages once you've actually linked to a page.

Here's one more tip: If you can't connect to a particular Web site (e.g., you get a message like "404 not found", "cannot retrieve . . ." etc.) try lopping off one or two levels from the end of the Web address and request access again. Sometimes this does the trick.

Tillman has all sorts of useful Web search advice and tips on her own home page. Link to it (http://www.tiac.net/users/hope).

Here's a final caution in using search engines. Because search engine sites are the places that Internet users turn to locate Web sites, they have developed into a source of power on the Net—not just for researchers, but for advertisers and companies that want to ensure that their sites are located by Internet searchers. Advertisers, then, are attempting to make their presence known on these sites by purchasing "banners" and adding certain keywords over and over to their Web pages in the hopes that a search engine will list their sites toward the top of the list returned to the user. Be on guard against possible manipulation, then, either by sites that get a high ranking but don't seem to deserve it, or by paying close attention to distinguishing banner advertisements on a site from the actual "hits."

If you want to learn more about keyword and Boolean searching, the appendix of my book, *Find it Online* (Windcrest/McGraw-Hill, 1994), has a thorough discussion on the topic.

REVIEWERS AND SUMMARIZERS

Keep in mind that in your journeys around the Web, you will come across some sites that seem like search engines, but are not truly. These are the Web site reviewers, summarizers, and clearinghouses. These can be valuable, too, and we'll take a brief look at these, but they are specialized sites, and not comprehensive Internet search tools like AltaVista, Yahoo, and the others.

The Reviewers

Reviewers, well, review! They examine a selected number of what the editors of the service feel are the most popular or interesting Web sites, and then review and rate them against some set criteria. These criteria vary, but typically include things like substance of content, design, ease of use, interesting use of links, credibility, and so forth. Many employ a star rating system to make their judgments.

Reviewers are useful in the Web, just because they represent at least some effort to help you filter out the good stuff from the junk. Of course, these sites can't begin to examine anywhere near all the sites on the Web, so their usefulness is somewhat limited. But that's okay—limited usefulness on the Web is pretty good these days! Here are some of the most popular Web site reviewers:

- **Magellan.**
    http://www.mckinley.com
- **Pointcom.**
    http://www.pointcom.com
- **iGuide.**
    http://www.iguide.com
- **Cyberhound.**
    http://www.cyberound.com
- **GNN.**
    http://gnn.com

My personal favorite of the above is Cyberhound, since the people behind this service, Gale Research Co., are long-time informa-

tion experts and are well-regarded as a publisher of top-quality library, business, and other directories. As of this writing the service was still free; however, it may eventually become a fee-based service.

News Filters, Personal Broadcast Networks, and Intelligent Agents

Just about the hottest portion of the Internet are software products that automatically scour the Web, newswires, and various electronic information sources to find and deliver, right to your desktop, only the information that you personally want. So, for example, if you are only interested in being alerted to new information on, say, human rights in China, chili peppers, Marxist theory, gardening, and salmonella, you can set up a service to automatically search for mentions of only those words or concepts and regularly get information just on those subjects delivered right to your PC.

This is a fast moving area and is still in its infancy. In fact, even the words used to describe this emerging industry are still evolving. When these devices were first introduced around 1994, they were only a couple and were usually called Customized News Clipping services. They were mainly limited to searching for items from electronic newswires and electronic newspapers. But by early 1997, there were literally dozens of these services, and many were delivering not just news items, but Web page sites, Internet newsgroup postings, abstracts from databases, and even information retained on company Intranets (an Intranet is basically an internal Internet that organizations set up so their workers can easily share information).

Personal Broadcast Networks (PBNs) and Webcasting are the buzzwords being used to describe the latest batch of these products. This makes sense because they really resemble a broadcasting medium more than a print one: That is, they deliver not just text, but also graphics, audio, video, and other multimedia. Some even offer "channels" of information. Another buzzword is "information push" (getting information delivered to you), which is replacing "information pull" (finding information yourself).

One of the promises that the vendors of these devices have been making is that they are a potential cure for our modern curse of information overload. The idea is that instead of you having to search all over the Web to try to come across the information you need, filters and PBNs will do that work automatically in the background, screen out the junk and irrelevant information, and deliver only what's of interest to you alone.

There are dozens of competing products on the market. The one that's made the biggest splash is Pointcast; but others include NewsPage, NewsHound, InfoSeek Personal, My Yahoo!, Paracel, BackWeb, IFusion, Intermind, Berkeley Systems, and Marimba. It's expected that the big players in the industry—America Online, Netscape, and of course, Microsoft—will all soon have their own information filtering and broadcasting devices as well. (By the way, don't confuse these filters with a different type of automated Web surfer, generally called "off site browsers." These products don't really hunt for topics of your interest, but will automatically link to and download to your hard disk the Web sites you specify that you'd like to monitor regularly. This allows you to browse those sites at your leisure, while offline. Two of the leaders in the off site browser categories are Freeloader: http://www.free loader.com and WebWhacker: http://www.ffg.com

There are some significant differences between the various filters. Some are geared for consumers and others for business. Some are free, and some are quite expensive. Some search only Web sites, others search Web sites plus electronic newswires (such as AP and Reuters), and others scan a wide range of online databases. The way these devices deliver the results to you differ too. Some provide your news in your E-mail, while others have a Web site you can link to. Some create a mock up of a newspaper, while others automatically display news items and data right on your PC's screen as a screen saver, or in a corner of your screen like a stock ticker.

The most advanced of these devices are called "intelligent agents" since they are supposed to be able to actually learn of your work and information habits and desires by observing and analyzing your decisions. There is a great deal of research going on in the use of intelligent agents (much of it is being conducted at the renowned MIT Media Lab in Cambridge, MA), and there

will likely be some impressive developments in this area before the year 2000.

Do these devices really work and are they a solution to information overload? They are certainly a useful tool for finding obscure information, for tapping sources you normally would not check, and for staying up-to-speed on relevant breaking news. But I feel that they also have inherent limitations. For one, they still cannot compare with the ability of human judgment to determine whether a particular article, Web site, or piece of information is truly relevant given your broad contextual needs. They also, paradoxically, represent yet another source of information (actually, they point to multiple sources of information), which will not help your information overload problems.

On another more philosophical point, having an automated system deliver to you a narrowly focused set of subjects is not necessarily conducive to maintaining a broad view of the world. Much of what we find to be valuable information, we find seredipitously when browsing the newspaper or a journal. And these days, the most useful information leads to insight, which is not likely to come from raw data—no matter how well filtered. Automated systems also cannot provide you with the higher level analysis that an expert whose judgment you trust can offer. These people could be newsletter editors, columnists, or librarians. The human filter is still superior.

ELECTRONIC DISCUSSIONS AND NEWSGROUPS

So far we've concentrated almost all of this chapter on "just" one section of the Internet, that is, the Web. And although there are countless incredible Web sites filled with all types of useful information, the other part of the Internet that can be just as valuable as the Web, and in some ways is even more valuable for the researcher, are the electronic discussion groups.

If there's one area where the Internet lives up to its hype, it is in its capability to help you find experts and people who may know answers to your questions. The Internet's "culture," so to speak, is

an information-sharing one. If you know something about a topic and someone posts a question on it and you can help them, you do so.

The best place on the Internet to find experts who can answer questions is in one of the thousands of discussion groups (technically called "usenet" and "mailing lists" or "listservs") where people with similar interests link up electronically to exchange ideas and debate current issues. Again, as with everything on the Internet, the scope of these discussion groups runs the gamut. You'll find newsgroups discussing offbeat and arcane topics from alien sightings and yo-yos to traditional business-related subjects like investment strategies and international trade to scholarly areas ranging from communication theory to zoological research. There's a group called alt.baldspot for men (and women, I suppose) interested in balding, and there's alt.x-files for fans of that television show.

What's great about these discussion groups is that you can throw out a question that may seem nearly impossible to find an answer to, and what's likely to happen is that you will find other people who either have answers, know someone who does, or at least has also been looking into the same subject and has begun gathering information on the topic.

Here, for example, are some questions that members of the "business librarians" (or BUSLIB) list have asked their colleagues—and successfully found answers:

- When was the first corporate stock split?
- Where can I find information on a Brazilian plant called *Coulteria Tinctoria* used for hair straightening?
- Does anyone know how to get a videotape that Bill Gates used in his opening talk at the Comdex conference?
- Where can I get a videotape of the Challenger disaster?
- I need a list of worldwide producers of yellow phosphorus
- What would be the value of $100 today, if invested in the S&P 500 in June of 1993?
- How many golf carts and forklifts are operating today in the United States?
- I need to find information on companies or plants that bottle liquor or beer.

I personally have had many, many success stories in finding answers and/or leads to information that I thought would be impossible to track down. For example, for many years I had tried unsuccessfully to track down a copy of an old, relatively obscure (early 1960s) MGM children's 33⅓ album that my brother and I used to listen to before going to bed when we were children. I tried secondhand stores, catalogues, special clearinghouses, MGM itself, resellers and distributors—but nothing. Ah, but this was before the Internet. But this was tough even for the Net! I posted my question on some "vinyl LP" and collector discussion groups, and though I got some helpful leads, none led me to the actual record!

Then I heard about a list called "stumpers"—an eclectic group specifically designed to help people who were stumped by a particular question! So I posted my question there, and among the leads I got were messages from two people who suggested that I call Bowling Green University's library of popular culture, which, amongst its collections, contained thousands and thousands of recordings. After tracking down the phone number, I was connected to a very helpful librarian, who looked up the title in his computer catalog, found that indeed it was included, and then for just $9.95 or so sent me a cassette tape of "The Bear That Wasn't" along with a photocopy of the album's cover. Eureka! (To send an E-mail message to Stumpers, send an E-mail message to Stumpers-L@crf.cuis.edu.)

As mentioned earlier, there are actually technically two different types of Internet discussion groups: usenets and mailing lists (listservs). The main difference in the two is the method in which you can access, read, and send messages. For the former, you need a special "newsgroup reader" that your Internet Service Provider makes available, and for the latter you only need an E-mail account, since the messages come to you as E-mail in your mailbox. For a lot more detail on this, see one of the Internet books recommended in the appendix.

How to Find a List of Interest to You:

There are several ways to find out the names of usenet groups and mailing lists. If you are a member of a consumer online service like America Online or CompuServe, that provider should have a feature where you can search for an occurrence of particular discussion groups, and then sign up. If, instead, you are reaching the Internet

through an independent Internet Service Provider, you can either find a list by using a feature on your browser (e.g., Netscape, Explorer) or by linking to certain Web pages that let you search or browse by name or subject. Here are the key sites:

1. **Dejanews.**

   http://www.dejanews.com

   Dejanews is actually a search engine, like AltaVista, described above. The key difference though is that Dejanews contains an archive of newsgroup postings. So although it is not really a site for doing an efficient search for specific newsgroups, you might find one that is relevant to your research by doing a search on Dejanews and seeing what comes up. For example, if you were doing a search on techniques for training people to use the Internet you might find that several postings related to that topic were found on a group called "Nettrain."

2. **The Argus Clearinghouse.**

   http://www.clearinghouse.net

   This is an extremely valuable listing of important Internet mailing list groups. It is not a comprehensive list, but is a selection of some of the most scholarly and important ones in the field. The directory is broken down into dozens of subject categories, including agriculture, anthropology, art, astronomy, botany, business, chemistry, communication studies, computers, environment, education, engineering, genetics, geology, history, humanities, jobs, journalism, languages, Latin American studies, law, library and information science, linguistics, literature, mathematics, medical practice, military science, music, philosophy/ethics, physical education, physics, political science, popular culture, psychology, publishing, religious studies, social activism, sociology, theater/film/television, transportation, weather, women's studies, writing, and more. Each group identified is described, and information on how to sign up is provided.

3. **Listwebber.**

   http://www.lib.ncsu.edu/staff/moran/about-listwebber2.html

   A searchable collection of listserv archives.

4. **Liszt.**

   http: //www.liszt.com/

   A directory of over 23,000 listserv and other mailing lists.

5. **"Thousand of Mailing Lists."**

   http://scwww.ucs.indiana.edu/mlarchive/

   A keyword searchable directory of nearly 12,000 mailing lists.

6. TileNet.
http://www.tile.net:2001/news
Search or browse thousands of Usenet discussion groups.

One other interesting feature you can perform on these newsgroups is to create an ongoing monitoring system so that when someone posts a message on a particular topic, you can automatically be alerted to that message, and obtain a link to it. A Web site called "reference.com" (previously part of Stanford University and called "SIFT") offers a free system whereby you can specify keywords that describe topics or concepts that you want to continually monitor, and Reference.Com will automatically scan thousands of online discussion groups on a daily basis and alert you with an E-mail message in your mailbox of new relevant postings.

The advantage of using a system like this rather than (or in addition to) signing up with a particular newsgroup, is that because Reference.Com searches such a wide range of discussion groups, it can find the odd mention of your topic, which you would otherwise never know about. So, though you may be, say, researching solar energy and have signed up with a solar energy related newsgroup, you would not have known about someone posting a message on, say, a home buying newsgroup that mentions a new solar technology. (You can link to this site at http://www. reference.com)

DRAWBACKS AND PROBLEMS IN DOING RESEARCH ON THE NET

So far this chapter has been telling you all the wonderful things about doing research on the Internet. Well, they are wonderful! But wonderful doesn't mean perfect! Far from it. Let's just quickly tick off what I see as the ten major problems of doing research on the Internet.

1. **Data Quality and Reliability.** You often don't know who posted the information or where it came from. This is a biggie! Yes, there are galaxies of information out there on the Web, but how do you know how reliable the information is, how credible the person is who posted the information, and so forth? Barbara Quint, an expert searcher, has said that

researchers need to follow "mother's first rule: If you don't know where it's been, don't put it in your mouth—or your ear or your mind." Unfortunately many Web sites don't explicitly state who or what organization is behind the information you've located. It's up to you to go that critical extra step to find out who the person or institution is. Then you can apply some of the evaluation criteria outlined in chapter 9 to assess reliability and credibility.*

2. **Flea Market Browsing.** The Web is mostly filled with useless stuff and fluff. This problem, though, becomes less relevant as search engines become more sophisticated and can cut through the junk to find the gems.

3. **Links.** Hyperlinks can be useful, but are often distracting and can throw focused research off track. (For an interesting analysis of hyperlinks, see "I Link, Therefore I Am," from the May 4, 1996, issue of *The New York Times* online technology news service CyberTimes.

    http://www.nytimes.com

4. **Slow.** The Web can be a tremendous time drain. It's easy to spend hours on the Web and, at the end of that time, have only a little bit of information to show for it. You may wish to set some limit, like 30–60 minutes of Web searching a day.

5. **Inappropriate Research Tool.** The Web, because it is so easy to log on, is generally free to search, and is fun, too, can be used as a substitute for other online sources or print sources that would actually be a better choice for doing research. Sometimes the best place to go to get what you need is still just an encyclopedia, the latest issue of a newsstand magazine, making a phone call, and talking to real live people. On one

---

*Although it is certainly true that finding information on the Web opens up a can of worms for evaluating credibility, the other side of this coin is that the Internet also allows many, many people who do have something very valuable and significant to say to a large audience the ability to do so! This has created access to a new type of knowledge: personal experiences and anecdotal information that until now was unavailable from so many people and so easily. This knowledge is not based on traditional authority like a Ph.D.; instead, it is based on an intense personal interest, or personal hands-on experience.

electronic newsgroup that I subscribe to, someone posted a message about the time and difficulty in finding zip codes on the Web. Another member wrote back about how fast and simple it is to find zip codes by having just a good old Rand McNally Atlas nearby!

6. **Weak Database Substitutes.** Sometimes the information that the major data producers put up on the Net is just a poor substitute for a much more complete database available online from one of the major data producers. Many publishers and databases only put "top line" or aggregate data on the Web, just to have a presence on the Net and to promote its full line of information products. If you just stop your research with what you find on the Net, you will miss out on the real depth information available on Dialog or one of the major online vendors.

7. **Decontextualization.** It's great to search and find a snippet of data buried deep in some 500-page government report. But as it becomes easier and easier to find bits and pieces of data, you also lose more and more of the original context of which that data was part. That context provides the broader meaning that is important for understanding.

8. **Emphasis on Speed.** One of the primary, if not *the* primary, characteristic of digital information is its speed and its ability to be accessed and transmitted nearly instantaneously. While speed is certainly an advantage, as we move faster to try to keep pace with the speed of the microprocessor something else can suffer. That "something" is often time: taking time for reflection—to think, plan, and analyze.

9. **Style over Substance.** Nobody enjoys scrolling though screen after screen of text on their computer. Internet publishers are quickly discovering this and are presenting less actual information—and more white space, design, and multimedia elements. What this means is that Web publishers are deemphasizing content. What one finds more and more on the Web are easy-to-read summaries, briefs, excerpts, and overviews. And while graphics and design do convey knowledge, words are still the primary mechanism we have for conveying the full breadth and subtleties of the issue at hand.

10. **Lack of Historical Perspective.** Relying on information online often means only locating the newest data. Most information on the Web only goes back to about 1994 or so—that's hardly a comprehensive backfile. Be sure to supplement your Web research with print or even traditional online sources that have a longer history.

Another point to keep in mind is that one of the most significant differences between information found on the Web and information from print journals is that often (though not always) the key element missing on the Web is not the expertise of the author, but the role of the *editor*. The editor's job typically includes assisting the author with matters of focus, organization, and clarity.

When the editor's role is removed, it is up to you to take on the burden of the editor's job yourself. This means trying to extract the essence of the information, looking for gaps in reasoning and logic, resolving inconsistencies, and so on. This is particularly tricky to do when trying to evaluate anecdotal information and personal views posted on the Web.

One editor who needs to evaluate information on the Web and online, Karin Coek of Gale Research, has said that she maintains an open mind but a healthy skepticism when looking at anecdotal information on the Net. She looks at whether the person's reasoning is sound, and also finds out whether opinions are based on a single incident or something that occurred over a longer period of time. You may also want to follow up with questions of your own to help you evaluate someone's opinions or views on the Net. You can send that person an E-mail and ask for additional information. What were the specific experiences or incidents that led to that person's conclusion or views? Such follow-up questions can help you ascertain credibility. And you can post your own questions to a newsgroup to find out if others have had similar experiences.

PROFESSIONAL ONLINE SERVICES

Although it may seem so, the Internet is certainly not the last word in electronic research. In fact, in many ways it is quite inferior to

the traditional professional online services, which have been delivering high-quality data to information professionals for many years. These services, while overshadowed by the mass popularity of the Internet, still offer the most efficient system for doing precision research.

Professional online services differ from both the Internet and consumer online services in several ways: They concentrate on providing information databases almost exclusively—no games, chat lines, clubs, etc.; the databases themselves are top-notch for researchers in that they represent thousands of in-depth journals, reports, and studies. The catch, though, is that these services are very expensive, and they can be complicated to search well, so it takes some practice to get good. However, the popularity of the Internet is putting pressure on these professional services to remain competitive, so they are generally getting easier to use, and less expensive to search.

The big names in this arena are Dialog and Lexis/Nexis, though there are others. Dialog offers more databases—well over 400— than any other online vendor in the world, and the databases themselves range from aerospace to zoology and most everything else in between. Lexis/Nexis is a powerful online service, and is the first choice for many lawyers, newspaper reporters, and librarians. Other big names in the field include DataStar, which specializes in European information (and is actually owned by Knight Ridder, which also owns Dialog); DataTimes, which offers the full text of many daily newspapers; Dow Jones News/Retrieval, which specializes in timely, in-depth business information; and NewsNet, which offers access to hundreds of professional industry newsletters.

Contact information for each of these services is provided at the end of this chapter.

THE CONSUMER ONLINE SERVICES

What about the consumer online services: America Online, Prodigy, CompuServe, and Microsoft Network? As mentioned earlier, all offer a gateway to the Internet, but they also offer their

own databases and information files. Are these suitable for doing in-depth research? All of them allow you to search encyclopedias, dozens or even hundreds of magazines, useful business information databases, and popular files like travel resources, health information, and so forth, and each have their own online discussion groups. Still, none can really hold a candle to the Internet or the professional online services in terms of what they offer.

However, out of the bunch, there's no question that CompuServe offers the most for the serious researcher. Its major offerings here include the Information Access Company (IAC) "plus" database, Knowledge Index, and IQuest.

The IAC "plus" databases are a series of superbly designed full text databases created with outstanding search capabilities. These include Business Database Plus, which provides the full text of 1,000 business journals and 600 newsletters; Computer Database Plus, which offers the full text of 150 computer magazines; Health Database Plus, drawn from about 750 major health and consumer-oriented publications; and Magazine Database Plus, which provides complete articles from over 450 popular periodicals and sources.

Knowledge Index is a subset of about 100 databases culled from the professional online host Dialog, but available at a much lower rate than if one searched Dialog directly. The only catch is that you can only use Knowledge Index at night or on the weekends. And you're not allowed to use it for any kind of profit-making resale work, such as "information brokering." If you can live with these restrictions, the Knowledge Index service is a superb bargain.

Finally, IQuest is an electronic "gateway" to several hundred professional databases available from a handful of professional online services, including Dialog, NewsNet, DataStar, and others. Databases available include business directories from Dun & Bradstreet, credit reports, patent research, demographic data, government publications, international company financials, and much more. IQuest is quite pricey, though, and so is suitable really just if you are willing to shell out some pretty big bucks for the privilege.

Finally, CompuServe offers a neat feature called the Executive News Service, an interesting customizable electronic "news clipping" service that monitors the Associated Press, UPI, Reuters,

and the *Washington Post*. To use it, you input keywords and concepts that you want the service to track. The service continually checks the wires for matches and, on a daily basis, provides you with a list of relevant headlines. You then scan the headlines and determine which, if any, you want to read in full.

Contact information for each of these services is provided at the end of this chapter.

ANOTHER OPTION:
THE INFORMATION BROKER

What is an "information broker"? It is a firm that offers computer search services and/or other research services for a fee. Such a firm accepts inquiries from users and then tries to come up with the answers by searching online databases and the Internet and, sometimes, by tapping into other information sources like associations and library resources.

A benefit of an information broker is that you are able to tap into the power of a computer search without needing access to a computer yourself. However, because it may be cheaper to do the searches on your own, using these firms is probably most appropriate for people who have only a one-shot information request or for those who need to make inquiries only very occasionally.

Information brokers vary enormously with regard to their staff size, research capabilities, and fees. Some brokers are simply individuals who own a personal computer and subscribe to an on-line database vendor. These people often get their customers by placing ads offering computer search services at a low cost. Other information brokers are large corporations with extensive staffs and resources. These firms may charge well into the thousands of dollars for their services. Some information brokers specialize in a particular type of information search, while others handle any topic or search request.

Because the capabilities and resources of information brokers vary so widely, it's important that you select carefully. Before deciding which one to use, compare brokers using the following criteria:

- What databases does the broker have access to? Do they cover the subjects you are interested in?
- What is the broker's experience in performing information searches? How long has the searcher been doing this kind of work? (You don't want someone to be practicing at your expense.)
- What credentials does the information broker have? A degree in library science? Has the broker worked as an information specialist in some capacity for another firm? Does he or she belong to the national trade association, the Association of Independent Information Professionals (AIIP)?

Another important factor is the amount of time and attention a broker pays to discussing your information project. A good information broker will try to learn as much as possible about your needs. The person who will actually be doing the search should discuss with you the details of what you need to find out, where you've already looked, why you're trying to find this information, what you're planning to do with it, and other details.

You can find information brokers by checking a variety of places. Some are listed in the Yellow Pages under the heading "Information" or "Research." Check writers' magazines (e.g., *Writers Digest*) and look for advertisements under "Professional Services" or a similar heading.

You can also check the *Burwell World Directory of Information Brokers*. This handbook lists hundreds of firms around the country and around the globe that will do research for a fee. The directory includes helpful information such as subject specialties, specific services provided, as well as full contact information. You can order a copy from Burwell Enterprises, 3724 FM 1960 West, Suite 214, Houston, TX 77068; 281–537–9051. And if you yourself are interested in *becoming* an information broker, I recommend getting *The Information Broker's Handbook* (Windcrest/McGraw-Hill) or get hold of *The Information Broker's Resource Kit*, available from Sue Rugge of the Information Professionals Institute in Oakland, California.

Also, sometimes nearby university libraries will offer online search services. Fees may be less than private firms, but the extent of services available is also likely to be more limited.

CONTACT INFORMATION
FOR VENDORS

The following are the addresses and telephone numbers of some of the most popular consumer and professional electronic database vendors.

Consumer Online Services

America Online
8619 Westwood Center Drive
Vienna, VA
800–827–6364

CompuServe Inc.
5000 Arlington Center Blvd.
Columbus, OH 43220
614–457–8600
800–848–8990 or 800–848–8199

Microsoft Network
Microsoft Corp.
One Microsoft Way
Redmond, WA 98052
206–882–8080

Prodigy Services Company
445 Hamilton Avenue
White Plains, NY 10601
914–448–8000

Professional Services

Dialog and DataStar
Knight-Ridder Information
2440 El Camino Real

Mountain View, CA 94040
415–858–3785
800–334–2564

Dow Jones News/Retrieval
Dow Jones Inc.
PO Box 300
Princeton, NJ 08543
609–520–4000

Lexis-Nexis
PO Box 933
Dayton, OH 45401
513–865–6800
800–543–6862

NewsNet Inc.
945 Haverford Road
Bryn Mawr, PA 19010
215–527–8030
800–345–1301

PART II

Experts Are Everywhere

6

Identifying Experts
Who They Are, Where to Find Them

QUICK PREVIEW: IDENTIFYING EXPERTS

An expert is simply a person with in-depth knowledge about a subject or activity. For most information-finding projects there are ten types of experts worth tracking down and contacting:

- **Book authors** are solid sources, but be sure those you speak with have stayed up to date with their subject.
- **Periodical staff writers and editors** can be excellent information sources. Technical and trade publication staffers are typically more knowledgeable in a specific field than are journalists who work on popular interest newspapers and publications.
- **Experts cited in periodical articles** make excellent information sources.
- **Convention speakers** are another potential top information source.
- **Federal government personnel** may take time to track down, but once you do, you'll find them to be surprisingly helpful.
- **Association staffers** are superb information sources—knowledgeable, helpful, and very easy to reach.

(continued)

- **Experts at private companies** are often valuable sources, but they may be hard to find and reluctant to reveal their knowledge.
- **Consultants** are often very knowledgeable, but typically not fruitful resources for the researcher, because they normally charge a fee for sharing their knowledge.
- **A "hands-on" expert** actually performs the activity you need to find out about.
- **"Non-expert experts"** are ordinary people who've had some personal experience in what you're trying to find out. They can offer interesting anecdotal reports but you need to be careful in assessing these person's credibility.

Identifying and using written source materials is only the first step of the information-finding process. The next step is to locate and talk to the experts behind the sources. Here's why:

- Reading written information means wading through piles of published materials to try to isolate the information you need. But talking to an expert gives you the opportunity to pose questions and zero in on specific issues that concern *you*. In essence, the information you receive from the expert is "custom designed" to meet your needs.
- If an expert makes a point that's confusing, you can ask a question to clear it up—not so easy to do with a magazine article or book!
- When you talk to an expert, you receive the timeliest information possible. You can find out what has happened in the last couple of days or couple of hours.
- Talking to an expert is simply more interesting and fun. You get the kind of live opinions and candid remarks not ordinarily found in published materials.

But before you begin, you need to learn the best techniques for getting to the "best" experts.

LOCATING THE EXPERTS

Experts are everywhere. An expert is anybody who has in-depth knowledge about a particular subject or activity. A few of these experts are famous—someone like a Benjamin Spock or Julia Child—but the overwhelming majority are not. The experts that you'll be talking to are most likely to be businesspersons, government workers, technical writers, shop foremen, teachers, and other ordinary persons with special know-how, skills, or background.

Here is a quick overview of ten of the best types of expert to track down and talk to. The pros and cons of each type are examined; and strategies are provided on how best to make contact.

✔ Book Authors

PRO: Book authors typically have a solid and in-depth understanding of their subject. They possess a broad view of their field and can provide excellent background information.

CON: A book author may no longer be up to date on his or her subject. This can be especially true in fields that change very rapidly (such as computer technology). Book authors can also be hard to find.

How to Reach:

The standard approach for contacting an author is to send a letter in care of the book's publisher. The publisher is then supposed to forward your letter to the author. This can be a slow and unreliable approach to making contact: It's possible that your letter will sit for days, weeks, or even months at the publishing house before it's mailed out—especially if the book is an old one. It's better to call the publisher and talk to the book's editor to find out where *you* can contact the author.

✔ Periodical Staff Writers and Editors

PRO: Staff writers and editors of magazines and journals are typically nontechnical types who are easy to get hold of, easy to talk to, and very helpful. They usually keep up with developments in their field and are good at pointing out other places and people to contact for information.

TIP: Tracking Down a Book Author

• You can often find the editor's name mentioned in the "acknowledgments" section in the front of the book. If you don't find it there, you can call the editorial department of the publisher and ask for the editor's name. Just be sure to make it easy for the publisher to help you. This means providing complete information on the book title, author, and date of publication. (If you cannot reach the editor, the next best person to speak with is probably someone in the publicity department.)

Will the publisher give you the author's address and phone number? Although many publishers have house rules prohibiting the release of this information, these rules are flexible. One key to getting the information is to make it easy for the editor or other staffer to help you: Again, be sure you have as much information about the book as possible. An editor at a major publishing house told me that her decision on whether to release information about an author often depends on *why* someone wants it. So think a little beforehand about whether your reasons for wanting to contact the author sound legitimate and important.

If you are trying to find the author of a paperback book, first check the book's copyright page to see if a different publisher put out a hardcover edition. If so, it's best to contact that publisher instead.

CON: While an editor or staff writer for a *technical or trade* publication may be quite knowledgeable about a field (such people have often covered a specific field for so long that they become experts themselves), newspaper journalists or writers or editors of publications geared for the general public (*Time*, *Good Housekeeping*, etc.) may not be. They may indeed write an article on a technical topic, but their knowledge of the field can still be somewhat sketchy, because they are usually journalists first and subject experts only through their contacts and interviews. But they can still be helpful sources. For example, I recently contacted a popular magazine's staff writer about an article he wrote regarding the overnight delivery services industry. Although the staffer had a good working knowledge of the field, the real value of speaking with him was getting his referrals to the true experts in the industry that he spoke with when researching the piece.

How to Reach:

When you read an article that's of interest to you, look for the writer's byline at the beginning or end of the piece. Then turn to the

periodical's masthead (normally found in the first five pages of the magazine) and search for the writer's name. Contact the publication and ask to speak with that person. If the person is not on the masthead, he or she is probably a freelance writer. The editorial department of the magazine will be able to tell you how to make contact.

Another way to utilize magazine staff members as experts is to look at the masthead of a publication devoted to your subject of interest and try to zero in on a specific department editor (e.g., "technology editor" or "new products editor") who sounds as though he or she covers the kind of information you need. If you can't pick out a specific department editor but want to speak with someone on the magazine, ask to speak with the editor or the managing editor. If you are a subscriber, or at least a regular reader, it will help your cause to say so.

✔ Experts Cited in Periodical Articles

PRO: Virtually all periodical articles quote experts when examining an issue. For example, an article about a decline in the public's attendance of movie theaters, published in *Theatre Industry News*, quotes an industry expert on why moviegoing is declining, what can be done about it, what may happen in the future, and so forth. This makes your job of finding a knowledgeable source easy. The magazine has already done the necessary research to find an expert and bring his or her opinions and expertise to its readers. All you need to do is make contact. Such people are typically leaders in their field and can be extremely valuable sources. They can provide you with a wealth of information and are one of my favorite types of expert.

TIPS: Zero in on the Best Expert

• Take special care to note those articles that are written concisely and clearly enough to be easily understandable for the nonspecialist (i.e., you!). Chances are that the writer of these articles will be equally clear and enlightening to talk to.

• An excellent source of experts on lesser-known and privately held companies are editors and reporters of regional business publications. You can get a free listing of these publications by contacting the Association of Area Business Publications, 202 Legion Avenue, Annapolis, MD 21401; 410–269–0332. Ask for a free copy of its *Directory of Members*.

CON: Occasionally, you might run into a very knowledgeable source who is not so adept at communicating his or her expertise. This can make for a confusing information interview. If you encounter a confusing source, try to get the person to define any buzzwords or jargon.

How to Reach:

When an article quotes an expert, the piece normally provides the reader with his or her name and place and city of work. It is then a simple task to call up directory assistance in that city and obtain the phone number of the organization. (You can get the area code of any city by calling the operator.) If the article does not provide the expert's place of work or the city, call the publication directly to ask for it.

✔ Convention Speakers

PRO: People who are invited to present technical sessions at professional conventions are often real leaders and innovators in their field. They should be intimately informed about the topic of their presentation.

CON: Again, you may encounter a top-notch authority who is not as talented at communicating his or her expertise. Otherwise, there is no real drawback with this sort of expert.

How to Reach:

You can find out where conventions are being held on your subject by checking a library copy of the *Directory of Conventions* or by scanning an "upcoming events" column in a relevant trade publication. (See page 53 for more information on conventions.)

✔ Federal Government Personnel

PRO: Many experts in government view sharing information with the public as an important part of their job. What is surprising to many is that government experts are sometimes the most helpful of all sources. In fact, there is actually a law requiring government personnel to be helpful to the public!

CON: If you don't have an expert's name, it can be time-consuming and frustrating to track down the person you need. If you do telephone, be prepared to be transferred around a bit.

How to Reach:

See pages 106, 107, and 110 on finding your way around Washington, and chapter 3 for an overview of obtaining information from the government.

✔ Association Staffers

PRO: As explained earlier in this book, people who work at professional associations are one of the very best sources of information. They are normally very knowledgeable, helpful, and easy to reach.

CON: An association executive might slant his or her remarks to advance the association's particular industry or cause. In addition, some association personnel are true experts in their field, while others are more oriented toward administrative or public relations work. Be sure you dig for the real experts. (Sometimes the true experts do not work in the association office itself, but work in private industry while maintaining a position with the association. It's fine to contact these people at their regular place of work.)

How to Reach:

Simply look up your subject in a library copy of the *Encyclopedia of Associations.* Call the association and ask your question.

✔ Company Personnel

PRO: Whether it's the person who buys tomatoes for Ragu, or the employee in charge of computer keyboard quality control at Texas Instruments, sometimes the "inside" information you need can be provided only by a specific person at a particular firm. If you're researching a type of *product,* a good place to start getting information is a company that makes it. I've found that salespeople for manufacturers are more than happy to educate interested people about their product, and they don't mind if your questions are elementary.

CON: It can be hard to identify the precise people you need to reach at a company, and if you do find them, they may be reluctant to reveal what you want to know. (See page 247 on obtaining "sensitive" information.) When interviewing company personnel, you also have to be on guard against receiving information that's biased toward promoting their firm.

How to Reach:

To find the names, addresses, and phone numbers of companies, consult Dun & Bradstreet's *Million Dollar Directory* or Standard & Poor's *Register,* found in the library. Once you have a company's address and phone number, you can try to get the information you need by calling its public affairs or public relations office; if the people there don't have the answer, they should be able to connect you with someone who does.

✔ **Consultants**

PRO: Some consultants are outstanding experts in their field and can provide a great deal of inside information, advice, and in-depth knowledge.

CON: There are a number of disadvantages in using a consultant in a research project. First, it can be difficult to determine how good a particular consultant truly is (however, see chapter 9 for tips on evaluating a source's expertise). An even bigger drawback is that unlike the other types of expert described in this chapter, most consultants will want to charge a fee for sharing their knowledge. This is understandable, because a consultant's livelihood is based on selling access to his or her expertise. However, few researchers are in a position to spend a great deal of money in gathering information, and in fact, as described in this chapter it is normally not necessary to do so!

How to Reach:

To locate a local consultant, you might just check your Yellow Pages. To find others located nationwide, check either a library copy of *Consultants and Consulting Organizations Directory* (Gale Research Company) or call a trade association of consultants by checking the *Encyclopedia of Associations* and asking for referrals.

✔ **The "Hands-On" Expert**

PRO: This is the person who actually performs an activity that you want to learn about—the fashion designer, master chef, computer programmer, and so on. Such people understand the subject in the intimate and detailed way that comes only from hands-on experience. You can really get a sense of the nitty-gritty by talking with them.

CON: These people's opinions will naturally be based on their own unique experiences. They are not like the journalist or industry observer who forms conclusions by gathering data from a wide variety of sources. You might receive a narrower, more limited view of the subject.

How to Reach:

Sometimes a professional association can refer you to a member who is a hands-on expert. Or just use your ingenuity. Ask yourself the question, Who would know? Let's say you wanted to talk to a top-notch auto mechanic. Try and figure out what type of organization would need to have a top-flight mechanic on its staff. You could call up United Parcel Service, ask for the fleet department, and then talk to the head mechanic. Or let's say you needed to learn about custodial techniques and products. Maybe you'd call Disneyland's director of grounds maintenance. Experts *are* everywhere.

✔ The "Non-Expert" Expert

PRO: The non-expert expert is simply another person who has had some personal experience with whatever it is you are researching. For example, say you were scheduled to have a hip replacement operation and were wondering how much mobility you'll likely have after the operation. If you can speak to one or more people who had this operation, you will likely learn some useful information and get some helpful advice.

CON: When you obtain anecdotal information like this, you need to be particularly careful in evaluating it for reliability and credibility. Obviously, it can be hazardous to draw broad conclusions from one person's personal experiences. However, if you hear the same reports from many people who appear to be trustworthy, then you may determine that such anecdotal information is worth paying attention to.

How to Reach:

Probably the best way these days to quickly and efficiently tap into the experiences, opinions, and views of millions of people is to post a message to a relevant Internet discussion group ("usenet" and "listserv" groups). See the discussion regarding "Electronic Discussions and Newsgroups" in chapter 5 to find out more on how to find the right group.

TIP: Directories of Experts

• Here are a few interesting sources. *The Yearbook of Experts, Authorities and Spokespersons,* published by Broadcast Interview Source in Washington, DC, is used by journalists to find experts on scores of subjects ranging from adult education to zoos. The reader looks up his or her subject of interest, and the directory provides the name of the association, company, school, or other organization that has volunteered to be contacted as an information source. For example, if you look up anti-Semitism, you find the Simon Wiesenthal Center and a person who can be contacted for information. The guide is free to working journalists ($37.50 to everyone else and is available from Broadcast Interview Source, 2233 Wisconsin Avenue NW, Washington, DC 20007; 202–333–4904). Anyone can search the information for free, though, over Broadcast Interview Source's Web site at http://www.yearbooknews.com

Other useful lists of experts are available on the Web including http://www.experts.com and the University of Southern California's Experts Directory at http://www.usc.edu/dept/News_Service/experts_directory. html

7

Making the Connection

Getting Access to an Expert

QUICK PREVIEW: MAKING THE CONNECTION

- Prepare for your talk with the expert beforehand. Do some reading on the subject, make a list of questions, and think how to best probe each particular source's specific area of expertise.
- Don't contact the leading expert first. Instead, talk to someone who is not too technical and is accustomed to explaining concepts to nonexperts. One such source could be a journalist.
- Decide if you will tape-record your conversation or take notes.
- Experts are not as hard to reach as you may think. All you need is a lot of persistence and a little luck.
- Telephoning rather than writing the experts is normally the best way to make contact. It's quicker, and you can ask questions and have a dialogue. E-mail is another option for contacting people who are very busy and hard to reach.
- Tips for reaching a hard-to-find expert: Get the secretary interested in your project. Talk to the expert's assistant. Call a related office. Be patient and keep plugging.
- If you call an organization's general phone number to try to identify an expert, figure out how to get the switchboard operator to help you.
- Don't be too quick to accept an "I can't help you" or "I don't know" response to your request to talk to an expert. If necessary, call and try again some other time.

How do you best prepare for your talk with the experts? What's the best way to track them down? What should you actually ask? Here's what you need to know:

GETTING READY BEFOREHAND

It's important that you don't contact the experts without first doing some preparation. One expert in library science who is frequently interviewed for information told me that if the inquirer has done some reading and checking around first, it makes her job a lot easier, and she can be much more helpful.

As mentioned earlier, you should first do some reading. Although it would be helpful to find and read anything the expert you're about to speak with has written, it's not absolutely necessary. It is important, though, to have done some kind of reading and research on the subject first; otherwise, you won't know what questions to ask and you may end up wasting your time and the experts'.

Before you contact an expert, also take a couple of minutes to think about how best to present what you're doing to this

---

TIP: You May Be Helping the Expert
• Think about any ways you may be helping the expert. For example, if the information you gather is going to be published, or presented to a group of influential people, let the expert know it. If you quote or cite an expert, or include the person in a list of sources of further information, it may be an aid to his or her reputation or business. This point is especially important to get across when you interview a vendor or consultant of some kind. These people normally charge for their expertise but will usually give you their information for free in hopes of getting customers through your information report. (This technique works equally well when you need assistance from an organization. Think of ways you will be letting others know of that firm's services.)

So be sure to figure out in advance exactly how your work can help publicize a person. And offer to send a final copy of anything you put together so that the expert can add it to his or her professional credential file.

---

particular source to encourage help. What should be stressed? What should be downplayed?

It's important that you spend a few minutes thinking about the best kinds of questions you could ask. These questions should reflect:

• Matters that are confusing and unclear to you after you've read information on the subject.
• Areas in which you need more detailed information.
• Problems or subjects unique to your needs that have not been addressed in any materials you've looked at.

Also, be sure to use this opportunity to probe for a deeper analysis of your subject and to search for the significance of the information you've acquired so far. For example, if your research on the airline industry turns up the fact that "currently, corporations do not negotiate with airlines for volume discounts," you'll want to find out *the reason why not* from the experts. If, in your study of the problems of the elderly, you discover that Medicare payments are planned to be reduced, you'll want to dig out *the implications of that policy* once it's instituted.

When you make up your questions, you should also consider what kinds of queries best probe a particular source's specific area of expertise. Let's say you had to find out everything you could

about the subject of tents. If you are interviewing a product design expert at a leading manufacturer, a question about the characteristics of various tent materials would be very appropriate to that source's expertise. If the next expert you interviewed was a top-notch camper, then a question about efficient strategies for quickly setting up a tent would be very productive. Of course, if you value a particular source's overall knowledge, there is nothing wrong with asking questions outside his or her exact expertise. But it is important to think carefully beforehand about what a particular source's real specialties are, and then try to zero in on them.

I've found that it's helpful to actually write up a list of all your questions and have them in front of you when speaking to an expert. (If you plan to contact an expert by mail, you can write up and send the questions; see page 225 for more on phone versus mail contacts.) The purpose of writing up your questions is to allow you to do all your planning and thinking ahead of time. This way, during the conversation, you'll have time to concentrate on what the expert is saying. You won't have to worry about what to ask next, or whether you've asked all your questions, because they will be written out on a sheet of paper in front of you. Each time you ask a question, just cross it off your list.

TIP: Sound Natural
• Try to avoid making your discussion sound like you're reading a list of questions—it's better to sound natural.

Once you've written up the questionnaire, you're ready for the talk.

SELECTING THE FIRST EXPERT TO SPEAK WITH

How do you decide which expert to talk to first? I've found that it's usually not a good idea to contact the leading expert in the field first. It's normally better to wait until after you've spoken with

some other people. This way, by the time you speak with the premier expert, you'll know enough about the subject to ask the most incisive and probing questions, rather than basic questions you can get answered by other sources.

A good type of first source to contact is often a nontechnical person, for example, someone who has written a clear and concise article that provides an overview of the field or someone in an association's educational division. As you learn more and become more confident, you can speak with the more technical experts in the field.

NOTE TAKING VS. TAPE-RECORDING

Finally, the last decision to make before you actually talk to the expert is whether to take notes or tape the conversation. This decision really comes down to a personal preference. I prefer note taking; to me, it seems like a bother to set up a tape recorder and then play back the tape to hunt through the whole conversation to find significant statements. I find it easier and more efficient to quickly jot down the important points as the expert makes them. The information is then right in front of me on a piece of paper, ready to be used whenever I need it. But if you prefer taping, you can buy devices at electronics stores that attach to the phone receiver and tape the conversation. You should inform the person that you are making a tape. (That's another reason I'm not crazy about taping. Many people get nervous and withhold information.)

A couple of strategies on note taking: Try not to make your notes too cryptic. Write them as if you were penning them for another person. Otherwise you may later find yourself desperate-

---

TIP: Tapes Plus Notes
• If you do decide to tape, you can make it easy to find specific statements by using a tape recorder with a numerical indexing counter. Whenever the expert makes an important remark, just jot down the number displayed. Later you can locate those statements simply by fast-forwarding the recorder to the numbers you noted.

ly trying to decipher your own handwriting. Also, it really does help to read over your notes immediately after the interview is over; they will make a lot more sense to you than if you read them a day or two later. Another benefit of reading notes immediately is that sometimes during an information interview you'll be writing so fast that you won't be able to write full sentences. Immediately after the conversation the details are still fresh in your mind, and you'll be able to fill in the gaps.

MAKING CONTACT

Most people think that it's very hard to reach experts. Not true. It may take a little persistence, or a bit of digging, but that's about it. As mentioned previously, most experts are not celebrities, and they can be reached easily. It's also true that people who are fairly prominent can often be reached without extraordinary effort. The trick is simply to try. Let's look at a couple of examples.

I recently needed to find information on wasteful purchasing practices going on within the U.S. Department of Defense (remember the $600 ashtray and the $400 hammer?). One day there was an article on this topic on the front page of *The New York Times*. The writer was identified with a byline at the beginning of the article, and I decided to give him a call. *The New York Times* switchboard operator asked me whom I wished to speak with, and I gave her the writer's name. She rang his direct line, he picked up his phone, and our conversation began.

So what? The point is that, although this writer was of no particular fame or prominence, many of us would incorrectly assume that it's a big hassle or even impossible to talk to someone writing front-page stories for the *Times*. But it's usually simple to do so. It's easy to forget that most of these "experts" like the rest of us sit in an office, with a phone on their desk. When it rings, they answer it. This isn't to say that you'll get right through to a national figure, but even then, you still never know. I once heard the story of a resident of New York who had some kind of complaint against his state government. So he decided one evening to call Governor Cuomo in Albany and air his grievance. Cuomo was working late that day,

223

heard his phone ringing, picked it up, and spoke with the resident. Nobody likes to hear a ringing phone. . . especially one's own!

But most experts are not famous, and you won't even need extra luck to get hold of them. What you will need, however, is a little patience. Don't get too upset if you keep missing someone, or if you get transferred on the phone a few times. This is part of the process. If you can accept that, you'll be better off.

Finally, try not to be too intimidated about calling an expert. If you think about it, you really have nothing to lose.

The following are a number of strategies that will help you make contact with the experts you need.

Finding Phone Numbers and Addresses

What do you do if you read an article that cites an expert but does not tell you where he or she works or can be contacted? If you run into this problem, you'll want to contact the magazine or journal and have a little patience. For example, I recently was researching the subject of "finding free software" and found a very interesting article in *Inc.* magazine that quoted an expert on the topic. Unfortunately, the article did not say where this person worked or where he could be reached. And to top it off, there was no writer's byline accompanying the article.

I decided to call up *Inc.* magazine to try and track down the expert. I found *Inc.*'s phone number by checking the masthead and then called the magazine and asked to be connected with the editorial department. A woman answered the phone, and I gave her the issue's date, the page number of the story, and the head-line. She then checked her files, found the writer of the piece, and gave me that reporter's direct phone number. I called the writer and told her what I was trying to find. She was able to look up the story in her files and inform me that the expert was a professor at the University of Texas. She gave me his phone number.

The lesson is, if you have trouble figuring out where to find an expert, don't be afraid to contact the source that cited that person to get the necessary information to track him or her down.

Phone Calls vs. Letters vs. E-mail

Is it better to write or telephone experts? And what about E-mail? My own recommendation is to use the telephone whenever possible. It's faster, and, more important, you can have a dialogue. You can ask questions, respond to what the expert says, pick up nuances, and do so much more than can be done by mail.

TIP: When to Write
• There may be certain cases in which a letter is more appropriate. If you want to reach a superstar celebrity, for example, you're not as likely to get that person on the phone. If you do write, keep your letter simple and short, and don't ask for a lot. Make it as easy as possible for the person to respond. Enclose a stamped, self-addressed envelope. Another tip is when writing to an organization or business for information, write to the top or one of the top people. Your letter will then be funneled to the appropriate office "lower down" and will receive more attention since it came down from a higher office.

Phone calls are also more demanding of experts than letters, which actually works in your favor. One frequently consulted expert in microcomputer technology who lives in Southern California told me that it's always much more difficult to say no to a person on the phone than to a letter, which may sit for some time before being answered.

E-mail is a more modern option, and it offers a few advantages, too. Although I still prefer using the telephone, because it lets me conduct a more natural dialog, I have found that E-mail can be useful for contacting people that are extremely busy and/or for those who are accustomed to doing most of their correspondence electronically. There are some people who you would find extremely difficult to track down by phone but who will check their E-mail every day and quickly respond. I've found that the easiest way to find someone's E-mail address is just by telephoning that person's office and asking to speak to his or her assistant or secretary, and then simply asking. There are E-mail directories on the Web that can be worth trying (for example, Four11 at http://www.four11.com), but these can be spotty in their coverage or contain older, out-of-date data.

TIPS: Cutting Phone Costs

If you are concerned about running up big phone bills by telephoning experts, here are a few tips to keep costs down:

• Some companies and organizations have a toll-free 800 number but do not publicize it well. Call 800–555–1212 to find out if there is a listing for the organization you want to contact.

• If you need to call an out-of-state organization, and it is large, it may have a closer branch office. Check the listings for the larger cities closer to you.

• Send an E-mail message with your questions. Make it as personal as possible, since you don't want the recipient to confuse it with junk E-mail!

Is there a best time of day to call? One *Fortune* 500 executive told me that he responds better to unsolicited inquiry calls early in the morning. He says that early in the day he's fresher, and that no unanticipated meetings or little crises have had time to come up and push his schedule back. Although this executive's preference is clearly a personal one, I would agree that many people respond best to early morning calls. As for the best day of the week to call, the standard advice is never to call first thing Monday morning, or on Friday afternoon. (In the summertime, you may want to avoid calling anytime on Friday—especially in the warmer parts of the country.)

Okay, now for a popular question: How do you "get past" the secretary? First of all, unless you're calling a very high level official—say, a company's chief executive or someone very near the top—the secretary is really not so much of a barrier. In fact, a survey done by a temporary personnel service revealed that 68 percent of top executives' incoming calls are *not* screened by a secretary or assistant.

Persistence will eventually get you the person you want. But if you do run into secretarial problems, here is some advice:

• If you're returning the boss's call, be sure to say so. That should get you through automatically. Similarly, it can help if you were referred by an office or person "higher up."

• It can help if your call sounds pressing or dramatic. For example, if you're in New York, and the secretary is in California, be sure you say that you're calling long-distance.

- Politely explain to the secretary why it could be in the boss's best interest to take the call. For example, "his views on the subject may not be correctly represented," "his competitors are all included and his firm will not be represented," and so on.
- Try to place your call when the secretary is out of the office and the boss must pick up his or her own phone. Usually the best time is right before or right after regular working hours, when the secretary has not arrived or has just left. Lunch hours are another possibility but may not be quite as fruitful.
- Another, and probably better, approach is to think of the secretary as an ally and not an enemy. Try to get the secretary interested and enthused about what you're doing. Explain why you're trying to reach the boss, what you hope to get out of the conversation, and why the project is so important to you. If the secretary gets interested in what you are doing, you should find access to the boss easier. (You may also get additional background information that will help you with your upcoming conversation.)

Although one school of thought is that it's best to be gruff with secretaries, it seems much nicer to be extra pleasant instead. One researcher I know told me that when she speaks to secretaries she always refers to them as "assistants."

If you really get stuck and can't seem to get to the boss at all, the next best thing to do is to ask to speak to his or her staff associate or assistant. Often you can get much of the same information from this person. In fact, occasionally you'll find that assistants actually know more details, and if there are questions they can't answer, you'll probably be turned over to the boss.

Here are some points to remember if you're having trouble getting your expert on the phone:

- If the person is out of the office when you call, it is generally preferable to try phoning again rather than leaving a message—this is to avoid being called when you are unprepared. But it is certainly not unacceptable to leave your phone number for a return call. As mentioned earlier, it's fine to do this, as long as you leave an encouraging message. If the person does not get back to you, just try again.

- Try calling a related office. Often, someone who works nearby will know the person you're trying to reach and will be able to pass along your message.
- Double-check the original source where you obtained the expert's location and phone number to make sure there was no mistake.
- Be patient. Keep plugging. You'll find that you'll almost always get to the person you need *if* you're persistent enough.

Sometimes you know *where* you're likely to find an expert (e.g., a particular company or association), but you don't have anyone's name. Here are some strategies for finding an expert in these cases:

- If you know the name of the department in a company that can help you, ask to be connected with the "director" of that office. If you don't have a department in mind, ask to be connected with "public affairs" or "public relations." Although a spokesperson there will probably give you fewer details than someone who works in another department, you may still get some helpful information. Calling the public affairs or public relations department is also helpful when your inquiry relates to something that affects the company as a whole; for example, if you wanted to find out about a company's new product line or the closing of a branch office.
- When calling an organization's general phone number, be careful how you phrase your information request to the switchboard operator. This person is usually very busy and will not have the time to help you figure out who you want to speak with.

Let's say you need to find out about new technologies in light-bulbs. An excellent information source would be a major lightbulb manufacturer like General Electric. If you called up GE's main number and asked the switchboard operator, "Who can I speak with that can help me find out about new technologies in light-bulbs?" you risk getting a discouraging "Sorry, I don't know" or, if you're lucky, "I can connect you with someone who can take your name and address and mail you some of our sales brochures." That's not exactly what you wanted. So, instead, try to help the

switchboard operator by providing some guidance as to where to send you. For example, you might say, "I have a technical question on your incandescent lightbulb products. Which department can help me?" Now the operator can feel more comfortable switching your call to a technical or engineering department. Or describe by function the "type" of person you want to reach: for example, "the person in charge of selecting new store sites" or "the manager of your computer systems." You can even try to guess the department you need—for example, by asking for "new product development"—and you may discover that the firm actually has a department like the one you guessed! Or the operator may find a similar-sounding department—for example, "planning and development"—and ask if he or she should connect you there. If it seems close, you should agree. Once connected, ask to speak with a manager or director of that division and pose your question. If that individual can't help you, he or she may be able to refer you to the appropriate division.

If you're calling a professional association, nonprofit organization, or public institution, there are certain departments common to many of these bodies that are especially fruitful information sources. For example:

The in-house library. The reference librarian is an excellent source of information and can search published resources for you.

The education department. This department is typically found in associations. Its role is to inform members and the public of the resources of the organization.

The publications department. Here you can usually get an index of what the organization publishes, and sometimes what's about to be published.

There is one final important point to keep in mind when you're trying to make contact with an expert. When you talk to the switchboard operator, an administrator, or whoever else picks up the phone, don't be so quick to take "We can't help you" or "I don't know" as an answer to your request for an expert. Often the problem is just that you've been unlucky enough to catch someone in a bad mood or someone who is not too knowledgeable about the organization's resources. Try politely rephrasing your question a couple of times if necessary to get some help or ask, "Is there

another person in the organization I can speak with who might know?" If this does not work, then consider calling another time, when someone else may answer.

The person you speak with initially may want to turn you over to a publications department. This may not be so bad, because you may find that there indeed are some relevant publications available that will help you. But do not feel obligated to end your search at this point. You should still ask to see if there is an expert available.

8

Talking with Experts
Strategies for Getting Inside Information

QUICK PREVIEW: TALKING WITH EXPERTS

- Never assume an expert won't talk. Most of the time the person will be happy to help you.
- Present yourself properly to the expert by identifying who you are and by asking if it's a good time to talk. Be serious, get to the point, admit any ignorance on the subject, and ask *specific* questions. Let the expert steer the conversation; put off tough questions until later.
- Think of ways you can heighten an expert's interest in what you are doing. For example, can you publicize his or her work to others or share any information that you come up with?
- During the conversation, question things that don't make sense to you, ask for definitions of technical terms, and see if the expert can help you define what it is that you really need to find out.
- Once the conversation is moving, get control and steer it to where you want it to go.

(continued)

- At the end of the conversation, ask if there is anything important that hasn't been discussed, request written information, and ask for the names of other experts.
- As you learn more about the subject, update your questions. Periodically review your overall goals and strategies.
- Always keep the "big picture"—your ultimate objective in the information-finding project—in mind as you proceed.
- If you encounter an expert who's suspicious of you, try gaining his or her confidence by revealing more about yourself and by offering to show a copy of anything you write up.
- If you encounter a hostile source, try to build up trust. Consider sending a written inquiry, share your findings, be as nice as possible, and let the person know how he or she is acting.
- Use the strategies outlined in this chapter to handle those experts who say, "I don't have time" and "I don't know," and who "tell no evil."
- You can try to obtain "sensitive" information by rephrasing questions, asking peripheral questions, asking for "feelings," taking a position on an issue, and keeping the conversation "off the record."
- You may confront ethical dilemmas when attempting to obtain "inside information" from knowledgeable sources. Often these dilemmas involve the issue of misrepresenting your affiliation and/or the purpose of your project. If faced with such ethical concerns, you should first make sure you've exhausted all public sources, identified easily interviewable experts, and confirmed the importance of the data you are seeking. Don't assume you need a ruse to get information—the truth usually works fine. Misrepresenting yourself is not advisable.

After you've managed to make contact with the expert, the next trick is to get that person to talk to you, and share his or her knowledge. Although most people assume that experts are too busy and uninterested to spend time helping strangers find information, *this is not usually true.*

Whether the topic is fine china, poodle breeding, or Norwegian economics, experts have a great interest in their topic, and they enjoy discussing it. Remember, these people have devoted a great portion of their lives to learning and exploring their field. When someone approaches them needing information, they're almost always pleased to oblige.

Adding to their inclination to talk is the fact that, no matter how mundane a subject may seem, there is always some kind of controversy that excites the experts. For example, I recently discovered in the course of researching the sexy topic of water meters that an intense battle was being fought between those favoring plastic meters and those who liked bronze ones! The important point to remember is, never assume someone won't talk to you. Always try.

Unfortunately, though, since the first edition of this book was published in 1987, it has become increasingly the case that

workers have become more and more overloaded and have less time to spare. This has made it somewhat more of a challenge to get people to carve a chunk of time out of their very busy schedule to speak with you at length. I've found that it has become quite important, then, to use the initial phone call to set up a phone appointment for sometime in the near future, where the expert can then block out a specific time when he or she knows your are going to call. Many people will also appreciate it if you could fax or E-mail your questions ahead of time, as this will also allow them to prepare for your interview and think more carefully about your questions.

Here are some other, more general strategies for approaching experts to smooth the interview procedure and encourage their cooperation.

PRESENTING YOURSELF TO THE EXPERT

Okay, the secretary has just told you that the boss will be on the line shortly. The expert picks up the phone and says hello. Now what?

No, don't hang up. Here's what to do to get the conversation off to a smooth start:

Identify Yourself. You've got to identify yourself—clearly and precisely—and explain why you are calling. This is very important to do to allay the natural suspicion we all have when a stranger contacts us. Don't start off your conversation by saying, "Hello. Can I ask you some questions about oil futures trading?" Infinitely better is, "My name is Karen Johnson, and I'm calling from (hometown or firm and city). I'm currently collecting information on the benefits of oil futures market trading (for a possible book or for a report for my firm or to learn about career opportunities), and I read your recent article titled 'Why Trade Oil Futures?' I wonder if I could have just a couple of minutes to ask you a few questions?"

It's also helpful to explain your goals and which sources you've already checked. The more information the expert has on why

you're calling, the easier his or her job will be, and the more you'll get out of the conversation.

Ask the Expert If It's a Good Time to Talk. You don't want to interview someone who's in a rush to get it over with. If it's a bad time, set up an appointment for a formal phone interview at a specific time a day or two in the future. This gives importance to your phone interview and legitimizes it. In fact, it may not be such a bad idea to make an initial call solely to set up an appointment for a future formal phone interview.

Be Serious. You need to convey the impression that your project is important to you, not a lark or a trifling matter.

TIP: Be Sensitive
• When presenting yourself, don't make the mistake I once did of conveying the impression that you're attempting to become quickly knowledgeable in the expert's field. I had about eight weeks to write a comprehensive report on the topic of micrographics. I explained this to one of my first expert sources. He refused to help and told me that such a project couldn't be done. He was wrong, but I learned my lesson. It's kind of insulting to say to somebody who's been in a field for twenty, maybe thirty, or more years that you are going to become an "instant expert" in a matter of weeks. Instead, it's much wiser to say that you're *collecting* information and advice from experts in the field, or reporting on what the experts are saying, or anything along those lines. In essence, that is really what you are doing anyway.

Get to the Point. People want to know why you're calling. I find it's more relaxing and enjoyable to save friendly conversation about the weather and so forth until after the interview is completed.

Admit Your Ignorance. If you are unsure about your subject and do not feel confident, it is *much better to simply admit that to the expert up front*. It's fine to say something like "I am just starting to learn about this subject, so please excuse me if my questions sound elementary." The worst mistake you could make is to fumble around trying to sound knowledgeable with a lot of "uhs," "well I guess sos," and so on. These only serve to arouse

suspicions—the expert may think you are trying to hide something! If you are asked a question to which you don't know the answer, simply say "I don't know" rather than trying to make believe you do know! Don't feel embarrassed or guilty that you do not know more—the whole idea of finding information is to learn! Also, once the expert knows that you are a novice, he or she is more likely to avoid using jargon and buzzwords and will attempt to explain concepts to you more clearly.

Be Specific. This is quite important, especially at the beginning of the conversation. Here's an example of what I mean. Suppose the topic you need to find out about is the "future of baseball in this country." If you began your conversation by posing such an overwhelmingly broad question, you'd be starting off on the wrong foot. It's too difficult and vague a question to answer, and your source will feel on the spot. Instead, start off with a more specific question that can be answered easily, such as "Do you think that the drug problem in baseball has lessened during the last few years?" or "Are the followers of the baseball scene predicting that a new commissioner will have an impact on the players' rising salaries?" Even if these questions are not vital to you, they will get the ball rolling, which *is* vital to the conversation. Later, especially toward the end of the conversation, when a rapport has been established, you can throw in the "future of baseball" question. By then, the expert is warmed up, and the answers given to your earlier questions make him or her more responsive.

Follow the Expert's Lead. At the beginning, let the source take the lead in directing the conversation. If the person feels comfortable talking about something that's not exactly on the right track for you, show interest anyway. Later on in the discussion you can redirect the conversation to cover the precise areas you are interested in.

TIP: Be Nice!
• Another important point is attitude. The importance of politeness should be obvious, but it's a point worth stressing. Your attitude really will make a difference. Don't ever be demanding or impatient. Try to sound confident, cheerful, and professional—present yourself as though you were interviewing for a job.

Delay Tough Questions. Don't begin the conversation with questions that may stump your source. If you think you've asked such a stumper, don't press for an answer. Drop it, and go to another question. Later on in the conversation you can try bringing it back up. Similarly, if you think any of your questions could be considered offensive, save these for the end, too.

GETTING THE EXPERT INTERESTED

Everyone wants to feel important. You can help the discussion along by making the source feel good. Show some sincere appreciation, give some praise, and tell the expert how helpful the information and advice is.

A good way to get experts to open up is to heighten their interest in what you are doing. Here are a few strategies:

- As mentioned earlier, be sure you figure out in advance any way the expert will be helped by talking to you.

TIP: Don't "Survey"
- People normally don't like to be "surveyed," but they like to give "opinions" or their "thoughts" on a matter. It's more personal.

- If you work for or are on assignment for a well-known publication or company, it may help to mention it. Often people feel excited about being consulted by a prestigious organization. This doesn't mean that experts always prefer talking to someone calling from a well-known organization. Some people are actually *less* disposed, either because they prefer to do a "public service" and help out an amateur information seeker or because they do not want their remarks to be widely circulated. It's a personal preference that will vary among your sources.
- A good way to heighten the expert's enthusiasm is to let the person know of any interesting bits of information you've come up with so far in your research. Often the information

you've discovered could be used by the expert for his or her own purposes. Similarly, you should offer to share your final findings with the expert. Remember, you're doing a lot of in-depth digging in the expert's field; what you ultimately come up with should be of interest to that person. (Note: Again, this can be a sensitive area. Don't make it sound as though your research will be groundbreaking. Just humbly offer to send whatever information you come up with.)

TIP: Be Persistent
• If your first couple of interviews don't go as smoothly as you hoped, don't despair. It's really a numbers game, and the process is such that some interviews will be great, some good, and some not so good.

• Attempt to interest the expert enough so that he or she really *wants* to help you. For example, if you wanted to interview an interior design consultant about some art-oriented question, you could get the person interested in talking to you by letting him or her know that talking to you will enable the viewpoint of a representative of the profession to be "heard" in your project. A different approach is to appeal a bit to ego. When you let a source know that your work is identifying the very leading experts in the field, it is very flattering, and the source will naturally want to be included in such a listing. It's also complimentary to ask for someone's ideas on a subject, especially if you mention that you'll be passing along those thoughts to others as expert opinion.

• Finally, try to get a feel for whether your expert would be excited about being quoted or would prefer to remain anonymous.

GETTING THE MOST
OUT OF THE INTERVIEW

Here are some specific pointers to keep in mind during the actual conversation:

Question Things! If an expert says something that doesn't sound right, or that contradicts something else you've been told, ask for more information. (For example, if an expert tells you matter-of-factly that so-and-so's theory on the link between attitude and illness is preposterous, ask the expert *why* he or she does not believe it. What are the *reasons?*) Questioning statements with a "why," instead of accepting them at face value, is one of the very best ways to deepen your understanding of any subject. Don't let questions "hang" unanswered. Politely press for reasons and explanations.

Probe for Specifics. Try not to accept general, unproven statements. If an expert on computers tells you that IBM makes the best computer on the market, ask him or her to tell you *why*. If you're then told that it's superior because the firm provides better service, ask *how* it provides better service. If the expert tells you that IBM's service is better because its response time to problems is quicker than that of its competitors, find out *how much* quicker. Again, if an expert tells you that it would be extremely unlikely for someone to get sick from eating too much of a certain vitamin, ask whether, in fact, it has *ever* happened; if so, what was the situation or condition that made it occur.

Ask for Definitions of Technical Terms. If the expert throws in any terms or buzzwords you don't understand, ask for a definition. Asking for explanations is nothing to be embarrassed about. It may be important for you to know the definitions of certain words, as they may be standard terminology in the field. Tell the expert that you want to define the term precisely but in layman's language.

Ask for Help. Early on in your project, you'll be trying to figure out exactly what you need to know to understand your field. You can enlist the experts' assistance in better defining exactly what you need to find out. If you have a good rapport with an expert, you can ask that person to help you isolate the critical issues on which you need to become knowledgeable.

Let's say you're digging up information on dream research. Initially you probably do not know what the important issues are in that field and may not even be sure what questions to ask. But

an expert will know the issues. He or she may say something like, "Well, if you want to find out about the latest in dream research, you should ask experts about some recent findings in 'lucid dreaming' and discoveries about the Senoi Indian dream techniques." What you're doing here is asking the expert to tell you which issues are important in the field, and what *questions* you should be asking other experts. In a sense, you are trying to find out the answer to the question, What should I be finding out? And there's nobody better qualified to tell you than the experts themselves. (Because this type of question is somewhat offbeat, you should not begin your conversation with it, but work it in toward the middle or end.)

Keep in Control. You've got to keep the interview on track. Occasionally a source may think that you are interested in a subject that is actually of no concern to you. He or she will try to be helpful but may go off on a tangent and talk a blue streak about something of no interest to you. Listen politely, but soon you'll have to rein the expert in and ask a question you *are* interested in. It's up to you to keep the conversation on course. You have a limited amount of time for each discussion, and it's important to make the most of it. Otherwise you'll be wasting your time and the expert's time. (Note: As discussed earlier, at the *very beginning* of a conversation you may want to allow the expert to talk about almost anything just to get the ball rolling. But soon you've got to move in and get the conversation on track.)

Wrap it Up. *At the very end of an information interview*, there are three questions you should ask:

- *"Is there anything important we haven't discussed?"* It's possible that your source has some additional important information to discuss but hasn't mentioned it because you didn't ask. This provides the expert with the opportunity to talk about it.
- *"Do you have any written information you can send me?"* Often the expert has written articles on the subject or keeps clippings of relevant materials.
- *"Who else do you recommend that I speak with?"* This is an extremely important question that you should be sure to ask all your sources. There are many reasons why this is such an

important question. One is that it is a quick way to get the name and phone number of another expert. Even more important, however, is the fact that you now have a referral person you can cite when you contact the new expert. Be sure to let that person know that you were referred by the mutual acquaintance. If you leave a message for the expert, it's worth mentioning the contact's name in the message to encourage a call back. There's almost no better way to reach someone than through a direct referral like this.

Another reason that it's so important to ask to be referred to other experts is that often the more people you are referred to, the more likely it is that you'll be speaking with someone who has the specific expertise you seek. Say that you have to find out all about new technologies in camera light meters. And say that you've decided to call a camera manufacturers association to try to find the information. Well, maybe the association's technical staffperson Tom will tell you that he keeps up only with general industry developments. But when you ask him for a contact, he refers you to his friend Pat at Nikon, who is involved more in day-to-day technological advances. You thank Tom and give Pat a call. Well, it turns out that Pat does have some good technological know-how, and you get some information from her, but she's not a real specialist in light metering components. She refers you to Bill, who heads that division, and he, in turn, refers you to the expert, Joe, on his staff.

So the process is such that when you get referrals, you often zero in on someone whose expertise is more appropriate to your inquiry. (The process can be frustrating, too: It often results in your best sources coming at the very *end* of your information search, when you are trying to wrap it all up!)

TIP: Confirm Your Facts
• The end of a conversation is a good time to clear up any confusing points the expert may have made during the discussion. You can use this time to confirm important facts, state your understanding of the issues, and get them verified.

STAYING ON COURSE AND REDIRECTING FOCUS

Throughout your interviews, it's important to keep on the course you've charted. To do so means asking the right questions and directing your energies to get you where you want to go.

The questions you pose to the experts will need to be constantly revised and updated as your interviews progress. Some of your simpler questions will be answered the same way by everyone, and it won't be necessary to keep asking them. At the same time, you'll also find that you'll have to add *new* questions as you go along and experts bring up issues that you weren't aware of. You'll notice as you speak with the experts that the important issues will emerge automatically as their conversation gravitates to critical matters. You'll then be able to incorporate these issues into your questionnaire. You'll want to create questions about these new issues and ask them of future sources. So your questionnaire will be a flexible one, and it will be modified throughout your information search to reflect the major issues as you see them emerge.

If you come to a point where you start to predict the answers from the experts, it's a sign that it's time to step back a little from the information-gathering project and assess where it's going. Think about whether it's necessary to alter the direction you're heading in and, if so, in what way. Think about whether your goals have changed since you began the project and, if so, how. Are there gaps in your information that need to be filled? Are there new angles to explore? Think about any new types of sources that you haven't tried yet that should be approached. Take stock of where you are and how things are going.

For example, let's say you're digging up information on careers in journalism. After interviewing a dozen or so experts, the time is ripe to assess where you stand in the project. As you step back, maybe you realize that, although you've interviewed people in the newspaper and magazine industry, you haven't spoken with anyone in television journalism; your efforts can now be directed toward reaching those sources. Maybe you'll discover that your overall goals have changed, too. When you started the project, you were interested in finding information about all types of journal-

ism careers. Now, after a dozen interviews, you realize that you want to pursue information specifically about the career of newswriting. So you redirect your questions and choose sources to reflect that new goal.

TIP: Read Your Old Notes
• Reading over the notes you've taken during interviews up until this point will stimulate you to think of new questions and fresh angles you haven't yet pursued.

Keep the "Big Picture" in Mind. At all times during your project, keep your ultimate goal in mind as a guiding force. Try not to get sidetracked into pursuing routes that have nothing to do with why you are conducting your information search. If, for example, your goal is to find information that compares the quality of the various long-distance carriers, and you're talking to a telecommunications expert, try to avoid being led into a long discussion on, say, the legal precedent behind the breakup of AT&T. Although that topic is related to long-distance service, it really is not pertinent to your specific goals. It's fine to change your goals as you go along, but just be sure that all your activities serve that goal.

CRACKING THE TOUGH NUTS

Now, what do you do if you have a source who's really a tough nut to crack and it's important that this person share his or her information?

The great majority of experts *will* talk to you and give you the answers you need. But it's possible to run into someone who is not so helpful. There are a number of reasons why someone would be unhelpful. Maybe you've called at a bad time. Maybe the person is simply someone who is not the helpful type. Or maybe you've encountered someone who is protective of his or her knowledge and doesn't want to share it.

Whatever the reason, if you encounter someone like this, sometimes the easiest thing to do is to abandon the interview and move

on to the next one. As mentioned earlier, not *all* of your conversations with experts are going to be perfect, so it's no big deal to drop a difficult one. But what if this one is important to you? In that case, you shouldn't give up. There are a number of strategies you can use to turn a difficult interview into a productive one.

TIP: Handling a Hostile Source

• How do you handle a hostile source? It's very rare to encounter someone who is outright belligerent, but it can happen.

Chances are, the person is hostile because he or she is a little nervous and suspicious of you. One thing you can do to help allay suspicions is to explain as specifically as possible *who* will be receiving the information that you are gathering.

Another strategy is to offer to send a written inquiry on your letterhead or your company's letterhead. There are a couple of reasons why a letter is more reassuring to a hostile source. For one thing, an expert who sees a specific letterhead feels more certain that you are who you say you are—letters are more "solid" than phone calls. In addition, letters provide the person with time to think. One reason a source may act hostile is fear of saying something later regretted. Now a response can be made more carefully.

It's possible that your source is hostile because you're being viewed as a competitor of some kind. There are a couple of ways you can try to overcome this problem. One strategy, if your work really does compete in some way with the expert's, is to be sure to offer to share your findings. Another strategy is to downplay the competition by emphasizing those aspects of your project that differ from the expert's.

What if all these strategies fail and your source is still hostile? Be *extra nice.* I've found that if you are unrelentingly nice—even if it kills you!—most of the time you will disarm the hostility. It may not be easy to do, but if a hostile source's information is very important to you, just grit your teeth and smile.

If this fails, too, you have little choice but to politely let the source know how he or she is acting. You might say something like, "It sounds like this is a bad time for you. Would it be better if I call back?" Or you can be blunt. One time I was interviewing a vice president of a major tobacco company in hopes of finding out more about its innovative use of copiers. For some unknown reason, the vice president was very belligerent toward me. Finally, I just asked, "Why are you so hostile?" That question confronted the issue in a nonaggressive way and let the man realize how he was being perceived. He then became much more helpful.

Remember, hostile sources are *rare.* The great majority of people are very helpful.

In this section we'll examine the ways to get through the rockiest interviews. This includes strategies for dealing with reluctant sources and strategies for dealing with difficult questions and topics.

Building Up Trust

A source who is unwilling to talk to you is often suspicious. Even if you've identified yourself clearly and explained why you are seeking information, the person may still be suspicious of who you *really* are and what you're going to do with the information. From the expert's perspective, you are just an anonymous voice on the phone; you could be a competitor or someone up to no good.

One strategy you can take to help allay suspicions is to simply stay on the phone longer and keep talking. Reveal more about yourself and why you're gathering information. Slowly, the expert will get a better feeling for who you are, and you'll become less anonymous and less threatening. As you reveal more about yourself and what you're doing, the unhelpful expert often loosens up somewhat and starts to talk.

Another way you can calm the fears of a suspicious source is by offering to send a copy of anything you write before it's published or presented to anyone. A big concern for some people is being misquoted or misunderstood. Some experts feel better if they know that they can correct errors or have some control over their remarks. In fact, their review can benefit you, too, because it should serve as a check on the accuracy of your information.

Specific Problem Areas

Here are ways to handle some common tough interview spots:

The "I Don't Have Time to Talk" Expert. What do you do if your source says he or she doesn't have time to speak with you? One strategy is to ask to be given just a minute or two. This will reassure the source that the whole morning won't be used up on the phone with you. But an interesting thing you'll find is that once that expert starts talking, most of the time he or she will continue to talk for twenty, thirty, forty minutes, or more!

Another way to reassure experts is to tell them to tell *you* when they want the discussion to end. If you give them the control of stopping the conversation, they're likely to be reassured.

A different tactic is to set up a future day and time for a formal phone interview. This enables the source to budget some time to allow for a few minutes with you.

The "I Don't Know" Expert. How do you handle a source who is answering a lot of your questions with "I don't know" and you think the person really does know. Sometimes the "I don't know" syndrome occurs when an expert does not want to mislead you with an answer that's not precise. But often all you're really looking for is a general idea. If this is the case, try asking for a "rough estimate" or a "ballpark figure." This will take the pressure off your source to be exact, and it may yield the general information that you're looking for.

The Expert Who Will Tell No Evil. Sometimes in your information interviews, you'll need to find out the negative or bad side of an issue. For example, you are interviewing a trustee of a college, and you want to find out what the school's problems are. Or let's say you're interviewing a representative of the American Advertising Executives Association, and you want to find out the negative aspects of a career in advertising. In both of these cases, the sources will probably feel uncomfortable giving you this negative information. In general, people prefer telling you the good, rather than the bad. It's safer, especially when one is representing a particular institution, product, or cause.

Here's a way to make it easier for the expert to reveal the negative. Ask for "the best points and the worst points," or the "strengths and weaknesses" of the matter in question. By asking experts to talk about—and indeed emphasize if they wish—the good, you allow them to dilute the bad, making it easier to divulge.

The "Too Smart" Expert. Occasionally, the very leading expert in a field may be so intimately knowledgeable of all the details of a subject and so aware of all the permutations that affect it that the person will sincerely have difficulty answering basic questions. For example, once I was writing a report on how companies

can reduce their travel and entertainment expenses. One of the premier experts in the field answered many of my questions with, "That is too complicated a matter to respond to simply" or "There is no one answer to that question" or "It really depends on the situation." Although he was technically correct, he was unable to come down from his lofty plane and work a little to provide some kind of help. If you get an expert like this, don't give up. You should still be able to glean some good information out of the conversation and get a feel for what the "big picture" looks like.

Obtaining "Sensitive" Information

In many information searches, it becomes necessary at some point to ask an expert about some controversial or sensitive matter. Although you'll be surprised at how often people will freely discuss this type of information, you'll want to have some strategies for getting as much cooperation as possible.

Don't Begin with Sensitive Questions. You should not begin your conversation with a controversial or sensitive question. These are best situated in the middle of a conversation when the expert is warmed up a bit and feeling more relaxed. It's also best not to end with a very sensitive question, unless you feel it is so sensitive that it may cause the expert to terminate his or her conversation with you.

Rephrase Questions. If you've asked a controversial question that the expert is unwilling to answer, try posing it in a different form. Let's say you received a "no comment" to your question, "Will Bill Jones be next in line to be president of the National Restaurant Association?" You could then try asking something like "Is Bill Jones a leading contender for the presidency?" or "Will Bill Jones be playing an important role in the association during the next few years?"

Go from the General to the Specific. This is one approach for getting answers to sensitive questions. For example, once I needed to find out how much money, if any, a particular company saved by implementing a "telecommuting" program—that is, a

system where employees can work at home via the use of a computer and a phone line hookup. Instead of asking the company how much money the program had saved, I asked a series of questions: Overall, was the program a plus for the company? Did it save the firm some money? Was it a significant amount? Roughly, about how much did it save?

Ask "Peripheral" Questions. This is a strategy to get bits and pieces of information that may shed light on your query. Again, in the Bill Jones example, you could ask questions about the vice presidency, previous association voting patterns, and so forth to try to piece together a picture.

Ask for Ballpark Figures. When you need to find out some sensitive numerical fact, you may find that it's easier for experts to provide rough estimates or a "range" rather than precise numbers. Another strategy for getting sensitive figures is to suggest a few numbers yourself to get a reaction. Often an expert won't volunteer the information, but will respond to your estimates.

Ask for "Feelings." You may find it easier to get an answer if you try to elicit an emotional response. Ask the person how he or she *personally feels* about a controversial topic.

Take a Position. This is an old news reporter's trick. Suppose you're trying to find out from an oil company executive whether there's any truth to the rumor that the firm is lowering its imports by 2 percent next year. If you bluntly ask the question, you're likely to get a "no comment." Instead, try taking a position on the question—state it as a fact—and continue the conversation. You might say "Since your company will be reducing imports by 2 percent next year, will there be a corresponding increase in domestic production?" Your source may have to bite his tongue to let your assumption go unanswered—especially because he may fear that you will later think you got the information from him! You may not get a definite answer on the subject through this ploy, but you may get more than if you just asked the question bluntly.

Keep Your Conversation "Off the Record." Sometimes an expert source won't mind talking about controversial topics but doesn't want

to be identified as the source or see the remarks in print. If you think this is the case, be certain you assure the expert that his or her remarks will be off the record, if so desired. Most of the time, it doesn't matter a bit to you if a source speaks off the record—you just want to have the information for your own knowledge.

If you decide that under no circumstances will your source divulge the sensitive information you want, you should consider contacting other people who may have access to the same information.

TIP: Negotiate an Agreement

• If you do need to quote a source or write up certain sensitive information, you can often negotiate with the expert how much or what type of information you may use. For example, although an expert may want remarks to be off the record, you might ask to use only one particular statement made during the conversation. Many times you'll discover that the expert will agree. Similarly, you can negotiate exactly how you will identify the source. For example, the expert may not let you use his or her name, but may not mind being identified as "an employee of Jax Manufacturing in Boston," or something similar. The more choices you can give the expert, the more in control the person will feel, and the more comfortable he or she will be about agreeing to some type of attribution. But remember, most of the time it's not necessary to work out attribution arrangements. All you need to do is to get the source to share expertise with you.

Offensive Questions

What do you do if you have a question or remark that you think may offend the source? You should always try to phrase your questions diplomatically to avoid insulting the expert. For example, if someone tells you "It's a scientific fact that wearing wool hats causes baldness," you can express your skepticism politely. You might say ,"Do you think your opinion on this is in the minority? Why don't you think there is more support for this view?"

Here are two other strategies to keep in mind. First, if you think the question is offensive enough to cut off the interview, save it for near the end to prevent the conversation from ending early on.

Second, use another reporter's trick: Pose the question in the third person. Don't, for example, ask, "Since you have never been invited to present your research results to the scientific community, isn't your information of dubious value?" Instead say, "Some people have said that since you have never been invited. . . "

ETHICAL ISSUES IN
OBTAINING SENSITIVE INFORMATION

What do you do if you need to interview someone for information but do not want to tell the person who you are or why you need it? Sometimes this happens when you want "insider" information on a specific firm or competitor company—and the only place to find that information is by talking to individuals who work at that company itself!

This is an issue that professional researchers who conduct "competitive intelligence" have recently been grappling with. (There is even a trade association of competitive intelligence professionals!) It's a tricky issue, because it revolves around the definition of what is and is not misrepresentation. There may be gray areas where the researcher does not out-and-out lie, but is tempted to withhold the "whole" truth out of fear that such disclosure would discourage the source from sharing his or her knowledge.

What should you do if faced with this type of situation? There are a number of questions worth asking yourself:

- Have I truly exhausted all public, published sources? As outlined in this book, there are scores of government documents, computer database records, trade magazine articles, and other public information sources available just for the asking. Make sure you have thoroughly researched the existence of all these potential sources.

- If you are sure no published information exists that can answer your question, try to identify persons you can interview where you feel more comfortable revealing who you are and the purpose of your project. For example, if you need to find out facts about a company's future strategic plans, you

can obtain insights by interviewing Wall Street analysts, trade magazine editors, and other types of experts.

- If those persons still do not have the information you need, ask yourself how vital it really is that you find that specific piece of information. Are there related data that could be helpful? Is there peripheral information from which you can piece together a picture?

- If you are sure that you still need that precise information, you may be convinced that the only way to get it is to misrepresent yourself. But this is not always so. Say, for example, you need information on a competitive company. You just might find that if you call the knowledgeable source, are up front, polite, and gracious, you may get unexpected cooperation! The source may help you for any number of reasons: He or she might have questions to ask you; the person may just enjoy talking; or he or she doesn't think what you are asking is particularly sensitive—who knows! The point is, don't assume you need to make up some ruse—as Mark Twain said, "When in doubt. . . tell the truth." You may be pleasantly surprised at the results!

If, finally, you are certain that the only way to obtain the information you need is by hiding who you are or by making up a story, you should ask yourself whether you really want to take that approach. Here are my arguments as to why misrepresenting yourself or even withholding relevant information (e.g., the nature of your research project) is *not* advisable:

Self-interest

- An unethical research activity may eventually be revealed to others. How will this affect you or your organization's reputation?

- Unethical data-gathering activities will eventually cause organizations to become so suspicious of researchers—with good reason—that sources of information will dry up. The job of the researcher will become much more difficult.

- With no standards set in this area, you and/or your own organization can become a target for unethical information gathering.

Personal Ethics

- Take a hard look to see if any research activity you are considering will violate your own personal code of ethics. For example, most of us

would not consider telephoning someone and misleading them into sending a check for $500. But today, information is as valuable a commodity as money. We would all like an extra $500, but we recognize legitimate boundaries in how to obtain it. Don't the same standards hold true for precious information? You should put yourself in the other person's shoes and ask yourself how *you* would feel if you were the recipient of what you are considering. Would you feel that you were dealt with fairly?

Finally, it is important to remember that just because there are ethical guidelines to follow, excellent research can still be performed by legitimate methods and by intelligent and thoughtful analysis of data.

9

Information Quality

Evaluating Sources and Determining Accuracy

QUICK PREVIEW: INFORMATION QUALITY

- As more information has been created and disseminated, it has become more difficult to distinguish good from bad information.
- When evaluating published documents, consider the *type* of document (whether it is a primary or secondary one) and the purpose of the publication—why is it being published?
- You should also scrutinize what you read to determine whether you are getting all sides of the story and whether the author of the piece is attempting to influence you with loaded words and other techniques.
- Other important considerations when evaluating published information is determining how the information was collected, if the data are presented in a logical and organized manner, and the manner in which the report is marketed.
- Polls and surveys are fraught with hazards. You should be sure to check whether the sponsoring organization is nonpartisan,

(continued)

---

what type of selection criteria was employed for selecting the sample, if any questions are "loaded," and the placement of questions.

- Also ascertain if memories or recollections are asked for and if any of the questions are complex, vague, or ask persons to reveal any sensitive information (all of these can elicit unreliable answers).
- In addition to evaluating published data, you can also evaluate the experts that you interview. Look out for biased sources. Be aware of an expert's affiliations and loyalties. Try to supplement potentially biased sources with more objective ones.
- Beware of those who have a very narrow scope of expertise or who are out of date, too far removed from the subject, unaccountable, or confusing.
- Evaluate your sources by noting whose names are cited frequently in leading trade publications. Ask experts for their opinions of others' work, use certain sources as "yardsticks," and probe for facts behind general statements.
- Evaluating the quality of your information means being a critical thinker. Critical thinking means not just believing something because everyone says it's so, or because something is repeated often or the first opinion you hear. Critical thinking also means questioning, probing, and looking for connections between data until you yourself are convinced of the truth of the matters under investigation.
- In cases where evidence is nonexistent or unconvincing, you can still examine related information to make a rational determination on the validity of the subject under investigation.

ENSURING THE QUALITY OF YOUR INFORMATION

Ironically, as more and more information is created and disseminated, it has become even more difficult to be able to discern the good information from the bad. One of the most critical issues of the information age is information *quality*. Today, the researcher's problem is not simply *where* to find information but how to *evaluate* the accuracy and reliability of the facts and data collected. In a sense, information has become another "commodity," and users need to become "informed consumers"!

The issue of data quality has grown more important with the increase in information available from computer databases and, of course, the Internet. Data viewed on a computer screen may appear more "official" and reliable but, of course, is not—in fact, in certain instances there is room for an increased number of errors. (For more information on reliability of electronic information, see pages 195–198.)

Information accuracy is an important and complex subject, and a full treatment deserves an in-depth and extensive discussion.

Although such a treatment is beyond the scope of this book, some basic advice is provided in the following two sections, "Evaluating Published Sources" (this includes information "published" electronically online) and "Evaluating Experts."

EVALUATING PUBLISHED SOURCES

The following are some key considerations to note when determining the accuracy of published data:

What Is the Type of Document? There is a critical distinction between a *primary* and *secondary* data source. A primary source is the originator of the data, and a secondary source secures the data from the original source. A researcher should never terminate a search with the secondary source. Secondary sources often delete the methods employed in collecting data and sometimes fail to reproduce significant footnotes or comments that may qualify the data in some way.[1]

What Is the Purpose of the Publication? A source is suspect if published to promote sales, to advance the interests of an industrial, commercial, or other group, to present the cause of a political party, or to carry on any sort of propaganda. Also suspect is data published anonymously or by an organization on the defensive, or under conditions that suggest a controversy, or in a form that reveals a strained attempt at "frankness."[2]

Are You Getting All Sides of the Story? Try to determine whether the article, report, or book is presenting only one side of an issue when there is clearly more than one point of view. For example, an article that cites *only* the problems associated with, say, national health insurance, without at least referring to potential benefits could not be viewed as a balanced presentation. That piece may still be useful, however, for example, to learn of the

---

[1]Nemmers and Meyers, quoted in Churchill, Gilbert A., Jr., *Marketing Research: Methodological Foundations* (Hinsdale, Ill.: Dryden Press, 1987).

[2]Ibid.

claims of those opposed to such a program, for finding out about other studies cited, and to obtain leads for further research. The point is, it should not be used as a single source of information.

Note that this issue of "balanced coverage" is tricky, however, and it's not always easy to determine what constitutes balanced coverage. In fact, one can even make the case that presenting both sides of an issue is not always legitimate. For example, if one is writing about a clearly outrageous case of child abuse, does the best coverage give equal time to the abuser to give his or her side of the story? These kinds of questions are thorny journalistic and sociological issues beyond the scope of this book. Suffice it to say: *Be aware* as to whether you are getting all *reasonably legitimate* points of view on an issue, and if it is clear you are not, do not use that source as a definitive one.

Is the Author Trying to Subtly Influence You? It's not enough to determine simply whether coverage of a topic is "balanced"; it's also critical to be able to detect the more subtle ways that an author may be trying to insert his or her views into a piece. Choice of words, placement of names, and other techniques can be employed consciously or unconsciously by the writer to influence the reader.

For example, see how the choice of the following words that mean the same thing can connote totally different feelings and elicit different reactions.

Free enterprise	Capitalism
Persons incarcerated	Criminals
Mixed drinks	Hard liquor
Spiritually renewed	Born again
Stronger defense	More money for missiles
Increased revenues	Higher taxes

Even something as simple as the insertion of quotation marks, or the use of a different word, can subtly change connotations. For example, compare these two sentences:

- John Doe, director of public affairs, said that he was instituting the clean-up committee to make headway in cleaning up the environment.

- John Doe, director of public affairs, claimed that "helping the environment" was the reason he was instituting the clean-up committee.

By setting Doe's words within quotation marks, the writer seems to imply that his remark should not be read as a fact; it almost seems like the writer is winking at the reader. The word *claim* is another way to cast doubt on the speaker's trustworthiness. The writer could have also shown his or her skepticism by beginning the sentence with the innocuous words *according to*, which again would add a subjective element to the sentence, decreasing Doe's credibility.

Keep your antenna up and be attuned to these subtleties—again, if you detect that information is being presented in a slanted manner, it does not mean you have to disregard the material; keep an open mind and just try not to let yourself be influenced by the *manner* in which a piece is written. You will need to make up your own mind after consulting a variety of different sources.

Is the Information Presented Logically and Is It Well Organized? Are the data internally consistent? Are conclusions supported by the data and evidence presented? Look for data presented in a well-organized manner, tables clearly labeled, and lucid accompanying explanatory material. Typically (although by no means always), these elements reflect a well-thought-out study.

Is the Information Based on a Poll or Survey? The quality of individual polls and surveys vary enormously. There is a science to accurate data collection that involves technical considerations such as sample size, rate of response, sampling and nonsampling errors, and more. It's important to find out how the information was collected (e.g., mail questionnaire or phone), who was interviewed, and the other details behind the study.

Polls and surveys that purport to measure people's views and behaviors are so fraught with hazards, in fact, that some observers believe that even the finest and most well-known survey organizations cannot overcome the great number of barriers that exist in accurate reporting. For these reasons, polls, surveys, forecasts, and the like should be utilized by researchers only with a great deal of caution.

Dr. Jared Jobe, director of the Collaborative Research Program at the U.S. National Center for Health Statistics, notes that there are a number of areas where polls and surveys can be misleading or inaccurate. The following are some of the most common problems:

- **Partisan sponsoring organizations.** Organizations that have a motive to manipulate surveys to achieve a desired result are obviously suspect.

- **Selection criteria.** By what mechanism and approach was the group selected? Was it a random sampling? The key point is whether the respondents were a *representative* sample of the particular population of interest. Jobe advises researchers to watch out for mail surveys, magazine subscriber surveys, and telephone call-in polls, because these are often biased by the fact that only persons with a particular reason for responding will answer the questions (those with extreme positions on an issue may be over-represented).

- **Loaded questions.** Jobe's research has shown that people's opinions are greatly affected by the tone, manner, and choice of words of the interviewer. Other studies have shown that people will provide totally different opinions depending on whether the words the interviewer uses contain positive or negative connotations. For example, according to one study, public opinion shifts if asked about favoring more spending "to aid the *poor*" compared to spending more for *welfare*. Sometimes, responses differ even when alternative words are used that do not seem to be loaded. For example, people were found to be less willing to approve speeches against democracy when asked whether the United States should "*allow* public speeches against democracy" than when asked whether the United States should "*forbid* public speeches against democracy."[3]

- **Placement of questions.** Question placement can affect the way people respond. For example, say a subject was asked whether defense spending should be increased by 10 percent. If he or she replied no, the subject might then be more inclined to say

[3] For further discussion and examples, see Rich Jaroslovsky, "What's on Your Mind America," *Psychology Today*, July/Aug. 1988, 54–59.

yes to a follow-up question as to whether the United States should increase defense spending by 5 percent. Had the respondent *only* been asked whether defense spending should be increased by 5 percent, he or she may have been more likely to have replied in the negative.

• **Asking for memories and recollections.** Jobe says that people are notoriously poor at remembering their past actions and activities.

• **Complex questions.** People will often answer questions they do not understand.

• **Vague questions.** Questions that are open to more than one interpretation obviously make for poor research results.

• **Sensitive questions.** Queries that ask people to admit to socially unacceptable behavior are less reliable. For example, today people often do not like to admit that they smoke.

• **Misleading conclusions.** Sometimes the survey process is fine, but the conclusions are misleading. For example, Jobe cites the commercial that says "no toothpaste gets your teeth whiter." Such a claim can simply mean that the brand is no worse than all the rest.

The best way to guard against these problems is to get a copy of the actual questionnaire utilized and study it to try to detect any of these pitfalls. Jobe advises researchers to look at many surveys, conducted by more than one organization at different times. If these surveys reveal generally the same findings, then you can feel fairly confident about the results.

EVALUATING EXPERTS

When you interview a "live" expert, how do you evaluate that person's credibility and knowledge? Here are some strategies.

Signs of a Good Source

Here are a few helpful indicators of a good source:

Peer Recognition. Has the source had anything published in trade journals or spoken at industry conferences? If so, it's an excellent sign because it signifies recognition by peers. Peer recognition is one of the very best indicators of an authoritative source. If you don't know whether a source has written or spoken on the topic, there is nothing wrong with politely asking. Use your judgment when applying this rule. If an expert has made a brand-new discovery or just finished a research project, it may take time to be recognized.

Referrals. How did you find the source? If you were referred by a recognized expert in the field, or someone you felt was a worthy source, it is a good sign. Good experts typically refer you to other good experts.

Repetition. Does the source repeat things you've heard before that you know to be true? If so, it's another good sign.

Attentiveness. Does the source pay careful attention to your questions and respond sensitively? I've found this to be a sign of a good source.

Sources to Beware of

The Biased Source. Bias is a tricky matter. The critical thing to be aware of is where a particular source is "coming from." For example, is he or she a salesperson for a product, a political appointee, or a representative of a special cause? Take this into account when evaluating the information. This doesn't mean that people with certain viewpoints or leanings are not going to be truthful or accurate. It simply means that each person's perspective must be uncovered so that you know how to evaluate his or her information.

For example, once I was digging up information on how certain cities cut their energy costs by forming fuel-buying cooperatives. One of the people I talked to was the president of a regional association of fuel dealers. He told me co-ops were a very bad idea; he said that although the participants might cut their purchasing costs, they suffer in the quality of their service. I noted his objection seriously, but at the same time realized that because he represented a group of fuel dealers, his constituency would have the most to lose if this co-op idea really caught on. I decided to call the individual co-op members directly to find out if they had indeed encountered service problems. It turned out that none had.

You must also stay on guard against organizations that do not easily telegraph their biases. These organizations often have impartial-sounding names but actually promote a very specific stand on an issue. For example, you locate an association innocently called "Citizens for Energy Awareness." The name suggests merely that the committee wants to help spread information. But it's possible that the committee's sole raison d'être is to advance the cause of nuclear energy or to ban it. To check for such biases, find out what kind of people the association is composed of. Are most of the officers of the "Citizens for Energy Awareness" executives at nuclear power plants? If so, you can guess why that organization has been created! Take a look at some of the organization's brochures and research reports. Do its studies and findings unfailingly reach the same conclusion and support the same side of a controversial issue? You might still get some good information from this special-interest group, but be aware that you will not get a balanced picture.

Another type of biased source that you need to be on guard against is the "overly enthusiastic" source. This kind of person is typically involved in implementing a new project of some sort. You're sure to get rave reviews from this person when you ask how the project is going. Nobody wants to express doubts about the success of his or her new ventures, so you have to be careful not to take glowing reports as gospel. In the above case of the fuel cooperatives, for example, the co-op members themselves may want to paint an overly rosy picture of their project. Probe for as many hard facts as you can.

When you run into cases in which you feel your sources have too many personal interests to be totally unbiased, try to supplement those sources with more disinterested experts. Again, in the case of the fuel-buying cooperatives, I would probably get the most objective information not from the fuel dealers or the co-op members, but from a government expert in the Department of Energy or another more unbiased authority on fuel.

The Overly Narrow Source. Let's say you are trying to find information on crime trends in the United States, and you find an expert on supermarket shoplifting. You'll have to ask yourself whether that person's opinions go beyond his or her area of expertise and extend to overall U.S. crime trends.

The Out-of-Date Source. Are you looking into a field that is constantly changing? If so, you want to be sure your sources have kept up with the changes. Try to find out the last time the person was actually involved in the subject. In certain fields—microcomputer technology, for example—information from only six months ago is quite dated.

The Too-Far-Removed Source. High-level sources with very broad administrative duties are often too far removed to provide you with the nitty-gritty details you need. For example, if you are digging up information on upcoming design trends in small automobiles, the head of the public affairs department of General Motors would be able to give you only the sketchiest and most basic information. You'd be much better off talking to design engineers to get more specific details. (Calling the public affairs office can still be worthwhile, if only to ask to be referred to a technical expert.)

The Unaccountable Source. The opposite of talking to a high-level official, like a public affairs executive, is the problem of talking to someone lower down on the company ladder who is not as accountable for what he or she says. While the public affairs person may not give you the nitty-gritty that you want, the person is careful about what he or she says, and the information you get should at least be accurate. The shop foreman may not feel so restrained and cautious and will give you the details you want. But

try to get those "facts" confirmed by other sources before relying on them as indisputable.

The Secondary Source. Is your source a true expert or just someone who is reporting on the experts' work or reorganizing existing information? Secondary sources *can* be helpful, but they are not ordinarily as intimately knowledgeable about the subject as primary sources.

The Confusing Source. If the person talks only in technical jargon and is unable to communicate his or her expertise to you, you're not going to get much out of the conversation. Move on to the next one.

Evaluation Strategies

Here are a few methods you can use to help evaluate your sources:

- Note the names of people who keep appearing in the articles that you read. When you see somebody quoted often, and in a variety of periodicals, it's usually a sign that the person is a leader in the field and has something valuable to say.
- It's fine to ask experts for their opinion of other sources. Just be diplomatic about how you ask. One way is to ask if they "agree" with so-and-so's conclusions about the subject in question.
- Think about using certain sources as yardsticks. If you've spoken with someone you feel is a top-notch authority, you can measure other sources' responses against that person's.
- If a source makes a statement you're skeptical of, politely ask where the information comes from. His or her research? Hands-on experience? Something read somewhere?
- If you doubt someone's expertise, you can test the person by asking a question to which you already know the answer.
- Does the expert say something definitively that you already know is absolutely incorrect? If so, that is obviously not a good sign!
- Have you had a chance to read anything the expert has written? I have found that the most useful experts to speak with are those that can write a clear, well-organized article or report.

- Does the expert simply repeat what everyone else says or does he or she have some fresh perspective on the issue? I've found that the truly superior experts can take an issue and not just describe the current situation, but see implications and add some new angles. The best experts provide insight into the underlying "why" questions which lead to broad implications. For example, when I was researching the topic of publishing on the Web, one of the best experts I spoke with early on told me that the *reason* why Web publishing was going to be significant was that before the Internet, there were two strong barriers of entry that made a mass-publishing operation difficult: 1) the need for a printing press; and 2) the need for some distribution mechanism, such as delivery trucks or a satellite system. The Web eliminates the need for either of these, demolishes the barriers to entry, and therefore makes it possible for anyone with a PC and modem (or even just access to one) to broadcast their information to a worldwide audience—and do so virtually instantaneously.
- I've found that one intuitive way to evaluate an expert is simply to ask yourself after you've had your interview whether you feel satisfied.

CRITICAL THINKING

Much of the advice given in this chapter could fall under the heading of "critical thinking." Being a critical thinker is vital for a researcher. But what does critical thinking really mean?

Critical thinking means a number of things. It means:

- Not just believing something because everyone says it's so.
- Not just believing something because you have heard it repeated so often.
- Not just accepting the first opinion you hear.

Critical thinking means constantly asking questions, probing, and digging deeply into a subject to learn more and more until *you yourself* are satisfied of the truth of the matter.

Critical thinking also means looking at bits of data, pieces of information, and bodies of knowledge and searching for connections and differences. It means sitting down and simply thinking hard about all that you've uncovered and trying to figure out what it all has in common. What are the threads that link the data? How do they differ?

What about the concept of trust or faith? Can a critical thinker ever decide simply to believe what someone says just because he or she trusts a person's judgment? I think yes. However, the trust will be an *intelligently placed one*. The experienced researcher sometimes intuitively feels when to trust a source and when not to. But this is a very difficult task, and it may not always be possible to make a decision on whom to trust. But you can ask yourself certain questions to help you explore your "gut" feelings:

- Has the person proven himself or herself to be reliable and accurate in this subject in the past?
- Does the rest of his or her work show integrity?
- Does the person have an ax to grind in this case or does he or she seem unbiased?

When Evidence Is Not There

What does the researcher do when he or she does not find any hard evidence to support a claim or position? Must the researcher dismiss any conclusions or findings as simply unproven and therefore not worth accepting? Let's look at a scenario where such a situation might be faced.

Let's say I came across a scientist who claimed that his work and analysis showed that there was a strong link between levels of air pollution and the onset of heart disease. Say that currently the medical establishment had not proven any link between the two, and in fact, there was no evidence at all linking the two phenomena together. How would one evaluate the scientist's claims?

Obviously, few researchers are in a position to definitively determine whether or not this person's claim is valid. There are scientific methods of discovery that are performed extremely carefully under intense scrutiny to determine whether a reported phe-

nomenon is indeed a reliable finding. However, you may find yourself in a position where you must make some kind of unscientific judgment on such a matter.

Although the judgment will be unscientific, it can still be of great importance, because it is these types of informal, unscientific but rational judgment that can provide enough interest in a subject to get the gears in motion for the scientists to set out and create their rigorous tests to discover truths. There is a lag time between the discovery of a phenomenon and its proof (or disproof), and the researcher can be a vital link in the process for assisting in facilitating the movement from the stage of initial theory or discovery to the stage of proof.

Let's look at an example. Say you start reading a scientist's claims about the link between air pollution and heart disease. Her conclusions are unproven and unaccepted by the scientific community, but you need to determine for yourself the likelihood of the theory being correct. What would you need to do? There are a number of paths you could pursue. First, you could find out the answers to these types of questions:

- What is the manner in which the person is presenting his or her findings? Is it in a sensational way, making claims like "revolutionary. . . fantastic. . . unbelievable," or are the claims presented in a more reasonable and rational way? Does the author of the study provide advice on how to best interpret her work or just run down a list of amazing benefits?

- Are there backup records available to document claims? If the research is very new, is there at least an attempt to carefully collect records and document findings for the future?

- What types of outlet is the person choosing to publicize her findings? For example, does she advertise in the classifieds of *National Enquirer* and ask people to send in $10 to get her secrets, or does she approach the mainstream media and/or scientific community? What kind of audience is she trying to reach—a gullible one or one that will provide intense levels of scrutiny?

- Does this person make all of her records and findings open for anyone to inspect, or is much of it "secret formula" claims that will not be released?

- What else has this person worked on? Does the scientist show evidence of achievement in related fields? Is she respected by peers?

As you can see, most of these questions do not ask you to analyze the actual claim itself, but to look at relevant peripheral information that can be an aid in making the judgment. And, of course, it is possible that even someone who fits all the "right" answers will ultimately be proven incorrect (or vice versa, but less likely). But you may need to make a judgment call. Finally, your role as a researcher cannot be to comment on whether the claims are correct, but whether a phenomenon does or does not deserve serious scrutiny and attention from the larger community. And this is no insignificant job.

10

Wrapping It Up

Organizing and Writing Up Your Results, with the Benefit of the Expert Review

QUICK PREVIEW: WRAPPING IT UP

- You'll know it's time to conclude your talks with the experts when you can predict the answers to your questions and when you're putting out a lot of energy but not receiving much new information.
- Before you consider your project complete, have one or more of the best experts you've spoken with review your work for accuracy. This is a *critical* step in the process.
- Organize the information you've collected by subject rather than by source. This will make it easy to arrange your final work.
- When deciding what is worth including in your final report, select information that's relevant and reliable.
- Make conclusions whenever appropriate.
- Always remember to be fair—search for opposing views and be complete and honest.

Eventually you'll come to the point in your interviews when it is time to start winding down your information search. But there are a number of critical steps that still need to be attended to at this late point. Here are the things you need to know.

KNOWING WHEN TO CALL IT QUITS

How do you know when you've done enough work? Here's a guideline you can use: Be aware of when you can predict how the experts are going to answer your questions. As discussed earlier, when this first occurs, it's a good time to step back and redirect your focus. But if you've redirected once or twice already, and you can't think of any new paths to pursue, it's usually a sign that you've covered your subject well, and you don't have to go any further.

Another guideline you can use to decide when it's time to quit is when you discover that you are putting in a lot of work but not getting much new information. When you reach this point of diminishing returns, it's also probably time to wrap it all up.

One other rule you may decide to use: If you are approaching a

deadline and you're out of time, you may have no choice but to quit! I've found that you need to budget something along the lines of 80 to 85 percent of your total allotted time for research and 15 to 20 percent for writing up the results.

Be aware, though, that typically the very best information in a research project comes more toward the very end! The reason is that as you do more and more research, you naturally learn more and more about your topic. This then allows you to better define your project's scope, better refine your questions, and get referred to people who have increasingly more of the specific type of expertise you seek. So don't wrap things up too fast if the good stuff is just starting to roll in, either. It's better to have completed an excellent research project that's a little late than a mediocre one that's in right on time.

MAKING SURE YOUR FINAL INFORMATION IS ACCURATE

After you decide to end your talks with the experts, the next critical step is to make sure you've covered your subject effectively and that the information you've gathered is accurate and complete.

The first thing you should do is to think back to your early expert contacts. Were there top-notch sources you spoke with but did not know at that early stage what kinds of questions to ask? Now that your knowledge of the subject is deeper and clearer, it might be worth going back to those people to talk to them again. Write an outline of your findings. Where do gaps still remain? Think of which sources you could consult to fill them.

Another step you might take at this point is to confirm the accuracy of certain discussions. Say, for example, that you spoke with an expert but you're not quite sure you understood the person completely. Jot down your interpretation of that source's points and send it off for confirmation.

The next step is very critical to complete this whole talking-to-the-experts process and make it really work. This is the "expert review" procedure and it works as follows.

If you are writing up your results, write a draft. If you are not

writing up your results, write a rough draft anyway. Now go back and review all the different experts you've spoken with during the course of your information interviews. Select one or two that were especially knowledgeable and helpful—your very best sources. Get in touch with these people again and ask them to review your work for accuracy. Tell them that all their comments, suggestions, and criticisms are welcome. Be sure to tell the reviewers that they have indeed been specially selected. Ninety-five percent of the time these people will be flattered that you've singled them out, and they will be more than happy to take a few minutes and read your draft. You can even type in questions at locations in your draft where you are unsure of certain points.

If you are going to be writing up your results, you should acknowledge the expert reviewers' assistance somewhere in the work, and tell them that you plan to do this.

Your reviewers will almost never ask for a fee to do this job for you. A big reason for this is that you have been very selective in your choice of reviewers. You'll find that in any information-finding project you will always "hit it off" with at least a couple of experts along the way. The process is such that about 10 to 15 percent of the people you talk to will not be too helpful or knowledgeable, 60 to 70 percent will be quite helpful and provide you with very good information, and 10 to 15 percent will be of superb assistance. There is always that percentage of extra-nice experts who go out of their way to help you in any way they can. *These are the people you get in touch with again* to ask for this review.

I usually prefer two or three reviewers, each with a different perspective. For example, after I wrote a report on the topic of microcomputers, I sent one draft to a computer programmer, another to a consultant, and a third to a vendor. If you know of an expert who specializes only in one aspect of your study, you can send just that particular section of your work to that person.

There are two ways you can actually carry out this review procedure. One way is to mail your draft to your reviewers and ask them to mark it up and send it back to you. This is okay, but I prefer another approach. I would recommend that you send the draft and ask them to read it and mark it with comments. Then you should get on the telephone with each reviewer, have a copy of your draft in front of you, and go over the draft page by page with

the expert. This way, you can ask the reviewers questions about any of their points you don't understand, and you can explain yourself on any points in your report that weren't clear to the reviewers.

In essence, this expert review is completing the circle—the experts are now reviewing the expert information that you've gathered. At this point, if you've done a thorough job, you should feel like an expert yourself.

NOTE TAKING AND ORGANIZATION

As mentioned previously, whenever you consult a written source of information, or talk to an expert, you'll want to take notes and keep your information organized.

There are naturally many different approaches you could take to organizing information. I've found that one particular method seems to work quite well for the purpose of organizing a lot of unfamiliar information gathered from a multitude of sources.

The way it works is as follows: Get a pad of paper, and for the first batch of written-information sources you consult (say, five to eight) take your notes on a pad, clearly marking at the top the name of the source, where it can be found, and the pages consulted. After you've finished with this first batch, you should be knowledgeable enough to be able to define the key subtopic categories within your subject and fit all future information you collect (from both written sources and talks with experts) into those categories you've established.

For example, let's say I was trying to find out everything about the sport of ballooning. After reading and taking notes on a number of articles on the topic, maybe I'd determine that there were fifteen critical subtopics within the subject. These might be purchasing a balloon, setting one up, safety considerations, fuel, and so on. My next step would be to get a stack of index cards and write each subtopic on top of a different card. Then I'd go back to my pad and copy the notes onto the appropriate index card. So if one sheet of the pad contained notes about a number of subtopics (fuel, safety, etc.) but were drawn from one source, I'd break up

those notes into those categories and copy them onto the appropriate index cards. This would eventually result in my having a stack of cards, each containing information about only one subtopic, but gathered from a number of different information sources. In theory, all my future notes should be able to fit into one of those categories.

As you continue to uncover information, however, and become knowledgeable about your subject, you may find that you'll need to modify the categories you originally created. Some subtopics may prove to be very minor and can be incorporated into a larger category. Or there may be additional categories to add as new topics arise that you hadn't considered.

This method of arranging information by subject, rather than by source, will make the final organizational steps simple. You can just shuffle the index cards until you're satisfied that the subtopics are arranged in a logical and smooth order. Then, if you are going to be writing up your results or making an oral presentation, you have an outline already created.

You may find it convenient to continue to take notes on large pads of paper even after you've created your index card categories. That's fine. Just be sure to copy the notes on the appropriate cards.

WRITING UP YOUR RESULTS

Here are some pointers to keep in mind if you plan to formally write up the results of your information search.

Sort the Gems from the Junk. As you read through all the notes you've taken—notes from magazine articles, government reports, talks with experts, and all other sources you've consulted—you'll need to decide which pieces of information should be included in your report. How do you discern the valuable from the not-so-valuable? How do you decide which fact is important and which is useless?

Although this is a common concern among first-time information seekers, if you've done a thorough job in your search, you will understand the subject well enough at this point to know which

information is important and which is not. But here are three guidelines that can help you make a decision:

- Pay particular attention to the information that you've gathered and the notes that you've taken during the last 10 to 20 percent of your project. As mentioned earlier in this chapter, for several reasons, the best information usually comes towards the end of a project, and you'll want to make sure that that information receives the highest priority when finalizing the scope, focus, and conclusions of your work.
- A critical question you need to ask about any piece of information is whether it is *relevant* to your investigation. Does it add information, shed new light, suggest a trend, or provide background for your subject? If a piece of information, no matter how interesting, does not advance the specific goals or fall within the scope of your project, it should not be included.
- When evaluating your information, think about who provided it. Was it from a source you considered reliable or did it come from a biased or otherwise suspect source?

Be Complete. When you write up your results, don't tease with a remark that leaves the reader hanging. It's very important to fully explain your points clearly, and preferably with a concrete example. A statement like "the Model W skis are the best because they meet all important criteria" would only be helpful if you explained what the important criteria actually are. Anticipate the questions your statements will elicit from a reader, and then do your best to answer them.

Make Conclusions. Another common question among beginning information gatherers is whether it is appropriate to state one's opinion or make conclusions on a controversial issue. Let's say you've just spent three months learning all about the racquetball industry. You've spoken to club owners, association executives, sports columnists, and equipment manufacturers. You've read articles in leading trade publications and in the general press. As you read over your information, you begin to come to the conclusion that indicators are pointing to an imminent drop in the popularity of the sport. Are you qualified to state that conclusion?

In most cases, I would definitely say *yes*—with a couple of small cautions. If you've done a thorough job digging out information on your subject, you are certainly justified in drawing conclusions and stating them. If you realize that the facts point to certain trends, or add up to certain conclusions, you should state them. In fact, findings like these are one of the most important things that can come out of these information-finding projects.

Now, although you can draw broad conclusions, it's best to quote the experts themselves on factual data and opinions. Let's say you are doing a study on the fight against some rare disease. A statement in your report like "this disease is not at all contagious" should be attributed to a particular expert, or at least preceded by words like "according to experts I spoke with. . . ."

But in any information-finding project you are certainly permitted to step back, look at the big picture, and give your opinion. You should then indicate in some manner, however, that this is *your* conclusion. In the racquetball case, you could phrase your statement along these lines: "After investigating the industry and talking to numerous experts in the field, this author feels that the game will soon be decreasing in popularity. The major reasons for this, I believe, are. . . ."

What do you do when there are arguments and evidence on both sides of an issue and you're not sure who is correct? I recently worked on a project that required finding information on potential health hazards of video display terminals (VDTs). There were two distinctly opposing viewpoints: Government and industry tests all showed that radiation levels fell well within safety standards; but unions and certain workers organizations claimed that there was little information on the long-term effects of the VDTs' low-level radiation, and they cited cases of higher-than-expected health problems among certain VDT workers.

It was not totally clear—to me at least—what the "answer" was regarding the safety of this equipment. So I decided to present the arguments of both sides as clearly as possible and leave it up to readers to draw their own conclusions.

In many information searches you'll run into these gray areas; you'll want a simple answer, but there won't be one. That's okay. Just present the facts as you see them.

Also be sure to ask yourself whenever you write about a con-

troversial or sensitive issue whether you are being *fair*. Fairness is pretty tough to judge, but I think the *Washington Post Deskbook on Style* defines it well. According to the editor of that book, being fair includes the following guidelines:

- **Search for opposing views.** In other words, don't be lazy and accept the first opinion you hear. Get both sides of the story.

- **Be complete.** Don't omit facts of major importance. Otherwise, your reader will be misled.

- **Be relevant.** Unnecessary information will cloud an issue.

- **Be honest.**

To Quote or Not to Quote

People often wonder when it's necessary to attribute information to an expert or a written source, and when it's acceptable to use the information without attribution. Although one wit claimed that "to steal ideas from one person is plagiarism; to steal from many is research,"* the general rule is that when you use somebody's own idea or work, you must attribute it to that source. But if somebody provides facts or general information that can be obtained from many sources (e.g., Death Valley, California, has the highest recorded temperature in the United States), it is not necessary to do so.

What about obtaining permission to quote the experts that you've interviewed? If you are writing a very sensitive piece, you can play it safe and specifically ask each expert for their permission, but normally it's not necessary. As long as you've identified yourself to the expert, explained that you are writing an article or a report, and made no off-the-record agreements, the expert should realize that you are using his or her remarks for publication.

Another common question regards obtaining permission to excerpt or quote published information. Here the general rule is that you may make what is called "fair use" of published materials without seeking permission. In general, "fair use" allows you

*Arthur Bloch, *Murphy's Law Book 3* (Los Angeles: Price Stern, 1982), p. 50.

to quote a few lines of a short article or a couple of paragraphs of a longer piece or book *with attribution* but without getting permission from the publisher. If you want to use more than this, you should send a letter to the publisher explaining exactly what information you want to use, exactly where it is located, and why you want to use it. The great majority of the time, the publisher will *not* charge you for the use of the material, but will require that you print a specific credit line. The publisher may also want you to send it a copy of the final work.

These general rules are exactly that—general. Each case is different. The best rule is to use your common sense and, if there is any doubt at all about attributing information or obtaining permission, to err on the safe side.

If for some reason a publisher is unwilling to grant permission, try to track down the author of the piece yourself. Then you can interview that person for information, and the expertise will be available to you without a hassle.

Libel is a much more complicated matter, and a full discussion of the topic is beyond the scope of this book. It's worth noting, however, a concise definition that was published in the *Washington Post Deskbook on Style:* "Basically, a libelous statement is a published statement that injures a person (or organization or corporation) in his trade, profession or community standing." Although traditional defenses against a libel charge have included "truth" (i.e., the information published was accurate) and "reasonable care" (on the part of the writer), it is impossible to generalize about this topic. The *Post* advises writers to again consider simply whether they are being fair. Did you give the party a chance to respond?

One last point: Be sure to show your appreciation to the experts you speak with. If you can think of any way that you can help them, or return the favor, offer it. And if someone ever comes to you with an information request, remember how much you appreciated the experts who helped you and try to do likewise.

11

Troubleshooting

Typical Questions Information Seekers Ask

Here are some of the most typical questions I am asked by researchers who are undertaking an information-finding project.

How do I know where to begin my information search?

There is rarely any single *perfect* place to begin your research. The Information Seeker's Map on page 285 should help you get started. The key is to get started on your research and begin learning about your subject. As you begin to gather information and understand your topic, the question will become irrelevant.

How do I know whether to use print or electronic databases when starting my research?

This can be confusing, especially since many periodical indexes and publications today can be found in print, online, and on the Internet. The basic rule of research stays the same, though: Start off with basic sources and build up your knowledge gradually. So whether you choose print or electronic, your initial sources should be nontechnical and geared for the popular user. Keep in mind, too, that print sources still retain certain advantages over

electronic: There's still *more* information in print, especially on more obscure topics; they go back further in time and provide historical perspective; they are usually cheaper to use; they are *always* full text; they are generally more pleasant to read from; and you don't need a computer!

I know that there must be some information on the topic, but I can't find anything!

It's extremely doubtful that *no* information whatsoever exists. One possible cause for not finding anything is that you might be unaware of any standard terminology that your subject would be categorized under. For example, say you were researching the topic "static electricity"—you would need to know that "electrostatics" is the standard scientific term for that phenomenon and that all indexes and materials will categorize that topic under that heading. Also, make sure you check as many sources as possible before you conclude there is nothing available on your subject. If you still cannot find anything, look up related or broader subjects. In the rare instance where there is truly absolutely nothing written on your subject, it could mean you are onto something interesting, and the results of your research could add to the body of knowledge!

I've found some articles on the subject, but I can't understand them.

Don't worry. Keep on researching the topic and look for articles written for a more general audience. If you can't find any at all, try finding a description in an introductory textbook or encyclopedia. Then call some experts, and explain that you are a layman on the topic and have some very basic questions to ask.

I'd like to call some experts, but to tell you the truth, I'm afraid.

You are certainly not alone! Just about everyone who gets into this field gets very nervous about calling strangers and asking for information. But think about it—you've got nothing to lose. Chances are, the person is going to help you out, and if worse comes to worse and the phone conversation doesn't work out, you can always say "thanks for your time" and hang up. It took me almost

two years' of talking to experts before I felt really relaxed before making these kinds of calls, so don't be too hard on yourself!

I can never get hold of these experts—either they are out or they don't return my calls!

It's not that you can't get hold of them, it's just that you haven't made enough calls! The process of reaching experts is, to a great extent, a numbers game—call enough people and you will always reach at least a certain percentage. It's a time-consuming process, but it works! If the person is very busy, though, try calling his or her office and ask for an E-mail address, and send your queries that way. This makes it unnecessary for the person to be available when you call, and also allows the person to respond when he or she is already in a mode of replying.

I got the expert on the phone, but he talked so fast I don't think I wrote it all down.

Don't worry. Note taking is a skill that improves with practice. After you speak with a number of people, you'll intuitively know how to capture the key points. And it really does help to read over your notes *immediately* after the conversation, so you can fill in gaps while the talk is still fresh in your mind. If it looks like you missed something critical, just call the person back to go over those issues again.

How do I know when to stop doing research?

There is no perfect time, but as mentioned earlier in the book, when you feel you can predict the experts' answers, have reassessed the direction of your project, and are expending a lot of research time but getting little new information, it's probably time to wrap up. You can try writing a draft of your findings to see if there are gaps still remaining that require additional research.

Help! I think I may have collected too much information! I'm swamped with articles, notes, and other data!

Your problem is probably not too much information, but not enough organization. Start going through your notes and begin

categorizing each statement of fact under a topic subheading and transcribe all related facts under each heading. This will make your big stack of information more manageable. Get rid of information that, although interesting, does not directly relate to the scope of your project or advance its mission.

Uh-oh, I've got conflicting information in my notes. How do I know whom to believe?

This is common—often there is more than one opinion on a subject. See chapter 9 on evaluating information sources. Sometimes you may simply have to present both points of view and allow the reader to decide the merits.

I really enjoy doing this kind of research. How can I find out about careers in this field?

That is a very interesting question, and it is one I have been asked many times. There are a number of different careers that involve digging up and analyzing information. The most obvious and well-known field involving finding information is library science—however, many researchers do not wish to work in a traditional library environment. Some ex-librarians have started "information broker" businesses (see pages 201–204) and sell their research skills to businesses and organizations for a fee. Other careers that involve heavy amounts of research include certain types of journalism, private investigator services, new business or product development, and market research.

One area you haven't really given any advice on is how to find information on getting a job. Any thoughts here?

Yes. Although the question of how to find a job goes beyond the scope of this book, I think the question is important and relevant enough to merit a few pointers. The main point I'd like to stress is that you can use the sources described in this book to first learn about organizations that appeal to you as a place to work and then utilize the phone-interview techniques to track down department heads, managers, directors, vice presidents, owners, and others who have the power to hire. Ask to speak with them about

thoughts you have on how your background and skills might be of value to their organization and then send them a written letter outlining your ideas, along with a statement of your qualifications. Try to approach the process as one professional seeking to establish a relationship with another.*

After reading this book, you may find that all of the sources and strategies described are a bit overwhelming, like there is just *too much* out there. But don't worry about trying to memorize the whole book. Just take a look at the Information Seeker's Map on page 285 to get a feel for the entire process, start some research at one of the "easy start" sources identified in chapter 1, then go with the flow and consult the book for help if you run into problems. And remember the basics:

- The information you seek is almost certainly available for the asking.
- There are experts around who will talk to you and answer your questions.

---

*For much more information on how to go about finding information on jobs and careers, I highly recommend *What Color Is Your Parachute?*, by Richard N. Bolles (Berkeley, CA: 10 Speed Press, 1997). Also, you can learn much about different careers and jobs by consulting the *Occupational Outlook Handbook* (U.S. Bureau of Labor Statistics, Washington, DC). Most libraries carry both of these books.

12

A Researcher's Road Map
Project Planning and Source Selection

As the online world and the Internet become more popular, it becomes increasingly confusing and difficult to know what type of source is best to use for what kind of research. Do you start with a book or a magazine article? Should you browse magazines in print, or try searching them on a CD-ROM? What about the fact that some magazines are now on the Internet, too? Or should you just call an expert and ask him or her your questions?

This is a complicated matter, and there is no one perfect solution. However, I will try here to provide two ways to make these decisions easier. The first is to offer a general step-by-step strategy in how to approach a research project; and the second is a description of what I see as the special strengths of the major print, electronic, and other sources described in this book.

PROJECT PLANNING

Although every information-finding project is different, in most cases the *process* of learning about a new subject follows a similar path. Generally, the trick is to build your knowledge of the subject by first using nontechnical sources and gradually proceeding to more advanced and technical ones. Any information-finding pro-

ject I undertake generally goes through *six steps*, outlined below. Although in practice these steps will overlap, I've found it useful to keep them in mind separately when planning my investigations.

1. DEFINE YOUR PROBLEM

✓What do you need?
✓Why do you need it?
✓What will you do with it?

2. LOCATE YOUR SOURCES

✓Pick the right library
✓Check basic indexes
✓Read articles and note experts' names
✓Identify and contact an association

3. OBTAIN TECHNICAL SOURCES

✓Check technical indexes
✓Identify and obtain trade journals

4. MAKE LIST OF QUESTIONS/ CONTACT & INTERVIEW EXPERTS

✓Gather expert names
✓Jot down your questions not addressed in literature
✓Start with non-technical experts
✓Identify yourself clearly
✓Be persistent but polite

5. REDIRECT FOCUS & EVALUATE PROGRESS

✓Have goals changed?
✓New questions to ask?
✓Untapped sources to contact?

6. WRITE DRAFT/GET EXPERT REVIEW

✓Send to experts
✓Get comments
✓Final changes

Information Seeker's Map

1. Define your problem. Break it down into its component parts. Determine *why* you need this information and *what* you plan to do with it. This will make your information search clearer to you and easier to conduct.

2. Locate basic sources. Because you probably know very little about the topic at this stage, you'll first want to obtain definitions and understand basic concepts. The best information sources to consult at this early step are nontechnical ones that explain unusual concepts and terms clearly and without jargon. Such sources can include newspapers and magazines geared to a general audience, reports published by the government for the public, and literature for consumers from manufacturers of products. A CD-ROM search can be an easy way to access some of these basic sources.

Print out any articles you've located. Underline what you feel are the significant points.

Review what you've underlined, and try to create topic categories to help provide structure and focus to your research (see pages 273–274). Don't, though, let these categories *limit* the extent or scope of your research. You may need to create new categories as you continue your research.

TIP: When reading your printouts, try to conduct an imaginary dialogue with the authors as you read them—in other words, if what you read prompts a question, write it in the margin. If you agree with something note it; if you disagree, write why. This dialoguing and questioning spurs you to advance the authors' arguments and brings you to the next, higher level of discussion.

---

3. Obtain technical sources. Now you're ready to seek out more specialized information. After you've grasped the basic terms and concepts of your subject, you're ready to dig into more technical material. Sources to check at this point could include trade publications, research center reports, and transcripts of convention presentations. At this stage, you may wish to go online and search a professional vendor like Dialog if you can afford the fees, as well as perform some research on the Web and on the Internet's newsgroups.

4. Make list of questions, contact and interview experts. While you were doing your research and reading, you should have been noting the names of experts to interview. Once you've done enough reading to feel fairly confident in understanding the basics of your topic, you should be in a good position to come up with some thoughtful questions to pose to the experts you've identified. When you've gotten all you can from published material, you should feel confident enough to begin contacting some experts to get answers to the questions you still have on the subject.

5. Redirect focus and evaluate progress. This is the time to step back and review your progress. Compare what you've learned with what you decided you wanted to learn in step 1. Make adjustments or redirect your focus, if necessary. Go back to earlier steps to fill in gaps, if needed.

6. Write draft/get expert review. Get one or more experts to review your work for accuracy. Don't neglect this very important step.

TIP: Identify key words and terminologies to allow for more precise searching. You can do this by simply reading about your topic and noting keywords as they pop up. For example, if you were studying how businesses prepare for the future, you would discover that key phrases include "forecasting", "strategic planning," and "anticipatory management." Then you could conduct your searches by using those keywords.

Now, congratulate yourself for having completed your information-finding project and succeeded in becoming an "instant" expert!

SOURCE SELECTION

The list below is designed to help you determine how the major types of information sources discussed in this book compare in

terms of special strengths and potential drawbacks. This can be useful for short projects or quick-answer research when you don't need to consult many sources and are only looking for one or two to check.

Print Sources

- **Textbooks.** Provides basic definitions and clarifies terms. Useful for obtaining a basic understanding of complex matters—especially at the beginning of a research project. Drawbacks include a possible time lag in reflecting the very latest news and movements in field.

- **Reference books.** Statistical data, definitions, numerical data, and basic facts.

- **Nonfiction books.** In-depth coverage of a particular topic. Useful for obtaining a deeper understanding of complex topics. Drawbacks include length of time to get through and absorb an entire book during a fast-moving research project.

- **Directories.** Lists, rankings, compilations, and addresses. Good for overviews, snapshots, and finding contact information (for companies, magazines, products, etc.). Drawbacks include the short life span of most directory data, making it necessary to find and use the latest edition (or no more than a year old).

- **Newspaper articles.** Local coverage of events not covered elsewhere; cites experts; usually written in nontechnical manner. Drawbacks include occasional superficial coverage of complex topics.

- **Magazine and journal articles.** More depth than newspapers. Best overall general research source. Also readily available electronically, which offers the advantage of searchability. However, print remains easier to read, usually provides fuller context, and sometimes may be even timelier than electronic versions due to lag time between publication of some journals and their availability on electronic systems.

There are three major categories of magazine and journal articles: popular, trade, and scholarly. Popular magazines include those you would find on a newsstand and appeal to the widest audience. Trade magazines are more specialized and are usually targeted to those working in a particular field (aerospace, nuclear engineering, wastewater treatment) or who have a special interest. Scholarly journals are normally written by professors and academicians for other professors and academicians. Though all of these types of periodicals can be useful for researchers, trade magazines most often balance depth of coverage while still being understandable for the intelligent layperson. (Another category of print periodicals are newsletters, which are highly focused discussions and analyses of news and events in specific industries, technologies markets, products, etc. They are "insider" type sources that specialize in offering implications and analyses of the latest and most significant developments in the field. They are usually very expensive and are not as commonly found in libraries as the other types of publications.)

Electronic Sources

- **Professional online.** Sophisticated, powerful search capabilities; massive databases. Best for highly targeted searches of major and leading popular, trade, and scholarly literature, as well as government data and other highly focused, data-intensive sources, including newsletters. Drawbacks include high cost to search and difficulty in learning system.

- **Consumer online.** Easy access to popular consumer magazines (e.g., *Time, The Atlantic, Sports Illustrated,* and so on). May be able to access electronic version as soon as or even sooner than availability of print. Drawbacks include lack of sophisticated search options and short back archives for many databases.

- **CD-ROMs.** Free (at the library) and relatively easy access to large information databases; supports sophisticated searching of major, leading print journals in many fields. Drawbacks

include the 4 to 12 week lag time to updates, and the lack of full text on some systems.

- **The Web.** Amazingly eclectic, diverse, and alternative information sources. Great for finding obscure information, free and cheap government data, information presented graphically, and the state of the art on the Internet and related technology. E-zines, or publications available only on the Web, are coming into their own as legitimate periodicals, especially those that cover the Internet, technology, and computer-related information. Drawbacks include difficulty in conducting precision searches, the mixture of commercial and substantive sites, the amount of time it may take to find useful data, and difficulty in evaluating credibility and even the source of some data.

- **Online discussion groups.** Excellent for locating experts, up-to-the-minute developments in a field or on countless topics, and anecdotal reports. Drawbacks include a high noise-to-signal ratio; evaluating credibility of anecdotal reports.

Other Key Sources

- **Government and university research.** Free or inexpensive access to in-depth studies, often relating to issues in science, technology, or matters of public policy. Drawbacks can include difficulty finding what you need and the age of the study.

- **Associations.** Free or inexpensive access to industry surveys, news, and overviews, as well as potential referrals to experts. Drawbacks include possible bias on the part of association personnel in favor of their industry.

- **Experts.** Customized, up-to-the-minute live information. Need to assess the expert's knowledge, credibility, and potential biases.

You may wonder if it is possible to know *which* of the many information sources uncovered in this book will be best for *your*

project. Unfortunately, it is almost impossible to know for certain which sources will turn out to be the most fruitful for a specific information-finding project. In one case you may find that your best sources turned out to be research centers and museums; in another, a specialized bookstore and a trade magazine; and in other projects, different sources. The only way to know whether a particular source is going to pay off for a particular search is to try it. Dig up as many relevant library resources, "supersources," federal government sources, business information sources (if appropriate), and finally, the experts themselves, until you feel you've found what you were looking for.

This is not to say that you cannot make some educated guesses and choose sources that seem *more likely* to pay off. For example, if you need information on some very timely matter, it would likely be covered in a newspaper or magazine; a more obscure scientific matter, at a laboratory or research center. Similarly, a public-policy or consumer-oriented issue is likely to be covered somewhere in the federal government, an art-related issue at a museum or maybe a university, and so on. So you don't really have to fly blind. Read the descriptions of the sources in this book, and use your best judgment to try to zero in on the ones that will most likely cover your subject.

APPENDIX

Sources of Further Information

The following is a selected listing of books, magazines, and associations that can assist you in learning more about research and information finding. Most of these sources are inexpensive or free. However, a few of the online magazines and journals are geared more to the professional researcher and will cost more.

Some resources related to the Internet and online research are discussed in detail at the end of this appendix.

BOOKS

BARZUN, JACQUES AND GRAFF, HENRY F. *The Modern Researcher,* 5th ed. (Harcourt Brace Jovanovich, 1992; $21.50). A classic book on the art of conducting research. Provides great food for thought on the problems, dilemmas, and challenges in the researcher's quest for truth.

BOOTH, WAYNE C., COLUMB, GREGORY C., AND WILLIAMS, JOSEPH M. *The Craft of Research* (University of California Press, 1995; $12.95). A very thorough and detailed approach to conducting a research project. Topics covered include asking questions,

reading critically, making good arguments, claims and evidence, drafting a report, communicating evidence visually, research ethics, and more.

BRADY, JOHN. *The Craft of Interviewing* (Random House, 1977; $12). Another classic; this one on how to conduct an interview. Aimed especially at journalists, this book provides strategies, tips, and advice on how to reach sources and then get them to cooperate with you.

FULD, LEONARD. *The New Competitor Intelligence* (John Wiley, 1994; $32.95). Leonard Fuld is one of the country's leading experts on the topic of competitive intelligence—finding facts on competitor companies. This book lists basic reference sources, provides creative information-finding strategies, and discusses the reasons for competitive intelligence activity in today's business world.

GARVIN, ANDREW. *The Art of Being Well-Informed*, 2nd ed. (Avery Publishing Group, 1996; $14.95). Written by the president of the worldwide research and consulting group Find/SVP (and co-authored by me), this 243-page paperback is geared to raising the "information consciousness" of businesspersons. It offers advice and case studies as to why research and information gathering systems are critical to businesses today, and provides a listing of a number of sources. The 2nd edition also examines the role of the Internet in business research, and provides specific strategies for battling information overload.

KING, DENNIS. *Get the Facts on Anyone* (S&S Trade, 1996; $15).Written by an investigative reporter, this book will help you locate missing people, locate credit and financial information, uncover court records, and use databases to find information that relates to people.

LESKO, MATTHEW. *Lesko's Info-Power III* (Visible Ink, 1995; $29.95). Lesko is nationally known for his expertise in finding information sources from the U.S. government. The book identifies thousands of sources of information and assistance from U.S. federal agencies and departments.

SCOTT, ROBERT. *The Investigator's Little Black Book* (Crime Time Publishing, 1996; $19.95). An intriguing little paperback book that identifies hundreds of sources for researchers. Some of these are databases and directories, but others are lesser-

known or unusual sources, such as where to find very old phone books, video archives, military records, and much more.

SCHWARTZ, PETER. *The Art of the Long View* (Currency/Doubleday, 1996; $15). Not really a research guide, but a fascinating business book on how organizations can develop scenarios to better prepare for the future. A key component, though, to constructing scenarios is research and information gathering, and chapter 4 of the book, titled "Information Hunting and Gathering," is one of the best treatises on the art of research anywhere. A few other excellent business books that stress the role of information and knowledge management are *Competing for the Future,* by C. K. Prahalad and Gary Hamel (Harvard Business Press, 1994); *Jumping the Curve,* by Oren Harari (Jossey Bass, 1994); and *The Learning Organization,* by Peter Senge.

For some critical and thought-provoking perspectives on the intersection of society, information, and technology, you may also want to check out Alvin Toffler's *PowerShift,* Bill McKibbon's *The Age of Missing Information,* Stephen Doheny-Farina's *The Wired Neighborhood,* and Neil Postman's *Technopoly.*

MAGAZINES

Most of the magazines that I read about research these days relate to doing online and Internet searching, and are discussed later. However, an excellent broader business publication that consistently provides incisive articles on topics such as evaluating and analyzing information and where to find the latest data sources is *American Demographics,* which is published in Ithaca, New York, by Dow Jones. American Demographics also has a superb Web site (http://www.demographics.com). A spinoff from *American Demographics* called *Marketing Tools* focuses on the use of information in effective marketing and market research.

PROFESSIONAL ASSOCIATIONS

If you really are interested in learning more about research and information gathering, you should contact one or more of the following organizations. In addition to their regular services, all publish various newsletters or magazines and hold regular conferences.

Association of Independent Information Professionals
Suite 2103, 245 Fifth Ave., New York, NY 10016
http://www.aiip.com
This organization's membership consists of *independent* information professionals (sometimes called "information brokers") who make their living doing computer and manual organization, retrieval, and dissemination of information. This would be the organization to turn to if you are interested in learning how to start your own information-brokering firm.

Investigative Reporters and Editors Association
100 Neff Hall, University of Missouri, Columbia, MO 65211;
314–882–2042
This organization is an excellent resource for learning how to gather information, interview sources, and perform online research. One of its books, called *The Reporter's Handbook*, edited by Steven Weinberg is a superb guidebook filled with sources and strategies for uncovering a wide range of hard-to-get data.

Special Libraries Association
1700 18th Street NW, Washington, DC 20009; 202–234–4700
A leading and highly respected organization of librarians that work in corporations, technical organizations, and various institutions outside the traditional public library.

Society of Competitive Intelligence Professionals
1700 Diagonal Rd., Ste. 520, Alexandria, VA 22314;
703–739–0696
SCIP consists of about 3,000 business professionals who evaluate competitors and competitive conditions and wish to improve their skills.

FOR FURTHER INFORMATION
ON THE INTERNET

Chapter 5 focused mainly just on research and finding information on the Web and from electronic discussion groups, and is in no way a complete introduction to the Internet. To learn more, you can scan the computer shelves of nearly any large bookstore and you'll see dozens, if not hundreds, of books on the Internet. Keep in mind, though, that books on the Internet are dated the instant they hit the shelves. Even a superfast book production schedule takes at least 4–6 months from the time a book is written to the time it is published, and on the Internet, that's a long time.

Still, if you don't pay too much attention to the actual Web addresses and material that's more technology dependent, reading at least one good book is still worth the time. Some classics are *Zen and the Art of the Internet* (Prentice-Hall, 1996), *The Whole Internet Catalog* (O'Reilly, 1994), and *The Internet Unleashed* (SAMS, 1997). My personal favorite, though, is *The Little Web Book*, by Alfred Glossbrenner (PeachPit Press, 1996). It's a simple yet complete and crystal-clear introduction to using the Web and the Internet. Glossbrenner is an old hand at taking complex technical topics and making them accessible to the layperson. This book does this for the Internet beautifully. As I mentioned in chapter 5, my favorite search engine is AltaVista. The firm behind that engine, Digital Equipment Corporation, has published a very useful book called *AltaVista Search Revolution* (Osborne/McGraw-Hill, 1997) that can be a very handy guide for learning the ins and outs of effective searching on AltaVista.

You should also consider subscribing to a few magazines and newsletters that will help you improve your search skills. Everyone, it seems, knows about *Wired* magazine, and it's certainly a valuable resource for finding some of the cutting-edge thinking about the digital age. Frankly, I don't read it that often myself, for two reasons. The first is that it doesn't really focus all that much on the research aspects of electronic information, and the second is that trying to read the words through all of *Wired*'s hyperdesign, dayglo color, and vibrating graphics gives me a splitting headache.

You can, though, get some good cutting-edge stuff about the Net from *Wired*'s Internet site called HotWired (http://www.hotwired.com). Among print publications, I prefer *Online User*, published by Online Inc. in Wilton, CT. It is geared to the serious, but nonprofessional online and Net researcher. *Internet World*, by Meckler in Westport, CT, is also quite good, though it focuses less on the pure research aspects of the Net and more on new developments and the whole Internet scene.

If you really become a hard-core regular user, you may wish to look at subscribing to a couple of professional newsletters that are geared for more advanced Internet searchers. The CyberSkeptic's *Guide to Internet Research* is an excellent one (published by Bibliodata in Needham Heights, MA), as is, I must say, my own newsletter, *The Information Advisor*, published by FIND/SVP in New York City. Both of these publications, though, are rather pricey and are geared mainly for the business researcher, which may or may not be your primary focus of interest. The two leading professional trade journals, which are actually read mostly by business librarians, are *Online* and *Database*, and these are both published by Online Inc. in Wilton, CT. Another prominent and well-respected publisher of magazines and books on electronic research is Information Today in Medford, NJ. Its publications include *Link-Up*, *Information Today*, *Searcher*, and *Information World Review*. With the exception of *Searcher*, which is written by industry expert Barbara Quint and geared mainly to proficient online professionals, Information Today's publications are more accessible to the more casual online searcher.

Online Inc. has also recently published several very good books on online searching and research on the Internet, under its book publishing moniker, Pemberton Press. One is called *Secrets of the Internet SuperSearchers*, by Reva Basch, herself a nationally recognized expert information searcher. Another book, *The Online Deskbook*, by another renowned searcher Mary Ellen Bates, provides tips and strategies for searching not just the Internet, but a whole range of online services, such as the consumer online services, the professional ones, and some smaller lesser-known ones as well. I have written a book called *Find It Online* (Windcrest/McGraw-Hill, 1994), which is rather out of date when it comes to the Internet, but would still be useful for its discussion of CD-

ROMs, online search strategies, and issues related to information quality.

Also, with all the hype surrounding the Internet, it's a good idea to inoculate yourself at least a little bit by reading some works that are skeptical of the Internet. Here are my favorites:

- *Silicon Snake Oil* (Doubleday), by Clifford Stoll. Stoll is well known in the Internet insider community. He wrote a book in the early 1980s called *The Cuckoo's Egg* about his adventure tracking down a German spy ring over the Internet, which became kind of a cult classic. But since then, Stoll has soured on the Net, and this new book examines why life online is so inherently less satisfying than real life. (I know, I could have put the words "real life" in quotes like that, but we haven't come that far yet, have we?). Anyway, Stoll makes some good points about how you can't experience things like planting a garden online, and that reading hundreds of E-email messages regularly is hardly a path to self-actualization.
- *The Cult of Information: A Neo-Luddite Treatise on High Technology, Artificial Intelligence, and the True Art of Thinking*, by Theodore Roszak. This book was first published in 1986, and was updated in 1993. Roszak was alert enough in the '80s to see the potential dangers of a society smitten and hypnotized by the dazzle of technology, and his update in 1993 makes the work even more timely. Roszak looks at how we as a society have turned over critical matters like educating children and research to digitalization, and how easy it is to forget that computer information is not the same as knowledge.

Keep an eye out, too, for *anything* written on this topic by Neil Postman, the chairman of New York University's Department of Culture and Communications. Although as of late 1996 Postman did not have a book specifically on the Internet, he is the modern day's equivalent of Marshall McLuhan, and his critiques of television and technology (*Amusing Ourselves to Death, Technopoly,* among others) are about the best out there accessible to the public. My guess is that he's going to have something out there on this topic very soon.

Some other thought-provoking material on the social and philosophical implications of the Internet can be found in a fascinating

article titled "What Are We Doing Online," published in the August 1995, issue of *Harper's* magazine. The article is actually a debate among several thoughtful experts in the fields of technology, online, literature, and knowledge, with one side arguing the benefits of the new online world, and the other side the drawbacks.

Finally, these days an emerging area of study are courses in how to search the Internet. Some are affiliated with libraries, others with colleges and universities, and others with private organizations. I currently teach a 9-week, 3-credit course on how to do research online for the New School for Social Research (New York, NY) distance learning (DIAL) program.

Index

military history, 80, 102
Million Dollar Directory, 26, 126, 215
minerals, 14, 87–88
minorities, 75, 78–79, 83–86
Minority Business Development Agency, 78–79
Modern Researcher, The (Barzun and Graff), 295
Monthly Catalog of U. S. Government Publications, The, 58
Moody's *Manuals*, 27
MSN News, 174
museums, 67–69. *See also* non-profit organizations

NAFTA (North American Free Trade Agreement), 152–53
narcotics, 65, 83–86, 122
NASA. *See* National Aeronautics and Space Administration
NASA Access Help Desk, 102
NASA Industrial Application Centers, 101
NASA STI Products and Services at a Glance, 101–2
NASDAQ Fact Book, 137
National Aeronautics and Space Administration (NASA), 101–2
National Agricultural Library, 78
National Archives and Records Administration, 102
National Association of Securities Dealers, 137
National Association of State Information Resource Executives, 65
National Center for Health Statistics, 85

National Clearinghouse for Family Planning Information, 85
National Computer Systems Laboratory, 79
National Criminal Justice Reference Service (NCJRS), 89
National Directory of Addresses and Telephone Numbers, 20
National Directory of Nonprofit Organizations, 36
National Economic, Social and Environmental Data Bank (NESE), 44
National Endowment for the Arts and the Humanities, 102–3
National Fax Directory, 21
National Health Information Center, 84–85
National Institute for Occupational Safety and Health (NIOSH), 85
National Institute of Justice, 89
National Institute of Mental Health, 85
National Institute of Standards and Technology, 79
National Institutes of Health (NIH), 84
National Library of Medicine, 86
National Newspaper Index, 42
National Oceanic and Atmospheric Administration, 79
national parks, 87–88
National Park Service, 88
National Science Foundation (NSF), 103–4

The NIGHT
of the
WEEPING
WOMEN

The NIGHT of the WEEPING WOMEN

Lawrence Naumoff

A MORGAN ENTREKIN BOOK
THE ATLANTIC MONTHLY PRESS
NEW YORK
•

Published simultaneously in Canada
Printed in the United States of America
FIRST EDITION

Library of Congress Cataloging-in-Publication Data

Naumoff, Lawrence.
  The night of the weeping women / Lawrence Naumoff.—1st ed.

  "A Morgan Entrekin book."
  ISBN 0-87113-187-0
  I. Title.
PS3564.A8745N5   1988
813'.54—dc19   87-28074

Design by Laura Hough

The Atlantic Monthly Press
19 Union Square West
New York, NY 10003

FIRST PRINTING

Part I

THE FAMILY THAT EXPLODED

Part II

THE NIGHT
OF THE
WEEPING WOMEN

Part III

THE HOSTAGE CRISIS

Part I

The FAMILY That EXPLODED

One

Humming a song on a Saturday morning was not the kind of aggressive act that could easily be explained in a court of law as an understandable reason for murder, but it struck Ervin Neal that he might finally have to kill his wife, or get rid of her in some way.

He sat up in his separate but equal bedroom and listened to that mindless warbling, which just went on and on. He swung out of bed. The mattress creaked. The humming stopped and both people paused. In the pause and for a brief moment, their passage through the interminable rites of late middle-age was suspended. Each listened through the walls of the separate bedrooms and gauged the state of the other. Like old-time actors getting ready to enter the stage from opposite wings, each planned the look on the face, the set of the mouth, the cast of the eyes, the angle at which the head would be held. Each planned the complicated details of posture that would set the tone for their first face-to-face meeting of the day, so that by the quickest, most indirect glance, Ervin would know what he was in for and Margaret would know, as well, with an absolute precision, what amount of bitterness or anger had been held over from the day before.

In that moment of suspension, then, as each listened to the movement of the other and each prepared to meet, the day began, two weeks before Thanksgiving, in the port city of Wilmington, North Carolina.

She left her room and he determined she was coming toward his room and he held his breath as she stopped in front of his door.

"Do you want breakfast this morning?" she asked.

"Uhhh," he moaned, unable to speak to her yet.

"Does the 'uhhh' mean yes?" she asked. "If it does, do it one more time."

"Arghhh," he bellowed and charged the door.

"Thanks," she said, and walked off as he stopped midway across the room, barefoot and lost now that the charge of death was over, just an old man with bony toes and thin, hairless ankles, and nowhere to go.

Having nowhere to go with all that hatred was hard on Ervin Neal. It left him with the taste of frustration so bad it was like chewing tinfoil with his lips wired shut. He couldn't spit it out. He couldn't swallow. He just had to live with it, and he withdrew to a spot where he could nourish his deceived and disappointed soul and where he sucked on his bitterness like a toothpick.

"I'm making waffles," she called, "and we'll eat in twenty minutes."

He put his fingers in his ears to obscure her voice and went into the bathroom and washed and shaved.

"Ready," she called. He left the room for the first time since seven-thirty the night before, since the moment she had joined him on the couch, after doing the dishes, to watch television and he had quickly left to watch it alone in his room.

He sat across from her. She served him two round waffles, swimming in syrup, and he looked up slowly, across the table, first at the fat, plastic shape of Mrs. Butterworth, and then, at the real thing herself.

4

"Sleep well?" she asked.

"Uh huh," he said.

"I had an awful night. After you went into your room," she began, talking fast, "I changed the channel and watched the Billy Graham special and then, like some lazy thing, I stayed right where I was and watched this whole three-hour movie about murder and sex and I dreamed about it all night."

He nodded his head and kept on chewing.

"You didn't go to bed till late, did you? I heard the TV when I woke up in the middle of the night."

"I don't remember," he said.

"You never do. You take those sleeping pills and you never remember anything. You must have fallen asleep and left it on. It was off this morning, though, wasn't it? I didn't hear it."

He nodded again.

"You must have gotten up in your sleep and turned it off. Maybe you did that when you went to the bathroom. That was around three. I looked at the clock."

He glanced at the old waffle iron and Margaret looked that way, too.

"Oh gosh," she said and jumped up. "I forgot."

She lifted the top and the waffle came with it and then dropped back onto the bottom grill when she poked it with a fork.

"I'll eat this one," she said. "I'll make you another one. You don't like it crisp, do you?"

He motioned for her to bring it on, waving his hand in the air as if he were directing traffic, come on come on come on, and she carried it to him and slid it onto his plate. He finished that waffle and his fourth sausage, pushed his chair back, took his plate with one leftover sausage to the sink, set it on top of the mixing bowl, and left the room.

Margaret continued to eat, taking little bites and sipping coffee. She took her plate to the sink and daintily

picked up his leftover sausage and nibbled on it, and stared out the window.

She stared across the open space of the backyard and into the pines behind it and she drifted pleasantly away, until she felt him standing behind her.

"One hour," he said and put on his jacket and went out the back door.

They were leaving in one hour to visit Sally and Robert. She was glad for that. She wanted to see her daughter.

Sally and Robert Zilman had settled in rural Chatham County, 150 miles from Wilmington and 20 miles from Chapel Hill, where they had both gone to school. Like the children of many middle-class parents, they stayed around the college town after they graduated, taking their time deciding what next to do.

That Saturday they began cleaning the house.

"It's impossible to get this old house really clean," she said.

"It looks fine to me."

"It won't to them, though. Especially Daddy."

"Forget it," he said.

They lived in an old and ruined Victorian farmhouse on twenty-six acres of land. The house was ruined because the heirs remodeled it in the late fifties with sheetrock and linoleum tile and then ran out of money and abandoned it, eventually selling it to a timber merchant who then rented it to the crews who worked at his sawmill.

"We'll do the best we can and we just won't worry about it," Robert told her after lunch when they were halfway through cleaning. "They never actually say anything about it."

"I can tell, though."

"Let them stay in that damn camper, then," he said.

"They will. At night, anyway."

6

They had bought the place five years ago, when they got married, but had not yet saved enough money to do anything with it. It hadn't cost much because no one wanted to live that far out in the middle of nowhere, but even with the cheap price, they just barely made their payments each month.

"Get the dog and cat out," she said.

"I'll go out with them," he said, "and mow the yard."

He got out the lawnmower. He started cutting the thick fescue grass. He pushed the mower a few feet then stopped, just before the engine died, and then, after it revved back up, pushed it a few more feet.

After fifteen minutes, the engine overheated and shut off and wouldn't start again. As he was pushing it back to the barn, he heard something on the driveway, which was nine hundred feet long and badly rutted, and every rain made it worse.

"They're coming," he said, running in the door.

"They can't be," she said. "They never come before three."

They looked out the window. He noticed the corncrib door swinging open. He ran to close it. Sally watched her parents' camper slowly coming down the driveway. It swayed and rocked, like a ship in high seas, like an enormous aluminum monster from a nightmare, relentlessly bearing down upon the dreamer. It went from one side of the road to the other, picking its way around the deepest ruts and potholes and scraping bottom when it had no way to get around a bad spot.

"Damnit to hell," she said.

The camper rounded the curve at the bottom of the hill and started up the last hundred feet to the house. Sally turned away. She stood for a moment. She closed her eyes. The old upright Hoover vacuum cleaner roared and vibrated beside her. She could feel it through her bare feet. She

7

picked it up and shoved it across the room and into the closet. She kicked the door closed.

She went into the bathroom. She scrubbed furiously. She cleaned the sink and the floor and wiped the specks off the mirror. She scrubbed the brown stain the iron pipes from the old well left in the bowl and then, taking out new towels and wash cloths, put one of the towels in her mouth and bit down on it as hard as she could, and then screamed into it, a muffled distant scream that died right there in the towel.

After a moment and a deep breath, she washed her face, put on a smile and trotted out to greet her parents.

Ervin drove past the parking spot to the side of the house and then backed in. He had bought the camper soon after the young couple had bought the house because he couldn't stand to sleep in the filthy old place or even use the bathroom.

"The toilet, did you see the toilet?" he had asked his wife after the first visit. "It rocked back and forth so bad I thought it was going to fall through the floor."

As he backed the camper in, he had to watch for two maple trees and his daughter's car on one side and a ditch on the other.

"Goddamnit, sit still," he yelled at Margaret, who had twisted around when she saw Sally run out and was waving at her.

"Don't yell at me," she said.

"Then be still. I've got all I can handle right here without you jumping around."

He finally got in place. As he turned off the engine Robert came out of the house carrying a twelve-gauge extension cord. He plugged it into the outlet on the porch and carried the other end to the back of the camper.

"That's the way to do it, boy," Ervin said.

Sally ran to her mother's door and hugged her and then hugged her father. She and Robert and Margaret started in.

"Hold it a minute," Ervin called. "I need some help with this stuff."

"I'll do it," Robert said, and Sally and her mother went in.

Ervin handed out a pile of plastic tables with removable legs he had bought on sale at K Mart. He stacked them on Robert's outstretched arms.

Sally saw Robert struggle with the door and ran to help. Her father came next, carrying a large ice chest.

"Steaks tonight," he said. He put it on the counter and then handed a bag to Sally. "This is for you."

It was four pairs of pantyhose.

"They were on sale, along with those tables. I know women always need stockings," he said and opened the ice chest and pulled out a garbage bag in which he had wrapped the steaks.

"I'll just get these trimmed and some seasoning on them," he said, and went to work.

Sally and Margaret took a walk down the driveway. The dog and cat went with them. The woods on either side belonged to other people and the Zilmans had a deeded access through them. The woods were undeveloped and, except for coon, squirrel and rabbit hunters, provided a buffer of privacy and the sense of a large estate.

As they walked, Sally scrapped rocks into the ruts with her shoes. The cat scooted ahead and laid traps for the dog, leaping out with extended claws and arched back.

"It's always so good to come up here," her mother said. "I'm always glad to have you. You know that."

"I know, but if I came as often as I wanted, you'd be sick of me."

"Of course we wouldn't, Mother. You're not any trouble

9

at all. And you're looking great, you know. Have you changed your hair? What is it?"

"Not my hair," she said. "I've lost weight. Just a few pounds, though."

She thought about it for a few seconds, looking at herself in an imaginary mirror, and then added, "But I do look good for my age, I think. I really do," she said and fluffed her hair. "Of course, all the women in our family age well. You will too," she told Sally.

"I hope so."

"It's amazing I've held up so well."

"I know."

"It's a matter of perspective, though. And forgiveness."

"Yeah. If you can do it."

"I'm not alone, you know. I have help."

"You mean . . . ?"

"The church, of course. It's a strength. Young people don't think they need it."

"Maybe they don't."

"Everyone needs it. It just takes a hard time in your life to see it, to realize it. But that's the way of the Lord. He's there when you need him."

"I'll remember that."

"Don't mock me."

"I'm not. I promise I'm not. I understand exactly what you're saying."

"You see," she said, switching the subject but only horizontally, "your father doesn't mean half the things he says. He just can't stop himself."

"I'll say."

"He needs somebody to stop him. Lately, I've been thinking about doing that very thing."

"Don't get in trouble, Mother."

"I'm not scared of him. I'm the one person who really has his number."

* * *

10

"How do you like the tables?" Ervin asked when the women walked in.

"Great," Sally said. "Really great."

"They're a little low, aren't they?" Margaret asked.

"Not a bit," he said. "Not one damn bit."

"Don't start cussing, Daddy," Sally said.

"Well, she finds something wrong with everything I do."

"I do not. I was just making an observation. Anyone can see that they're lower than end tables usually are."

"See?" he said, looking at Sally. "She never lets up."

"They're fine," Sally said. "Mother may be right, but we're not trying to win any awards in this house."

"See," he said.

At four-thirty the conversation ground to a dead stop. No one could think of a thing to say. It was too early for supper. Everything was already prepared, even the tossed salad, which Ervin had mixed and brought in a large plastic container.

Robert looked at Sally. She looked back and cocked her head, as if to ask, What next? He shrugged. Ervin rustled his newspaper. Margaret shifted in her chair. She lazily swung one leg over the arm of the chair and left the other one on the floor and when Ervin looked over at the dark inside of her thighs he popped up off the couch as if he'd been ejected.

"I was just thinking of this joke I heard a fellow at the post office tell the other day," he said. Ervin was assistant superintendent for postal services.

"Two men from down South were up in New York for a visit," he began. "Early one morning they were looking out the window of one of those high-rise hotel buildings and they saw this great big open truck collecting trash.

"Now down below, these nigger men were throwing the trash in the back of that truck and one nigger man says to the other, 'Look heres, Mr. Brown, that trash gonna blow away if we don'ts do something. You climb up there and lay on top of it, you hear me?'

11

"So the other man climbed up there and lay down on the trash, spread-eagled like, to keep it from blowing away, and the truck drove off.

"And the two men up there looking out the hotel window watched that truck drive off and one of them says to the other, 'Look yonder at how these Yankees do up here. They have throwed away a perfectly good nigger.' "

Ervin laughed. He laughed hard. He looked around the room for a response.

"That's awful, Daddy," Sally said. "Those kind of jokes aren't funny anymore."

"I think they are," he said.

"I don't," his wife said.

"I don't care what you think," he said.

"You've got to understand," Sally said, "that things are different now. People are sensitive to things like that, even if you don't really mean anything by it."

"A good joke is a good joke, no matter who or what it pokes fun at," he said. He walked into the kitchen and fussed with the steaks.

After supper, when the evening hit another dead spot halfway between digestion and time for bed, Sally suggested they play Scrabble, forgetting that her mother took so long to make a word the game would go to hell before it was finished.

"Great idea," her father said and they set up the game on the kitchen table. It was a small table. There was hardly room for elbows. Sally passed behind Robert on her way to get ice tea and bumped his chair. He winked without looking up. When she came back and served the tea, she reached over his shoulder and bit him on the ear.

"Ouch," he said.

"Just trying to perk the old boy up," she said and took her seat. She was ready for the evening to end and to get to bed. The game began.

" 'Yo' isn't a word, I don't think it is, anyway, Mr. Neal," Robert said twenty minutes later.

"It is too."

"Time for the dictionary," Sally said.

"Yo-ho-ho and a bottle of rum," her father said as she came back with it. "It's the first word of that."

"But not a real word," she said, showing him the place on the page where it should have been.

After Margaret had struggled through the early stages of the game making simple, short words, her rack was filled with letters and when this turn came around she was stumped.

"It's your go," Ervin said.

"I know it is. Just give me a minute."

He watched the electric clock on the wall above their old refrigerator, which they had given to Sally and Robert, and when the second hand came around again, he said, "Time's up."

"Not yet," she said, and everyone shifted into a more comfortable position. She was thinking hard. She was trying to use up as many of her letters as possible, and, for a moment there, looked as if she had something as she moved one letter off the rack toward the board. She put it back, though, and in the silence, time stopped. Faucets dripped. The dog moaned in a dream. Ervin stretched. He moved his long legs under the table. His knee fell over against Sally's. She froze. In her mind she assembled legs and feet and knees under the table, trying to determine whose it was and when she was sure it was her father's, slowly eased away and stood up.

"More tea, anyone?"

"I'll take a little," her father said while Margaret shifted more letters around and pointed to spaces on the board. Ervin reached up to his breast pocket to get a cigarette, and finding his pocket empty, remembered he had quit smoking.

13

"Ah well," he said, and made an elaborate pantomine of lighting a cigarette and taking a deep breath. "I'll just pretend."

"Can I help you, Mother?" Sally asked after she sat back down.

"I've got it now," she said. She put out all her letters. She spelled, starting from a "c" on the board, an l . . . i . . . t . . . o . . . r . . . u . . . s. Then she looked up.

"I'm sorry," she said. "That's the only word I could think of that would use up all of the letters."

Sally looked at the board and when she realized what her mother was trying to spell, laughed and said, "Oh my God, Mother, that's a first for family Scrabble."

Just after the words left her mouth, Ervin yelled out, while grabbing at the letters, "That's not spelled right," and he shoved them back at her and knocked the board sideways, scattering everything on it.

"Well, how is it spelled then?" she shouted back.

Ervin glared at her and when he didn't say anything, Sally offered to look it up.

"Forget it," he said. "The game's over."

Ervin, cooling off now, began to pack up the game.

"I guess I really scrambled that Scrabble," he said, and Robert beeped a little laugh, like a honk of a bicycle horn.

Ervin and Margaret went to the camper. While Ervin was in the tiny toilet closet, Margaret undressed and put on flannel pajamas and got under the covers. When he came out she watched him take two Unisom sleeping tablets and wash them down with a hit from a bottle of NyQuil.

"You're only supposed to take one," she said. "And that NyQuil will give you bad dreams."

"Shut up and leave me alone," he said, and climbed up into the loft that was the closest thing within the camper to a separate room and, in the dark, took off his clothes, got under the sheets in his underwear, and after tossing and

14

grumbling and cursing under his breath, eventually fell into nightmarish sleep. Margaret lay still until she heard him go, and then just as she was thinking she would never get to sleep, dropped off without even knowing it.

Outside the house, the dog and the cat waited to be let in. The dog scratched lightly on the screen door and the cat paced under and around him, stroking him with his tail as he walked back and forth.

Inside the house, the rooms were dark except for a lamp in the bedroom on a table beside the bed, and the light in the bathroom, where Robert sat with Sally, who was taking a bath.

"The thing I can't understand," he said, "is why he gets so nervous."

"It's Mother. She makes him nervous. She always has."

"Always?"

"Well, nearly as long as I can remember. Maybe not when I was young. It seems like we all got along well back then."

"I don't think it's her," he said. "I think it's you."

"Wash my back," she said.

"Maybe it is her," he said, and washed her with his hand, "but it's a damn mystery, whatever it is. I've been watching him ever since we got married and I still can't figure it out."

She dried off. She put on a white cotton gown and ran through the hall and jumped in the bed. Robert finished his bath, and he came in with the towel wrapped around his waist.

"Move over," he said. "I'm freezing."

She threw back the covers, naked from head to toe.

"Come on down," she said like the game-show host.

"I almost didn't make it," he said. "I nearly fell apart right there at the table."

"I'm glad you didn't."

15

"It was too much. I don't think I could have paid the old woman to do a better job on him than she did."

"Daddy's very uptight about sex."

"Do tell," he said.

"Spell me some words," she said. "So I can do better at Scrabble next time." He did. After that they laughed and carried on and then, out of the blue, she asked him, "Why do you like me?"

"Well, I just do," he said.

"But why?"

"Because you're fun. You're nice. You're smart. You're good looking. Everything."

"Then why do you love me?" she asked.

"Well, because, I guess, because of who you are."

"And who am I?"

"You're the person I know. And you're mine."

"And that's all?" she asked.

"That's a lot."

"Because you know me and because I'm yours?"

"It's what I know about you that makes me love you," he said.

"And what does it mean when you say, 'because you're mine'? What does that mean?" she asked, snuggling in his arms.

"It means that you're not anyone else's."

"Well, you know that."

"Yeah, but it means that you never have been," he said.

"I might have been married before. You might not know it. I might not have told you."

"But were you?"

"But would it make a difference?"

"I don't know."

"Would I still be yours?"

"Sure, but wait a minute. Were you?"

"Don't be silly. Of course not. I was just trying to get you to tell me what you meant."

"Why are we talking about this?" he asked.

"I was just thinking about it. In terms of my parents, you know."

"Yeah."

"Want me to turn off the light?"

"I guess so."

"Want me to do anything else?"

"Yeah."

"What?" she asked.

"This," he said, and showed her a little thing or two he'd been thinking about, and a little while later, she showed him a few things as well.

Meanwhile in the driveway of the old, dilapidated house, within the smooth aluminum skin of that frigid sideshow of married life, all of this occurred unknown but, it seemed, not unfelt, as a series of cries and jerks rocked Ervin Neal while his wife slept soundly with a faint smile on her lips. She was tucked in toward the wall on the narrow bench, like a baby sleeping in a dresser drawer, a sweet sleep where a part of her life was going well, and where hidden away, she tried to make it last, and where, in the remote, uncharted regions of her dreams, she began to plan for something different.

"Anyway, if they're not up," Ervin said, after he had changed clothes in the tiny bathroom, bumping and scraping against the sides like buried alive and trying to get out of the coffin, "I'll just wake them up." Margaret stayed in bed until he left, then washed and dressed.

Every time the portable electric heater came on in the camper, the lights in the old farmhouse dimmed.

"I wish they'd turn the damn thing off," Robert said to Sally.

They were at the table in the kitchen drinking hot tea, and Sally asked, "Does it hurt the wiring?"

17

"No, but it bothers me. It'll blow a fuse before it does anything bad."

Ervin opened the door and looked quickly around the kitchen.

"Good. You haven't made breakfast yet. I'm going to make you my special leftover-steak and eggs dish."

"You don't have to do that, Mr. Neal," Robert said.

"Yes I do. That's why I saved the drippings."

He went to work. Margaret came in. She had some coffee.

"I don't suppose you're going to church," she said to Sally.

"No. I guess not."

"I didn't think so. I wish you'd come home on Christmas and go to Christmas Eve services with me."

"Let's talk about it later," she said. "You'll be back up for Thanksgiving. We can decide then."

Just before they left Ervin looked at the house and shook his head.

"You know," he said, "it wouldn't take much to paint it. It sure would do a lot of good. We could give you the money for Christmas," he said.

"Thanks anyway," Robert said, "but we've been saving for it and were planning on doing it anyway."

"The offer stands," Ervin said and drove off.

"Why'd you tell him that?" Sally asked.

"I don't know. It just came out."

They sat on the porch. The porch faced east. The maple trees that had been planted around the house when it was built created a canopy of shade during the summer and now shone red as they stood full of leaves ready to drop.

"It's so quiet," Sally said. The cat was on her lap and the dog was in the yard in a sunny spot.

"It always is," Robert said, "after they leave."

"I know," she said. "It's almost like when the radio or

18

television's been on real loud and suddenly you notice it and turn it off."

They put their feet on the rail and they rested. Next weekend they had to visit his parents. The week after that the Neals returned for Thanksgiving. After that, Christmas. A solid month of madness. They shared the quiet morning then, anticipating what lay ahead.

Two

Ervin spent a lot of time in convenience stores. He spent time in them the way a person who loved art might spend time in a museum. He strolled the aisles. He looked for new products. He looked for old products in new packages.

These stores were just right for the South, where they took the place of the neighborhood bar and served people who, brought up in that generalized Baptist world of denial and abstinence, poured in junk food as merrily as red-faced alcoholics, only the store was better, because you never knew what you were going to find on the shelves. Potato chips au gratin. Corn nuts. A Mickey Mouse ice cream bar with chocolate ears.

People like Ervin passed each other in the aisles and looked at each other and stared, waiting for the other to speak. They moved in the same way and they looked for the same thing, but, unable to ask for it, they continued on. They were travelers in the neighborhood museums of the commercial arts.

Ervin's favorite store was the Pantry, where wide aisles and bright lighting and shrink-wrapped magazines of the

forbidden naked female beckoned. Even on his bad days, in his worst moments, he only paused at the rack, never for a moment letting on how much he missed the sweetness of a woman, the touch, the look, the understanding smile, the comfort of someone to talk to.

It was his favorite store partly because the clerk who worked the day shift treated him so nicely that, for a moment each day, he felt a little better.

He opened one of the glass doors and reached for a can of Gatorade, but just as his hand gripped the cold orange can, he saw a sign taped on the adjoining door advertising alcohol-free beer and he closed the door where he was and stared transfixed at the new product.

"That's great stuff," the nice clerk said.

"What? That?"

"That near-beer, or, I mean, not near-beer, but whatever they call it," she said and walked through a side door and appeared behind the racks of cold drinks where she quickly, like a machine built especially for the task, racked up a whole shelf of six-ounce orange juice bottles.

Ervin pulled out one of the cans. It had a foreign-sounding name and he read the ingredients and the rest of the label.

"I wonder if it'll make my breath smell," he said. He was on his lunch break.

"I don't think so," she said as he put the can on the counter and reached for his wallet. "There's no alcohol in it."

"I guess not," he said, and paid for it.

"Come back," she called after him and he waved and took the new beverage to his car. It was a cold day, but with the windows rolled up, the inside of the car was warm as a greenhouse. As he drank, he rested sections of the free classified shopper on the steering wheel and read all the ads, even the help wanted, when the last thing he wanted was another job.

The beer was highly carbonated and he began to burp. He let it roll, and as he felt one coming on, he worked it up and let it loose, one after another, smacking his lips at the taste and swallowing again, waiting on the next.

He slumped back in the seat of his old Dodge and continued reading. He actually felt a little drunk, loose and warm and cozy in his private little world in his car in the sun. He finished one section of the shopper and tossed it onto the floor with the empty can and put the second section against the steering wheel. He opened it, felt a bit of discomfort from gas, and leaned over toward the door to let it escape.

At the same time he leaned over, he looked up to see if anyone heard and not fifteen feet from his window and walking toward him was the new woman who had come to work at the post office.

The smell was absolutely fierce. He quickly looked away. He fiddled with his keys as if he were going to start the car and when she tapped on the window he acted as if he didn't hear her, and then looked up, surprised.

"Oh, hi," he said through the glass.

She said something. He pointed to his ear and waved his hands around as if he were deaf.

"Roll it down," she said, and made a cranking motion with her hand.

"I can't," he said, and made as if to try, and acted as though it were stuck.

Meanwhile the smell had come purely out from between his hips and the seat and filled the car like poisonous gas.

She walked around to the other side and he thought, Holy cow, what am I going to do? She tried the door and then looked at him strangely. She pulled in the air beside the door lock, lifting it and pointing at it.

"Wait a second," he said, and turned the key to accessory and the blower on, and then pointed to the mess on

the floor and began to throw the cans and wrappers and old newspapers into the back seat. He swept the seat itself off with his hand, and then suddenly realized his escape. He opened his door and leaped out, and then slammed it closed so hard the old car shivered and twanged like a dropped guitar.

"The car's so messy," he said, sprinting around to her side.

"I wanted to ask if I could have a ride back. I took my car to the shop and was going to take the bus but it doesn't come in time and then was going to take a taxi when I saw you over here."

"Oh sure," he said, "you can have a ride."

"I'm Angie," she said.

"I remember," he said. "You started a few months ago."

"Right."

"Do you want to buy anything for break?" he asked, stalling for time.

"I don't think so," she said, and then paused, when during a lull in the traffic, she heard a whirring from his car and looked in. "Something's on in your car," she said.

"Oh," he said, and reached for the handle. "I left the blower on. I was just getting ready to leave when you tapped on the window."

He pulled on the door and it hung for a moment halfway open and then snapped, loud as a gunshot, as it cleared the spot where the hinges were bent and the door dug into the supporting post.

"Yeow," she said.

"Sorry. It always does that. Old piece of junk," he said and reached in and turned off the key, leaning over at the same time and unlocking her door.

"We better go," she said and got in. He could still smell it.

"I've go so much trash in this old car it smells like a

23

garbage truck," he said. "I just never get around to clearing it out."

"Mine's the same way," she said, and looked for her seatbelt.

"It's, uh . . ." he said, and searched in the crack of the seat for it, ". . . it's, uh, right here, I think," and he pulled on the silver buckle, but in pulling on it made a fist and couldn't get his hand back through.

"Never mind," she said. "It's not far," and they drove off, Ervin stiff as a brick and uncomfortable in the cold air blowing in through his window, and Angie, rather innocently riding along beside him not knowing, of course, having no way of knowing, of course, that she was the first woman in years, outside of Margaret and Sally, to be alone with him. He felt downright giddy and didn't know what to make of it.

Three

Sally and Robert visited his parents once a year. It was 120 miles to Charlotte from their house. Robert's father was a dentist. He was famous for having convinced his patients, when the high-speed drill was introduced, that they no longer needed novocaine. By convincing them of this, he cut ten minutes of chair-time from each visit. He could see nearly a third more patients. He smiled and chatted happily while he drilled the tears right out of their eyes.

"There it is," Robert said, driving up to the grand house the high-speed drill had helped pay for.

"Stately mansions," Sally said.

"What's that from?"

"A book? No. A hymn, I think. I can't remember."

They parked behind the two cars already in the garage.

"This is it," he said.

"I guess it is."

"Teeth brushed?"

"Check."

"Hair combed, all lint and stray particles removed?"

"Check."

"Then we're ready," he said and they walked down the slate walk to the back door. It was locked.

"That's strange," he said. "They were expecting us. Weren't they?"

"I think," she said. "You took care of it."

"I hope it's not the wrong day."

He rang the bell. He heard his mother's high-pitched voice. It was aimed at his father.

"You know that's the back-door bell. The front bell," she said, "goes ding-dong and the back bell goes dong-ding."

Sally moved behind Robert and pulled on his shirt, hiding but letting him know she was there.

"You're late," his mother said. "What happened?"

Robert's father patted her on the shoulder, as if to say, Calm down, calm down. She was so upset at Robert for having disappointed her in so many ways that no matter what she told herself each time she was going to see him, no matter how she and her husband planned what they would say and what they wouldn't, she just spilled it all out anyway.

"Now, now," Dr. Zilman said. "They're not too late, are you?"

"I don't think so," Robert said.

"Come in and sit down. Tell us what you two have been doing," Dr. Zilman said and led everyone into the den. While the three of them talked Mrs. Zilman watched her son, who had not been close to her since he was a teenager. She had the same feeling she had always had about him that if she could just break through to him, just shake him loose from whatever it was that had possessed him, if she could just save him from whatever it was that had turned him cold toward her, then the family could be back the way it had been when Robert and his sister were young.

"Will you stay the night?" she asked and saw her hus-

band look away, as that was one of the questions they had decided not to ask anymore.

"No, I don't think we can," Robert said. "We've just got so much to do."

"Like what?" she asked.

"Well, I mean, Sally's got her job and I've got mine . . ."

"You don't work on Sunday, do you?"

"No, but I mean . . ."

"And what kind of job is that, anyway, for someone like you, construction work, I mean, it's just not right," she said.

"It's not construction work," he said. "It's carpentry."

"Whatever."

"There's a difference."

"It's still not a career."

"Sally's got a career," he said.

She was a graphic artist at the university in Chapel Hill. She had majored in studio art at UNC and then, after a few years to play around, married Robert and took the job.

"That's not what I mean."

"How's Reecee doing?" Robert asked about his sister.

"Beautifully," his mother said.

"She's Phi Beta Kappa already."

"And just a junior," his mother said to Sally, as if she didn't know and gave her a lemon smile.

"Four-oh average," his father said.

"She always was good with books," Robert said.

In the lull, Dr. Zilman took out a thick, old Havana cigar, lit it and began to puff. Mrs. Zilman turned on an air purifier. As Dr. Zilman puffed, billows of smoke rose in the sunlight coming through the window behind him. The smoke played in the light and drifted lazily across the room. They all watched this smoke, suspended and hypnotized and warmed for a few moments by its graceful flow and by the rhythmic puffing on the cigar.

"Phi Beta Kappa," his mother suddenly said again, as if coming out of a dream.

"Double major," his father said.

"Might go into dentistry," his mother said.

"We always thought it'd be you," his father said.

"I guess that's the way things go," Robert said and noticed his mother looking at him strangely.

"What's that?" she asked and rushed over and grabbed the neck of his sweater. "Look at that spot. What is it?"

She pulled on the material and stretched it out to see it better.

"What?" he asked, looking down like an old man with bifocals trying to see what it was.

The whole family converged on him, Sally included, knowing it would be her fault he had the spot. They offered their opinions.

"It's a burn," his father said.

"It's not," his mother said.

"It's grease," Sally said.

"Grease? What kind of grease leaves a black spot?" his mother asked.

"Automobile grease," she said.

"Oh," she said and let the material pop back.

"I got that on me this morning when I was adding some oil," he said.

"And you let him wear it looking like that?" she said to Sally and rushed out of the room and then back in again carrying a spray can of K2-r.

"I'll fix it," she said and pushed Robert's head to one side and said, "Watch it," and sprayed him like a bug, whirling the can in a circle as the white foamy spray, which smelled like burning Easy-Off, obliterated the spot.

"There," she said. "Wait awhile and then we'll brush it off with the cap." She pointed the spiked plastic top at him. "I hope it's not ruined," she said and pulled on it again.

28

"Let me just take it off," he said.

His mother took his sweater in the kitchen and he and Sally went upstairs to his old room, which had new furniture.

"See that roof?" he asked. "That's how I used to sneak out."

"You jumped from there?" Sally asked.

"I was tougher then."

"And had more to run away from, too."

"That's right, baby," he said and pulled her down on the bed.

"Don't."

"Why not?"

"They might come in."

"Let them."

They went down for a late lunch his mother had prepared while waiting for the spot remover to work, but before she served them, she guided Robert into the other room.

"I just want to ask you one thing."

Here it comes, he thought.

"What's that?"

"I told myself I wasn't going to worry about it this year, but I have to know. I just have to."

"The answer is no."

"No to what?" she asked.

"To what you're going to ask me."

"How do you know what it is?" she asked, truly dumbfounded.

"Because you ask me every year."

"Ask you what? Go on and tell me if you're so sure?"

"If I went to Yom Kippur services this year. Right?"

"That is right," she said. "But I never remember asking you. Never. I worry about it, but I never remember asking you."

"He started to go," Sally said and Mrs. Zilman spun

29

around to see her leaning in the doorway. "He talked about it, anyway," she said.

"I did talk about it," he said. "But I didn't make it."

His mother went out the other door to the room and circled back to the kitchen and started serving lunch.

When Robert had told them he was marrying Sally, and even after they met her, his mother had said, "Well, if you do that, you're finished. You'll be sorry for the rest of your life."

She had a low opinion of the Christian world, based mainly on an undefined sense of competition and a two-week vacation she had spent as a college student with one of her Christian friends, which she never got over and whose faults she ascribed to everyone outside of her faith she ever fell out with.

"They don't live like we do," she had told Robert. "All you'll hear is Jesus, Jesus, Jesus from her family for the rest of your life. They keep dirty houses. Your father tells me they have bad teeth. They run around on each other. They hold the liquor bottle in one hand and the Bible in the other."

So far, Robert had found none of that to be true.

The children left immediately after lunch.

"We've got to get home before dark," he said. "I think one of my headlights is burned out."

The only thing that was really burned out was the relationship, and as far as Robert was concerned, there was no fixing it and he hadn't worried about it in so long the visit once a year was more or less on the same level as paying taxes.

"Well," he said, as they drove up Interstate 85, "one weekend I get to see your parents fight it out on a Scrabble board and the next weekend I get this."

"It's all my fault, of course," Sally said.

"Some trip," he said.

"Promise me something."

"Anything, baby," he said.

"Promise me if we ever get that bad, we'll just go our separate ways."

"Promise me something, too."

"Okay."

"Promise me if I ever get like your father you'll shoot me."

"I can't promise that," she said.

"Well I'll shoot myself, then."

"It's strange," she said, and put her feet on the dash. "When you think about people being married, you think about people being in love. But then, what happens?"

"Beats me."

"Wonder why people stay together when everything's gone sour."

"My parents love each other," he said.

"Oh, I guess they do. It's mine I'm talking about."

"I don't know."

"I'm glad we have what we have," she said, and leaned over and kissed his cheek. "It's the most precious thing in the world to me," she said, and looked down the road ready to get back home and get on with her life, and to get past Thanksgiving, Christmas and New Year's.

They drove up to the old house just as the sun was setting. It looked good in subdued light, but with the trees losing their leaves, it looked much worse during the day as the sun illuminated the peeling paint and rotten underboxing and patched clapboards.

"I know," she said. "Let's get the house painted before Mother and Daddy come up for Thanksgiving."

"How can we do that?"

"We just do it."

"Have we got the money?"

"Barely. Maybe."

"But what about the payment?"

"We've got enough for that, too."

31

"I hate painting. I hate scraping. Have you ever done it?"

"I did ours with Daddy when I was younger."

"Your house is brick."

"It has siding halfway up around the windows and along the back, remember?"

"Oh yeah."

"I'm determined to do it," she said.

"I can tell."

"I'll do anything to get it done before they get here."

Four

That Sunday morning Ervin was dragged from his drug-induced sleep by the sound of organ music and choir singing. The hymn was upbeat. It was the opening theme song to a praise-the-Lord-and-pass-the-money show that Margaret watched while getting ready to go to church, where the entertainment, while not as slick as television, was good enough.

Because Margaret was going to church, Ervin wasn't. That left the whole morning to kill before the "NFL Today" program and, if things were in his favor, six to seven hours of nonstop action.

"Have a good rest while I'm gone," Margaret called to him when she heard the car horn. She didn't drive, and hadn't for years. Ervin came out when he heard her drive off.

"Good rest, my ass," he mumbled at the departing car. He flipped across the channels and paused for a moment on the East Carolina coach's show, and then turned it off and dressed.

Margaret assumed he stayed home and rested and made the most of being alone. He never did. He always went somewhere, but finding interesting places to go on Sunday

33

morning in the coastal plains of eastern North Carolina where everything was shut up tight took ingenuity and creativity.

One of the places he often went was a hardware store in a rural community about sixteen miles from town. It was open 365 days a year, from morning until night, and sold guns and ammunition along with hardware, soft drinks, crackers and groceries.

He wandered around in the store. He knew a few of the regulars by sight, enough to nod and establish that he meant no harm, this stranger to the community. He stopped this morning in front of the gun racks. Rifles and pistols were displayed behind a locked, glass-paneled door and, within, were locked once more through their trigger guards with a chain. He bought a small Coke and a pack of Lance salted peanuts and, while he stood there, he dumped the peanuts in the Coke and then sipped on the bottle, first letting a little of the drink slide in and then opening up for a mouthful of nuts.

When he finished, he went to the hardware section and bought a tiny grease gun and a tube of grease, intent on silencing his car door. He checked his watch and then left the store in time to get home before Margaret. On the way, his car died suddenly, as if the impulse to the spark, and the gas as well, had simultaneously shut off. It didn't sputter. It didn't fire again, and he coasted to a stop in a dirt parking lot in front of a closed restaurant surrounded by fields of blueberry bushes as far as the eye could see.

He stood beside his car with the hood up and soon caught a ride into town, and then took a taxi to his house, where he saw Margaret at the window.

"My car broke down."

"But where were you? I didn't know you were going anywhere."

"I just went out for a ride in the country."

"To see who? To see what?"

"Just a ride. Just killing time. Don't worry about it."

"You better not be up to anything," she said, trying to see through him.

"Forget it," he said. "We've got to get the car."

"What do you mean?"

"Ride out with me in the camper and I'll take a chain and pull it back to Wart's garage. He can work on it Monday."

"I can't drive."

"Just steer it. You can do that. A child could do it."

"I can't. Call a wrecker."

"Cost too much," he said and handed her her coat and started out the door.

"Let me change clothes."

"No time. Something might happen to the car. It's sitting in the middle of nowhere."

"I might get dirty."

"Listen," he said, and turned around. "You're just going to sit in the car and hold the steering wheel and that's it. You don't have to crawl under it and work on it."

He couldn't find the old chain he thought he still had from years ago so he took the bag of tire chains he had never used and tossed it into the back of the camper.

"Let's go."

The road was old. It was narrow. The land on either side was flat. Small communities of blacks lived along the road, left over from the days of tenant farming. Each community had a church. After church, the black families walked back down the road to their houses. They were dressed in their best clothes. As they walked, they paraded their finery, and waved and talked back and forth to each other on either side of the road and to the families already gathered in the front

yards of their houses. They barely minded the cars coming down the road.

"Get the fuck off the road," Ervin said through the windshield.

"Don't talk like that around me," Margaret said.

"Look at them. We gave them the vote, we gave them the schools, and then we gave them all our jobs and they're still just niggers."

"I won't listen to that," she said. She turned her face to the side and smiled pleasantly at the people they passed, hoping to counter Ervin's scowling looks.

"The ones over in Korea weren't so bad," he said, remembering blacks he had fought with, "but I guess it was just the army keeping them in line."

"You used to write to, what's his name, you know, when you first got back."

"Yeah, but he was different."

"What ever happened to him?"

"How should I know? Things are different now. He's probably got uppity by now, like the rest of them."

"You were nicer then, to everybody," she said, thinking about herself in particular, and feeling awfully discouraged about what they had lost. "We had such a happy family."

"Don't get started on that crap," he said. "You're just here because I need someone to drive the car. I didn't bring you along to have to listen to that weepy crap about the way we used to be."

"You better be nice to me or I won't drive."

"If you won't drive, I'll leave you out there all alone and then you'll see how nice your black folks are."

"Do it," she said. "I want you to. I wouldn't have a minute's trouble. They can tell what I think of them. They can tell I'm not prejudiced."

"Bull," he said and slowed down. "After we get stopped just get in the car and I'll hook us up and pull us home. You

steer and when you see me hold my hand up, like this, it means I'm getting ready to put on the brakes."

"Then what?"

"Then you get ready to put on yours so you won't ram into the back of me."

"The power brakes won't work with the motor off, will they?"

He let her out. He backed up to within a few feet of the old car. He took out the tire chains, hooked them together and managed about five feet of length and then hooked one end over the ball of the trailer hitch on the camper and the other around the bumper of the car.

"Put it in neutral, here," he said and reached in and did it, "and take off the emergency brake," he said and reached down and did that for her, too, but in doing so touched her leg. "Get out of the way. Move over. I can't get the brake off."

"Drive slowly," she said.

"I will."

The car was so close to the camper that Margaret could not see the road between them. She felt as if she were going to ram into the back of the camper and almost immediately, she waved her hand for him to stop.

He looked in his outside rearview mirror and saw her and rolled his window down and waved her away. He took it up to forty-five miles an hour and checked back. She was still waving her hand so he gave her the braking signal and pulled over on the shoulder.

"What is it?"

"I can't do it. I can't see the road. I can't see where you're going or which way the road is going up ahead. All I can see is the back of the camper."

"We can't stop now," he said. "Just follow me. That's all you have to do."

He got back in and took it up to fifty. Margaret quickly looked at the speedometer, afraid to take her eyes off the

camper, and when she saw how fast he was going, applied the brakes. They had little effect though she mashed as hard as she could.

He felt the car drag and waved his arm back and forth and she let off. He took it up to sixty then and the car began to tremble, like the steering wheel was going to shake loose.

"I can't make it," she said out loud to herself. "He's got to stop." She rode the brakes steadily. Ervin felt it and took it up to seventy, grinning as his big V-8 overcame the drag behind him.

At seventy, the old car began to shake as if it were coming apart. Margaret forgot all about the brakes and just held on for dear life to the steering wheel, which shook so violently it jiggled the loose flesh under her arms and on her face like she was hooked up to the belt of an exercise machine. She held on tighter and she opened her mouth so she could breathe better. She looked like she'd grabbed a high-voltage wire as her cheeks slopped back and forth like an old woman with a bad case of palsy.

Ervin looked in his rearview mirror and thought, What the hell, and then remembered how badly out of balance the front tires were and he chuckled and took it up to seventy-five.

"Oh Jesus, help me get through this," she warbled in vibrato like a singer on a warped recording.

The camper and the car sped by the black families on the side of the road and in their front yards. The two vehicles drew attention not only by their speed but by their extreme proximity and by the smoke and smell of burning asbestos as Margaret mashed on the brakes.

In the front yard of an old frame house with a sagging front porch and a cleanly swept dirt front yard and a giant green John Deere tractor parked beside the house, and nearly larger than the old dwelling, which sat on the edge of

a field owned by the farmer who owned the little house and the tractor, as well, the extended clan of the old couple who lived there stopped in midsentence as they heard the approaching vehicles and, like the teeth of a gear rotating slowly, all turned and watched the sight.

"What's that coming?" one of them asked.

"I don't know."

"There it come," the first one said.

"Look," another said.

"I never seed nothing like that before," the first one said, pointing as the two vehicles sped by with what looked like the driver of the first one laughing and the driver of the second crying.

"Is that man pulling that car?"

"Yeah. He pulling it."

"What's that smoke?"

"He burning up his engine."

"Must be them white folks from up North, going South for the winter," one of them suggested.

"Yeah," the first one said, satisfied with the explanation. "They always is in such a hurry."

When they got to the edge of town Ervin put out his hand and signaled, braked and slowed down. He kept to the speed limit once inside the city, and as the car stopped shaking, so did Margaret, so that by the time they got to the parking lot of Wart's garage, the only signs of her fright were the dried tracks her tears had made in her makeup.

"I will never talk to you again," she said when she got out on shaky legs.

"Of course you will."

"I will never do anything for you again. Don't even ask."

"Don't blame me if you don't know how to drive. You are the one who got scared and quit driving."

"I want to go home. Take me home."

39

"And look what you did to the bumper, putting on your brakes when you weren't supposed to." He pointed to the bumper, which had bent out like the prow of a ship.

"Just take me home."

Back in the house, Ervin turned on the NFL, got a Coke from the refrigerator and a bag of Doritos, nacho flavor, and settled down for a perfect afternoon.

Margaret went into her room, took off her coat, took off her shoes and sat on the edge of the bed. She remained there in the stillness of the darkened room, trying to ignore the football game in the other room, and trying to decide what next to do.

Five

Friday, coming home from work early, Sally and Robert began scraping. The house was a story and a half. It was in two sections. The sections were built into each other and formed a T. The back section had a large dormer on both sides of the roof. The roof was tin and painted red. The rest of the house was basically one story.

She had decided to paint it a pure yellow-ochre color, a deep and rich yellow that was like the most golden color of the sun before it turned red.

They scraped until their arms ached, getting nowhere with the stubborn, old lead-based paint. They went inside to rest and saw, while glancing through a Sears catalog, a paint sprayer with a sandblasting attachment.

"Let's get it tomorrow morning," she said.

The old truck, a 1955 Dodge, wouldn't make it the forty-five miles to Durham so they took her car. When they got to the store they discovered the one advertised on sale wouldn't handle a sandblaster well enough for what they needed, so they bought a five-hundred-dollar outfit with the intention of selling it when they finished with it.

After they got all the way back home Robert couldn't make the plug fit.

"It's for a two-twenty outlet," the salesman said when they called him.

They loaded the heavy thing back into the trunk and drove back to Durham.

"You'll have to buy this five-horsepower gasoline-powered model," the salesman told them.

"It'll sandblast?" Sally asked.

"Absolutely."

A man in bib overalls was listening to the conversation. He had a paper cup in one hand. About the time the salesman went off to do the paperwork, the man spit into the cup and came over to Robert and Sally.

"Was you talking about sandblasting?" he asked.

"Yeah," Robert answered.

"You going to use that?"

"Yeah."

"Of course it's none of my business, but I don't believe I'd do that if I was you."

"Why not?" Sally asked.

The man had on a cap with a frayed bill exposing the cardboard within and the cap had an emblem on the front with two rebel flags crossed like swords and the faded words, "Martinsville Speedway," above the flags.

"It won't last," he said and looked down at Sally and more or less into the bill of his cap, as if talking to a strange woman was a difficult thing. "It just won't hold up no time at all. Them seals go bad, see. That engine's aluminum. It can't take much heat."

"Well, what would you suggest?"

"Buy mine. I got one I'll sell you for the same as that."

He spit into the cup and even though Sally tried not to, she saw the filthy brown tobacco juice.

"I don't really want to sell it," he said, "but I got down in my back a few months ago and can't use it no more."

"Where can we see it?" Robert asked.

"Over at my place."

"Where's that?"

They talked it over and then Robert said, "Well, we weren't really planning to spend quite that much when we came over here."

"I can sell it to you for less."

"It'd have to be a lot less."

"We can talk about it," the man said.

After the salesman refunded their money, they followed the man out to an old Ford pickup with homemade wooden sides piled to the top with pieces of machinery and old tires.

"My name's Delbert Johnson, by the way," he said, leaning out the window. They followed him for miles. They drove completely out of Durham and then out of Durham County and onto Highway 70 and west for ten more miles, then north beyond Hillsborough.

"Bad sign," Robert said.

"You want to stop?" she asked.

"Too late now."

"I guess we might as well see what he's got."

Finally Delbert stopped and pointed to a narrow, rutted driveway that was worse than theirs. A couple of hundred feet down they suddenly came to a clearing. The house was one story with asphalt siding. The siding had been manufactured with a brick-veneer pattern. In the yard were two pulpwood trucks, a dozen old cars and a pile of machinery and appliances and lumber that just went on as far as they could see.

"Bad news," Sally said.

Six dogs came out from under the house. They ran at the car. Delbert yelled and threw a radiator hose at them. "Don't mind them, folks. Just go ahead and get out. They won't bother you none."

"You've got a lot of stuff here," Robert said.

"I save everything and anything. You wouldn't believe what people throw away."

They walked behind the house. The dogs sniffed them. One of them rammed his nose up Robert's ass and then walked around in front of him and looked him in the eye as if he'd smelled something peculiar and wanted to check out the face that went with the smell.

"Here it is," said Delbert. He pointed to a four-cylinder diesel air compressor mounted on a two-wheel trailer. "It's old but it'll really do a job."

·"But what is it?" Sally asked. "I mean, what was it?"

"It's an old state-surplus compressor. They used them to run jackhammers to tear up roads."

"It's bigger than we imagined," she said.

"Yes ma'am, but you need it if you're going to sand-blast."

The machine was buried in vines and blackberry briars. They couldn't see it clearly.

"Let me get my old Farmall and pull her loose," he said and set off at a limping trot toward a shed, like Grandpappy Amos on "The Real McCoys."

"We're in trouble," Robert said.

"Let's just look at it and be polite and then hurry on back to Sears and get the other."

Sally looked back at the house. She saw a woman standing in an open doorway. The woman stared at her. She waved. The woman never moved. Delbert came back. He was driving a rusty old Farmall-A tractor, and dragged a chain behind it which he hooked to the trailer to pull it free of the growth.

"We'll have to jump her off." He attached the jumper cables to the tractor battery. "They're both six-volt," he said and got a can off the porch and came back, looking over his shoulder at the woman.

"Don't worry about her. That's my wife's mother."

He returned to the porch and filled a can with oil from the tank on stilts beside the house.

"Heating oil is the same as diesel fuel," he said and then sprayed ether from an aerosol can into the air cleaner and mashed the starter.

Blue smoke puffed and wheezed out of the stack on top of the engine but it wouldn't start.

"It'll start, I swear it will. I had that thing running just the other day."

Delbert's mother-in-law appeared in front of them.

"Will you be wanting lunch?"

"Not yet."

"It's lunchtime."

"Just not yet, that's all," he said and straightened up from the motor.

The old woman walked off.

"She don't talk much," Delbert said and went back to work.

He tried the starter again. The motor fired.

"I told you," he said.

The noise was so loud they couldn't think. Delbert pointed to a set of gauges and explained how they worked. He dragged a long red rubber hose from under the machine. He hooked it onto the air outlet, all the while talking incomprehensibly. He put a tire chuck on the end of the hose and filled the slack tires of the trailer on which the whole thing sat. It was an enormous steel trailer with a tongue that had been resting on a concrete block before he pulled it out of the bushes.

After he filled the tires, he went into the bushes and came back with a splattered paint sprayer and hooked it up. It worked. Then, with the motor still wide-open and the heavy diesel smoke settling around the house and yard like fog, he hooked up the sandblasting attachment. He sprayed

from an old bucket. He sprayed the bushes. Branches ripped off like they'd been machine-gunned, leaving the bushes bare and stripped. Then he cut off the motor and looked over at them and laughed.

"I told you, boy. I told you it'd work. I just bet you didn't believe me when you saw it. Now tell me. Did you?"

"We weren't sure," said Robert, the first words either of them had spoken in the half-hour, mind-rattling display.

"It'll eat up that little Sears machine and spit out the parts," he said and laughed again.

"Can we talk about it?" Robert asked Delbert.

"You just suit yourself," he said.

"It worked," Sally said.

"I know, but . . ." he said.

"But it worked. It really did."

"You mean you want to buy it?"

"Why not? We can strip the paint off the house this afternoon and have it painted twice before Thursday."

"And then what?"

"Sell it."

"Let's do it, then."

"How much do you want for it?" she asked.

"I'll take six hundred. Everything included."

After he said that, he let fall a wet, black, compacted mass of chewed-up tobacco. It rolled out of his mouth and fell like a dog turd onto the ground. He spit. He stuck his finger in his mouth and wiped out the insides of his cheeks. He pulled a single toothpick from his shirt pocket and used it and then took a pouch of tobacco from the other shirt pocket and mashed in a fresh chaw.

"That's too much," Robert said.

"We can't afford that."

"How much can you afford?" Delbert mumbled through the tobacco.

"About two hundred," Robert said.

"Done," he said and grabbed Robert's hand and shook it. "A handshake's good enough for me," he said.

After he shook his hand he leaned to one side and spit a stream of fresh juice that looked like some kind of liquid disease.

"Can I write you a check?" Sally asked.

"I can't cash no check," he said, more to Robert than her. "I don't have no bank account."

Robert had that much in his wallet, having just cashed his paycheck.

"I've got it," he mouthed to Sally, who nodded for him to pay him, after which it occurred to him that they had no way to pull it back to their house.

"Can you pull it for us with your truck?" he asked.

"No sir, I can't do that. I'd like to, but what with the wife sick and all, I just can't."

"Well, how are we going to get it home? If you can't get it home," Sally said, "you'll have to give us our money back."

"Now it's not my fault about that," Delbert said, suddenly getting tough. "But I tell you what I'll do. I'll drag it over to the front and help you hook it up to your car. It won't be no trouble."

He pulled it with the tractor. The tongue dragged the ground and plowed a furrow as it went. It took all three of them to lift the heavy tongue and get it level with the bumper of the car.

"I thought you had a trailer hitch," Delbert said.

"Nope."

"Well, never mind. I'll work something out."

Robert held the tongue steady on top of the bumper while Sally pushed from behind to keep it from rolling away. Delbert returned with some electric-fence wire. He tied the tongue to the bumper and then wrapped it around and around and through the bumper and through every hole and slot he could find. When they stepped back, they saw that the

weight of the tongue had flattened the back springs of the car and raised up the front so that it looked like a speedboat at full throttle.

"She's heavy, all right," Delbert said.

"You think we'll make it?" Sally asked.

"Sure. Just take it easy."

They started off. After a few feet, Robert applied the brakes. The trailer slid forward and rammed into the back of the trunk.

"Hold a second," Delbert said and ran toward the house. He looked on the ground and then ran to the porch and saw one of his grandchildren's toys, a brown, furry teddy bear. He mashed it in between the trailer tongue and the trunk. The bear squeaked when he mashed it in.

"That'll keep from scratching that up," he said and off they went. All the way down the drive they heard the little bear squeaking as the trailer rammed back and forth against the trunk. At the state road they went around and looked.

"Jesus H. Christ," Robert said. "What have we done?"

"I don't know."

They leaned against the car. Through the trees they heard Delbert's tractor.

"I feel stupid," Sally said.

"Yeah."

"I guess it's not going to fall off, though," she said, pulling on it.

"You want to go?"

"Might as well. At least it'll work. Do we have enough sand?"

"He said we did."

"Let's go, then."

They crept along until they found Highway 70 and had been on it no more than a minute when they had a line of cars behind them. They were going thirty miles an hour. The temperature gauge in the car read danger.

"I've got to stop," he said.

"Wait until we find a good place," she said, looking back at the machine as it lumbered from side to side no matter how they tried to keep it straight. The bear squeaked and squealed and screamed, "Help, help," as the car lurched and jerked over the bumpy road. The weight of the trailer made the front end so light they had hardly any steering. Soon the bear quit crying. Soon after that they pulled over at a road-side picnic table.

"Oh hell," he said.

"Look at that," she said, as the line of cars accelerated past them.

The trailer had crashed through and wedged into the trunk. The tongue had mashed the little brown bear through the metal. The end of the hitch stuck through its stomach.

They drove the rest of the way as if they were returning from the funeral of a close friend. The trailer, wedged firmly now, pulled better and they made it home without additional trouble.

After they got it loose from the car and jacked the tongue level they got out their jumper cables. The dog dreamily sniffed the wheels of the trailer, mesmerized by years of strange urine.

They hooked the jumper cables up and tried to start it. The cables melted. Robert went to buy new ones while Sally climbed the ladder and began scraping.

"I'll just kill some time doing this," she said.

When he returned with the heavier cables it still wouldn't start. He remembered the ether.

"I better go get some," he said.

"I'll just keep scraping," she said.

"Back to town," he said.

"Yep," she said.

With the ether the engine fired and then died. It kept firing and then dying.

"Damnit," Sally said.

"I know what it is," he said.

"What?"

"No fuel. It must have leaked out."

"I'll do a little more scraping," she said.

"Be right back."

He put the fuel in and then sprayed some more ether. It turned over but would not start. He called a mechanic who had a shop nearby.

"You've got air in the lines," he told him.

"Is that bad?"

"It's not bad," the mechanic said. "It's just that a diesel won't start with air in the lines."

"What do I do?"

"You'll have to bleed them."

"Could you tell me how?"

"I can't explain it over the phone. You got to bring it on over here if you want me to do it now. I can't leave the shop and I hate to work Saturdays anyway."

Robert told Sally about the conversation.

"This is madness," she said.

"I'm sure not going to try to pull that thing anywhere again," he said.

"No. We can't do that."

"Well. What then?"

"Let's just quit. Let's just forget the house and forget the compressor."

"But we can't. The house looks worse than ever now, half scraped like that."

"I don't care. I mean, so what? Really. What difference does it make?"

"But."

"But I know. It was my idea."

"What'll we do with this old piece of junk, then? We can't leave it here."

50

"Get the truck and drag it around behind the barn. Maybe we can sell it. Maybe it'll start when it gets covered with vines."

For a moment before he moved it, their house took on the look of a Delbert Johnson homestead, in its early stages.

Later, after resting, they began scraping again, and did it all day Sunday as well and started painting Sunday night. Her parents were coming Thursday.

Six

Ervin's car was fixed right away. His points had broken in half. Wart fixed that and mashed the bumper in and the car was back in service. On Tuesday, as Ervin walked down the hall to leave the post office, he glanced out the window and saw Angie waiting for the bus.

Minutes later, Angie turned as she heard tires screeching and saw Ervin's car coming around the corner. It pulled into the road a half block ahead of the bus and stopped in front of her.

"Need a ride?" he asked.

"Sure," she said and got in. "Which way are you going?"

"Any way you want."

"Well, I'm going home. To the Brookstone Apartments."

"I know where they are," he said, and started off.

The bus pulled up behind him, and the crowd that had been waiting boarded. Ervin watched them in the rearview mirror.

"I didn't know you rode the bus," he said.

"I don't usually. My car's completely broken down. The guy says it'll cost too much to fix. More than it's worth."

"What'll you do?" he asked.

"Save my money and get another one. Later."

He got into the left lane and the bus pulled up beside him. It was packed and toward the back people were standing.

"I don't mean any disrespect by this," he said, nodding at the bus, "but you're new in this area and all that, and you wouldn't know, but down here, people just don't ride the bus."

"What do you mean?" she asked, looking at a bus full of people.

"I mean white people don't ride the bus. It's just not safe. That's why I rushed around to get you."

"Oh," she said, with a puzzled look on her face.

"Where are you from, anyway?"

"Originally from Cleveland," she said, "but I lived in Fayetteville for five years. My exhusband was stationed at Fort Bragg. Still is, I should say."

"I see," he said.

"I took the postal exam shortly after we separated and then when I got a notice about this job, my daughter and I moved here."

"Uh huh," he said, now having to imagine the daughter as well as the exhusband.

"She's seven," she said. "And a real sweetheart."

"I bet," he said.

"Here it is," she said, and pointed to Building C. "And there's my little girl. Waiting with Mrs. Scholtz at the bus stop."

"Who's Mrs. Scholtz?"

"She's a retired woman who keeps Darlene after school."

"I see."

"And there," she said and pointed to a rusty old Plymouth sedan, "is my old heap. Dead on its feet."

"That reminds me," he said. "I know a pretty good

mechanic I could take the car to, if you want a second opinion."

"It's not worth it. It was Bill's car. I knew it wasn't any good when he gave it to me, but it was all I could hope for from the settlement."

"Well then, how about this? I'll take you home every afternoon."

"Can you do that?"

"Sure."

"I'll pay for the gas, then."

"No way."

"You've got to let me do something," she said.

"It'll be my pleasure. I like to help people. If I can do something nice for someone, it just makes my day."

"All right, then," she said. "See you tomorrow."

After he drove off, he thought, How stupid am I, I didn't arrange for her to get to work in the morning. She still has to take the bus then.

He was so excited about this new arrangement that instead of going home he drove to a 7-Eleven across town, where he bought a Coke, two oatmeal cookies and a Hershey's Big Block and celebrated. Then he went home, saw Margaret in the backyard working in the garden and turned away when she waved. He took out the Tupperware pitcher with the tea in it, already sweetened and lemoned, and poured a glass. As he sipped, he watched her working in the plant bed and noticed the flex and pull of her thighs as she bent over.

He put the tea pitcher back and turned the cap around past the notation for closed, past the notation for pour, and positioned it so that the top would fall off when the next person used it.

"How do you get to work in the morning?" he asked Angie that afternoon.

54

"I caught a ride this morning with Mrs. Scholtz's daughter. She said she could take me mornings if I was out there at the same time."

"Good," he said.

"She didn't seem to mind taking a dollar from me," she said, and held one out for him.

"No ma'am. Not for anything would I take it. This is on me."

Angie was twenty-seven and had married her husband, after she was pregnant, when she was nineteen. She had never known, in any way, really, another man. Her husband had been rough, hard-drinking and demanding, and Ervin's politeness, his courtliness, she thought, like an old Southern gentleman, delighted her.

"You're very kind. I don't pretend that money isn't precious to me."

"Of course it is. A single girl, all on her own. Of course it is," he said. "Now we won't say another word about it."

"All right."

He was late coming home again Wednesday, the second day in a row, and although Margaret had said nothing about it yesterday, she wasn't going to let it slide by today.

"You're late," she said when he came in.

"Late for what?"

"You know what I mean."

"How can I be late when there's nothing to be late for?"

"Listen," she said. "You were late yesterday. You had a funny look on your face. You're late today. For the past, I don't know how many years, you've come home like clockwork, so don't tell me you don't know what I mean."

He began whistling a song and walked over to the window. He whistled old songs, such as "Annie Laurie" or "Old Folks at Home," which Margaret used to love to hear as she lay with her head on his shoulder while they drove along, young and in love.

Now, though, he used the songs to block her out, to mock her, and when he struck up with "Row Row Row Your Boat," she screamed at him.

"Stop that damn whistling." She pulled him by the arm so that he had to look at her. "You better not be messing around."

"Oh?"

"You know what I told you."

"What did you tell me?" he asked and walked into the kitchen, where he opened the refrigerator door and looked in.

"You know."

"I can't remember," he said in a childish voice. "Please tell me again so I'll know."

"I'll not do it," she said.

"Sorry," he said, and walked to the back door.

"Where are you going?"

"To the mall. They're having a sale. I want to check out the fishing tackle."

"Take me with you."

"No," he said in a whining voice. "I don't want to take you with me."

"I want to go. I never go anywhere. I never get out of the house all day."

"That's not my fault. Get your license back."

"Just wait a minute while I get dressed."

"Sorry," he said. He let the storm door slam. The plexiglass panels rattled as if they were going to fall out.

She ran at him, still in her housecoat and bare feet. He sprinted to the car. He jumped in. She pulled on the passenger door handle but it was locked.

"Ha ha, got you," he said through the closed window. She beat on the window.

"I can't hear you," he said and held his hand to his ear the way he had done with Angie that time. He started the

engine. She ran around and stood with her knees against the back bumper.

"Get out of my way," he screamed with an ugly, red face.

"If I can't go, you can't go," she screamed back.

He rolled his window partway down and yelled, "I'm going to run over you. I'm going to kill you if you don't move."

"Go ahead. You want to, anyway. You've wanted to for years."

He put the car in neutral and stomped the accelerator to the floor. The car shook against her legs as if she were really stopping it.

"KILL ME," she screamed. "GO AHEAD AND DO IT," she yelled at him through the back window.

He let off on the gas momentarily, put the car in reverse and then, with his foot down hard on the brake, stomped the accelerator again. The car twisted and reared up on one side. Black smoke poured out the tail pipe. Particles of metal and rust from the exhaust sprayed all over her.

"GET OUT OF THE WAY," he yelled.

"DO IT," she screamed, and then, trembling like the car itself as it began to die out, she said again, more quietly, "Go on and do it."

The motor idled roughly and then died. Ervin got out. "Okay," he said. "You win. Get dressed. We'll go to the mall and have supper and do some shopping."

With her head held high, she went in the back door. Ervin leaned against the trunk of the old car, which he had bought from the city when it sold its worn-out police cars. On the ground behind the tail pipe was a bare spot where the force of the exhaust had cleared away all the pine straw. In the spot, which was as clean as if it'd been swept, he noticed the soot and bits of metal.

Damn near blew up my engine, he thought, and looked

toward the house. Margaret was standing at the window, still in her housecoat.

"Go get dressed," he said and waved her away.

She left. He looked over his shoulder. The couple who lived next door were standing at the window. He waved to them. They waved back. They left the window. Hope you enjoyed the show, he thought, and looked around to see if anyone else was watching. He looked across his yard. The yard had no grass. It was covered with needles from the longleaf pines. The longleaf pines dropped pinecones, as well. Margaret gathered them and made displays, or dried them and varnished them, thinking to give them as presents. The closets and attic were full of them.

The neighborhood was quiet now, as if with the death of the roaring engine, all other sound had ceased as well. He heard water running, a distant gurgling sound that came, he decided as he looked at the house, from the vent pipe in the roof over her bathroom.

She's just flushed the toilet, he thought, and in a quick move, got in the car and backed out. She heard the engine. She ran for the door.

"You promised," she yelled as she opened it and saw him going down the street.

"Come back," she said and chased him and nearly caught him by cutting catty-corner across the yard but he zoomed off and she found herself standing on the side of the road, abandoned and betrayed.

"I'll just walk," she said, and set off toward the mall. If he's not there, she thought, then I'll know he's running around on me, and if he is, she told herself, making a fist, there'll be trouble.

Ervin drove into the Fast Fare and bought a Coke and oatmeal cookie and a package of six miniature powdered doughnuts. He ate while he drove around and then, actually on the way to the mall, saw Margaret, walking barefoot, on the

shoulder of the road. He parked and watched her. She never turned around. She walked with determination, as if she meant to get there.

I can make it, she told herself. I haven't walked this far since we went to New England twenty years ago but I can do it. She stepped on a sand spur, a ball of spikes. She balanced on one foot and pulled it loose from the other.

Damn fool, Ervin thought, and drove up beside her. She looked away.

"Get in."

"I'm going to the mall."

"Barefoot? In the dark? In the cold?"

"So what?" she asked, and held herself as dignified as one could, given the circumstances.

"Just get in the car," he said. "You don't even have your damn purse with you."

"I guess I showed you," she said. They started home.

"I guess I showed you," she said again.

"You didn't show me a thing I didn't already know," he said.

"Some men tried to pick me up," she said.

"Oh really?"

"Yes. Back at that house, with all the cars in the front yard. I was walking along and they called to me."

"What did they say?"

"They said something nasty."

"Uh huh."

"They did. They wanted me to come inside with them."

"Pretty damn hard-up men, I'd say. Yelling at a fat, fifty-four-year-old woman."

"I'm not fat."

"Hell."

"They liked me."

"Sure thing," he said. "Tell me another one," he said and laughed all the way home.

Seven

Sally and Robert painted Monday and Tuesday after work and then stayed home Wednesday and finished most of the second coat by that afternoon. Sally left him and went to town to the grocery store to buy what she needed for Thanksgiving.

The traffic moved slowly and she was mad, not at the traffic or the house or the painting or Robert or even the visit, but at herself and another damn period starting.

Of course, it was not the end of the world. It could be considered a new beginning. It could be looked at that way, the way losers were taught to look at things so they wouldn't drive right off the bridge or pull out the gun; it could be looked at that way if you were a believer with the kind of faith that allowed the fourteen-inch fist of a nonbeliever to be jammed through your teeth and halfway down your throat while you stood in front of him spouting the words of holy men.

It was the operation, of course, that was to have fixed all that, and damnit all, it did nothing, just ripped her up some more. Damn the faith healers and the holy medical men and their healing powers and damn the sales pitch heavy with

the syrup of sucked blood, engorged with the tumescent bulge of wallets throbbing with the thrill of another surgical procedure and damn the spinal paralysis of the long needle, the foolish conversation of Valium-induced merriment and damn the promise of that zero-to-forty-percent chance looking better all the time in the narcotic dreams in front of her eyes, the promise of tubes so clean and swift eggs would dance and sing their way to conception, and all the infections of the past would be gone.

Damn all those things Sally Zilman thought as the traffic moved slowly, the line turning into the parking lot moving in coordination with the line at the other end leaving the lot, as if there were only room for one car entering as one left, only room in the store for one person as another left.

Soon she found a space. She bought a fresh turkey and stuffing mix and cranberries and sweet potatoes and a bag of marshmallows and a bottle of wine. She bought and she bought, knowing she had to because everyone expected all the right things.

Thursday morning they both painted furiously and by ten o'clock they were finished and the latex paint would dry in a few hours.

"Now," she said, "I've got my house the way I want it."

At eleven, her parents arrived.

"They must have left at daybreak," Robert said, "or before."

"Well, they're here. Let's go."

By the time they got to the camper, Ervin stood beside it with the door closed and Margaret nowhere in sight.

"Where's Mother?"

"She won't get out."

"Why not?"

"Because I won't open the door for her."

"Well, go open it," Sally said.

61

"I can't."

"I will, then," she said. "Come out, Mother."

"Not until your father opens it and helps me down."

"But Mother. He never does that. He never has."

"He used to. He will again."

"She won't get out," Sally said to Robert and her father.

"Let her sit," her father said and grabbed the handles of his new cooler, which was as big and heavy as a baby's coffin.

"Steaks," he said.

"Steaks? For Thanksgiving?" Robert asked.

"For tomorrow morning. Steak and eggs."

Ten minutes later, inside, the three of them stood in the kitchen talking when Sally, who could bear it no longer, asked her father if he noticed anything different about the house.

"Looks like you finally painted it," he said, and flipped open the cooler. "Bright color, that yellow."

She walked out so as not to blow up in front of him. She opened the camper door, where her mother rested her feet on the dash. It was warm inside.

"I'm a flower," she said. "I need a lot of attention."

"We're all flowers, Mother."

"And your father's a tree. He's hard and brittle, like the rough bark of a tree."

"Okay. That's fine," she said. "You're a flower and he's a tree but let's get out and get on with the day."

"I will not."

"Well, if you won't get out, then at least tell me what you think about the house."

"I think it looks a lot better but I wouldn't have painted it yellow," she said. "But it does look better."

"Thanks a lot," Sally said.

"Tell him to come get me. He'll listen to you."

"I will, but why all this now?"

"Because I saw this couple on the Donahue show and the

62

woman said their marriage worked because her husband still treated her like he was courting her and I thought, Of course, I'll treat him that way if he'll treat me that way, but he has to start first. He stopped first, so he has to start back first."

Forty-five minutes later Sally persuaded her father to get her.

"Come on," he said.

"Take my hand," she said and extended it. "Help me down properly."

He took it. He had to fight off the impulse to jerk her to the ground and stomp on her.

"Thank you," she said. She walked in like a grand lady on escort.

"Don't thank me," he said and leaned close and whispered, "because when we get home I'm going to fix you but good."

"Of course, you'll do no such thing," she said.

"Now that wasn't so bad, was it, Daddy?"

"It was bad enough."

"He's stubborn," Margaret said.

"Do you help your wife in and out of the car?" he asked Robert.

"I would, I guess, if she wanted me to."

"Hear, hear," Margaret said and Ervin left the house. He wandered around in the yard and looked at the house and thought what a godawful hippie color they had painted it. He stood with his back to it and wanted to smoke, but put it out of his mind and just walked around waiting for the womenfolk to get the glands calmed down. Hell to pay, he thought, on those certain days, and felt sorry for all the men in the world like himself who tried to do battle with female hormones.

Around the back of the barn he came upon the Delbert Johnson landscape.

"What's that?" he asked back inside.

"That," Sally said, "is exactly what it looks like."

"A piece of junk?"

"It is an air compressor that we used to scrape and paint the house," she said, which was, in the distant reaches of the truth, accurate, because they had used it to force them to scrape and paint it.

"You never," her father said. "That old thing wouldn't blow my hair."

Boy, just give me the chance, Robert thought. I'd blow you into a damn hole and cover you up.

"Suit yourself," Sally said and went on with cooking. They ate at three-fifteen. The wine loosened them up. Her father soon started the jokes. At first, they were not too bad.

"How many Carolina students does it take to change a light bulb? Three. One to hold the bulb, one to unscrew it, and one to hold the beer."

After that, they got worse. Sally called time-out for dessert. Then it was time to clean up. Everyone helped. She wanted to do it alone. She wanted them out of her kitchen. Four people were too much. They were tight as if they were crammed in a closet. They bumped and scraped by each other and filled every horizontal surface with dishes and pots and leftovers and glasses and plates of half-eaten pumpkin pie.

They crawled over each other. Ervin began talking non-stop. He started in on the jokes again. Margaret switched to her soap opera queen act and fixed a smile on her face, determined to be gracious.

From the other room, a football game on the television laid a background of cheers and music, excited talk and so forth. Georgia versus Alabama. Carolina versus Duke. Who knew who was playing? Who cared?

Ervin reached over Sally. He grabbed at a dishtowel

from the rack over the sink. He mashed her into the cabinet. Margaret walked behind him and knocked him loose, pushing him against Robert, who was already jammed into the corner against the hot water heater, trying to stay out of the way. They bumped each other around the room like people inside a pinball machine.

"It's getting crowded in here," Ervin said, and began another joke. "Did you hear the one about the grapefruit?"

No one answered.

"See, there were these two boys walking down the street and one of them has this grapefruit in his hand and he takes out his pocket knife and he's getting ready to cut it open and eat it. Suddenly the other boy stops him and points up to a Jewish synagogue."

Oh shit, Robert thought. Here it comes.

"He says to the boy with the grapefruit, 'Don't you ever eat a grapefruit in front of a synagogue.' 'Why not?' the other one asks. 'Because if you do, all the juice will run out.' "

Ervin laughed. He was the only one laughing.

"Now that," his wife said, "was certainly not funny."

"You people wouldn't know funny if it hit you in the face," he said, turning on her fast.

Sally dried her hands. Robert looked down and thought, What do I do? Kill the old man, or what?

"Listen, Daddy," Sally said. "You're just going to have to stop it with those jokes. In this house, anyway, you're going to have to stop it."

"What for? They're just jokes. If a person can't joke about things, he might as well give up."

"Those aren't jokes, though," she said.

"No, they're not," his wife said and he glared at her.

"What are they, then?"

"Mean and vicious stories."

"You people are just knee-jerk liberals," he said. "Anything a nigger does is right and anything a white does is wrong."

"What's that got to do with it?" Robert asked.

"We're just talking about good manners, Daddy. We're talking about good manners and treating people with respect."

"Boy," he said. "The day my own daughter, who I taught how to have good manners from the day she was born . . ."

"What about me?" Margaret asked. "I taught her, too."

". . . from the day she was born, starts teaching me what's right and what's wrong, well, I tell you, that'll be the day."

He looked around the room. Robert looked at the floor. The two women looked at Ervin. "I can see I'm not wanted," he said. "I better leave if that's the case."

He walked to the door. On the way through, he said, without turning around, "I know exactly where I'll go," and he let the screen door shut by itself, pulled back quickly by the spring hooked to the jamb.

The dog and the cat had been waiting outside for the leftovers and as soon as he cleared the door, they charged in. The cat ran through the dog's legs and slowed him down and the door slammed on his hindquarters. He yelped, and slipped through.

"Is he really going?" Sally asked her mother.

"He better not be," she said as he drove off.

"That's a first," Robert said. "He's been out of control, but never that much."

"I think he's got a girlfriend," Margaret said.

"Not seriously, Mother. Not really."

"I think so. He's been coming home late."

"From work?"

"Yes. And he used to always come home at the same time. Like clockwork."

66

"Does he go out at night?"

"No."

"On the weekends?"

"No."

"Then when does he have time to have a girlfriend?"

"I think she must work with him."

"What makes you sure?"

"I've been married to him for thirty years."

"Oh."

"That's a pretty good argument," Robert said.

"Well, Mother, really, I'm sure it's nothing. Whatever he's doing, he's probably doing just to get at you."

"That doesn't make it hurt any less," she said.

"Just ignore him. I'll bet he'll stop."

"I can't ignore him."

Her lips quivered and her nostrils flared and turned red and she left the room.

"That's the saddest thing I've ever seen," Robert whispered. "He treats her like dirt and she still loves him."

"Of course she loves him, you stupid dope."

"Hey. Don't start on me. I'm not your father. I just can't see how she can still love him."

"She loves what they used to have. What we used to have. Together. As a family."

"But I mean, enough is enough."

"She wants it back. She can't let go of the idea that she can get it back. You remember my grandparents?"

"I never met them."

"I know, they've been dead for years, but what I'm trying to tell you," she said and looked toward the bathroom to make sure her mother was out of earshot, "was that she grew up in real bad circumstances."

"I knew that, I think."

"Her father was hard on her and her brothers. Real hard. And when she met Daddy and left to marry him, her

67

whole world changed like she had only dreamed it would."

"She told you this?"

"Many times. She would take out the pictures of Daddy in his uniform before he was shipped off to Korea and talk about things back then. It was so good, coming from what was so bad, that to her, it's worth waiting for again."

"You guess."

"I guess."

"We don't really know."

"But I think I'm right."

"She could be planning to leave him any day now. She could have a lover."

"No way," Sally said. "That's not mother. That's just not her style."

Ervin drove to Chapel Hill. Along the way, yards full of cars and parents and children reminded him it was, indeed, Thanksgiving, the day to be with the family and give thanks for what one has.

Of course I'm thankful, he said to himself. I'm grateful for all I have. I'm no ingrate. That's one thing I'm not, he told himself and thought about Angie, probably alone, and how sweet it would be to be with her.

Everything was closed in town. There was nowhere to go. He eventually found a FastFare. He parked. He called Angie on the pay phone. There was no answer.

He went inside. He had eaten too much and the turkey was squawking around in his stomach like it was trying to get out.

"I sure would like a cigarette about now," he announced to the woman behind the counter as he entered. She wore a red-and-cream-colored FastFare smock and she was eating a candy bar and reading a magazine and sitting beside the cash register.

"What kind?"

"Oh I can't really do it. I just said I wished I could."

She looked back.

"I gave it up a few years ago. Just like that," he said and snapped his fingers. She nodded.

They were alone in the store. He stood in the middle of the checkout area. A large wood-look plastic tub full of ice and beer cans leaked on the floor just behind him. He moved his heel out of the water and heard a strange, electronic musical sound. He saw a single video game against the wall. It was called Pole Position. He walked over and, as if by magic, the moment he stopped in front of it, a voice came out of the machine and said, "Insert your quarter now."

It was an awkward, pinched voice, without pitch or variance. After it spoke, the music began again, and a trial run of the race started.

He put a quarter in the slot. A musical fanfare blasted the quiet store. The instructions rolled on the screen. He put the gearshift in low and applied his foot lightly to the pedal. The game began. He wiggled and twisted his hips as he maneuvered the car through the difficult and tricky course. Soon he shifted to high and soon after that wrecked his car for the last time. The game stopped. A voice said, "Game over. Insert your quarter now."

"Ah well," he said and turned to the woman. "I'm not as fast as I used to be, I guess."

He put his hands in his pockets and jingled his keys and walked to the aisle where the individual packs of cookies and cakes were. It was the same in every store. It was easy to find. As he walked over, he whistled, "Oh My Darling Clementine," and he wagged his head from side to side, keeping time.

Oh my darling, oh my darling, oh my darling Clementine, he thought as he whistled, you are lost and gone forever, he thought and then stopped whistling in front of the candy, still jingling the keys in his pocket.

"I really shouldn't have anything," he said out loud, and reached for a peanut butter Twix, which he had just seen on television and wanted to try. Just then a man rushed in the store and asked, looking all around, where the charcoal lighter was. The woman pointed and Ervin spoke up.

"It's over here," he said. "I'll show you."

The man thanked him, paid and left. Ervin walked over to the checkout counter.

"Is that all?" she asked.

"Yes. I believe it will be."

"Forty-one cents."

He paid her and then turned sideways to the cash register and peeled the wrapper off the two thin, chocolate-covered wafers and took a bite.

"You know, I've got a daughter about your age."

"Is that so?"

"Have you tried this new Twix yet?"

"Sure haven't," she said, without looking up.

After he finished the last bar he had a twinge of heartburn and went to the medicine aisle and bought a bottle of Maalox, which he took to the camper and drank straight from the bottle, as if it were soda pop.

It was six-thirty and dark when he returned. They heard him drive up. He looked at the house as he parked. He saw three faces in three separate windows.

"Well, I'm back," he said.

It was an awkward moment. It was as awkward for Robert as the time he threw up all over the girl beside him in third grade and then, after leaving the room to clean up, had to come back and sit beside her. He felt that embarrassed for the old man, who had essentially thrown up all over everyone, rushed out to clean up, and then returned.

It was awkward for Margaret, as she saw the remains of the man she married trying to crawl through the brambles they had grown around each other. She was sorry for him.

It was awkward for Sally, who wished she were not there and hadn't seen or heard all that she'd seen and heard that afternoon and wished that she were not going to be put in the middle and have to hear any more of it. She feared what would come next, and wondered how she would ever get away from this crazy family.

"Well," he said and cleared his throat, "what I've brought for you is this. I realized out there how good it was to have a family to come back to, and I've brought each and every one of you an apology. I apologize to you all if I hurt your feelings or said something wrong."

He crammed the apology down Robert's throat by walking over and shaking his hand. He forced it into Sally by kissing her on the cheek and he floated over to his wife and put his arm around her and pulled her to him.

"Just one of those days," he said.

"Well," Sally said, becoming the arbiter of the family, "I guess that's what families are for."

"How's that?" Robert asked.

"They're places where you can look bad and make a fool of yourself and still come back to."

"Hey, here now," her father said. "Let's not go too far, how about it."

He laughed. He laughed hard enough to force a weak and polite laugh out of everyone else, and with the laughter things returned to normal, as normal as four naked people in a room could be.

Eight

The Neals left Friday just before lunch. Sally went to the garden and looked at the dead vegetable plants, withered tomato vines and the thick weeds.

"I think I'll turn the garden," she said when Robert came out to join her.

"I was going to."

"I'd like to. I need to shake the visit out of my system."

She went to the shed beside the old corncrib and, with one hell of a jerk that lifted the Rototiller off the ground, pulled the starter rope and fired the engine on the first try.

"At least this thing starts," she called over the noise and then walked the tiller on its tines across the side yard and across the driveway and into the garden. The soil was dry and hard. The tiller bounced on top of it and bounced her with it. Robert watched from the porch. The dog and the cat watched from the porch, too. After a few minutes, the tiller cracked through the red clay crust into the moist soil below.

She went down one row and up another. She stopped and untangled the weeds from the tines and began again. She rolled up her sleeves, tied her shirt at her waist and

72

pulled her hair back and worked for an hour without stopping and had a third of the garden finished when the tiller ran out of gas. She got the can, filled it, and started again.

Robert walked into her line of sight. She stopped. She killed the motor.

"Take a break," he said.

"I'm going to finish. It makes me feel better," she said, and fired it up again with a single pull of the rope.

"I'll cook supper," he said. "When I see you're about finished, I'll run a hot bath."

She nodded and continued down the row. She finished. She took her bath. She ate. She felt relaxed, physically.

"But I'm pissed off," she said. "I don't think I'm going to be good company tonight."

"I guess it's not a good time to talk about how we're going to get out of going down there for Christmas, is it?"

"Not a good time," she said and went to bed, looking especially good to Robert, flushed and loose and fiery, just right, but no way, not tonight.

He turned on the television. "The Dukes of Hazzard" were on one station. "Washington Week in Review" was on another. He flipped back and settled down to watch Daisy Duke walk around in her short-shorts and try to keep her breasts inside her blouse. He wondered if this would be the night she and Bo and Luke finally made it on camera, cousins or no cousins.

Bo jumped the General Lee right over Hazzard County pond. Roscoe landed in the middle, sputtering and spitting water as he climbed on top of the car.

"He's all right," Luke said to Bo, looking back.

"Yeah. He's okay," said Daisy, who was in the back seat.

"Now let's do some fucking," said Bo, and Daisy took off her blouse and made room for Luke as he climbed back with her.

Ah, thought Robert. I was right. This is the night.

After Luke was through with her, Bo climbed in the back, and, as the scene faded, Daisy's legs appeared spread from one side of the car to the other and hooked over the back of the front seat. Bo disappeared from view. Robert climbed in through the window with Luke.

"Leave a little for me," Robert said to Bo. "I think I'm heading for a dry spell back home."

Daisy looked up from watching Bo work and said, "Sugar, come on back here right now. I've still got a mouth and two hands free."

"I think I'm going to have to move to Hazzard County," he said when it was all over and he looked in the bedroom where the light beside the bed cast a glow over Sally as she lay on her side with her long hair spread out like the halo of a glamorous movie star.

"But you know what happens around Christmas," she said to Robert Monday morning as they prepared to go to work. "Mother gets wackier and Daddy gets meaner."

"Well you tell me how we're going to get out of going and I'll back you up. They're your parents."

"Right."

"At least with mine, they know not to expect anything out of me. One visit a year."

"That's what comes from marrying me."

"Best thing I ever did."

"But Christmas, see, is this really tender time for Mother and she's already asked me to go to Christmas Eve services with her."

The matter remained unresolved when Robert left for work. He had to be there an hour before she did. He was doing trim work on a large apartment complex, and the job was big enough to last all winter, a good thing because it was all indoor work.

When Sally got to work she flipped on the lights. The

fluorescent fixtures buzzed and flickered and then caught. She sat at her desk unenthusiastically as her eyes got used to the fizzy carbonated glow, and at exactly eight-thirty the phone rang. It was Adrian. Adrian was a very particular customer and she had fouled up a job for him.

"But it wasn't me," she told him.

"You're in charge."

"I suppose."

"Then it's just the same."

"What can I do about it now?" she asked.

"Do the whole job over."

"Impossible."

"Why?"

"Do you know, can you imagine how busy things get just before Christmas, with the semester ending?"

"Yes, I can imagine, but my butt is on the line over here and you put it there."

Disgusting, she thought. I wouldn't get near your butt for anything.

"I can't do the job over. I just can't. Mistakes happen. The announcement's not ruined, it's just not perfect."

"We shall see what you shall do and what you shall not do," he said and hung up before she worked up the courage to call him a tightass little pimp.

On the way home, looking for something to take her mind off her work, she decided to begin writing in her journal again, something she had let slide since the summer. It was her secret project to document her life, for her own edification only. Robert knew nothing about it, and it was best kept that way. She tried to remember everything, and she tried to make everything make sense. She made lists. She checked one against the other. How many were on each side? Were they equal? Did one good event weigh as much as one bad, or as much as two? How to know?

She wrote about her parents. She wrote about men, and

men and women, and husbands and wives and fathers and daughters and all the snaky trails left behind from the family history, from stolen moments with strangers, a look, a kind word, even, the gesture from someone never seen again that changed the day.

As Christmas grew closer, she withdrew more and soon Robert came down with the blues himself, just as if she'd given him the flu.

All of this went right over the head of Rocket, the cat, but Dreeno, the dog, knew something was up, and whenever either of them walked by, he looked sideways and weakly wagged his tail. He hated those long, drawn-out fights between the humans.

Nine

T. G. and Y. was a good store. It wasn't as big as a K Mart, but it had good prices and different items, some that Ervin saw nowhere else. He went to the automotive section. On the shelves were cans of oil and gasoline additives. Some of the cans increased power. Some stopped annoying valve and push-rod noise. Some of them cleaned out carburetors. Some of them sealed cracked rings and overhauled worn-out engines as you drove.

He studied the labels. He held the cans at his waist and tilted his head back trying to bring the small print into focus. He bought a can of Marvel Mystery Oil and took it to his old police car. The engine needed something. Wart had told him his timing chain was worn out or the tensioner was worn out but he didn't want to put that kind of money in the car. He poured the additive into his crankcase and then started the engine. He could tell a difference. He went back to work. Later, he took Angie home.

"Can you stay awhile?" she asked.

"A few minutes, I guess."

He stayed longer than a few minutes and was home late again. Margaret was still in her bathrobe, same as when he'd left that morning.

"I just never got dressed. So what?"

"People don't stay in their pajamas all day unless they're sick, that's what. Are you sick?"

"No, and you're changing the subject. You used to come home almost exactly at five twenty-five every day, in time to see "The Andy Griffith Show," and now you come home almost any old time at all and don't even care if you miss it. That's what we're talking about."

She was hurt much worse than she was letting on. She had slipped into feeling tender toward him during the day and had made him a special Jello salad from a recipe she found in *Woman's Day*. She put in fruit chunks and nuts and cream cheese and then whipped it and chilled it and had already had a little bit, just to make sure it was as good as it looked, and she had it in the refrigerator waiting for him. But now, she thought, just for that, he's not going to have any.

Ervin got into the kitchen first. He opened the refrigerator and saw it.

"Look at that," he said. He took it.

"That's mine," she said. "You can't have any."

"Finders keepers," he said.

"Mine," she said and grabbed for it. He held it out of reach and went to his bedroom, eating it on the way.

"This is good."

"I made that for myself. You can't have any."

He shut the door in her face and she opened it just as fast.

"Get out of here. This is my room," he said and took another spoonful.

"I will not leave until you give me my Jello."

"You stay away from me or I'll throw it on the floor."

"I'm not leaving."

"Then watch me eat if you want to."

She walked toward him. He backed into his bathroom and locked the door.

"Open up."

He smacked his lips and sighed about how good it was.

"Open up and give it to me or I'll never cook you another thing. Never," she said, pulling on the door.

"Ah," he said, "this is something else. I better save the rest until I finish my shower," he said, as if talking to himself.

The water came on.

"You better let me in," she said. She pulled on the knob. She twisted it. She jerked on it. She put one foot on the wall and both hands on the doorknob and pulled as hard as she could and, to her great surprise, it came off in her hands and she fell backwards. The inside knob hit the tile floor.

"What are you doing?" he called and leaned out from behind the curtain. "What in the hell have you done now?" He picked up the broken knob. "You've torn it off. How in God's name did you do that?"

"I don't know," she said. "It just came off."

He looked through the hole in the door. The latch was still in. The door was still locked but there was no way to release the latch or unlock it.

"Put the knob back and see if you can turn it," she said.

"It won't go. Try yours."

"It won't either," she said. "It's locked from the inside, anyway."

"Then tell me, you stupid old bitch, just how the hell I'm going to get out of here."

"Maybe you're not."

"The hell you say."

"This is what you get for coming home late and taking my Jello."

"Cut the crap and get me out of here."

"Not yet," she said. "For once I've got you right where I want you."

"You don't have me anywhere."

"I think this is a good time to have a talk."

"Hell with the talk," he said and looked for something to turn the latch.

"You know," she said, sitting on the bed a few feet from the door, "the time just after we got married was the happiest of my life."

"I'm not listening," he said and stuck a toothbrush handle in the latch.

"They were happy times for you, too."

"I'm still not listening," he said. The plastic handle twisted without success.

There was no window. The bathroom had been a walk-in closet. It had been remodeled into his private bath when he started sleeping alone. The only ventilation was a fan built into the light. Like any closet door, it opened out and the hinge pins were on the outside.

"Do you remember how absolutely sweet we were with each other? Do you remember rushing home after work just to be with me? Do you remember that?"

"I can't hear you," he said. "The fan's making too much noise."

She sat on the floor and talked into the knob hole.

"Do you remember buying presents for me, for no reason at all, just because, you said, you adored me."

"ADORED SHIT," he screamed. "GODDAMN YOU, LET ME OUT OF HERE!"

"Not yet," she said calmly. "There's so much I want to talk about. Do you remember when I was pregnant with Sally? How happy we were. And when she was born?"

"I don't remember anything," he said, "and I can't hear you, anyway." He turned on the shower and the faucet at the sink.

"I know you can hear me even with the water running. I know you remember, too."

"Get me a screwdriver."

"Not until I'm finished."

"Listen you bitch. You go get me a screwdriver and unlock this door."

She sat on the carpet and leaned against the wall. She pulled her robe over her knees and pulled her knees up to her chest. She held them against her with her arms crossed around them.

"The more you talk to me like that," she said in a calm voice, "the longer you'll have to stay in there."

"ARGHHHHHH," he screamed and went over to the toilet. When he heard her talking again he flushed it. Even with that, he could hear her and he put his fingers in his ears and hummed loudly, like a child drowning out a parent's lecture.

"I'm really serious, Ervin. It's time, it's really time for us to make up. It's just so wrong and so silly to waste what we had."

"Hummmmmm."

"You know, everyone makes mistakes. I've made some and you've made some, but people go on. They have to. You still love me. I know you do. And there's never been any other man for me but you."

"SHUT UP," he screamed.

"We don't even know what we're fighting about anymore. It's just a pattern, like a bad habit, and we've got to break it."

She looked through the hole and watched him and when he unplugged his ears and the toilet had filled, she spoke again.

"I read in a magazine about the need to break bad habits, how you just have to derail yourself off the bad track and get back on the good. You know what I mean?"

He looked at the ceiling and started whistling "Old Black Joe." She waited until he stopped and then asked, "Are you finished?"

"Are you?" he asked back.

This time, she did not answser.

"Okay. You're finished. You've had your say. Now get me the screwdriver."

Nothing.

"I know you're there." He turned off the water and the fan. "I can hear you breathing. I know you're there so quit playing around."

He stuck his finger into the hole and picked on the latch. He hooked his fingernail into what he hoped would release the lock, and turned.

"Goddamnit, now look what you've made me do. I've broken my fingernail."

"You're like Br'er Rabbit. The harder you try, the more stuck you get."

"I knew you were there. Listen," he said, "this is dangerous. There could be a fire. I could be trapped in here."

"There won't be a fire."

The door was solid core. It would be difficult to break it down. If he broke it down, he thought, then he'd have to buy a new one.

"The Jello's melting," he said.

"I don't care about the Jello," she said, worn out and beginning to accept she would get nowhere. She pushed the screwdriver into the hole. He pulled it through, turned it around, inserted it in the slot he suspected would release the latch, and opened the door.

"Now get the hell out of my room," he said and twirled her around by her arm and pushed her into the hall. She went to the living room and put her palm on the cold windowpane. It was nearly Christmas. It didn't look it. The pine trees looked the same year round. It wouldn't snow. It rarely

snowed in Wilmington. She wished she lived in the mountains, near the Blue Ridge Parkway, in a house that overlooked a valley. It would snow there, she thought, and as far
as she could see would be white and clean and peaceful.

A car backed out of the driveway three houses down. The
driveway was dirt. The car, driven by a teenage boy she had
watched grow up, spun its tires as it backed onto the road.
The car was lowered in the rear and had two chrome exhaust
pipes extended past the bumper. In the car the boy's
girlfriend sat so close to him they looked like one person.
The car was loud. As it accelerated by, she read the false
license plate mounted on the front. It said, "I LOVE COLD
BEER AND HOT WOMEN."

"Boy's going to kill himself one of these days," Ervin
said, startling her. "That girl sits so close to him there's no
way he can drive safely," he said and started out the door.

"Where are you going?"

"To the hardware. To get a new lock set."

"I'm coming with you," she said. "Wait for me to get
dressed."

She hurried. He was still there when she came out of her
room. This gave her hope. She felt good riding off with him,
doing something with him, being with him, even though he
didn't say anything all the way there and back, at least they
weren't fighting. It didn't feel as good as being sixteen and
wrapped around your boyfriend, but it felt like something.

Ten

Three days before Christmas, Robert and Sally decided there was no way to get out of going to Wilmington.

"And Mother wants me to go to that special church service."

"I hope I don't have to go."

"You won't. Neither will Daddy."

"Great, I get to baby-sit for him."

The next day was the last working day before Christmas vacation. The other people in her shop were art students who worked part-time and were already gone. She had one project to finish and she didn't want to do that.

A salesman came in. He sold paper. She had been doing business with him for five years. He was a curious fellow. Some days he really came on strong, obviously interested in her. Other days, he was strictly legit. He was in his fifties. He was well preserved. He played tennis. He played golf. He had told her about all of this over the years.

"How about tennis sometime?" he asked.

"You know I don't play," she said.

"You don't play?" he asked, making a desperate run at a double entendre.

One of those days, she thought.

"No. Not tennis."

"I could teach you."

"I don't think so."

"Then how about lunch?"

"When?"

"Today. Now."

She was curious how far he would go. She was also curious how far she would let him go before she stopped him. She had just that morning made another list. It seemed to her, she had thought, that her life had revolved around men. This man or that man or the next one, or leaving the previous one and getting clear, and so forth. She made a list of the men she had slept with, and the list had thirty-seven names. This disturbed her, because she could not now imagine sleeping with anyone but Robert. It disturbed her that she had taken so long to settle down and had given so much and gotten so little for it.

Imagine, she thought, if she could get all of them together now, see them now, all in one room or, one at a time, bring them in for an interview, for observation, unseen, behind a two-way mirror, take a look at these fellows. Imagine, she had thought, how absolutely horrible it would be.

Thank God it was over, she had told herself when she closed her journal that morning.

"Sure. Lunch? Let's do it," she said.

"You look really good today," he said when they were seated. The Carolina Coffee Shop was full. Out of the corner of her eye she saw Adrian with a slim young man with one long, dangling earring.

"Thank you."

"You look fit, too. You don't play tennis, but you must work out some way."

"I don't play any sports. I work in the garden. I clean house. I walk from the car to the office. That's about it."

"That's not enough," he said. "You know all they say about the cardiovascular system these days."

"Maybe I should do something," she said. "But finding the time is so hard."

"There's always the weekend. Or after work."

She began to watch him as if she were watching a scene in which she was, and was not, a player, anticipating his next moves and her own.

"After work is out. I'm ready to go home then," she said.

"The weekends are always nice," he said. "I always keep my weekends free in case anything comes up."

They ordered. They ate. He kept on. He went further than she thought he would.

"Of course, there're other kinds of exercise."

"Like what?" she asked, pretty sure what he was going to say.

"Oh, I was just thinking," he said, and laughed, as if what he were going to say was funny, but a little naughty, giving her a chance to get ready for it.

"What was it?" she asked.

"I was just thinking about what Mae West used to say."

"And what was that?" she asked.

"About what kept her young. You know. Her love kept her young."

"Lovemaking, you mean?"

"Yes."

Now what? she thought.

"You know," he said, "I've known you all these years and yet I don't feel like I really know you. Know what I mean?"

Yes. I know exactly what you mean, she thought.

"You don't know me?" she said.

"Not the way I'd like to," he said as they sipped coffee. "Tell me about yourself," he said.

"There's nothing to tell. There's nothing to know. You tell me about yourself."

He did. He talked a long time. He talked through a coffee refill. He wove, he thought, a perfect little web around her. He'd done it before.

"Now you tell me things," he said.

"My life's pretty dull," she said, and smiled at him. He fell for the smile.

"You know," he said, "you're a very pretty woman. Everything about you. Especially your hair." He leaned across the table and looked closely at her hair. "I really love your hair."

This is it, she thought.

"I've always wanted to touch your hair," he said. "Do you mind?" he asked, and before she could answer, reached across and stroked it, letting his fingers caress her neck as he did.

She stared at him. She cocked her head sideways.

"Are you kidding me?" she said. "You just reached over and touched me."

"Well," he said, sitting upright and looking confused, "I thought . . ."

"You thought you could just reach over and touch me?"

"Well, see," he said, "it's just that, I thought that . . . well, I was just looking at you. . . ."

"And you thought what?" she asked, rather loudly, and he noticed people listening.

"Just calm down a second," he said quietly. "People are staring."

"Tell me what you thought," she said, louder than ever.

"I thought," he said, quieter than ever, "that it was going to be all right."

"Let me tell you something, mister," she said. "Don't you ever, ever touch me. I mean in any way," she said loudly, and stood up, knocking her chair over. He looked up at her, holding his hands out, palms upward, bewildered that his technique could have missed so badly.

"DO YOU HEAR ME?"

"I hear you," he whispered.

"No one but my husband touches me, you hear?"

He nodded.

"Just because I went out to lunch with you," she said, looking at him but talking to everyone in the restaurant who seemed unable, by any means, to exercise good manners and look away, "doesn't give you the right to touch my neck. You understand that?"

"I understand," he said, a bit more firmly, trying to gain control. "I made a mistake. Let it drop, how about it?"

"See that ring?" she asked, still standing over him. "You've got one, too. You want me to call your wife and tell her? You want that?"

No answer. She grabbed the edge of the table and tilted it to dump everything on his lap. He caught it. He steadied it. He pushed it back against her. They glared at each other while the coffee spilled and the cups slid around in their saucers.

"NEVER TOUCH ME AGAIN!" she screamed and then walked toward the door, leaving him in his chair looking as if someone had beaten him half to death, embarrassed, ruined and nowhere to hide. She walked on, and then, without planning it, looked at Adrian, who sat wide-eyed and open-mouthed with his thin friend whose earring wiggled as if he were shaking, and she stopped and said, "That goes for you, too, you little pimp," and she rushed on, having wiped out, in one locally historic minute of restaurant agony, in one historic minute of public horror, wiped out and destroyed one self-confident nervy man in love with himself, and a little weepy drag queen.

"You bitch," the earring guy squealed at her; only when he said "bitch," he pronounced it, bee-utch, and then he grabbed Adrian's hand and like lovers running not through the field of golden grain, but through the gauntlet of hor-

rified disapproval and glaring disdain, pulled him into the bathroom, leaving the poor salesman to hide behind a cup of coffee, thinking, Boy, there's one fucked-up woman; but, of course, not daring to say it.

She walked up the alley beside the restaurant. The side of the restaurant was bricked up. There were no windows from which the diners could follow her and see what next she did.

Good, she thought. I'm glad I did that.

She went back to work. Would the salesman dare call again? she wondered as she sat at her light-table and fiddled with her T-square, sliding it up and down and feeling its smooth flow along its track.

Then, when she came home that evening, she told Robert about it and asked, "Now why did I do that? Really. It felt good to trap him like that, in there, and to embarrass him so badly, but then on the way home I thought, now why did I do that?"

"I don't know," he said. "But I'm glad you did. I don't want anybody messing with my baby but me."

"Still," she said, "I mean people flirt all the time. I mean, it just goes on."

"It better not."

"Not to that extent, but more subtly."

"I don't flirt."

"You look at other women."

"Not really. Maybe just a glance."

"I don't mind. I look at them, too. At men and women."

"I may have to kill that guy if he ever shows his face again."

"And that's the other thing," she said. "Unless he gets transferred, I'll still have to do business with him."

"I bet he'll stay on the other side of the desk."

"I imagine he will," she said, and walked out of the room and then stopped and came back and leaned against

the doorjamb. "Still," she said, "it's so unlike me. It was just too perfect, I guess. It was so easy to trap him and and he fell into it so fast, it just happened."

She leaned down and let her hair fall over, obscuring her face. She put both hands on her head and dug her fingernails into her scalp and scratched. "I've got to wash my hair tonight. We're going to Wilmington tomorrow. Remember?"

"How could I forget," he said.

"I'm so blue," she said on the way down. "I'm just worn out with these trips. I'm just worn out anyway."

"Maybe you're pregnant."

"Hey look," she said, "Don't joke about it. I can't take it, okay?"

"Sorry."

"I've got to figure out some way to break all of this."

"This what?"

"These trips, these parents, these things that enter my life over which I have no control."

"I saw something about that on the front of one of those magazines the other day."

"Look, I'm serious."

"I am too. Do you want me to turn around?"

"We can't do that."

"Sure we can. I just put my foot on this pedal and turn the wheel around and around."

"I know. I know. But we have to go through with it."

"That's what you always say."

"I don't know how to get loose. I don't know what I'm supposed to do. I hate being with them, but I feel sorry for them. I don't want to hurt them any more than they already hurt each other."

"It's up to you."

"It always was. I was always the peacemaker."

"Just do like I did," he said. "Just walk away and don't look back."

"I can't. I think about everything too much. About everyone. All the time."

"You're just too good."

"Right. I wish."

"Look," he said. "Let's pull in and eat before we get there."

"Good idea."

They pulled into the parking lot. The restaurant was in the middle of nowhere and was attached to a gas station which was attached by a chain link fence to a junkyard. They stopped the car. There were four other cars. Two men were standing in front of the cars and talking to each other. They poked and shoved each other playfully while they talked— salesmen, selling each other on something, so excited about being men they couldn't even remember what product it was they were selling that day, just talking and squeezing and pulling on their crotches and shifting around as if their shorts were caught up between their hips, and just having a time of it until Sally and Robert got out of the car and Sally walked around behind them wearing her long Guatemalan Indian dress and her huaraches and her long, fine and spar- kling hair, so beautiful in the sunlight there with all its colors the world's best hair dye couldn't even come close, brown and blond and a little red here and there, all of it hanging down her back and the two men had to stop, these two men out in the world alone, their wives back home, stuffing in the food out of desperation and loneliness, and they had to take a look at this woman, they had to take her in as she walked by, drinking her in as she walked by, wanting her so much she felt it and she had to work to keep from staring back at these men who, it seemed, might never have seen a woman before in their life, but, like, holy shit, looky here, what's this, a woman, holy shit, and they watched her

walk by and they shared her a little bit, looking back and forth and winking and thinking the same thing and letting each other know about it and all the time just getting more and more excited about being men.

"Creeps," Robert said once inside, and sat in a booth beside one of the rectangular plate-glass windows.

"What do you expect around here?"

"You couldn't pay me enough to live here."

"Nor me."

"I'm glad you left."

"I am, too," she said, "or I might never have met you."

"Let's eat," he said and they ordered and ate and thoroughly enjoyed barbecue sandwiches and slaw and hush puppies and ice tea and chocolate pie for dessert and it was all real good. At least, they did raise good hogs around there.

They arrived in Wilmington in the middle of the afternoon. The temperature was in the fifties but another cold front was due. Robert parked the car in a way he hoped would discourage Ervin from noticing the damaged rear end and he took their suitcase from the back seat—he couldn't get the trunk open—and followed Sally and her mother to the backyard, where her father was at work.

"Steaks," he yelled, standing beside a massive red-brick outdoor grill.

Steaks? Robert thought, and he peered past Ervin to see if they were the same as usual. They were. They were thin, a half-inch thick, and were some of that same bargain meat he had bought a year ago, a whole cow and about fifty chickens and two dozen rancid pork chops and a long tube of bologna, all for about three hundred dollars, and the steaks were just unrecognizable, just totally unrecognizable in shape or cut, as if the cows had fallen off the truck and died on the way to market or been run over by a train; and tough, so tough it was like chewing steak-flavored parachute cloth, bloody and so stringy you ended up with threads of nylon stuck between

your teeth or in your throat so that you went around for days afterwards hacking and coughing like a cat with a hairball.

"Steaks?" Robert whispered to Margaret. "Is that all he eats? Ever?"

"It was the war," she said. "He just didn't get any fresh meat over there for so long, so that ever since he's been back he's been crazy about steaks."

"I can't eat it," Robert later told Sally in her room, the same bedroom she had as a child. "I just can't."

"Try," she said.

"Oh. Try. Sure. Why not? It is Christmas. I guess I can gag down one more for him."

"You're sweet," she said, working hard to make everyone happy.

She later went to church with her mother while Robert excused himself and went to their room where he poked around in the drawers and in the closet, looking at mementos of his wife's childhood. He found a diary with the strap torn off. He looked through a stack of 45-rpm records. Dolls and magazines and books. It was like a museum. Everything had been preserved just as it had been when she left it.

"Yeah," Sally said later. "When I went to college, Mother said she was going to keep everything just as it was. She likes to live in the past, remember?"

"What about this diary?"

"Oh. Let me see it."

"There are some pages torn out."

"I know."

"How come?"

"Daddy. That was a big scene with Daddy. He found it one day, he didn't know I had one, and he read it."

"He read it?"

"He read it and I came in and found him reading it and grabbed it and ran into the bathroom and tore everything out and flushed it away."

93

"You mean he tore the lock off to read it?"

"Yes."

"I can't believe it."

"Things weren't too good back then, around that time."

"How old were you?"

"Fourteen, or so."

"What was inside?"

"Just the usual. I don't know how much he read."

"What did he do after you threw everything away?"

"Nothing. I don't remember. He was always messing around in my room, looking for things, trying to catch me."

"Doing what?" Robert asked.

"Smoking, anything."

"Smoking what?"

"Cigarettes, sweetheart. That's all we had back then."

"Right."

"Things happen, you know," she said, and began to undress for bed, "in families, and like, they must look awful, they must look weird and terrible to other people but for some reason, they make sense to the family involved. It's like, I mean, look at your family, for instance."

"You can't compare mine to yours."

"No, but . . ."

"I know what you mean," he said. "The private horrors of family life."

"Right."

"Now playing at your local theater."

"You got it," she said, and put on a robe and went to shower.

"It doesn't seem like Christmas," he said after the lights were out and they were in their separate beds.

"It's the weather," she said.

"I guess."

"What do you think they're going to give us?"

"I hope nothing."

94

"We could use money."

"I already saw three boxes in there. Yours, mine and ours."

"Uh oh."

"I'm beat," he said, suddenly exhausted.

"I'm not even sleepy," she said and a few minutes later, after a waking dream, she heard his regular breathing. "Goodnight," she said, but he didn't answer.

Later she turned toward him and felt in the air with her hand. She stretched until she felt the edge of his bed and then inched her hand along until she touched his back.

"You want to come over here?" she whispered, far too quietly for him to hear.

The hall light shone under the bedroom door. The streetlight shone through the windows. They were steel casement windows, roll-out types, through which she had sneaked out many times. The metal was pitted from the salt air, but the cranking mechanism still worked smoothly.

She heard the muffled and strained conversation of her parents in the other room. For a moment, she felt excited and anxious as if she were a child and Santa were coming and she couldn't wait for morning. Only for a moment, though. She chewed on a fingernail and almost bit it off before she realized what she was doing. She stood at the window, looking at the empty street illuminated by the arc lights spaced every five or six houses.

Later, after falling asleep, she jerked awake at the sound of a door closing. She listened, then walked across the room and leaned toward the door, trying to discern who was up or what was happening. When she heard no more, she looked out the window again. A lone dog walked down the middle of the road, walking fast, as if he were late for something. After he walked out of sight, she remained where she was and pressed her lips and cheek against the cold glass. Then she heard walking again.

Ervin heard something, as well. He crept out of his room and down the hall. He stopped at Sally's room and listened. He held his breath and leaned toward the door with his fingertips against the wall for balance.

He started back to his room and heard movement again. He waited. He heard nothing.

They better not be doing it in my house, he thought. By God, they sure as hell better not be.

He stopped by his wife's room and listened to her through the closed door. She snored lightly.

Just like a man, he thought. She snores just like a man.

He went back to his room. He knocked down two more Unisom tablets and slept right through a throbbing hard-on that would have bothered the hell out of him had he been awake. He would have had to either do something with it, or not do something with it. Either way, it would have been hell.

Sally started on the fingernail again and then stopped and decided she was not going to sleep anytime soon and went into her closet, closed the door, turned on the light, and, for almost an hour, read through a stack of old *Seventeen* magazines. Then, at three, she went back to bed and slept until eight.

Eleven

The first day back at work Ervin took Angie out for lunch. He had missed her something awful.

"We're an item," she said.

"How's that?"

"People talk about us."

"Let them talk."

She had a salad. He had a steak and a baked potato. They were eating in the Western Sizzlin.

"But if enough people are talking," she said, "people who we don't want to know about us might find out."

"Don't worry about her," he said. "I'm going to fix that."

"How?"

"Don't worry about it. I just am."

"You know what people are saying?"

"Tell me," he said and took a big bite of steak. It was number six, the sirloin strip, and it came with Texas toast and baked potato or fries.

"That we're having an affair."

"But we're not."

"But people think we are."

"But we're not, so it doesn't matter."

She mixed the salad in her bowl. She had taken lettuce

from the salad bar and then bacon bits, marinated green noodles, cherry tomatoes, mushrooms and chopped egg and grated cheese and topped it with French dressing. It was difficult to mix it without spilling and the cherry tomatoes rolled right out onto the table.

"Sorry," she said. She was trying to be so careful. She was also trying to stay slim. She'd been overweight for so many years that now, with her new life and a chance to start again with people who had never known her fat, she was determined to keep her weight down.

She was also being careful about how she handled Ervin. She liked him. More than she thought she would at first. He was gentle. He was courteous. He was slow. He was too slow, in fact. She was ready for more.

"My ex came up last night," she said.

"He did? What for?"

"To see Darlene. He came without calling. He's supposed to call. It's in the agreement."

"What happened? Did you let him in?"

"I had to. I didn't want a scene in front of Darlene."

"How long did he stay?"

"All night."

"I mean, what time did he finally leave?"

"And I mean," she said, "that he spent the night."

"Spent the night?" he asked and put his fork down with a piece of steak all ready to go.

"Uh huh," she said, looking down like a bad girl who'd been caught.

"But I thought, I mean, you know, I thought it was all over."

"I wish it were. It's so hard, being alone. You know what I mean? You're the only person I see. The only person I talk to."

"That's the way I want it," he said. "I want you to talk to me."

"You're nice."

"Now tell me all about it."

"I can't. I'm ashamed."

"Now you tell me, Angie. You tell me about it."

"Please don't make me."

"I need to know. I have to know."

"But why?"

"Because I do."

"Well, it was nothing," she said, and shifted her salad around, finally getting the tomatoes cut up without shooting the hard things off the bowl. "It was just something that happened. It got late. He was there. I was there. And then, it just happened."

Ervin had stuffed a giant bite into his mouth and he waved her to wait. When he got it chewed and swallowed, he said, "But that's not right. I don't blame you, but it seems as if he took advantage of you. He may have even come up just for that."

"He might have," she said. "He's like that."

"Then it's got to stop."

"I get so lonely, Ervin. I never go out at night. You're the only man I see," she told him again, and looked him right in the eyes. "I shouldn't have told you anything about it. Let's talk about something else." She was rather surprised how easily she had set the hook and how quickly he had bit.

"What do you want to talk about, then?"

"You," she said.

"Me? That's a boring story. You wouldn't want to hear that."

"But I would. I told you about me."

"Listen, if I were to dig down and tell you the story of my life you'd get up and run out the door."

"I would not."

"You would too."

"I most certainly would not. You underestimate me,"

she said and squeezed his arm. She squeezed hard. She dug her nails into his skin. She looked at him intently and smiled as she did. She dug her nails in until he stopped chewing and looked at his arm.

"You couldn't run me off that easily," she said, and dug a little deeper, quickly, a final jab that made him wince. After she let loose, there were four puncture marks in his skin.

"That hurt," he said. "You really hurt me."

"I meant to," she said, and speared a forkful of salad and put it in her mouth. The lettuce hadn't been cut up small enough. Part of a leaf hung from her lips. She stuck out her tongue and pulled it in. Seeing her tongue made him feel as if he'd seen her do something nasty. Between that and the red marks on his arm, he was so shook up he could barely work the rest of the day.

"Look at my arm," he said as she was getting out of the car at her apartment after work. "How'm I going to explain that to Margaret?"

"Keep your jacket on."

"But why did you do it? I don't understand."

"I did it because you don't understand. You really don't, you see, so I had to do something."

"What? What is it?"

"I like you Ervin. I don't know if it's your age or what, the difference in generations or what, but I've never," she said and moved so that her knees touched the side of his leg, "never, ever liked a man this much and not been further along. Do you get me now?" she asked, and she tilted her head around until she was leaning over him with her face next to his. "Do you get it?"

"Oh."

"Oh. Goodness sakes, Ervin. I like you, man. I've been sitting here telling you that and now what? Oh?"

"What?" he asked, actually bewildered.

100

"Is this a one-way thing?"

"No. I like you. I really do. I just didn't know, you understand, it's been so long. . . ."

"And, I know," she said, "I'm free and you're not."

"I guess that's it."

"I'm not being fair to you, am I, old man," she said and kissed him on the lips. His lips were dry and cracked and his breath was bad, but she hung in there.

"I don't know what to do," he said.

"You don't have to leave her, you know."

"But."

"Hey, listen Ervin, my big boy. I think this girl better slow down. This girl doesn't want to run off the only truly nice man she's ever known."

She pulled away.

"Do you really think I'm that nice?"

"Nice and good looking, too."

"Really?" he asked.

"Really. Now you know what you can do? Lean over and kiss me goodbye and think about it."

He did.

"By the way," she said, "Darlene's going to stay with her father this weekend." She closed the door. He watched her walk away. He drove home in a trance, as if he'd just seen an extraterrestrial being, which he had. He'd just had a close encounter with a passionate woman and it scared the hell out of him. By the time he got home he was ready to do better, to make up for being such a dolt.

But.

There she was, earthbound like a beached walrus in a chaise lounge, wrapped in a long coat with a blanket around her.

"I told you," she said, meeting him as he opened his door. He favored his arm as if it were broken.

"What now?"

"I told you about being late. Let me smell you," she said and stuck her head in the car and sniffed him.

"Get back," he said. "Get out of the way."

"I want to talk."

"Didn't you do enough of that the other night?"

"I want to talk and I want you to talk to me."

"I don't want to."

"But I do. I decided a few months ago that things were going to change, and they are."

"Talk to yourself, then. I've got to put some oil in the car."

"I don't want to talk to myself."

"Why? You do it all the time."

"So do you."

"I do not."

"You do so. I see your lips moving all the time."

"I'm singing if they are, or whistling to myself." He took a quart of oil from the shelf in the carport and opened the hood.

"If I talk to myself and you talk to yourself, maybe we should talk to each other more and we wouldn't be talking to ourselves."

"You lost me there, old girl," he said and punctured the can with a pouring spout.

"I want to talk about us."

"I know what you want to talk about," he said, mocking the sound of her voice, "but I don't."

"I want you to do this. I want you to tell me the things you don't like about me and I'll tell you the things I don't like about you. We'll make a contract, see, to change a certain number of things each way, to trade off, you know, get rid of some of my bad for some of yours."

"Where in the crap did you get that?" he asked, and laughed an ugly sneer at her and then pulled the breather

from the valve cover, exposing the oil-filler hole. "Another one of those magazines? Give me a break," he said.

"What if I did? What's wrong with it?"

"What's wrong with it is you. You're what's wrong with it. There's nothing you can change about you that would interest me."

"Then why don't you leave me?"

"Is that an invitation?"

"No. But why, please tell me, please explain why you have stayed with me so long if you don't even like me?"

"Because you're too damn dumb to leave," he said.

"I'm serious," she said and pulled on his arm.

"Now look what you made me do. I spilled the oil on the alternator, you dumb bitch. Move out of the way and let me get a rag."

"I'm not in your way," she said.

"Just move," he said, trying to avoid being face to face with her.

"I will not move until you answer that question."

"I answered it," he said, sliding along the bumper to get out from between her and the car.

"Why don't you turn around and face me," she said. "You're scared to."

"Bull," he said and slipped free.

"You're a coward. That's what it is. You're scared to do anything. You're scared to talk to me, you're scared to leave me. That's it, isn't it?" she said, and nodded an affirmative to herself, as if in revelation.

"Listen, bitch," he said. "The day I'm scared of you is the day I cut my throat."

He walked onto the carport. He came back with one of his shirts.

"Don't use that," she said. "That's one of your good shirts."

"It's torn."

"I can sew it up."

"Forget it."

She reached for it. She got a grip on it. He held the other end.

"Give it to me."

"I will not. It's my shirt."

"But I can fix it."

"You can't fix anything," he said and walked off, dragging her.

"Quit pulling me."

"Let go of the shirt."

"I can sew it up. I used to sew them up for you."

"You used to do a lot of things," he said and jerked her forward and ripped the shirt half in two. She fell onto her hands and knees.

"Help me up."

He leaned into the engine and wiped up the oil. He put the breather cap back on. Without making a sound and moving so fast it surprised him, Margaret came up like a lineman charging forward at the snap of the ball. She grabbed him around his back. She pinned his arms to his sides and squeezed for all she was worth.

"What the hell?" he said, trying to look around to see how she had him. "Let go of me."

She held on. He fought to get loose. She was up on his back and she wrapped her legs around his and had his arms pinned with hers.

"Get off," he said.

He hopped toward the carport. He tried to get out of sight. She held on. She bounced up and down with him. Her legs were wrapped tightly around his so that her heels were inside his thighs. As he hopped, the spotlight from the garage that was trained on the driveway illuminated them in the dark yard.

"Come here quick," the next-door neighbor called to his

wife as he stood at the window in a darkened room, watching.

"What is it?"

"Look. They're really at it this time."

"Oh my Lord," she said, and then let out a laughing sigh, kind of an "Ohoooooooo," but musical and high-pitched.

"What's she doing to him?" she asked.

"I can't tell. I'd just stepped in the room when I looked out and she come up from the ground real fast and grabbed him around his back."

"They are the oddest couple," she said.

"Always have been."

"Look at his face," she said.

"She choking him."

"It's about time."

They jostled each other for a good position at the window, while outside, Ervin struggled on.

"Get off me. Let go."

"I will not. I will not let go until you agree to talk with me."

"Never," he said and hopped along toward the carport, panting and red-faced. "Now you're choking me," he said in a strangled voice. "I can't breathe."

"I am not. I'm not even touching your throat."

"I can't breathe, damnit," he moaned and looked to the carport to see how far he had to go to get out of sight.

It was forty feet from where she grabbed him to the carport. It was the longest forty feet of his life. It was longer than forty feet of North Korean hell.

He made it. He hopped around to the far side of the camper. He fell against it. His legs trembled. She weighed nearly as much as he did. As he fell against the camper, he wedged Margaret between him and its side.

"Now. Get off me."

"If you will come inside and talk, I will."

"Just get off."

"Not until you say yes."

"I can't think."

"You think I don't know what you're doing, don't you?" she asked.

"What? What do you mean?"

"Coming home late."

"Listen," he said.

"You have a girlfriend."

He slid onto his knees. She unwrapped her legs, but stayed on his back like a cowgirl resting on her stomach on a horse.

"Is that what this is all about?" he asked.

"I told you before. I told you long ago. If it's not going to be me, then it's not going to be anyone."

"You're crazy," he said.

"Not any more than you," she said, with her head resting on his back. He was still on his hands and knees. When he felt better, he crawled to the back door. She rode him upright holding on to his shirt at his shoulders and letting her feet slide along the concrete floor for balance.

"Who is she?" she asked.

He crawled to the steps. There were three steps. They were concrete like the carport floor. They led to the side door. He put one hand on the bottom step and said, "I can't get up with you on my back."

"Why are you going in?"

"So we can talk."

"I don't believe you."

"I've had it this time," he said, swaying from her weight as he rested one hand on the bottom step. "You win. Maybe it's time we worked something out."

"You promise? You swear to God?"

"I do. I'm worn out. I can't fight you anymore. Just get off."

She stood up and he crawled up the steps like a dog.
"Why are you crawling?" she asked. "Stand up."
"I can't. You've killed me. I can't walk."
He reached for the handle of the aluminum storm door and pulled it open. It had a strong closer and shut against him immediately.
"Will you hold this for me?"
"Sure," she said.
She stood on the floor to the side of the steps and held it wide while he crawled in. As soon as he got past the door, he whirled around and slammed the wooden entrance door in her face and locked it.
"Ha ha and double ha," he yelled at her. The door had three separate narrow pieces of glass in the top half. They were set at an angle, like stripes, all going the same way. He peered through one of these windows and pointed at her and laughed.
"I'll never talk with you, you damn crazy bitch," she heard him say. "Never, you hear?"
Then she heard him locking the other doors to the house and then she heard nothing. She sat on the steps. She began to cry. She cried quietly. Then she fell over. She fell over like the Buddhist monk in Vietnam who set himself on fire in front of the cameras and then burned, in a sitting position, until he fell over, still sitting, and still burning. She fell, still weeping, with her hands over her face and she lay on the dirty concrete slab without moving.
Later she heard him inside. The floor creaked as he walked back and forth. She heard the television. She heard the refrigerator open and close. She heard the water running in the pipes. She was cold. She wanted to call Sally. She needed to talk to her. She knocked on the door. She had been outside an hour.
He opened it. He turned his back on her. She went to her room. They did not say a word. She called her daughter. Ervin picked up the extension.

"I don't know what to do with him."

"But Mother, what can I do?"

"I don't know. What would you do if it were you?"

"I don't know. I can't imagine it. I can't imagine things going that far."

"It happens slowly," she said. "You hardly know it until it's too late."

"But it's never too late," Sally said and then hated herself for saying such a dumb thing. "I mean, people have options."

"What are they?"

"They can leave, they can seek counseling, things like that."

"I can't. Don't you see? I can't explain it."

"You don't have to. I've seen enough of it."

"But it's worse now. I really think he's got a girlfriend and though I always considered it a possibility, it hurts so much now that it's real."

"Can you talk to the minister?"

"I don't want anyone to know."

"That's it, isn't it?" Sally asked.

"What?"

"That you don't want anyone to know. It's pride."

"Is it? Is that what you call it?"

"I'm not helping you much, am I?"

"It helps to talk. To anyone. I guess I should go see someone. He won't talk to me and everything's all bottled up and confused inside."

"Write it down," she said. "Make a notebook of things, of thoughts, you know, like a diary."

"I've tried. I just don't seem to have the energy. I sit down and then can't think of anything to say."

"It's hard, I know. Listen, Mother, it's always worse before and after Christmas. You know you always feel better in spring. I don't know what to say. I don't know what to do. I

feel for you, God knows I do, but I don't know what to say. I really don't."

They hung up. Ervin hung up. He heard Margaret in the bathroom. He quickly looked up Angie's number and called her. She did not answer. He looked it up again and dialed carefully. Still, however, there was no answer.

Margaret sat in her room on the side of the bed. It was late. She had eaten a tuna fish sandwich earlier and she kept burping up the smell. She gargled mouthwash and sat back on the bed. She stared at the carpet and began chewing on her finger. She worked her teeth under the nail and against the flesh and she rocked her finger back and forth against her teeth, not biting, just rocking, and she rocked herself into a trance, first on one finger, then another. She lay down. She couldn't sleep. She got up and went to the bathroom cabinet and took two codeine pills from a prescription left over from when she had back pain.

Soon she felt herself slipping, letting go, as if she were slowly dropping, dropping backwards, and as she dropped, the old unwelcome body tingled, sensuous again, and she drifted into a lonesome, sweet, delicious sleep.

As soon as Ervin heard nothing, absolutely nothing from her room, he called Sally. It was midnight. He woke her up.

"Daddy? What's wrong?"

"I just wanted to talk."

She knew, by the rules of the family, not to ask if he knew that Margaret had just called.

"Is something wrong?" she asked. She wore no clothes. She sat in the living room in the dark after lurching from the bed to the phone.

"Did I wake you?"

"I think so. Maybe I'd just fallen asleep."

"I'm sorry, baby," he said.

Baby? she thought. What the hell.

"What's going on down there?" she asked.

"I've got trouble with your mother."

"What is it?"

"I think she wants a divorce. She thinks I'm seeing someone."

"Are you?"

"Sort of."

"What does 'sort of' mean?"

"It means, I guess, that I am."

"Who is it?"

"Someone from work. A very sweet person."

"This is no good, Daddy. No good at all. I don't want to be in the middle of this."

"But you aren't. I just wanted to talk with you about it."

"But why now, Daddy? After all these years."

"I'm lonely, baby. I just am."

"But you said Mother wanted the divorce. That doesn't sound like Mother."

"Well, maybe we both do."

"Maybe you both better do nothing. Do you know how many years I've lived with your madness? Do you know?"

"I don't know what you mean."

"Of course you do. Let me tell you something. I'm worn out with it. I've got my own life. It takes all I've got to keep it going. I can't hold you two up any longer, don't you see?"

"But we never asked you. . . ."

"I've had to do it my whole life. One or the other of you has always come to me to figure out what to do with the other. You used to take me fishing and Mother used to take me shopping, or you used to go for a drive and then when I'm sitting there feeling great, come out with some crazy story about my very own mother, or she would do the same about you, and YOU KNOW IT," she screamed, and with that Robert rose out of bed as if he'd been electrocuted and ran into the living room.

110

"What is it?" he asked.

"Sorry," she said, covering the mouthpiece. "It's Daddy."

"Oh," he said.

"Get out of here," she said and waved him back.

"Are you there?" her father asked.

"Sorry, Daddy. It's late. I'm tired. I can't help you."

"I see I made a mistake calling you. I see my only child, my own daughter, doesn't want to help her father."

"It's not that. It's that I can't. I would if I could. But I can't."

"You're on your mother's side, I guess. You can't help it. You always have been."

"I'm not on anybody's side."

"You'd like her," he said.

"Who?"

"Angie."

"Angie. My God, is that her real name? Is she an angel?"

"In a way."

"This is too much."

"I'm going to try to get some time off to come up there and talk to you. Face to face."

"Don't do that."

"I'd like to bring Angie with me. I'd like you to meet her."

"Please don't do that. Just cool it for a while. Let's talk sometime again. Next week. And not at midnight, all right?"

After they hung up she stayed in the dark. She heard Robert breathing in the other room. She closed the bedroom door and then turned on a lamp. She walked through the kitchen. Two Christmas presents, a coffee-maker machine and an electric carving knife, were on the counter in a corner. She walked out onto the porch. The dog stood beside her.

She looked across the field. The house sat in a clearing. Back from the clearing, the dark woods shone in outline in

the moonlight. The house itself glowed, a little bit the color of the yellow moon. The dog followed her into the field.

She stood in the cold field like a nymph, a jungle woman with long hair and perfect form, tight, sinewy, ready to run, an interloper who had come upon this house glowing in the moonlight and must decide to go back or go on, a woman without cover, in flight, her dog against her leg.

The civilized world lived in houses. Within the houses the most uncivilized things took place. Family members ate into each other. They cut each other up and then ate from the leftover torsos with forks, all the while ignoring the screams of the children who knew they were next. A moment there, in the early life of the family, in the sweet young beginning of parent and child, the charmed, precious existence of one to the other balanced and held true.

That moment gone, the doors shut tight, the windows locked, the blinds and curtains drawn, and the orgy of punishment and betrayal and deceit commenced. One day it was lollipops, the next day flesh, and the incestuous carnage surfaced like a dripping monster from the depths of the decaying family.

The next day, at school, at work, the smiling face of the shattered life hid, shamed into cover, and raced through the day, and then returned, having fooled the friends and lovers.

So she thought as she imagined the private terrorism occurring all over the world behind closed doors, as she imagined the shock of the friend, the lover, the fiancé, the husband, who then, fooled by the passionate desperation of the ravished heart, entered the family, too late to run.

And so, the next morning, she got up with Robert even though she wanted to sleep late, even though she needed to, and cooked his breakfast and petted him and cooed to him and made him late for work, all the while, as she lay on her back in the solid old bed, under his weight, all the while fighting the presence of other men.

The other men haunted her like recurring nightmares, the faces, the force, the suffocating dryness of their strange bodies like skin sloughed off and sucked in as she tried to breathe, she remembered, like not breathing at all, she thought, as her darling, cherished husband gasped quietly and breathed in, easily, clearly and happily, the vapors of his strangled wife.

Part II

The NIGHT
of the
WEEPING
WOMEN

Twelve

"Out with the old and in with the new," Margaret said early on the morning of January 2, as she passed Ervin coming out of his room.

"Ugh," he said and retreated.

She filled the water container and inserted it in the coffee machine. She knocked on his bedroom door. He didn't answer but she heard the shower and walked in. She knocked on the bathroom door, and then she opened it. He stepped from behind the curtain at the same time as she entered.

"Oh look at you," she said. "I'd almost forgotten what you looked like."

"Damn your ass," he said and covered up. "How'd you get in here?"

"The door was open. It looks like you put the knobs on backwards," she said and studied the arrangement. "The lock is on the outside."

"I don't give a damn where I put it."

"Well, it certainly doesn't matter to me," she said cheerily.

"What the hell is up with you? What are you so damn giddy about?"

"I'm going to start driving again."

"Sure you are."

"I want the keys to the Dodge."

"And if I give them to you, you're going to go out and—"

"Don't say it," she said, interrupting him, ". . . almost kill myself again."

"Right."

"That was a long time ago."

"And you haven't driven since you totaled that brand-new Chrysler, the best car we ever had."

"I'm ready now. It's a new year."

"You make me sick," he said.

"Just give me the keys."

"Your license has expired."

"I'm going to get a new one."

"You can't drive down there on an expired license," he said and then stopped himself as he flashed on the potential for another wreck, "unless you really want to. If you're set on it, take them. I'll drive the camper."

"You mean it?"

"Sure."

"Thanks," she said and leaned over to kiss him.

"Back off," he said.

She took the keys from beside his wallet on the night table and walked out; as she did, he entered the bedroom, still drying himself with the towel, and looked to see if she had separated the car keys from the others. Then he dressed and left. Margaret watched him out the window as she put on slacks and a blouse and a sweater and running shoes and a warm jacket.

I can do this, she thought. I steered it that time when he tried to kill me. Surely I can drive it by myself.

It was like riding a bicycle or skating. It came back to

her. She drove slowly. She parked around the side of the license bureau. The lot was full. A notice on the door said sign in and wait. An old black man sat in a chair at the examiner's desk. His back was to the room. Margaret watched the old man. He was handsome and dignified and looked like an old darkie straight out of a Shirley Temple film.

"You don't have a license?" the examiner asked.

"No sir. That is why I am here," he said.

"Didn't I see you drive up in that car right there?" he asked and pointed to a big green car.

"Yes sir. You did."

"How can you be driving without a license?"

Margaret started to leave but just as she rose the examiner looked at her and said, "Just wait, ma'am, we'll get to you before long."

"You see, Mr. Offi-sir," the old man said, "I had my wallet stolen some time ago and the poe-lease man what stopped me inscructed me to come here."

There are people who just long for the good old days, they miss them something awful, but they keep quiet about it, having been inscructed by the federal government to do so, but it had been a long time since an old-time nigra who knew how to talk to a white man had come into that license bureau and it just touched the examiner's heart, it did, it just took him back, and the old man could not have made a better case for himself if he'd tap danced and sang and clapped his hands, he could not have done any better if he'd come shuffling in and ast him if he's got any yards work, "Yes sir, I sure do's appreciates it," it was just hard to imagine how good it felt to find an old black who could make you remember the good old days, hell, you'd give him about anything just to come in and visit once a week, and it just touched the examiner deep inside, and he said, as softly and nicely as he could, "Well, if that's the case, Uncle Billy, I

guess we will certainly let you have another license. Fill this out here. You can write, can't you?" he asked, hoping, God knows he was hoping Uncle Billy couldn't write so he could do it for him.

"I can write," the old man said, still dignified.

Margaret studied the book in her hand and worried about her own story. She had thought to read up right there and take the written test and then take the road test but now she had to worry about explaining how she got there and so she thought fast and said, when asked, "My husband drove me."

"And left the car here?"

"He rode to work with a friend who followed us over."

She had not lied in so long she was certain he could see right through her.

"And what if you don't pass?"

"Then I guess I will have to call him to come get the car," she said.

This was logical. He bought it. She passed and then waited while the laminating machine sealed her photo to the license and then she walked into the world, a registered mobile citizen once again.

All day Ervin laughed to himself, imagining the old woman in a wreck or in trouble for driving to the license bureau. It just made his day. He took Angie out for lunch again. He took her to a Chinese restaurant, the only one in town, and a place Margaret had always wanted to go.

"This is nice," she said as they were shown into a booth with a curtain that the host drew, sealing them off in their own world.

"You're nice to take me to lunch so often. You must let me take you out sometime."

"Wouldn't think of it," he said, studying the menu.

"Buddy wouldn't even take me out, not after a while. He

did at first, but then, I don't know, after Darlene was born, he just wouldn't go anywhere with me."

"Wonder why?"

"I never could figure it out."

"I know what you mean," he said, a bit distractedly, as he studied the menu, lost once he left steak and potatoes.

"You order for me," he said. "I trust you."

"Anything? Do you like anything, really?"

"Don't get me any squid or octopus or anything like that."

"Moo shoo pork is good," she said. "We can order extra pancakes and share it. And some Chinese wine?"

When it came, she prepared the pancakes with the sauce and the filling and set them, one at a time, as he ate, on the extra plate they had asked for. After he finished two, she fed him a third, reaching across the table and putting it right in his mouth.

"I'm glad that curtain's drawn," he said.

"You're just an old prude."

"I am. I am old. You ought to know that."

You're just right, she thought, imagining quiet nights and a fatherly warmth, not to mention a thirty-year civil service pension. "Even if you retire like you said you were going to, you're so healthy and young-looking you could do anything else you wanted."

"You paid for your lunch with that," he said.

She slid forward and her knee touched his knee and then, relaxed and feeling so comfortable in their private booth, she slid a bit further, straddling his leg with both of hers.

"I like you," she said, sleepily, dreamily, warmed up by the wine and the closeness. "It's so hard sometimes being alone. Of course, I'm not alone, but I mean with Darlene, all the time. I love her. I don't mean I don't, and I wouldn't take anything for her, but it gets so tiring. I had an awful fight

121

with her the other night. It was one of those days, you know, when she felt bad and I felt bad and she was just on me, all day. She never let up."

"That's bad."

"You know what I mean. You have a daughter. You remember those days when you can't stand another minute in the house with them, but then, if you leave, you can hardly wait to come back. It's kind of like that. A person needs something else."

"That's for sure."

"I like you because you pay attention to me. Because there's something there, the way we are together, that I've missed. I didn't think I'd miss it, not after all I went through, but I have."

"I miss it, too."

"Buddy was very selfish. He didn't mean to be, I don't even think he was aware of it. It was just the way he was. On certain nights he would be nice to me. Just a little. For just a little while, he would pay attention to me, and then, after I gave in, nothing," she said, and opened her palms to show what she meant. "Nothing, that is, until the next time. It was awful."

Ervin listened. The glass of wine was the first alcohol he'd had since he was in the army. He felt so different from any way he had felt in so many years he knew more clearly than ever before how much he wanted out and how much he wanted this sweet, lonely young woman.

"It's bitterness," he said.

"What?"

"Your husband was probably bitter."

"My ex, please. But about what?"

"Oh, I don't know. Something must have happened that put a bad taste in his mouth and he couldn't get rid of it."

"Why do you say that?"

"Just a guess."

"Is that what happened to you. With your wife?"

"Maybe."

"What was it, then?" she asked.

"Nothing. Or, well, I mean, everything, really. It wouldn't do any good to talk about it."

"But I want to know."

"Well, it's like she lives in a dream world. Of course, now that I hear myself saying it, it doesn't sound so bad."

"What's it like?"

"What's it like? Well, for instance, when I go home, I never know what to expect. She's all over the map. She's fine one day, calm and leaves me alone, and the next day, out of the blue, she's like a crazy woman. Chases me around the house. All kinds of things."

"That's awful."

"I don't know why I married her. I can't remember now. But anyway, I shouldn't be talking about it. It's not your problem. It's mine."

"Maybe it's ours."

"No. I wouldn't do that to you. There's no reason you should believe me, anyway. I might be making it all up. It might be me who's the crazy one."

"I doubt that," she said.

They lost track of time so that later they had to rush to get back to work and Angie, running out with him, saw them reflected in the big window of the camper as they ran toward it.

"We look nice together," she said. "Don't you think?"

"I do."

"Why did you bring this, anyway?"

"Margaret took the car."

"Oh. I thought you said . . ."

"She's got her license back. Or, she was going to get it.

The new year and all. She's always starting some new plan, always has some new idea. Big changes. All the time," he said, and made a grim face.

"One thing I always wanted to ask you," she said, thinking about the car.

"What's that?"

"Why'd you act like your window wouldn't roll down that first time I rode with you?"

"When was that?"

"After I took my car to the mechanic. When you were sitting there at the store and I knocked on the window?"

"Oh yeah. Right. That was when, well, it wouldn't then. I got it fixed."

"You acted like you didn't want to give me a ride. I thought, you know, before I asked you, when I walked up to you, that you'd be glad to give me one. You'd been staring at me for weeks."

"I had not."

"You had to," she said. "You just stared at me like I was the first woman you'd ever seen, or something. I didn't know what to make of it at first."

"I must have been smitten," he said.

"Now we both are," she said, and they drove off.

Margaret was home by one-thirty, in time to see her favorite soap. She shopped after she left the license bureau and took herself out to lunch. She had spent more than two hundred dollars.

"Don't pick me up this Sunday," she told Evelyn, her friend who took her to church.

"Are you going out of town again?"

"I've got my license."

After the soaps she went into her bathroom, and in one of the more courageous moments of recent life, dragged the scale from under the sink and actually stepped on it.

124

"Oh my God," she said out loud. "I never."

At four-thirty she watched an afternoon talk show, and as if God had heard her calling from the bathroom, listened to a man describing a new diet.

I'll do it, she thought. And I'll put Ervin on it, too.

Then, checking the refrigerator and the freezer and failing to find anything that strictly conformed to the new ultra-low-carbo plan, she drove to the grocery store and bought what she needed. Ervin would be home in a little more than an hour.

About the time Margaret checked on the chicken and tossed a light salad of lettuce and carrot strips, Ervin and Angie climbed into the camper.

"She went to get her license," he explained as he started off, "because it is a new year."

"A time for new beginnings, of course."

"But she shouldn't try it. She can't drive very well."

"I see," Angie said. She was eager for any kind of information on the wife.

"Anyway, that's neither here nor there."

"If you say so."

"I wish I didn't have to go home."

"I do too."

"But what can I do?"

"It's difficult," she said.

"It's not your problem, though. I shouldn't drag you into it."

"I am in it, though. In the middle, you might say."

"I hate that," he said.

"Don't hate things," she said. "It's not good for you."

They drove quietly along. Ervin took the long way home down Front Street, where previously declining grand houses now stood renovated, the Cape Fear River flowing behind them and, in the distance, across the shore, the battleship

North Carolina, open to the public and, during the season, lighting the skies with its reenactments of battles at sea.

"I love these houses," she said.

"They're nice."

"I wish you didn't have bucket seats."

"These are captain's chairs," he said. "They're not exactly bucket seats."

"But I can't sit close to you this way."

"Oh," he said looking at her.

"I like to be close. If you haven't guessed."

"I have a daughter your age," he said.

"I know that. I don't care."

"She might even be older."

"So what? People are ageless in certain ways."

"Such as?" he asked, looking in the rearview mirror as a car behind them illuminated his lined face.

"Such as in kindness, in generosity, in warmth, in love. Such as," she said, "in those things."

"It's been a long time," he said.

"For what?"

"For anything. For any of those things you just mentioned."

"Maybe you were saving it."

"Maybe so," he said, and drove on without speaking, all the way to the Brookstone.

"Where's Darlene?"

"Upstairs, I suppose. Why?"

"What if you were a little late?"

"It wouldn't matter. Mrs. Scholtz will stay until I get there. She knows to."

"Do you want to just sit here and talk?" he asked.

"I thought you'd never ask," she said, and climbed through the passageway between the seats and settled down on the bench along one side.

"Back there?"

"Why not. You've got a traveling home here. It's nicer than my apartment."

"Oh, it's not."

"It is. I could live here."

"Some people do. They put them up on blocks," he said as he joined her, "and hook into utilities and have a little house."

"Why not?"

"I can turn a light on, if you want."

"We don't need it. The light coming through the windows is just right."

"I don't know what to do, you know."

"Sit closer to me, for a start," she said, and he moved against her and she lay her head against his shoulder, snuggling under his arm. He sighed. Her closeness slowly worked through him, and with the sigh he lay his head against hers and breathed in the sweet smell of her hair, her neck, her skin.

At five forty-five, Ervin was fifteen minutes late. Margaret took out the chicken and unwrapped it, stuck it with the meat thermometer and watched the needle rise and then pushed it back in the oven and closed the door, turning the dial to the lowest setting of warm and left the kitchen.

She went into his room and searched through his drawers. She searched them neatly and methodically and looked in his closet and behind his clothes and in the dark corners and on the half-shelf above the rod. She looked for evidence and she found in his night-table drawer an updated list of post office employees. She knew all the names but two. She wrote their names and addresses on a piece of paper and got in the car, a licensed investigator now, and went to find her husband.

The first address was beside the name Chandra Alston and was in a part of town she knew little about and when she

saw through the lighted windows the family inside and no camper in sight, she backed out and started for the Brookstone Apartments to find out about this other name, this Angela Taylor.

The address was across town and would take fifteen minutes to get there.

It began to rain and from inside the camper Ervin remembered sleeping under the tin roof of his parents' farmhouse.

"It's raining," he said.

"I know it is. I like the rain."

"It's cold, though."

"Let's get a blanket around us, then," she said.

"I mean outside. It must be in the thirties. The temperature's been dropping all day."

"So?"

"It might freeze."

"Good," she said.

"I mean onto the roads," he said.

"That'll be just right, won't it, baby," she said.

"Do you think," he said, "I mean, do you want . . ."

"Yes."

Cars driving in and out of the parking lot swept the camper with their lights, searchlights on this couple inside the thin walls, kissing hard enough to make lips bleed.

"Take it easy," she said.

"I'm sorry. I don't know what I'm doing."

"Don't move. Just stay just like that. Let me."

He shifted while she was kissing him; he reached toward the window.

"What's the matter?"

"I want to close the curtains."

"Are the doors locked?" she asked.

"No."

"Then lock them."

"What about Darlene?"

"Don't worry about her."

He made the bench into a bed, a narrow single bed on which they entwined like snakes.

"I never . . ." he said.

"Never what?"

"Never thought I'd feel this way again."

"Do you like it?"

"I think so."

"Do you want to get undressed?"

"Do you?" he asked.

"Yes. Do you have another blanket?"

He got the blanket from the storage chest above the bed. The blanket was old and was from a double bed from long ago.

"Nice," Angie said.

They snuggled, still dressed, under the blanket and she pulled him over on top of her. She held him against her with her arms and her legs and she pressed against him so hard he couldn't move or think, he just held on and tried to stay with her.

"Let's take our clothes off," she said.

"Where?"

"Anywhere you want," she said and took hers off right then and there, proud of her new figure and showing it off for the first time since she had begun eating what must have been by that time a tractor-trailer load of lettuce and celery and carrots.

"You like me?"

"I like you," he said, and she slid under the covers.

"Now you."

"Okay," he said and looked toward the doors and the windows.

"No one can get in, can they?" she asked.

"No. I don't think so."

"Then come on baby. I've been waiting a long time for this."

He thought about his old-man body and his skinny little ankles and the bald places on his legs where the hair had fallen off and he thought about that little thing inside his pants and would it look right, I mean, did the men these days, I mean, he thought, was it the same? and he said, "I think I'll get undressed under the covers," and he climbed in with her and took off his shirt and as it came off she reached for him.

"You're shy," she said.

"Not for long," he said, and kicked until he got his pants off and then his boxer shorts and as soon as he had them off she reached for him, there, too.

"Whew," he gasped.

"Are my hands cold?" she asked, and put them to her lips.

"No. This stuff is a little new to me."

"You mean?"

"I mean."

"How long?"

"Oh, I don't know. Just not too often, is what I mean."

"Well we'll change that," she said. "You bring that little boy over here and I'm going to make him into a big boy," she said and went to work. She worked hard, there's no denying it, and she did everything just right. After all she'd had years of experience with her drunk-soldier husband, a recon man who could drop from a rope down the side of a mountain or free fall with a parachute until he was three thousand feet up and pop that cord and hit the target dead on, lots of experience, you see, even when dead drunk and still wanting it, she could get him there, the quicker the better, too, so they could go on to sleep, and so she knew just what to do.

"That's nice," he said.

"Just relax. Think about what you're going to do to me."

And still nothing was happening, like the nothing that would happen if you took some cold hamburger meat and sculpted it just so and then tried to force it into a steaming-hot slab of rump roast just out of the oven, that kind of nothing, about that firm, you see, like that cold pop-art penis, nothing, you see, nothing, when, had Ervin known it, he could have done anything to her, just anything, so much she wanted to be his at that moment, so close she was to having him just where she wanted him, she would have said yes to anything, to whatever he needed, baby, you know, I just want to, I just need to, you see, take this knife and slice your belly open a little, not too much, but just a little, all right, all right, just take me, just do with me, turn me over and do with me, stand me up and do with me, push me down and do with me, I'm yours, she had told him, but he just didn't know what it meant and there was still that cold piece of hamburger down there, and every time she reached for it, it practically disappeared, talk about something slipping out of your grasp, just gone, like that, and in its place in that tortured guilty mind sending the signals across synapses that hadn't seen a twitch in years, in its place a soft, fleshy statue of Margaret Neal appeared, like a pale, white bat she hung there upside down, staring back at him.

Angie was having her own troubles keeping her mind on things by then, thinking, there goes that thirty-year pension, there go the warm nights by the fire in the new condominium she had looked at one Sunday afternoon, just dreaming, just planning ahead, and here come more of those endless days in the post office walking on the concrete floor until the bones in her heels had pounded up into her brain, all of that not quite so distinctly, but she knew she was losing her momentum.

131

"You bitch," he said.

"What? Did you just call me a bitch?" Angie asked, sitting up.

"No. I certainly did not."

"You did. I heard you."

"Oh. I guess I was thinking of Margaret."

"But don't do that. Think about me."

"I want to. Believe me," he said, stalling for time and trying to find some way out of this humiliation, trying to find someone, anywhere, and who better to blame than the nemesis of his life, that queen of the housecoat and terry-cloth slippers, that woman who knew way, way, way too much about him, knew so much he couldn't ever get past it all, so he thought it was time, it was time like no other time would be, to tell Angie one of the reasons he couldn't leave the poor old girl and why this saint of a man couldn't betray her.

"She's crippled," he said, and Angie asked, "What? Who?" and he said again, "I just didn't want to tell you but I guess you need to know."

"You mean Margaret?"

"Yes. One of her legs is crippled and she has to wear a brace on it. I didn't want to say anything. I've tried to protect her. But you need to know."

"Oh, I'm so sorry."

"And every time I get fed up with her and try to leave her," he said, seeing it as he said it, "I just look at that leg and that brace and watch her clunk across the room and I just sit back down and I can't get any further than that, you know, like tonight, I just can't. I just don't know how I'll ever get away from her."

"Come here, honey," she said and held him against her. "I had no idea. I really didn't," and she began to see what he had been through, all that he had been keeping inside himself and she held him and rubbed his hair and rested against

his shoulder even though his armpits smelled like the inside of an old shoe, she gave what she could, both of them silent while they tried to figure out what next to say, what next to do, where, just exactly, they could go from here, both still and so quiet that when something bumped against the outside of the camper, they jumped like one person.

"Ervin," the thing that bumped called. "Ervin, are you in there?"

"Oh God," he whispered. "It's her."

"Margaret?" Angie whispered.

"Yes."

"Are you sure?"

"Ervin?" she called again and tried the door.

They dressed and put away the blankets and folded up the bed, all the while staying below the level of the windows.

"I can hear you in there, Ervin Neal. You open up right now."

"Get down," he said to Angie, who was on the floor.

"I am down."

"I hear voices," Margaret called. "What are you doing? Who's with you in there?"

She pulled on the door again. He remembered the bathroom door. He stepped over Angie and started the engine and drove off as fast as he could, bouncing over the curb and into the street while Angie rolled around like an empty pop bottle and Margaret stood in the rain for a moment and then started after him.

"Take it easy," Angie said.

"Stay down. She's coming after us."

"Lose her."

"I can't."

He cut in front of a line of cars and turned right. The cars slammed on brakes in chain reaction. Margaret was trapped behind them trying to get out of the driveway.

"That car's got a four-barrel carburetor and a high-

performance cam," he said, "and we'll never outrun her."

He drove around the block and ran a red light and stopped behind the apartment complex in the shadow of the buildings.

"Jump out," he said. "Out the back."

She leaped and he started off before she closed the door and it swung back and forth, and by the time Angie disappeared around the building and he turned the corner, Margaret caught up with him. She saw him as the door swung open. Her headlights lit up the inside of the camper and the back of Ervin's head and she could see his eyes reflected in the rearview mirror. Ervin hit his brakes but then quickly let off and the forward impact slammed the door shut as Margaret slid toward him on the wet street. He floored it and pulled away, but she caught him again and followed him, this time from a distance, all the way home.

"This is it, Ervin Neal," she said after they were both out.

"What? What's it? I didn't do anything."

"I know what you're doing. I know her name. Now where is she?" she asked and pushed by him to search the camper.

"You're making a fool of yourself," he said. "As usual."

"Don't lie to me. I'm sick of it."

"Be sick of it, then."

"Where is Angela?"

"Who?" he asked, amazed she knew her name.

"Angela Taylor, your girlfriend from the post office."

He walked to the house and she followed him. He walked in front of her in the blind terror a person felt on the sidewalk after sensing that someone had walked up close behind him and he was about to be mugged. Afraid, but more afraid to turn around and face it. When they were in the carport, she struck.

"Hey. Calm down. All right?" He had fallen against the

storm door and knocked the plexiglass panels out. "Look what you did now. You're tearing things up again."

"I'll tear you up if you don't tell me what's been going on."

"Okay. You've got me. Come on in and we'll talk."

"You mean you were with her?"

"Yes."

"You mean you admit you've been seeing her?"

"Yes," he said and she followed him into his room.

"And have you?"

"Have I?"

"Have you and her?"

"No. We haven't done that."

"You better not have."

"Don't worry."

"Don't worry, you say," and made as if to hit him again when suddenly she just dropped, lifeless, like a puppet whose strings had been cut all at once and she wept and she wept in such a deep, moaning way and with such force that Ervin, in spite of everything, felt sorry for her and he sat on the floor and held her.

"You don't have to," she said.

He held her with his arm around her shoulder and supported her until she stopped heaving and shaking and she looked up at him and he looked down at her and it was the perfect moment to kiss, to forgive, to make up, a scene from a movie, come true. It was six-thirty. Forty-five minutes had passed since the chicken went back in the oven to stay warm. Outside it was still raining, the temperature was still falling and was, at that moment, thirty-eight degrees.

At seven, raining harder in Chatham County than on the coast since the rain and the cold were coming from the northwest, Sally told Robert that supper would be delayed still more.

"It'll be worth waiting for," she said.

"I don't mind."

"It's the cheesecake."

"I can wait for that."

"We could eat now and then wait on dessert."

"Let's do it right. I'll take a bath."

"Okay."

"I'll light the gas heater."

"We've got to get some more wood in, as well."

"I'll get that later."

Sally's journal was on the clothes hamper where she had left it that morning. Robert picked it up. He didn't know about the journal since she only wrote in it in the mornings after he left.

What's this?

He read the open page. It read like the kind of nonsense he wouldn't read if he found it in a women's magazine but because it was his wife's nonsense, he read further and then flipped back to the beginning. The title had been written and erased a number of times. It now said, "Journal of My Flights."

What flights?

While he was reading he had the sense he should not be, but he continued on.

Just curious.

He filled the tub. He stayed in the water until it turned cold and then stood in front of the open, fire-bricked gas heater and dried off. He heard the floor creaking and put the book down and dropped his towel over it.

"It's ready now," Sally said, leaning in.

"Just a minute more."

"Did you fall asleep?"

"No. Why?"

"You've been in here half an hour."

"Just give me a minute to get dressed."

The kitchen table was arranged as if for a photograph. There was ambrosia and roast duck and wild rice and snap beans and sautéed mushrooms and, in the refrigerator, the cheesecake with blueberry topping.

"This is a kind of midwinter present," she said. "Twelfth Night, Russian Christmas, or what have you. Anyway," she said, "you've been so good putting up with Mother and Daddy and all the visits and the rubbery steak, I just thought I'd do it."

"Looks great," he said.

"Aren't you hungry? Let's eat."

"You left a book in the bathroom."

"What book?"

"The journal of your flights."

"Oh. That book. Well, thanks. Where is it?"

"Still in there."

"I'll get it later."

"I read it," he said. "I'm sorry, but I did."

"You shouldn't have done that. I wouldn't read something of yours I saw was personal. Not without asking."

"I know."

"Why didn't you ask me?"

"I don't know."

"So. What do you want me to say?"

"I want to know if it's true."

"Maybe and maybe not."

"Because if it is, something strange has happened. Because if it is, then you're not the person I thought you were. If all that stuff is true, then I don't even know you."

"That's ridiculous," she said, and tried to keep on eating. "It really is. I'm the same no matter what."

"But you're not."

"But I am."

"But, thirty-seven men. Really?"

"Oh hell. That would be the part you found," she said.

"Can that be true? I mean, you've got their initials down there, and dates, I mean, what in the hell? How could you do that? How could anyone sleep with that many different people? I mean, you'd almost have to be crazy."

"Not crazy," she said, embarrassed and humiliated. "Not crazy, exactly, but kind of desperate."

"Either way, it makes me wonder."

"Me, too. That's why I wrote it down."

"Come in here," he said and took her by the arm and guided her from her chair and the perfect meal and into the other room, while back at the table the ambrosia curdled.

It was the perfect moment to be kissed, there on the floor with the tear-streaked face and the broken heart and the protective arm of Ervin around her, but it passed, without the kiss.

It passed without the kiss because hard as he tried, much as he hated to see her hurt that badly, much as he hated her for so many things and as much as he wished he hadn't done or said so many of the things he'd done or said, he had to let the moment pass, because he had, during that moment, decided he needed Angie in his life and that he would be able, finally, to leave this worn-out old woman.

It was so important not to make mistakes with the person you loved, and there were so many mistakes already made with Margaret there was no way out of them.

"Wash up," he said.

"Why?"

"Just go wash up," he said and led her into the bathroom. "I'll get you a clean towel."

She filled the bowl with cold water. She cupped her hands and splashed it on her face. She heard the door close and found herself alone in the room.

"Ervin?"

"Sorry," he said.

"What?"

"I've got to do some things. I just can't have you interfering."

She pulled on the door but it was locked and when she reached to unlock it, looking for the button one would find in any bathroom-door lock, she found nothing. Yet, the door was still locked.

"Open up, now. This isn't funny."

"I know it's not."

"Where's the lock button?" she asked.

"It's on the outside. Remember? I put the knobs on backwards," he said, changing clothes, "and when I did it I thought I'd just change them around later. I see now," he said on his way out the bedroom door, "that there was a purpose to it."

She heard the bedroom door close. She heard him drive off and she sat on the closed top of the toilet seat with the green and purple cotton cover that matched the green and purple oval rug on the tile floor and she looked in the tub and saw a mass of hair caught on the drain guard and without knowing she was doing it, scoured it clean with her fingers and tossed the hair into the trash.

"Really," Robert said, "what does that make me? I mean, think about it. You know what it makes me? Number thirty-eight. That's what it makes me. Number thirty-eight."

"Of course it doesn't."

"I mean, you know, we don't expect our wives to be virgins nowadays, but then again," he said, and thought back, "then again, that explains why you are such an expert in bed. That explains a lot."

"It doesn't explain anything," she said.

"It explains how you know so much and what a damn fool I've been. I must have looked like a real jerk to you. Imagine how you've had to teach me everything. God-

damnit. That makes me feel like a real fool. I mean, you know, like I said, we don't expect our wives to be virgins, but then again, we don't expect them to have been professionals in the business, either."

The cat walked in. He walked toward Robert. The dog knew better and hid behind a chair but the cat walked right up and rubbed against his leg and got kicked across the room.

"Goddamn cat."

"Don't."

"Don't? Shit," he said, and then he said it three more times. "Shit, shit, shit."

"That's nice," she said. "That's really intelligent."

"Oh, you want to get tough?"

"No. I don't want to get tough. I just want it to be over."

"Then tell me about it."

"I don't want to do that."

"That's the only way it'll be over."

"Can't you see how embarrassing this is for me?"

"And can't you see what it makes me?"

"No. I can't."

"It makes me number thirty-eight."

"Don't say that again. Really. It's meaningless."

"Somehow it's not."

"But it is."

"Just tell me."

"You really want me to?"

"I do."

"But where do I start?"

"At the beginning."

"Let's eat first. At least let's do that."

"I'm not hungry."

"This is so strange," she said. "I ought to just go eat my supper and forget all about this."

"But you can't, because you know you're in the wrong. You've deceived me. You've betrayed me. I thought you were mine, but now I find out you were everybody's."

Ervin rang Angie's doorbell, and Mrs. Scholtz came out from next door.

"Are they home?" he asked. "Do you know?"

"They're not home. They left a few minutes ago."

"Exactly how long ago?"

"I don't know. Not exactly."

"Where'd they go?"

"I don't know that either. I just saw them get into her old car and leave."

"But that car won't run."

"It runs a little."

"Have you got a key you could let me in to wait for them?" he asked.

"I couldn't do that."

"Yes you could."

"No. I don't think I could," she said and closed her door and would not answer when he rang her bell.

"You tell her I have to talk with her," he yelled through the door. "Tell her it's important."

He drove to the nearest FastFare and bought a large cup of coffee and a box of Krispy Kreme doughnuts.

Meanwhile, Margaret had already tried the doorknob with force, hoping to tear it off, but it held. She pushed against the door with her shoulder the way police broke down doors on television but it would not open.

"Let me out," she said to no one but herself.

She beat on the wall. There was a wall adjacent to the hall, one adjacent to her bedroom, one adjacent to his bedroom and one on the outside wall. There was sheetrock, insulation, blackboard and four inches of brick between her

and the outside world. She yelled. Her voice was faint and a person would have to have been standing directly outside the wall to hear her.

"I was not everybody's," Sally said. "I have never been anyone's but yours."

"Sure."

"You don't understand it. You should, but you don't. I can see that. I have been loyal to you, so fiercely loyal to you. No one," she said, "was ever as loyal to a husband as I have been to you and it's because everything's so right between us."

"Was so right," he said.

"You just don't know. You just can't know, I guess, you just can't understand, I guess, unless you know what I've been through and what I've had to live with. I guess that's the way it's going to be. I'm surprised you haven't asked about that, too?"

"What?"

"If you're asking what, then I guess you haven't read the whole journal. I guess if you had, you probably wouldn't be here by now."

"What else is there?"

"Listen. If I tell you all this sordid stuff and we talk about it, will it be over? Can we just let it go?"

"I guess so. I don't know. But maybe."

"See, you wondered why it's been so hard on me that I haven't been able to get pregnant, why I went through that stupid arthroscopic surgery and all that. And, of course," she said, "Daddy figures into this."

"It's getting worse all the time, then," he said.

"He just has made such a mess of things. I don't know how he could do it. With Mother and with me. He just has done all the wrong things."

"I'm listening," he said, trying to close off any expression on his face and have that dead look the therapist had when the patient looked up and said, "But listen, you see, I've killed sixteen people, eaten little children for breakfast, fried them in a pan, I killed the Pope and ate his toes and there's nothing better I like than a real good thick shit sandwich," and the therapist just sat there and nodded, as if, "Of course, of course you did all those things," he sat there like that, waiting for whatever it was.

"Well," she said. "Talk to me. Say something," she said and reached for him and he pulled away.

"Don't touch me right now. My skin feels crazy. I can sit here but don't touch me."

"But baby," she said, "I want to be sure this is the right thing. I want to be sure we are closer, not further apart after all this is over. Don't leave me now."

"I'm right here. Just go on."

"Well, I was fourteen—" she began.

"Fourteen?" he cut in. "You were fourteen when you started?"

"Just listen to me, please. I was fourteen and we were living in Wilmington in that same house, and Mother and Daddy were fairly normal, still slept in the same room, I think, I'm not sure, anyway, they fussed and fought a lot but at the time I thought it was just the way things were, not knowing life could really be any different, hoping it would or could be, but not really sure.

"Anyway, that year things went bad for them, I don't know why, and Mother wrecked the car that year and quit driving, and they started fighting more and I started hating it so much all I could think of was getting out and getting away, graduating, having my own life, just anything but staying with them.

"So naturally, there I was, ripe for some nice boy to

143

come along and just do with me anything he wanted and that's what happened. I got this crush on an older boy, who was in the eleventh grade, and this led to that and so on and pretty soon we were sleeping together."

"At fourteen," Robert said, and shook his head. "A baby."

"I wasn't a baby. I was mature, but it was early. It really was. I think I was the first girl in my group of friends to do it. But you know, it wasn't like really making love. It was more like, I don't know, more like speeding in a car or sneaking out. It felt the same. A kind of rush. A kind of illicit thrill. It was not," she said and reached over and touched him on the back of his hand, which he pulled slowly away, "it was not," she said, "like what we do. Nothing was ever like that. You have to know that. Nothing was ever like that. It wasn't making love. It was more like the thrill of doing something wrong."

"I bet."

"And," she said, ignoring the remark, "I had that diary, the one you found with the pages torn out, and I wrote about it. I wrote about everything, but in the diary I romanticized it something awful and I knew at the time I was doing it, I mean, I knew I was exaggerating and so forth, but I wrote it that way because I wanted it to be that way. Look," she said, "I was fourteen."

"Right."

"Oh well, anyway, one night Daddy found the diary in my desk drawer. I think he must have pried it open and read something. You could pull it apart a little because the strap wasn't all that tight and you could read sideways into the pages. Anyway, the next thing I know I went in there and he was sitting on my bed, reading the thing with this awful, red-faced look.

"He put the book down and motioned for me to come in and told me to close the door and I was scared. I can't tell

you how scared I was. I don't know if I was ever that scared again, except when I had the abortion. . . ."

"The abortion?"

"Well, I'll tell you about it in time. So, I was in the room with him and I was scared, really scared, and he made me sit across from him and he kept on reading. And it was awful. Really awful, because as I sat there and he read, his hands were shaking, and he lit a cigarette and they were shaking even worse trying to do that, and I had to sit there and watch him read and every time I tried to say anything he would look up at me with this ugly face he'd never used on me before, would point his finger at me and tell me to shut up, and then, of course, I would, and he just kept on reading.

"I tried to read upside down where he was in the book and I could see he was already to the parts with Richard and me and, as I read upside down I could see he was getting to a part, I mean, he was already way past the part where I talked about going all the way with him, but I could see he was getting to a part that was really romantic, really phony and made-up and I just couldn't stand for him to know that much about me and I grabbed the book and ran out of the room and he chased me and almost had me except that Mother came walking through the hall just then and as I passed her and she saw him chasing me she grabbed his arm, in a reflex I think it must have been, like, hold on here, what's this about, and I got to the bathroom and locked the door and tore out the pages and flushed them away.

"And then when I came out Daddy must have been talking to her because they took me by the arms, one on each side of me, and led me into the living room and started in on me. Is this true? Is this true? They just kept on. 'Did you' . . . what is it they were saying, oh yeah, 'Did you fornicate with this boy?' That's what they kept asking me, fornicate, like it was something awful, I'd never thought of it that way, but I

145

did the strangest thing then, I just told them no, that it was all a lie and that I had been making it up in the diary just to pretend. And of course they didn't believe me and kept at me, giving me the third degree and it just went on all night and I kept denying it and Mother sided with me for a while and Daddy got madder and madder, said he knew I was lying and you have to remember back then how big a deal being a virgin was, I mean, it was like the ultimate sin to lose your virginity, and Daddy was getting madder and madder and, you know, thinking about it now I don't think there is anything I could have done that would have gotten them that upset. Not anything at all. Not stealing, not flunking a course, not anything. Isn't that weird? But, so it went on and I was crying the whole time and just absolutely worn out and they were just like, by the end, somehow Mother was on his side, furious that I'd done it, and I was crying and still lying, and the harder they pushed me the more I lied, the more furious they got and after a few hours I was so tired I was about to fall over right there on the couch and they were still going strong and then Mother said that they were going to take me to the doctor the next day and have him examine me to see if I was still a virgin and that all my lies would be exposed then."

Sally walked into the kitchen and drank the rest of her ice tea and reached for his. "May I?" she asked and he nodded yes.

"So they were in this fury, this compulsion to prove me wrong and Daddy said that we didn't have to go to a doctor to prove it, that he and Mother could examine me right then and find out and I just went nuts, let me tell you, I really did, and I started crying and running around the room, and they took hold of me and forced me to sit back down and said they'd give me one more chance, you know, that old thing, but I was so far gone with the lies I couldn't stop, so they took me, and I mean took, like dragged me, into the bed-

146

room and shut the door and Mother told me to take off my panties and I wouldn't do it and they both grabbed me, they hurt my arms they held me so tight, I remember they hurt for days afterwards, and they pulled me down on the bed and pulled up my skirt," she said and looked at him, but though he knew she was looking at him he wouldn't look back and just shook his head.

"You want me to go on?"

He shrugged.

"I don't have to," she said.

"Go ahead."

"All right. But let me say something. It's really strange telling this. I have never said a word to anyone about this, and yet in telling it, it's like I'm telling it about someone else. Like it happened to someone else."

"I wish," he said.

"So I was still fighting and Daddy had my wrists and Mother was down at my legs and I was turning and screaming, God knows I wonder what the neighbors thought, and then Daddy squeezed my wrists so hard and twisted them around to make me be still and I just went limp. I just gave up. I just went dead. I just wanted it over with. And Mother examined me and Daddy held me and I just lay there with my eyes closed and then, the strangest thing, after she claimed to have found out the truth, that I was no longer a virgin, everything let go, I mean, literally, he let go of me and the anger and madness let go, and after I admitted it was true, they seemed relieved. And happy. I swear they were. Everything changed, and Mother, who had been so vicious, as vicious as Daddy when I never thought she could be, held me while I cried and then ran a hot bath for me and took me in there and the night I never thought would end finally ended and I fell into the deadest sleep you could ever imagine.

"Except later," she said, and looked up as if she were

trying to see it more clearly, "either Daddy came back in or I dreamed it but it was like I couldn't breathe all of a sudden and I couldn't wake up and I halfway did and there was his mad face and then it was like one of those dreams where you can't get loose from something and you can't wake up and just at the point where you think you might actually never come back you do, like just short of real death, that was what it was like, and then, at six-thirty, when the alarm went off, I got up, got dressed, went to school and just kept on going. As if nothing had happened. Can you imagine that? Really. But I did it and no one ever knew a thing.

"And that's what's so crazy. Neither that nor anything else, like what I'm going to tell you next if you want to still go on, was ever talked about again. I mean, it happened, but it didn't happen. Like the shame of it all was just too much. For everyone. Know what I mean?"

"I guess so."

"Are you still with me?"

"Yeah."

"Can I come and sit beside you now?"

"No."

"Please."

"Not just yet."

"Then maybe I better not go on."

"I think you better."

"But you're pulling away from me. More. I can feel it."

"I'm not. I'm still here. I'm just waiting for whatever it is coming next."

"I don't know," she said.

"Do you want to tell me?"

"I do. I really do. I just want to be sure it's right."

"Then go on."

"Okay," she said. "I will. Because it's making me feel better."

"Good."

"So, after that, everything changed. Between me and my parents, I mean. I don't know, Daddy got weird, wouldn't talk to me, wouldn't look at me, acted like a jealous lover if you want to know the truth, like I'd betrayed him. He used to follow me on my dates. I mean, I knew it, and we'd see him, he would have found out from Mother where we were going and of course we never went where we said, but he'd show up sometimes, in the car, and we'd lose him, it would turn into a game, he'd chase us and we'd lose him and those poor little boys I'd be out with wouldn't know what to think, they just didn't know what they'd gotten into, but you know what?" she asked and was quiet for a moment as she thought about it. "You know what? If he hadn't been so crazy about it and so perverse about it, I wonder if I wouldn't have eased up a little. I just wonder."

"I don't know."

"They were both so puritanical and so all twisted up, about everything, really, they just drove me to it and what else could I do? I didn't have anyone. I didn't have anyone who wanted me or loved me."

"Seems like you found plenty of guys for that," he said.

"No. Not from them."

"Whose baby was it?"

"I don't know. I was so out of control I don't even know. But I got pregnant, I missed two periods and that made me, let me think, I guess that made me about ten weeks at the time I finally told my father."

"Why didn't you tell your mother? Why tell him?"

"I don't know. We were out in the car, I guess he was picking me up from somewhere, and I told him. It just happened. I couldn't keep quiet about it anymore, and he didn't say anything at first, but a little bit later, I swear I think he gloated, like, 'I told you so,' or, like, well, 'I knew it,' and he just did all the wrong things after that. He called me a bitch and a slut and was mad as hell and all I wanted was

understanding and help and he wouldn't let me tell Mother. He said it'd kill her and then I told him I wanted to have the baby, because by then, I had decided that. When I first thought I was pregnant, I immediately thought of an abortion, but you couldn't get them back then, I mean people had heard of them, had heard of people getting them but no one I knew really knew where to go or how to get one, but the more I thought about it the more I thought I'd just go ahead and have the baby and give it away to someone who wanted one, but then after I told him about it, he said no way. He said we'd all be ruined if anyone found out and that he'd have to see about getting it fixed. That's the way he said it, 'Getting it fixed.' And so a week later he took me down into colored town and had it done."

"Just like that?"

"Just like that. All I remember is being so scared I thought I was going to die, that I would never come out of that little house alive, and that I prayed that I would be forgiven and that I would live. But here I am."

"Yeah."

"And now I can't get pregnant. It's a punishment on me, but damnit, it shouldn't be on me. I was innocent. In a way I really was. I was crazy and I was wild but I was innocent at the same time. I didn't know what to do. I couldn't do anything, really. I could only do what people told me to do. That's all I knew to do. Only what people told me to do."

"Someone should have killed him long ago," he said.

"We can't think that. It's just that I wish, I really do, I could have come to you in better shape. If I could just make up for it. If I just could."

"It's a little late."

"But it isn't. That's why I've gone ahead and told all of this. Don't you see? I'm going to be better now. You can never tell what might happen. You know how things change. I've read in magazines about people who couldn't get preg-

nant and then they adopt a baby and then something happens and then they do. It's because they've let go of something and then it happens. Don't you see?"

"I don't know what I see. I see, on the one hand, that I ought to be magnanimous, but if you want to know the truth, I feel like shit. And I hate your father worse than ever now."

"But it won't do any good to hate him. You can't. I've tried. It doesn't work. It doesn't affect him. It doesn't change a thing. It just wears you out. He's still there and it's still there and he's always going to be there. You just have to let it go. Just like I just did. I feel so much better. The only thing I'm worried about is you."

"Thanks a lot."

"Come back to me, honey," she said and the phone rang and it was her father, who said, "I'm coming up."

He was calling from a pay phone.

"I have nowhere else to go. I can't go home. I can't find Angie. I've got to talk with you."

"Don't," Robert heard her say and knew it was him. "You must not do that. Not now. Not tonight. It's impossible."

"I am coming," he told her. "I have nowhere else to go."

"He's coming here? Now?" Robert asked when she hung up.

"Yes."

"But why?"

"He didn't say. He just said he couldn't go home."

"What's wrong at home?"

"I don't know. I think I'll call Mother and have her stop him."

"Can she do that?"

"If she wants, she can."

She called, but no one answered.

"I don't want to see him," Robert said.

"Neither do I."

"As a matter of fact, I don't think I will."

"What do you mean?"

"I think I'll leave."

"Don't do that."

"No. I think I will."

"But I need you now. I thought if I told you all about that . . ."

"I wish I had never picked up that journal. How things change once you know about something, when before, oh well," he said, "I just can't believe it. I feel absolutely trashed. Thirty-seven men. Which makes me number thirty-eight and what does that make me?"

"Just stop it. Please."

"Abortions and examinations on the bed and God only knows what else there is to find out and now he's coming up and if I stay around here I just might kill him. I really might. I don't know you anymore. I don't know who I am, either."

"But baby," she said, "I'm the same. I really am."

"You're not. And I can't face him tonight. Much less for the rest of my life. It seems like you two should have worked all this out before I came along. It seems like," he said, getting up and walking out, "you should have worked out a lot of things a long time before you met me. I'll leave you two alone to do it tonight."

"But if you leave now . . . I mean, please, what do you want me to do? He's still my father."

"Do whatever you want. Just leave me out of it."

At eight o'clock Margaret knew Ervin had really left her there for the entire night. She turned on the exhaust fan to air out the stuffy room. When she turned it on, she remembered that it vented out the roof into a sloped metal cage on top of the shingles above the bathroom. She yelled into the fan. She put one foot on the edge of the tub and the other on

the toilet and called for help. She tried to call in a dignified manner. She said, "Please someone. I'm locked in. Can anyone hear me?" Then she turned the fan off and tried it that way.

All I can do is wait, she thought. And hope.

She took the towels from the linen closet and made a mattress on the floor. She folded a pillow from them and lay down. The cold-water faucet dripped in the sink. She had not known it dripped. Ervin must not know it dripped because he would have fixed it. Any sound kept him awake. No. Not anymore. He took so many pills and drank so much NyQuil it was a wonder he woke up each morning.

The furnace ignited and warm air blew from the grill in the wall. It blew for ten minutes and then stopped. A half hour later, it blew again. She took off her shoes and put her bare feet directly on the grill. She leaned against the side of the tub. There was nothing to do with her anger but forget it. She was furious but had no way to show it.

She was hungry. She had not eaten supper and remembered the chicken and salad and wondered where Ervin was and imagined him in a nice restaurant, being pleasant with the waitress in a very low-key way, letting on nothing, a felon in flight, a murderer of possibilities, a thief of happiness, a man guilty of so much, yet never standing trial for anything.

On the road, in the middle of a tract of paper-company woodlands, the man in flight passed a solitary house. The house was back from the road a hundred feet and was dark except for one room where a single overhead bulb hung from a cord.

Ervin saw this as he sped by in the camper, his home on wheels, more elaborate and better-equipped than the old shack. He glanced briefly, but saw clearly into the house. An eerie white light shone from a television set. It glowed more

brightly than the bare bulb. A man in a straight-backed chair leaned his elbows on a green wooden table.

It was remarkable how thoroughly this man in flight, guilty of so much domestic violence, captured this solitary vision of home, this still life of the house on the edge of thousands of acres of trees, lit by a single light, illuminating one person in a room nearly empty of furniture save the chair and the table and the unearthly glow of the television.

Sally stood beside the knee-high plastic end table on which the telephone sat and watched as Robert came across the room, intent on leaving, ignoring her, going out.

"This is wrong," she said.

He did not answer. She followed him across the room.

"I haven't done anything to you."

He went out the door. She followed him onto the porch. She was barefoot. The porch was wooden and sagged in the center where the rain, which splashed off the flat rock that served as a step, had rotted the flooring and the sill beneath. The floor was cold but not as cold as the air.

"Get rid of that old man," he said.

He went to his truck. The engine fired immediately, still warm from the drive home. He backed out of the parking spot and out of the range of the porch light. He drove off and did not look back.

He did not look back because he did not want to see his wife standing on the porch barefoot and weeping, with her hand on the dog's head, resting gently as it had on his arm.

He did not look back because he did not want to see her lips move or hear her say, "Don't leave me," and he drove down the driveway, blinding himself by turning his head so that out of the corner of his eyes he would not see her raise her hand in a gesture for him to stop, or know that she was saying, once more, sobbing now from the betrayal of what childhood had promised to the possible end of her own

charmed marriage, sobbing now with the distant woods and the open field and the black cold sky a vision of emptiness, and saying into the night, "Don't leave me," and pausing, "Please don't."

She went inside. She locked the door. She took a blanket off the bed and wrapped herself in it and sat beside the dying fire of the woodstove, and she waited.

At eight-fifteen Angie got the message to call Ervin but there was no answer. At eight-thirty she left Darlene with Mrs. Scholtz and went to find out what was going on. She did not want to lose him. Disregarding the pension and the new condominium, he was the only man who had even been nice to her, been kind to her, talked with her, respected her, listened to her, and asked nothing in return.

She felt sorry for him and she felt sorry for Margaret and she was worried because there was no answer and she had to know where she stood, and so she drove to his house. She knew where he lived because she had driven by before to see what kind of place it was. His camper was not there, but the car was. She drove down the street and then back up, and from neither direction could she see any lights in the house.

She parked on the side of the road two houses down and walked right up. She rang the bell, certain no one was home and not wanting to look suspicious should anyone have been watching. She rang it again and then walked around back. She was afraid of what she might find.

She could see where she was going from the illumination of an area light on a utility pole in the backyard next door. She tried the door and then walked to the other side.

Margaret heard the bell ring twice. She called. She beat on the wall and called and yelled and Angie heard her and stopped.

"Hello?" Angie called, but not loudly enough.

She listened to Margaret beating on the wall and calling for help and then she picked up a rock and beat on the brick wall opposite the noise. Margaret beat back from the inside and called louder this time and Angie followed her directions to the spare key and came in the side door.

She turned on the lights as she went from room to room, and as she did, she noticed the furniture, the decor, the cleanliness of the house, the pictures on the wall, all the domestic evidence of the other woman in Ervin's life, and, lighting her way across the house, and following the sound of Margaret's voice, ended up in his room.

The moment she entered the room she knew his smell and she saw his bed and she knew from what he had told her he slept alone and she looked at the unadorned walls and she heard Margaret through the door directly in front of her and she feared coming face-to-face with this woman for whom she felt so sorry and whose marriage she was about to destroy.

"I'm here. Are you there?"

"I'm here," Angie called. "How do I get you out?"

"The lock is on the outside. My husband, oh, never mind, it's right there, in the knob. Do you see it?"

Angie opened the door. She looked at Margaret. She looked right in her eyes and though she tried not to look down at the leg, she did, and saw two perfectly formed legs.

"How did you hear me?" Margaret asked. "Who are you? I thought you were one of my neighbors."

"Oh," she said, scrambling to compute the good leg and figure out what next to do or say. "I, well, I was walking by, really I was looking for someone's house and I had come up to your door and after I rang the bell—did you hear the bell?—I heard you calling."

"Well, I'm glad of that. It was silly of me to lock myself in there. My husband's gone out of town and I don't know what I would have done without you."

Angie nodded.

"I'm Margaret Neal, by the way."

"I'm Sa—Sara Taylor," she said.

"Oh," Margaret said, and began to think.

"I guess I better go now. I'm glad you're safe."

"Why not stay a minute. Have some coffee."

"Well, I shouldn't really," she said.

"Oh come on. It's not every day you're a hero, is it?"

She sat at the kitchen table while Margaret made the coffee and looked at her in Ervin's chair with her legs crossed and looked at her legs, as well, drawn to them by the sight of those familiar blue-gray crepe-soled shoes postal employees who had to be on their feet all day often wore.

"You're not really Sara Taylor, are you?" she asked as she put her coffee down in front of her.

"Well of course I am. Whatever are you talking about?"

"You're Angela Taylor and you came here looking for Ervin."

"You're crazy," she said.

"You are Angela Taylor and you did come here looking for Ervin because the last time you saw him you were being chased down by me in that car," she said and pointed out the window, "sitting right there in the driveway. Right?"

Angie did not answer. Margaret studied her. She saw a woman older than her years, a woman who looked to be in her late thirties, but probably wasn't. A woman who'd had a hard life, probably much harder than hers. A woman with an acne-scarred face, at least fifteen pounds overweight, and with fingernails bitten, uniformly, all the way down to the quick.

"I've got to smoke," Angie said. "I'm trying to quit," she said, still lighting it.

"I'm right, aren't I?"

"Maybe."

"And you came here looking for Ervin? Is that what you

157

did? You came here looking for my husband," she said, staking the claim with the word *my*.

"Maybe I did."

"And what were you going to do if you found him?"

"Maybe I didn't care whether I did or not. Maybe I was just looking to see . . ." she took a big drag, ". . . what kind of woman would follow her husband and try to break his door down and chase him across town in a car. About what kind of woman that was."

"Me," Margaret said.

"Yes. I see. You."

"Yes, and I see something too. I see a woman who doesn't have the foggiest idea what she's getting into. I see a woman who's about to make the biggest mistake of her life."

"I doubt that."

"I don't. I know it. I'm married to him, don't forget. I see someone with her hands shaking who just better, for everyone's good, pack it up and forget about all of us."

"Ervin might have something to say about that."

"He won't have anything to say about it. Let me tell you something, girl," Margaret said, "you can't take him away from me. You can't because he doesn't want to leave. If he did, he would have left me years ago. You understand what I'm saying?"

"You're wrong," she said. "You're wrong or I wouldn't be here."

"Oh is that right?"

"That's right. If I didn't know he wanted me more than you, I wouldn't have come looking for him to save him from some crazy woman like you."

"GET OUT OF HERE!" Margaret screamed at her and Angie started out.

"THERE'S NOTHING LEFT BETWEEN YOU TWO," Angie screamed back at her and she ran out the door. "He loves me," she said.

Margaret chased her into the yard and spun her around by her arm.

"He doesn't love you. He can't. I'm the closest thing he ever got to love and it scared the hell out of him. If he left me for you, he'd make your life such hell you wouldn't know what hit you."

"That's your opinion," she said and pulled her arm loose.

"Stop," Margaret said. "I'm sorry I yelled at you. Don't leave yet. We really ought to talk about this."

"What's there to say?"

"You need to understand what's going on. What you're doing. Have you been married before?"

"Yes."

"Well," Margaret said and then realized they were standing in the cold rain. "Hey, why are we standing out here in this rain? Come on back in."

"I don't think so," Angie said.

"All right, then. Be that way. This is what I want to tell you. You don't know him. You can't imagine what you're getting yourself into. I know you think he's in love with you but he can't be because he can't love anyone. He's not able to. He just isn't."

"But you love him."

"I do. I love him for what he was, and what he might be again. Do you understand me?"

"I've got to go," she said.

"I'm trying to be nice to you, you stupid girl," Margaret said. "But if you want to be that way, I can, too. Don't ever come back here. Don't ever see him again."

"I'll wait and hear that from him," she said.

"Leave town," Margaret said to her back, following her. "Stay away from him and from me. Get another job. Do it for your own good. You can't have him. You won't get him. He's mine."

And Angie, having met the immovable force face to face, having met the octopus of possessive madness and tangled with it, drove home, astonished at the tough woman she had found when she thought she was going to just blow her away, astonished at the good leg and seeing a glimpse of the trouble she was getting into. She began to fear the entanglement of the desperate situation, fearing for herself and her daughter, fearing, having just been through it herself last year, the nightmarish reality of the eviscerated marriage, the dark presence of the deadly broken taboos and the lonely empty nights of the broken life.

She drove back, then, homesick for her daughter, for the steady trusting love that she shared with her. She drove home empty and shaking inside like waking from a bad dream where the revelation of what she'd seen cut too deeply to go any further and jerking awake was the only way out, and then, in the waking, the truth that had been made visible in the dream, the truth of the destructive madness of the unmended, selfish heart, the truth stayed with her as she drove home to her daughter, and as she held her and felt, at least there, a steady, perfect balance of love.

Sally waited alone. She waited in that desperate, paralyzed way the child waits to be spanked, having been told to do so. She waited in the same way the patient stands immobile for the needle, the way the victim waits before the hollow barrel of the gun, waiting to be shot.

She curled up under the blanket and fell asleep for a moment. The fire was out when she jerked back awake and she pulled up the afghan her mother had made and given her when she went off to college, and wrapped that around her, as well.

The dog scratched on the door and the cat jumped up on a table on the porch and looked in at her through the window. The dog scratched again and sounded a faint and pitiful

whine along with it and the cat put one paw on the cold windowpane and stared at Sally until Sally acknowledged his exotic countenance.

"I can't get up now," she said. "Just wait."

The dog scratched again and she thought how many coats of yellow ochre she had put on that door trying to make up for years of dog scratching and she arose looking like a rag lady or a refugee from the faded films of World War II.

"It's not much warmer inside," she told the animals, but it wasn't true. There were those soft chairs and the pillows and no cold wind and the animals knew where they wanted to be, with her, in the house, a place, she thought, she ought to leave.

If I'm not here, then what?

She opened the oven door and turned the dial to 450 and lit all the burners as well, and she pushed the kitchen chairs near the stove and sat on one and put her feet on the other and she thought about leaving until she realized that it was possible, quite possible, and, indeed likely, that Robert would return to be with her and how horrible it would be for him to meet that old man alone, and so she waited in the kitchen and listened for the sound of someone coming down the drive, and she even prayed a little, casually and without effort, making a few deals while she was at it, for things to come out right.

At nine Robert parked his truck in downtown Chapel Hill. He had failed to take a jacket. The heater in the old truck just barely worked, and the cold air from where the battery had rotted out the metal under the floor on the driver's side blew into the cab.

He sat in the truck and chewed on his knuckles and thought about a scene from his wife's journal, where she had written about a time on the beach on the Outer Banks where

she walked alone during one vacation when she was a fresh-
man in college, and saw, in the distance, someone come
down the empty and isolated beach and how she met him
and how she thought that one could not not speak, one could
not not talk and make contact, she had written, how one
could not, in the middle of miles of empty sand and beach,
meet another decent human being and not make contact
and recognize his existence, a metaphor come to life, how
one could not leave without giving something to the other
person, so that in the leaving, she had written, each takes
with him or her something that makes life a little easier, a
little better, if only for a little while.

And how it had hurt when he'd read that, because how
true it was and how truly touching it was and how truly like
the generous soul of his precious wife to see it and do something about it.

He got out and looked in the window of a restaurant
where a wide-screen television lit up one end of the room
and a basketball game was on. Further down the street a girl
stood in front of a clothing store. She wore knee-high boots
and a mini-skirt and stockings and a vinyl jacket with a
furry collar. She looked sideways as he slowed down to see
her better.

That girl's a whore, he thought. She's waiting for someone.

He stopped at the next window. The girl remained
where she was. He looked at her face. She was young. She
might have been sixteen or as old as nineteen. It was hard to
tell.

People passed behind them. The sidewalk was brightly
lit. He looked back at her and saw her face was red and puffy.

Drug addict, he thought. Or drunk.

"Excuse me," he said. She looked up. Hard as she tried
to hide it, he saw that she had been crying.

"I'm sorry," he said. "Are you all right?"

She nodded and then looked down.

"Can I help in any way?"

"I'm okay. Thanks, though."

Damn, he thought. The night of the weeping women. "You know, it's strange. I'm having a kind of bad night myself."

She nodded.

"Well, if you're really okay," he said, and started to leave.

"You don't have to go."

"All right. You want to get out of this rain and go somewhere?" he asked.

"Where?" she asked. "Where do you go to cry?"

"Good point," he said. "Where does a person go to cry? Well, let's see. I live too far away to go to my place, and it wouldn't work, anyway."

She noticed his wedding band.

"I guess not," she said.

"Restaurants and bars wouldn't be right, would they?"

"Not unless they served Kleenex."

"That's pretty good," he said and they both smiled.

"I just need to talk, really. That's what usually makes me feel better."

"We could sit in my truck. That's all I can think of."

They walked to the truck and stayed an awkwardly long distance apart, as if in fear of touching each other.

"Here it is," he said. "Not much, but it's home."

"You're kidding."

"I'm kidding."

The cab was high and rounded something like a dome. The seat was long and wide and high so that their legs hung straight down as if sitting in real chairs.

"This is a nice old truck," she said. "It is old, isn't it?"

"Yeah. About twenty years old."

"That's older than me."

"I thought it was."

"How old are you?" she asked.

"Thirty. Or so."

"So's my boyfriend."

"Oh."

"He threw me out."

"Literally?"

"What?"

"Did he actually throw you, like toss you out?"

"Oh sure. That's nothing new."

"Did he hurt you?"

"Not much."

"You can tell me about it if you want."

"It's nothing. Just one of those things I get myself into."

"What're you going to do?"

"I don't know. That's the problem. I don't have anywhere to go. I don't even have any money. He pushed me out the door and threw me my coat and my purse but I don't have, but, let's see, about eight dollars," she said, and emptied her wallet into her lap. "That's about it."

"Well," he said. "I've got a little and if you're feeling like it we could go to a restaurant. I'm starved. I kind of ran out without supper, myself."

"I don't know. I'm scared I might run into him."

"Oh."

"Let's just drive around. Back when I had my own car I used to drive around by myself, you know, when I got down, had a bad day, you know. Just ride around going nowhere, doing nothing."

"Sounds good," he said.

"You're nice."

"Thanks."

"You're a real nice guy," she said and patted him on his shoulder in a strangely unfeminine gesture, the way a man

164

might pat his son on the shoulder and tell him, "Good job, son."

He turned the blower to high and pushed the heater control all the way over. The fumes coming through the holes in the floor were bad and both of them had their windows down.

"I used to work there," she said, and pointed to a chicken-and-biscuit take-out restaurant.

"Did you?"

"Yes. After I quit the mill. I should have never quit. Long story, though. Lots of long stories in my life," she said.

"I think I'm just going to have to get something to eat."

"Okay. But listen, mister," she said, and then, as if just realizing it, said, "I don't even know your name."

"Robert."

"Mine's Catherine. With a C."

"Nice name."

"Listen, Robert. Don't get me wrong, or anything, but how much money do you have on you?"

"Not much."

"I was asking because here we are both riding around in the cold with nowhere to go and why, I was thinking, don't we just go to a motel, get a nice warm room and get comfortable. If you have enough money, I'd love to get off the streets."

Angie hugged Darlene so hard and so long the little girl wondered about it.

"Ouch, Mommy. That's too hard."

"I needed it. It felt good to Mommy."

"Where did you go? Why did Mrs. Scholtz have to come over?"

"I had to go somewhere," she said. "I thought I did,

anyway. But Mommy's back now. She made a mistake. Someone told her a lie."

"Who?"

"Just someone."

"What mistake?" Darlene asked.

"She almost got in trouble."

"What kind of trouble?"

"She almost got into something bad, just like something bad that happened to her a little while ago."

"But what?"

"It's nothing. Not anymore. I'm home and I'm going to be very careful now and you and Mommy are going to do lots of things together and we're going to have a great life."

"Here in this old ratty apartment?" Darlene asked.

"Maybe we better move," she said. "To a not-so-ratty old apartment. How about that?"

"To a nice big house? With an indoor swimming pool?"

"Maybe," Angie said. "Maybe we can do that someday. Right now, though, it's bedtime. Come on. I'll tell you a story."

"Which one," she said and climbed back in where she'd been when she heard her mother come in and send Mrs. Scholtz away.

"Your favorite."

"Okay. But let me tell it to you. I'll be the Mommy."

"All right. You be the Mommy."

"If you were a bird, and you flew away, I'd be a tree and you'd have to come back to me."

"That's right," Angie said.

"If you were a fish and you swam away, I'd be a fisherman and bring you back with a net."

"That's right, honey. Keep on."

"And if you were a bad bunny and you ran away, I'd make myself as big as the world and I'd always be with you everywhere you went."

166

And Angie curled up beside Darlene and together they went to sleep, balancing along that fragile line of parent and child.

The telephone rang and Sally answered it and it was not Robert and it was not her father. It was, of course, her mother.

"I knew he'd call you. I knew he'd go running to you. I just knew it," her mother said.

"Well, I don't know what to do about it. Where were you, anyway?"

"Locked in his bathroom."

"What?"

"I'll tell you about it when I get there," she said.

"Get where? Here. Not you too, Mother. I can't take it," she said and then thought about it. "But yes, maybe that's best. Maybe you better come on. Now. Hurry. Maybe that's the best thing that could happen," she said. "But how will you get here?"

"I've got my license now and I've got the car and nothing's going to stop me. And when I get there," she said, "I'll have him right where I want him."

"Can you drive this far alone? In the dark?"

"Of course I can. I've got maps. Why can't I do anything anybody else can do? You just hold him," she said, "until I get there."

"I don't think I'll do that," Sally said.

"Or get Robert to. I think I see the light at the end of the tunnel," she said. "I met his girlfriend."

"Oh no."

"It was good. I've got so much to tell you. It made me see things so much more clearly. Anyway," she said, "I'm coming now. I'll be there before you know it."

*　*　*

167

Robert gave Catherine some money and sent her to wait in line for a box of chicken while he went to a pay phone to call his parents to see if he could come home for a few days and get things sorted out. He also wanted to tell them they had been right.

When he heard his mother's voice, he thought for the first time that night he might cry. The sound of her voice took him far back and he wanted to say, he could hear himself saying as he saw himself running and being held and comforted while he wept, "Mother, Mother darling, I'm coming back, I'm coming home, please hold me, please take me in and tell me all is forgiven." He could feel that in the tightness of his throat as he told them, "In a way, I just wanted to say that maybe I've done some wrong things and made some wrong decisions and maybe, after all, you were right. Not entirely, but maybe I made a mistake and maybe I should have known from that first time when I visited her family and something told me things were just not right but I just kept on, I mean, it's so hard to see what people don't want you to see. And that's why I've called because I thought that maybe, if it'd be all right, I could come down. I don't know, for a few days and, I don't know, just get things sorted out."

"Of course you can," his mother said.

"Of course you can," his father said.

"But what's happened?" his mother asked. "Tell us what brought this about."

"I can't. Not now."

"Is it an affair?"

"No."

"Then what could it be?"

"Just a lot of things," he said.

"Well, I was afraid this might happen," his mother said.

"It couldn't have worked out," his father said.

"Not ultimately," his mother said.

"Well," Robert started to say.

"I don't mean she isn't just as nice and sweet as can be," his mother said.

"We don't mean that," his father said.

"It's just that you come from two different worlds," she said.

"Anyway, it's over," his father said, still on the extension.

"And we're here for you," she said.

"I didn't say it was over," Robert said.

"Well, whatever it is, we're here and we're ready to help and you come on home for a few days and tell us all about it."

"And if it is time for a divorce, we'll help you with a lawyer."

"We'll get you a good one," his mother said. "Half of everything is yours," she added.

"Even if she did pay for most of it," his father said.

"Don't let her get the farm," she said. "Even though we've never even seen it, real estate is always worth holding on to."

"You just work out a settlement with her," his father said.

"We'll talk about it," his mother said. "And if it really is over, then we can just thank God it's not been any worse than it has."

"You've learned something, anyway," his father said.

"He has," his mother said back to him.

"I knew he would pull out of it someday," he told her.

"I know you said that," she said back to him, and while they discussed him with each other he just kind of faded away on the other end of the phone as the sound of their voices brought him back from that scene of being held and comforted to what really was in store for him when he went back, days and days and maybe for the rest of his life of telling him what to do and with whom to do it, and it wasn't

too hard to go from there to just why he had fallen so in love with Sally and just what there was without her, just what there was where he had come from and while they talked to each other, completely forgetting he was there, he quietly and ever so lightly hung up the phone and walked back to Catherine, thinking, for a moment, until he saw her bright and expectant face, that he might just go on back to the farm.

"Ready?" she asked.

"Well," he said.

"Oh, come on," she said. "We'll have a good time."

"Okay," he said. "Just for a little while."

The motel had a double bed and a table instead of a desk and a wooden chair at that table and on either side of the table were two other chairs. One was a contemporary design, with black plastic cushions and varnished wood arms. The other was wrought iron with a canvas seat and was circular and looked like something that had once been on a patio or near a pool.

The carpet was brown and spotted. The room was cold and the air conditioner was also the heater. Robert turned the dial to heat and the fan to high and Catherine set the box of chicken and two cans of Pepsi on the table.

"It's not that bad, is it?" she asked.

"No. Not bad at all."

"No television, though. You have to ask for it."

"Never heard of that."

"They're afraid people will steal them. You can get one, if you want. It's just a dollar extra. They make you sign for it, though. Show identification, you know."

"Do you want one?" he asked.

"Do you?"

"I don't know. What's on?"

"What's today?"

"Tuesday. I think it is, anyway."

"Yes. It is. I remember now."

"I don't want to watch anything."

"I don't blame you. What do you do, by the way?" she asked.

"I'm a carpenter."

"My boyfriend hangs sheetrock. You don't seem like a carpenter to me. Not like the ones I've known."

"I am, but only temporarily, you might say. Passing through on my way somewhere else."

"That's neat. I like that. My boyfriend and this other guy he works with make a hundred dollars a day, sometimes. Each."

"That's more than I make."

"Sometimes they don't though. Am I talking too much?" she asked as he checked on the air conditioner–heater. "Or too fast?"

"Not to me."

"Sometimes I do. That thing'll heat up in a little while. It takes in the cold air here," she said and went over and pointed to the grills along the bottom, "and converts it to hot air and blows it out here, but it has to change the air in the room a couple of times before it can really start doing any good."

"How'd you know that?"

"My daddy was a furnace repairman. I used to go on the jobs with him when I was little. Before he left us."

"Oh."

"Let's eat," she said. "I'm suddenly hungry myself."

"Okay. White or dark?"

"White, if you don't mind."

"I don't."

She handed him a napkin and opened the drinks and he took the chicken from the box and gave her a piece. She put the pop-tops from the cans on her little fingers.

"I used to wear these when I was little, you know, pretending I was married, and all."

"Yes."

"I used to want to be married. Real bad. I dreamed about it all the time. Now I don't."

"I know what you mean."

"I used to watch my parents fight. My old man used to hit my mother, oh hell, he used to hit her so hard I couldn't believe she could take it. She never went down, though. I never saw her fall or flinch."

"Sounds awful."

"She'd hit him back later. When he wasn't expecting it. They fought all the time. I used to want to be married to show them I wouldn't be like them."

"That's common."

"Common?"

"People want to be different from their parents."

"Anyway, my boyfriend is just like my old man was. I can't believe I did that, you know, fell for someone just like him. When he gets drunk he slaps me around. He doesn't mean it, though. I don't think he does. Except," she said, contemplating further, "he slaps me around when he's sober, too."

"What do you do?"

"Leave. Usually. Well, sometimes. Sometimes I don't mind. I guess sometimes I deserve it."

The chicken was greasy. Robert used up his napkin. Catherine handed him another.

"I got to take these boots off. They're too tight. I knew they were too tight when I bought them, but it was the only size they had. I liked them, so I bought them anyway."

She pulled at one while holding the chicken with her other hand.

"Stuck?"

"Yeah. Can you help?" she asked.

He pulled them off. She wore pantyhose. The reinforced foot parts were torn.

"Thanks. Anyway," she said, "sometimes I deserve it, I guess, when I make him mad."

172

She was small. With her high-heeled boots off, she was no more than five-one, he thought.

"Is he big?"

"Real big. Bigger than you. Bigger than my old man. And mean."

"I gather."

"Mean to other people. He'd beat the hell out of another guy as soon as look at him. One time I was talking to this guy I used to know, in the parking lot, we were just standing there talking and L.C., which is his name, my boyfriend, I mean, came out of the parts store—he was rebuilding a motor for a friend of his—and he saw me talking with this guy and he just walked up and slapped him with this long box gaskets come in."

"No kidding?"

"He did."

She took off her jacket.

"I'm getting crumbs all over my good jacket," she said. She had on a blouse with two missing buttons.

"That's where he grabbed me when I ran," she said, noticing where he looked. "You can't really see my bra, can you?" she asked and looked down at herself sideways, trying to view her blouse as someone else would see it.

"I can't."

"I deserved it this time, I guess."

She sat in the round canvas chair. She turned sideways. Her skirt slid up as she slid down to get comfortable.

"You don't mind me sitting like this, do you?"

"Not at all. Make yourself at home."

"L.C. says I have a good body, but he doesn't want me showing it off. He gets mad when I wear tight clothes. Or short skirts."

"Is that what happened tonight?"

"How'd you know?"

"You're wearing a short skirt."

"Oh yeah. He came home and I was wearing this skirt, I

like it best, and he asked me where I'd been all day and I wouldn't tell him and then he grabbed me and tried to fuck me—oops, I'm sorry."

"That's okay. I'm over twenty-one."

"I'm not, but, anyway, he was trying to fuck me, right there on the floor, and he had that goddamn sheetrock dust all over him and he smelled bad and I wouldn't let him."

"I don't blame you."

"I mean, I wouldn't have minded if he'd took a bath first."

"Right."

"But I hate that dust. You didn't mind when I said 'fuck,' did you?"

"No. Why should I?"

"Some people don't like cussing, but I do. I love it. I cuss all the time. Even when I'm alone I go around cussing at things."

"It's a good way to get your frustrations out."

"I just like the sound of the words."

The room warmed up. The blower on the heater rattled as if something had come loose.

"You're nice to talk to," she said. "L.C. says I talk too much and too fast. Maybe I do. I like to talk. I like to talk about anything and everything. I'm interested in things, you know. I made good grades in school. I really did. I would have graduated if I hadn't run away."

"You ran away?"

"Yeah. Last year. When I was sixteen. I was thinking of going back. To that school in Durham."

"Which one?"

"Rutledge. I went over there once and talked with them. They were real nice. They wanted me to have my high school diploma first. I ought to go back one day. I'd be in the tenth grade, though. All my old friends would be graduating and I'd be in the tenth grade with all those creeps. That'd be hell,

wouldn't it? It sure is hot in here now. Mind if I take off my pantyhose?"

"Go ahead."

"You can turn around if you want. I don't wear underpants. I mean, L.C. used to get mad at me about it, but he said it sure made fucking a lot easier. I guess he wanted it both ways."

She stood up and reached under her skirt.

"That's the way I like it. Sometimes around the house I go around naked all day. You want another piece of chicken? It's good tonight. It's not as greasy as it usually is."

"Not right now."

"You're married. I see your ring. What's your wife like? I bet she's real pretty."

"Well. She is. She's tall and has long hair and nice skin and she works as a commercial artist."

"Wow. That sounds fabulous. Did she draw any commercials I might have seen?"

"I don't know. I don't keep up with it."

"Maybe I could do that. I got a B+ in art in the eighth grade." She got out of the chair and started across the room. "I'm glad the blower's making all that noise. I've got to go to the bathroom. I hate to hear someone in the john, don't you?"

The bathroom was in a corner of the room. It had a birch-veneer door. Some of the veneer was torn off. She stopped just before she went in.

"Listen," she said. "I like you. I really do. I'm feeling really good now. I was just wondering, do you want to fuck when I come back out?"

Ervin turned into Sally's driveway. She did not hear him until the dog barked. For a moment, as she watched the lights coming up the dark drive, she imagined it was Robert.

The size and bulk of the camper and the slow pace of its approach, however, dispelled that hope.

She had been awake since her mother's phone call. She had changed into jeans and a blouse and a wool sweater and a pair of warm hiking boots. The wood stove was out. The old ornate farm equipment thermometer tacked on the living room wall read fifty-one degrees. It was warmer in the kitchen where the gas oven and four burners were still lit.

Ervin tooted the horn and parked and Sally stopped in the middle of the kitchen as she heard him on the porch and watched the door thud against the lock as he tried to open it.

"Hey," he called. "Anybody home?"

She opened the door.

"What's the matter?" he asked as she pulled away from his embrace.

"I told you not to come up here."

"I know you did, but I had to."

"Well, if you've come up here, you're going to pay for it."

"I don't understand," he said and looked around the room after seeing the glow from the burners. "What's this?" he asked. "And where's Robert?"

"Never mind. Just come in here," she said. "Sit down there," she said and pointed him into a chair.

"Where's Robert?" he asked again.

"He's gone out for a little while. He heard you were coming and left."

"But why?"

"Because he's sick of you. Just like I am."

"I can't believe you just said that."

"I said it."

"But why?"

"You don't know, do you?"

"No I don't."

"I guess you don't," she said.

"I guess you're right," he said.

176

"Listen, Daddy. Don't push me tonight. I told you not to come up here and I'm real upset about it."

"I'm sorry."

"And about other things, too."

"But what have I done?"

"What you've done is not know what you've done. Ever."

"Listen," he said. "All I did was zip on up here to have a little talk with you. Granted it's a little late, but I had to."

"You're zipping-on-up days are over."

"You have never talked to me this way."

"I should have."

"What's happened? Who is this talking to me?" he asked the room in general.

"Listen to me," she said and slapped the table with her open hand. "You are not going to make me feel sorry for you with that look because you just can't anymore. You can't get to me anymore. You can't because I am through with this facade, this charade."

"I didn't know we were playing charades," he said.

"STOP IT!" she screamed. "STOP YOUR GODDAMN JOKES AND LISTEN TO ME."

He held up his arms as if to say, I surrender.

"It's time you started realizing what you're doing to the people around you and think about somebody besides yourself, and it's time you stopped treating Mother like dirt and it's time you stopped getting me mixed up in the middle of it all. You hear?"

He nodded.

"I mean, like, you don't even know what I'm talking about. I can tell by looking at you. I mean, it's like all that about painting the house and we kill ourselves to do it and you don't even say a word."

He shrugged.

"It's like, all my goddamn life you have just run over me and Mother and anyone else you wanted to and then when

things didn't work out like you wanted to, you have been, all my life, you hear, as long as I can remember, coming to me and putting me in the middle between you and Mother, always, since I was a child," she said. "Don't you know it?"

He shrugged again.

"IT'S TIME FOR IT TO STOP," she yelled. "It's time for you to get out of my life and off Robert's back and just disappear, how about it."

"Listen," he said and stood up, pushing off the chair like an arthritic old man, destroyed and frightened to hear this from the one person he thought he could always count on, wiped out in spite of his offhand manner. "Listen," he said, "if I'd known things were going to be like this, I'd have never come. I sure would have never come," he said, and started out the door.

She stopped him.

"You're not going anywhere."

"I'm going back to Wilmington. I'm going back to find Angie."

"No, you're not. You're going to stay here until Mother comes," she said and snatched the keys out of his hand.

"Your mother?" he asked. "But she can't be coming up here. It's not possible."

Margaret stopped in a little town. She looked at her map in the glow of the streetlight and saw she was in Dunn and was eighty miles from Sally's house. Maybe a little less. It was hard to tell from the map. It was nearly one A.M.

She drove on as if her life depended on it, as if her arrival would mark the end of a long fight, the cessation of hostilities, the end of the long battle of the sexes and she drove on as if she had, in the car, the evidence to convict and gain the confession of this man who had started it all, this guilty man, the end of the long delay in the trial, the judg-

ment in her hands, mercy and compassion with her, as well. She drove to claim him, to claim the family honor, to forgive him, to allow him room to return, and, in doing so, fulfill the manifesto of her life, of the dream, of the marriage and the love and the family, of the parables of patience and duty and devotion, and of the triumph of good over evil.

Robert was still on the side of the bed with a half-eaten piece of chicken in his hand when Catherine came out of the bathroom, completely naked.

"Do you like my body? I do. My breasts are small, I know, but they're real firm. My nipples get big when I get excited. Sometimes they get big just when I get cold or something rubs against them. They're not all the way big yet. They're getting there, though."

She looked at herself in the mirror, and then resumed talking, but faster.

"I thought my breasts would get bigger when I got older but I guess they won't. I wonder if I'll be able to make enough milk to nurse a baby. I want to do that. I read about it in a magazine. It's good for the baby and for the mother, too."

She posed sideways and pulled her elbows back.

"My waist's small, though, and that makes them look bigger. What's your name, by the way? I forget if you told me. Oh yeah, Robert. I remember now. What was your last name?"

"Zilman."

"That's interesting. I never heard that before. It kind of sounds like a Jew name. Is that what it is? Or a Catholic one? Which is it?"

"Jewish, I guess."

"Really. That's great. I never knew a Jew before. Oh, wait a minute. I did. This girl in school was a Jew or her mother

was, anyway, and she looked just like everyone else, you couldn't tell, not by looking at her anyway, but there was something different about her once you found out. People used to make fun of her but it never bothered me. I never minded niggers, either. Blacks, I mean. I try not to call them niggers anymore, like L.C. does. I call them blacks because they call themselves blacks, except I've heard them call each other nigger, too. A black boy fucked me one time. He was awfully light skinned, though. He was almost white, so I don't know if it really counts."

She put the leftover chicken in the box and took Robert's and wrapped it in a napkin and put it on top of the rest.

"I never had sex with a Jew before. This is going to be great. I love to do different things. That's one of the things that gets L.C. mad at me. I like to go places and meet people and do all kinds of things, and he just wants to stay home and drink. Or take dope. Do you drink? Oh yeah, you said you did, didn't you, or did I just make that up? I'm talking too fast again, aren't I? I'll try to slow down."

"You're doing just fine."

"I know I am. You're so nice. Do you want something to drink now? We could send out for something. A lot of men like to drink a little before they do it. I don't need to, though. Do you want anything? Good. L.C. says I come faster than any woman he was ever with. It's so nice and cozy in here now. I told you it would be. Aren't you going to take off your clothes?"

"Yes. I am," he said. "Let me go to the bathroom first."

"Sure. I did. I always go before I fuck. That way I don't have to get up when I'm finished and I can just lay there and feel it and just relax, you know, and it's so good, like it's one of the few times a person really feels relaxed, except when you do drugs, you know, some kinds anyway, but then when you come off them you feel worse, but I guess sometimes I feel bad after I've done sex, too."

When he came back she had put her knee-high boots back on but was otherwise still naked.

"You like this? I saw a woman posed in a magazine like this once, only she was on the bed, kind of like this," she said and lay on the bed and imitated the pose, "and it looked really neat. So sexy. I mean, if you think about it, why would boots make such a difference?"

"I don't know."

"I made love to a man once what kept his shoes and socks on. Talk about weird. He was real short and I guess he was trying to be as tall as he could, but talk about weird. I'm not kidding, I could feel his shoes and socks the whole time. Why don't you take your clothes off now?"

"I'm going to. I was just thinking for a second."

"I never think when I'm fucking. I just do it. If you start thinking about things it makes it harder to come, you know what I mean. You get messed up."

"I know."

"You do, don't you? You're the kind of guy what understands about women. I can tell. That's one of the things I like about you." She lay with her head toward the foot of the bed and put her feet on the wall over the headboard and looked at him upside down as he undressed.

"Oh look, you're not hard yet. L.C. always gets hard even before his clothes are off. Why aren't you hard yet? Don't you like me?"

"I do, but I was just . . ."

"Don't worry about it. I know what to do. Come on over here and get on the bed with me."

"Let me check the door first."

"Okay. What are you worried about? Nobody's coming in. Who even knows we're here?"

"Maybe L.C. followed you."

"The hell he did. If he had, he'd already be in here and would have killed you by now."

181

"Oh."

"You like the light on or off? I like it on so I can watch what's happening but we can turn it off if you want. That's good. Lie down beside me. I got a really great way to do it in mind. This man I met one time showed it to me. He was part Indian. His grandfather, he said, was a Lumbee Indian and anyway, this man showed me this kind of Indian way and I'll show it to you. You'll love it. Everybody I showed it to does."

"What do you want me to do?"

"Get like this," she said and then, for a second, for a long, long second, during which he saw L.C. coming through the door and during which he saw Sally weeping on the porch and during which he saw Ervin's ugly face and during which he saw, from a distance, himself, as well, for that long, visionary moment, he stopped.

"Mother is coming up here," Sally said.

"But," he said and looked closely at her, trying to determine how much she knew, "she doesn't even know where I went. She doesn't even know I'm here."

"Yes she does. She called and I told her you were coming."

"How could she call?"

"She used the telephone, like anyone else. Was there some reason you didn't think she could do that?" Sally asked.

"Well, not really."

"Of course there was. Don't lie to me," she said, "don't even begin to try to lie to me because I've got you this time and I know what you've been up to and this is the night, this is the moment when it's all going to stop and you're going to get your life in order and you're going to apologize to Mother and you and Mother are going to make up and you're going to forget this ridiculous thing with Angie and you're going

to, finally, you HEAR ME," she began to scream again and then stopped, "get out of my life. Get out from between me and Robert and out of it for good."

"Give me the keys," he said.

"I will not."

"Give them to me or I will take them from you."

"You'll have to if you want them. But if you touch me, if you lay one hand on me, I'll kill you. I swear I will."

"Just give them to me. I'll leave. If that's what you want, I'll certainly do it."

"Nope."

"All right, listen," he said. "Let's sit back down. Let's have some coffee. Let's talk about it. But then, let me have my keys and get out of here."

"Are you afraid of Mother?"

"No. Don't be silly. I can see you're upset. It probably has something to do with Robert's leaving. If I've been the cause of it, then I'll have to own up to it and I'll quietly leave and let you two get on with things. If that's what you want."

"You're not going to get out of it that easy."

"Look. Just sit down. You're still my daughter and I love you very much." She made a face. "And I'm you're father and I always will be and that's that. You can't get rid of me, so let's talk about whatever you want. But first," he said, "let's make some coffee. Let me shut this stove off and while I make the coffee why don't you get your woodstove started."

"I'm standing right here. I'm not moving until Mother comes. You're not going out that door. Make your coffee if you want."

"Okay. I will. But one thing," he said, "let me call Angie. Just a quick call. I'll charge it to our phone. It won't cost you a thing."

"You're not going to call."

"I have to."

"You should have thought of that before you came up here."

She looked out the kitchen window and when she did, took a breath, like the first time she'd breathed since he walked in the door, and Ervin, hooked to his daughter by all those tangled threads of blood, felt her let go and came up behind her and put his hands on her shoulders.

"Baby," he said and she swung around so fast it knocked him back.

"Don't."

"ALL RIGHT, I WON'T," he screamed at her. "But you owe it to me to tell me what started all this. You really do."

She told him about the journal. She told him about the conversation with Robert and she started in again on the night of the examination.

"Don't you see, you fool, you damn fool," she said, "that normal people don't do things like that? Normal people don't hold fourteen-year-old girls down and take off their clothes and stick their fingers up in them."

"Don't talk like that," he said.

"Don't you see how crazy both you and Mother were? Are? Don't you see what you drove me to? Have you never seen it? Have you never thought about it?"

"But I never . . ."

"You never did anything? But you did it all. You drove me away from you and you drove me crazy and you made me, finally, after all was said and done, you made me, you," she stumbled to find the right words, "you sacrificed me. You sacrificed me to save the family honor and the family had no honor."

"What do you mean?"

"You wouldn't let me have that baby. You made me go through hell. You almost killed me. Have you no idea what it was like? What I had to live with? What I still have to live with? Have you no idea?"

"I thought I was doing the right thing."

"The right thing? You took me to that dark filthy place and I went in one way and came out another. I went in myself and came out another person. And you've never said a word about it. NEVER ONE WORD. You never talked about it. You never let me say a word. I've had to live with it all my life and I was innocent. I was. I swear I was." She was crying now, and she looked at him and he looked back at her and raised his hands and opened his palms. "And still, now, you say nothing."

"I thought I was doing the right thing," he said again. "Believe me," he said and then neither said anything. For a long time they looked in opposite directions, lost in the coldness of betrayal and sadness, and when ten minutes was up, such a long time for silence when there was so much to say but no way to say it, Ervin asked, ever so politely and humbly, "Now may I have my keys back? Please."

"I feel great," Catherine said. "Let's just lie here and talk. I saw this movie once about the Holocaust, you know the death camps, and it was really something. Just awful. It showed these starving people, real films of them, and I mean, how thin can a person get and not die, I mean, it was just awful, and there was this one woman, Faye Dunaway, I think, I'm not sure, but anyway, she had this plan to kill this Nazi guy because he was doing all this bad stuff to people, and then making her fuck him, only she had to keep letting him do it so she could catch him at the right moment. Did you see that one?"

"I think I missed it," he said. Catherine hopped out of bed. She still wore her boots. She drank a long pull from her warm Pepsi and then got back in bed.

"Anyway, I watch a lot of movies. I learn things from them. We've got cable, well, we used to, anyway, but it got took out, but when we had it I watched movies just all day

long. It's cheaper than going to see them in town. They cost four dollars a ticket now. Do you have cable?"

"No."

"I loved it when we did. I saw this movie one time . . . are you getting tired? You look like you're falling asleep. It is late, isn't it? I can't believe how time flies. I just can't. Except when there's nothing to do, like in a waiting room or something, anyway, I'm tired, too. Sometimes I stay up all night and then feel fine the next day until about three and then I just crash. I mean, it's weird. It's like doing drugs and then coming off real fast. You just fall. Everything goes out of focus and like one minute you're fine and the next minute you're so tired you can't stand up."

"I think I better go," Robert said. "I thought earlier that I might stay a few days, but I think I better go."

"Are you really going to leave? Oh. I get it. You're going back to your wife. Right?"

"I think I better. She might be in trouble about now."

"How come?"

"She just might."

"It's the right thing to do. I can't go back to L.C. yet. I need to make him worry more. I think I'll just stay out a few more days. Do you have enough money to let me have a little to rent this room for a few more nights? I know I said I wasn't going to ask you for any, but you've been so nice to talk to and everything, I know you understand."

"I'll see how much I have."

"What are you going to tell your wife? You're not going to tell her about me, are you? Don't do that. When you love someone and find out they've been with someone else it makes you feel real bad. I know. One time this man I thought I loved did that to me. I was sixteen. He worked at Cone Mills in Hillsborough, where I worked, until it shut down, I was only working part-time, but anyway, he was real nice to me

186

and then later on I found that he was sleeping with a friend of mine's mother and, shit, I can't tell you how that messed me up, for a little while, anyway. I broke up with his ass, but fast, let me tell you that."

"I'm not going to tell her."

"Good. I bet she's really beautiful. I can just imagine what she looks like. From what you said. Like those women in the ads. Does she look like that?"

"Sometimes."

"I knew it. I knew somebody as nice as you would have a wife like that. How much are you leaving me?"

"How much is the room?"

"Fourteen. Plus tax."

"Here's forty. Is that okay?"

"Oh, that's great. Now I can really work on L.C. He'll get so drunk he won't be able to go to the job for a week. I like a man what doesn't have to drink all the time. Do you think if I went back to school and studied art I could get a job like your wife's?"

"Why not?"

"I don't know. I can't make up my mind. I hate sitting behind a desk all day. Take a shower before you go home. You better. Sometimes you smell like the other person. That's a dead giveaway right there. Do you like me?"

"Very much. You are an interesting person."

"I am. I really am, aren't I? It's all inside of me, though. I can't make it come out. I try to do all these different things, but I just can't. Like I can see myself doing all these different things, but I just can't make it happen."

She followed him into the bathroom and leaned in the doorway while he ran the water waiting for it to get hot.

"You want me to wash you? I do it real well. It'll feel good. You can't ever get your back clean unless somebody does it for you."

"If you want."

"Let me take my boots off. There. Just get in. Whew, that's hot. Good. Now turn around. You have a nice back. It's smooth. L.C. has pimples all over his. My back's smooth, like yours. I wish I had met you before you got married. If you weren't married, would you like me?"

"I like you anyway."

"But would you like me enough to stay with me?"

"Maybe."

"I know. It's hard to tell from just one night. We're different. Is it wrong for a Jew to fuck a Christian?"

"I'm not sure."

"I hope you didn't commit a sin. One time these guys in school made this Catholic boy eat meat on Friday. They held him down and forced it in his mouth. I don't know what happened to him, though. I guess it'll be all right, because he didn't mean to, wouldn't it? I know it would. When people do things to you you don't want to happen, it's like they're not really happening, like you're not really doing it. It's like you're not really there. You know what I mean. It's like it's not a sin because they did it to him and he didn't want to do it, so he didn't do anything wrong. He's innocent."

"That's true," he said. "All too true."

"I know it is. Turn around and I'll wash you in the front too. Just close your eyes and lean your head back. That's right. You can wash me when I'm finished. Are you going straight home? What time is it, anyway?"

"It must be about two."

"Ugh. Time to go to sleep. What are you going to tell her? I know. Tell her you got to town and you were real mad at her but after you walked around a little you realized how much you loved her and you had to come back. Wouldn't that work? I mean, just like in the movies. You can do it. And it'd be true, too. I can see it. Like, you run up to each other

and kiss but you kiss each other real hard, it's a really wild kiss and it just goes all through your body and then you look at each other and walk off together. Do something like that, okay?"

"I don't know if I can."

"Yes, you can. Wash me now. See how big my nipples get? I told you they did. You don't have to wash me if you don't want to. I'm so little, though, it won't take long. Sometimes I wish I were taller, but really, I don't know if I'd be prettier or not. What do you think?"

"You're pretty just like you are."

"I knew you'd say that. I guess you better go now. Where'd you put the money?"

"Beside the chicken."

"Why don't you take what's left. I ate more than you did, anyway. The rest is yours. Take it. Take it to your wife, then she won't have to cook tomorrow. Is she a vegetarian?"

"No. Why?"

"I don't know. I just flashed on it, for some reason. I'd like to meet her, but I know I never will. It's funny, though. You make love with some woman's husband and then you want to meet her, like you want to talk with her or something. I've felt like that before. I don't know. It's crazy. What would you say? You couldn't tell her anything."

"Curiosity, I suppose."

"You want me to dry you? No. I guess not. It's hard to dry somebody. Here, I'll take your clothes over by the heater so you can be warm when you dress."

She took the money and put it in her purse and then put on her skirt and blouse.

"I'm not going to sleep in these. It'll wrinkle them. I ought to wash them out after you go and hang them in front of the heater. I wish I had enough money to buy some new clothes. That'd make me feel better."

"I just don't have any more."

"Oh, I know you don't. I just mean I wish I had some money. Period."

"I know the feeling."

"Yeah. Anyway, you're great. I'm really going to remember you. You even kissed me. I love a man to kiss me. I was with this man once and he was fucking me and I asked him to kiss me and he said he wouldn't but he would pull on my hair if I wanted. Stupid ass. It didn't even feel good. You're real sweet, though. Think about me sometime, will you?"

"I will."

"I guess I'll never see you again, but maybe I will. If I do and you see me and you don't want me to talk to you, just turn away. I'll understand."

"I wouldn't do that."

"Tell your wife how much you love her. Tell her you're sorry you ran out. Tell her whatever she did you know she loves you, too. Be sure to tell her you're sorry, though. That's important."

"I don't know if I can."

"Of course you can. You just say it. Anyway, it'll be true. You do love her. I can tell. She loves you, too. You can tell when a man has a woman who loves him. There's just something there you know you can't get to."

"I wish."

"It's there. Listen. Where'd you put the key? Oh yeah, I see it. Here. Hug me for just a second. Oh. That's nice. Now you better go. Don't slam the door. I hate to hear doors slammed. Close it quick. It's really cold. Bye, now."

"We're waiting for Mother," Sally said, and went toward the bedroom. "But I've got to lie down. I'm so tired I can't even see. I've got to get some sleep. Do what you want in

here. Start the fire if you want. I'm dead," she said. "Just dead. Absolutely dead," she said and closed the door behind her and collapsed on the bed and Ervin stayed on the porch for a moment and then stepped into the yard and stood in the rain, getting colder and wetter by the minute but unable to think what to do, just stood there like a drunk, like a wino who had wakened after passing out on the sidewalk and found himself in a cold rain and rose up trying to get the two or three brain cells that still worked to tell him what next to do. He stood there like that, that empty of ideas, only the one Sally had given him current.

He carried in an armload of wood and started the fire, and after it was blazing, closed the damper in the pipe and the one on the stove and fell asleep on the couch. His sleep was troubled, this time not by cough medicine and pills but by the gauze unraveling from the plastic surgery he had done on himself to hide his confused and bitter face. Under that gauze all his skin was raw except for his erectile lips which had sucked the sweetness right out of his daughter and left her so empty she flew into the arms of anyone who would hold her, and left his wife so crazy she spent all her time trying to figure out what had happened or when it had happened or what next to do.

But you just don't know, Ervin thought, as he slowly woke up, how much I loved both of you and you can't know because this night would have never happened if you knew how much I've wanted to make things right, with both of you.

I can't even remember what it was, and I can't even tell you if I try, I don't even know when it was, that first moment with your mother, to whom I used to say, "We will never go anywhere without the other, we will never travel in a car, on a trip, or fly in a plane without the other because, what my dear, my darling little angel, would life be like without you,

what, my sweet and precious little thing, would I have to live for without you." I don't even know, you see, when that first moment happened, when suddenly the charm that had sustained us was lost, struck down by what? I don't know.

I never knew, my daughter, he would have liked to have said, when it started and I never knew with you, either, not even that night, because it was before then and I don't know when, but you have to know I wanted back, I wanted to come back, to both of you but I got so messed up I couldn't even stand to touch another person, could do nothing but scream at you and your mother, faded away is what I did, so that the person standing in front of you squeezing your wrists with that ugly face was not me, it was not even a person I knew, but it was, he wanted to tell her as she lay on that bed so deeply asleep, the person I could not get away from, and I hated myself, I swear to you I did.

You must believe me when I tell you that your mother is not without blame. She has a side you have never seen. She saved it for me because whenever I wasn't what she imagined a husband should have been, whenever she didn't get her way, she was meaner to me than anyone had ever been, meaner than you had ever seen, but so subtly you couldn't know it, and it was she who taught me how to fight, how to go cold as death right in her arms just as she thought she had me back. She taught me that. It was the coldness, you see, that drove me away, that froze me out of your lives that made me go mad because she killed me, because she wanted me dead rather than like I was and she wouldn't let me go and so she killed me, you just don't know it, he wanted to tell her, you just never saw it because she saved it for me, so don't blame it all on me, don't, because it wasn't me acting that way and saying those things, it wasn't even a person I recognized.

The stove glowed red hot, orange really, and puffed smoke out the loose bolt holes and around the worn-out door

gasket. Ervin opened the damper in the pipe and let the smoke up the chimney and went to the kitchen and opened the door to get some air and to cool off the place, it had gotten so hot during that awful sleep.

And in the other room, Sally was lost in her own sleep, lost in exhaustion, lost in confusion and worry that Robert might not come back, really might not, that everything she had tried so hard to make right, that the kindness and understanding she had found after so many awful nights in the skeletal arms of carnivorous beasts posing as men, as human, even, so far they were from knowing what she wanted, so far they missed she could hardly breathe while they took all they could from her and she gave it, not knowing what else to do, and with her worry and exhaustion she had the old elephant dream again, a stupid animal to dream about but there it was, ever since she was a child, the elephant-in-the-soap-dish dream and here it was again on this desperate night, the soap dish built into the tile wall and the naked little girl in the tub and the soap dish at eye level with the elephant coming, taking up the whole inside of the dish and swaying and rocking back and forth as it lumbered toward her and the trunk moving from side to side, and continuing toward her, a ridiculous dream, but there it was, year after year, and now again as she twitched and tried to get loose but was too tired and too lost to figure out even how to throw off the covers, just lay there and sweated and twitched.

And Ervin, in the kitchen, heard her moan and wanted to tell her, please forgive me, baby, please hold me, please let me take you in my arms and let's say it's all right, now, that it's over.

He so wanted it to be over. It hadn't been all his fault. He wanted to be forgiven for everything that he'd ever said or done that had been wrong. He wanted to get back to the better memories of himself, a long way to go back, maybe too

far, maybe no way, and just as fast as the remorse had come, it left, as he felt pissed off at the goddamn mess he had made of his life and at all the goddamn people who had helped him do it, and the realization he might never get loose, especially with Margaret on her way up.

He turned the knob on Sally's door. He turned it carefully. The old mortised latch pulled back. Never in its hundred years of action had it reversed itself so slowly, so quietly, and he opened the door and with the light from the lamp behind him, he walked over to her bed and looked down at Sally. He went to her dresser and carefully opened her top drawers and looked at her clothes and what he couldn't see he felt with his fingertips and turned to see if she had heard him and then went to the bed to see if she were really and truly asleep or just laying low, and decided she was gone, far gone, and he carefully, oh so carefully pulled back the top cover and then pulled back the wool blanket under which she slept curled up in the middle of the bed and he looked at her arms and her hands pulled against her breast and he put one knee on the bed and he leaned forward, right over her, keeping his balance with his other hand against the headboard as he reached for her hand, which held, still clutched but loosely now, his ring of keys, and as he slipped them loose she began to wake, to climb up from that deep sleep, struggling up, fighting to get awake like coming out of anesthesia, so lost she was, but brought back by the shock of another person's skin ever so lightly touching hers, and finally most of the way back, she smiled, still with her eyes closed and said, "Baby, I knew you'd come back," and she put her arms around Ervin's neck and pulled him down and then opened her eyes and shoved him back and rolled off the side of the bed and ran into the wall and spun around.

"WHAT IN THE HELL ARE YOU DOING?" she screamed. "WHAT ARE YOU DOING IN HERE?"

194

"I just wanted my keys," he said.

"TAKE THEM, DAMNIT," she said, "AND GET OUT OF HERE. I DON'T CARE WHAT YOU DO. JUST LEAVE!"

"I will. But let me talk with you first. Just for a minute."

"LEAVE. OUT."

He stopped just out of sight of the house and tried to throw up. He was trying to get rid of those hot dogs he had eaten on the way up, when he had pulled in at the sign which read 4-for-a-dollar, and which he had eaten even though they had tasted cheap and red and foul, but he couldn't throw up, so he just gagged and dripped spit and mucus and then got his breath and started out the driveway.

Margaret, at that moment, had just pulled in off the paved road and was starting down to confront this man. She was moving fast. She wanted to surprise him before he could think of some way out, before he would joke and cajole and worm his way out of what he had done, trap him in front of Sally, for once, where he would be exposed for the deceiver he really was, really had been, she thought, and Sally never knew it. She always took his side.

So with this in mind she cut off her lights and drove as fast as she could and still see the road and they met in a sharp curve halfway down the drive where his lights illuminated not the road or her car, but, because of the curve, the woods on the far side and they met in a collision so sharp and sudden Sally not only heard it but felt the concussion as well.

Margaret's lap-and-shoulder belt snapped tight as she was slung forward. The belt stopped her midway to the steering wheel. She sat in a daze until she focused on the camper and saw it was her husband.

"Ervin," she cried. "What happened?"

He was unconscious. His head was against the steering wheel and his body was jammed below it as if he'd been stuffed into the space between the bottom of the wheel and

the floor. He was illuminated by the dome light as she opened the door.

"Are you all right?" she asked and he woke up, not to the words of the princess who found this frog and brought him back to life, but woke up because the bump on his head had only been that bad, thirty seconds' worth.

"You," he said. "I hit you?"

In his crushed-down position he looked as if he'd been born again, only this time with severe birth defects, no legs, no neck, a head coming out of the chest, but tilted back forever in a tortured position. "I really hit you?" he gurgled and then having already wet his pants from the force of the steering wheel against his stomach, threw up four bright red hot dogs that gagged from his throat and out his mouth like giant, bloody, oozing trichinal worms, swimming up, finally, after years of internal feasting.

"Oh hell," he said.

"Don't worry," she said. She ignored the vomit and the piss and hugged him. She had him, by God. She stroked his face and stroked his hair and told him to take it easy, that she would help him.

"Just get me out," he said, his voice different from anything she had heard. "Just help me, please," he said as she pulled his arm to get him to roll out sideways from between the steering wheel and the seat.

"Oh God," he moaned. "You're hurting me." He whined like a baby just as Sally ran up with a flashlight and the dog.

"What has happened?" she asked.

"We hit each other."

She shined the light on her father and leaned over to look and the smell retched in her stomach. She backed away and shined the light on the two vehicles. The car, with its brakes on, had hit low into the camper, which, higher than the car anyway, had ridden up over its bumper and had

eaten into the front of the old Dodge as if it were taking a bite out of it, eating the lights and the grill and the top of the hood. The lights were smashed on the camper, as well, but the bumper on the big truck-chassied vehicle had absorbed most of the damage.

"Are you really okay, Mother?" she asked and shined the light up and down her body.

"I am, but help me with your father."

"I'm not going to touch him," she said.

"What?"

"You do it," she said and started off. "I'll get the house ready for you two. Just walk on down when you get him out."

"Sally," her father cried. "Sally. Sally. Sally, come back," he called.

The sound of her name coming from her injured father affected her like a magical incantation known only to members of a family, and she nearly lost her resolve.

"Come on," she told the dog, and they ran back to the house.

Mrs. Zilman punched her husband in the side and he turned over without waking. She kept a flashlight beside the bed and she shone it around the room.

She went downstairs. She passed the high-school-graduation portraits of her two children. The house seemed fine except her husband had left his cigar in the ashtray and the smell of the wet, chewed-up stub had fouled the air.

On the way back up the stairs she shone the flashlight at Robert's portrait and then hurried up and turned on the overhead light.

"Get up," she said.

"What?"

"Get up."

197

"Why?"

"Robert needs us."

"What do you mean. Did he call again?"

"No. But he needs us and this is one time we've got to do the right thing and help him out."

"But . . ."

"We've got to help him be strong."

"But he hung up on us."

"I don't know what that was all about, but I do know we've got to act fast. We're going up there."

"Now?"

"Yes. Now."

"Why don't we call first. Just to see if he's there."

"I don't want to do that."

"But we don't know what we're getting into."

"That's just it. Since he won't tell us anything, we can only assume the worst. We've got to find out what is happening up there and we've got to help Robert through this. He wouldn't have called us if he didn't want our help."

Dr. Zilman knew there was no stopping her but he was trying to slow her down a little.

"Can't we wait until morning?"

"No."

"Why not?"

"I can't sleep. I can't wait. I've got to know what's happening. He called me. Don't you see? He called us and asked us for help."

"But what about my patients?"

"We can be back by noon if we hurry."

"You want me to cancel the morning appointments?"

"Let's hurry," she said and soon they were on their way in the big Lincoln Town Car.

"I want some coffee," he said before they left town.

"Stop here," she said.

"That place?"

198

"I'll run in," she said, and she entered the Squawkin Walkin Chicken—take out or squawk right in—and bought two large coffees and two chicken biscuits.

"Sally," her mother said, "why did you walk away from us back there?"

They were in the kitchen. She and Ervin sat at the table and Sally stood with her back to the sink. Ervin's face was red and he had a bump on his forehead. The bump was blue and swollen and was bleeding. It bled until the ice pack stopped the bleeding and stabilized the swelling.

"That ice hurts as much as the bump," he complained to Margaret, who mashed the dripping towel with the ice against his head. "Just stop awhile. You're really hurting me."

"Not yet," she said, and looked at Sally. "Why?"

"Why? You should ask such a question. After what he did to you? Why didn't you just leave him there?"

"Because he needed my help."

"How did you get out, anyway?" Sally asked.

"Someone let me out," she said.

"See, Daddy. I know about it. I know you locked her in the bathroom."

"I had to," he said. "She was out of control."

"I was not," she said and mashed a little harder.

"Ouch."

"Just be still," she said. "You know who let me out?"

"Who?" Sally asked.

"I want Ervin to ask me. Guess who?"

"Okay. Who?"

"Angela."

He put his hands on her arm and pushed her back and looked at her.

"I don't believe it."

"But it's true," she said and she just glowed, like some-

one who had been keeping a secret for so long, so hard to keep it and not tell, and then finally gets to tell it, and there it is, the person's amazement, disbelief, there it is, the reward.

"How could she have possibly even known about it?"

"She didn't. She had come to find you and she heard me inside. And she let me out."

"I should have never come up here," he said and put his head down on his arms but forgot about the bruise.

"Damnit," he said.

"Don't cuss," Margaret said.

"What did she say?"

"She told me everything. And I told her that she wouldn't be seeing you anymore."

"You did? You told her that? And what did she say?"

"She heard me."

"Serves you right," said Sally. "That just serves you just right."

"Why are you so down on him?" her mother asked.

"Because we've had it out, and I was sure, I mean, at least I thought, that when you got up here you would have it out with him, too. I thought we were going to get all this cleared up."

"It is cleared up, isn't it, honey?" Margaret said to him.

"No. It's just starting."

"Oh no it's not. It's over. You and her are over. She'll leave town if I have anything to do with it."

"If I could just get out of here, I'd find out for myself what happened. Let me use the phone now, will you?"

"Not a chance," Sally said.

"Ervin," Margaret said, "You don't seem to grasp the situation. I drove up here to get you. To tell you it was all over. To bring you back."

"You won't learn, will you Daddy? He never learns. He's

been pushing me and pushing you so long he can't stop himself. You can't, can you?"

"I can stop," he said.

"I always thought you two were in cahoots against me," Margaret said.

"You don't know the half of it. If I hadn't spent half the night crying, I'd be doing it again now. You just don't know."

"What is she talking about, Ervin?"

"I don't know."

"Where's Robert?" Margaret asked, startled that she had just realized he was nowhere in sight.

"He left. Long before Daddy got here. But after he found out he was coming."

"But why? Where did he go?"

"I don't know, but I can tell you why he left."

"Don't do that," her father said.

"Don't do what?" her mother asked.

"I will tell you because it's time you knew," she said and she told her about the baby and the infections and the knotted-up tubes and the arthroscopic torture and the eggs that each month couldn't find their way past that wreckage and Margaret listened, absolutely astonished.

"And I never knew a thing," she said when Sally stopped talking. "How dare you," she said to Ervin, but in the calmest tone of voice, with finality, as if there could be no more proper and righteous thing to ask, but, how dare you, how dare you do this to her, to me, to us, behind my back and then live with it all these years, making the lie worse every day it went on.

"How dare you," she said again and threw the dripping-wet bundled-up ice compress on the table and stepped back. The ice spilled off the table and Sally cleaned it up.

"It was so long ago," he said. "It happened to a lot of people."

"It's not just that, Daddy. It is and was everything. Can't you see? It's all this pretending that everything's all right, that the way we've lived and the things we've done and the way you've treated Mother and the way you've dragged me into all the fights and trouble between you two, it's the pretending that it's all okay, that's what's so bad. Never owning up to it. Never admitting what's going on."

"I am just killed," her mother said. "I am just killed," she said again, both times to herself, but out loud.

"And that's why," Sally said, with her arms crossed, "you're not ever coming up here anymore. I mean it. Not without an invitation from me and Robert. Because your days of running over me and Mother are over. They're over because of your foolishness with Angie and they're over because finally, after all these years of my life, I have been able to tell you to leave me alone and mean it, because finally I have been able to look you in the eye and tell you all this. You owe me an apology and Mother an apology. You owe the whole damn world an apology."

"Just tell me what you want me to do," he said, seeing no way out, after hearing once more this litany from his daughter, after seeing that he would never get away from Margaret and thinking that even if she hadn't scared off Angie, she would make life such hell on them he would never make it. "Just tell me what to do and I'll do it," he said.

"Answer me this," Margaret said. "Answer me truthfully."

"I will."

"Why did you stop sleeping in the same room with me? Why did you move out?"

"I've got to go to the bathroom," Sally said not wanting to be in the middle of that.

"I don't know," he said. "Why bring it up? It's been so long ago."

"You said you would answer me."

"I can't."

"But it started about the time all this happened with Sally."

"It did?"

"Don't you remember?"

"Not really."

"Did you wean off me because of what you did to Sally?"

"Maybe," he said. "I don't know."

"Was it that? Because I think it must have been, because I have been piecing it together while we talked and it was almost exactly at that time. I am sure of it. Was it the guilt? Is that what it was?"

"It must have been," he said, and as he said it Margaret turned away and her face changed as this amazing revelation surfaced, this unexpected gift from this night of such madness, this unexpected relief that it had not been her he was hating, but himself. A light bulb could not have come on in the cartoon image of her mind that would have been bright enough to illustrate the intensity of that revelation, the immediacy of the release that she felt, that it had not been her but something else.

"I think I understand so much more now," she said, and went over to him. "I think I do."

"I'm glad," he said.

"Things are going to be different now," she said.

"All right," he said.

"You don't have to see Angela anymore. You don't need to. Okay?"

"If you say so."

"You'll never see her again. All right?"

"All right."

"We won't have any secrets anymore."

"All right."

"This thing with Angie is over. I told her and now I'm telling you and I can see now what has happened and I can

see now what to do. It may take a while, but we're going to have the life we have missed."

"Okay."

"When we get home, you will move back into our room."

"I will."

"I know you will. And then you're going to take me out to dinner twice a week. I've always missed that."

"All right," he said.

"I want to go on a trip soon. A cruise. A long cruise."

"Fine. If we can find the money for it."

"We have it. We'll spend it."

"All right."

"We do everything together from now on. I see that was a big mistake, just letting you go off on your own so much. We go shopping together. We go everywhere together and when you retire, we're going to move up to the mountains."

"I hate the mountains."

"And I hate the coast. We're moving to the mountains. It's only fair. It's only fair that I get my way a little now."

"Okay. What else?"

"I want a car. A new one."

"What kind?"

"It doesn't matter. We'll decide that later. And you're going to start going to church with me. Every Sunday."

"All right."

"And not only that, I want you to join the men's discussion group."

"Is that all?"

"For now," she said. As Sally came back into the room, Margaret drifted along the waves of the comforting revelation that had come to her as if by gift, as if in necessity all needs will be met, as if, after the long suffering, there is the knowledge and strength to make life come out right, to forgive and forget and to go on.

* * *

At a little after three A.M. Mrs. Zilman took a folded piece of paper from her pocketbook. It was a hand-drawn map Robert had sent them years ago of how to get to the farm.

"Slow down," she said to her husband.

"I am slowing down."

"Stop," she said.

"Is this it?"

"I can't see. I can't read this."

"Let me see it," he said.

"You can't tell where the turnoff for the driveway is from this thing," she said.

"Let me take a look at it," he said.

"It says to turn right just past a burned-out house with the chimney still standing."

"It also says it's a half a mile from that intersection," he said.

They backed up and measured the distance and made the turn off the pavement and onto the red clay driveway. The red clay was slick as ice and the Zilmans slid into the ditch.

"Why'd you do that?" Mrs. Zilman asked.

"I certainly didn't mean to," he said.

"Now what'll we do?"

"I'll get us out."

He put the car in reverse and floored it and the back end of the car slid further into the ditch and began to dig down in the mud.

"Great," she said.

"Just be quiet," he said. "I'll put it in Drive-Two. That's for snow and ice."

He moved forward about half an inch. The tire made a sound like a siren. "We'll have to walk."

"In these shoes?"

"What can I do?"

"Let's go then."

"It's pitch dark," he said after he turned off his lights.

"I've got my flashlight," she said.

"You're shining it where you can see but I can't see a thing," he said.

"Just keep going."

As they walked, their shoes stuck to the red clay and every time they took another step a little more clay stuck to them, so that soon their feet felt heavy as anvils and Mrs. Zilman's shoes pulled right off.

"These are my new stockings," she said.

"My shoes are ruined," he said.

"What's that?" she asked, shining the light up ahead at a looming presence in the middle of the road.

"I don't know."

"It's a wreck."

"A wreck?"

"Look at that."

"How could you have a wreck in a driveway?"

"Don't look inside."

"Just keep going."

"It's none of our business."

"That's not their car."

"They don't have a camper either."

"Who else lives down here?"

"I don't know."

"Who else would?"

"I can't imagine," she said.

"You know he never was the same after he married her," he said.

"It started before then."

"It did?"

"Of course it did, you dope. That's why he married her," she said.

"Well, let's get calmed down now," he said. "We've got to play this right."

"I'll play it right. Don't you worry about that."

"We don't know what we're going to find," he said.

"You may not," she said. "But I'm going to find my son."

The dog heard them and barked and Sally came out and saw a person with a flashlight. Ervin stepped out beside her.

"Who is that?"

"It might be Robert," she said.

"Oh. It probably is. He couldn't get by the wreck."

"Robert?" she called.

"He's not there," Mrs. Zilman whispered.

"It's the Zilmans," her husband called.

"Oh no," Sally said and thought, This is the night, this must be the night the world will end because what else can happen to me and what are they doing here anyway, and Ervin went back inside and told Margaret who it was and they prepared to meet these people for the first time ever.

"We're drenched," Mrs. Zilman said.

"I never knew you lived so far back," her husband said.

They charged in with four wet, red clubfeet, stumped onto the porch and right into the kitchen where they saw the Neals.

"Who are you?"

"We're the Neals," Ervin said and extended his hand.

"Who are the Neals?" Mrs. Zilman asked her husband, forgetting they were there and she could ask them.

"We're Sally's parents," Margaret said.

"That's impossible. Her name isn't Neal," Mrs. Zilman said, losing her resolve to stay calm and be nice in the face of this unexpected and disturbing development.

"Her name used to be Neal," Ervin said.

Sally came back into the room with newspapers and towels.

"I don't understand what you're doing here," Mrs. Zilman said.

"It's a strange time for you to drive up, as well," Ervin said.

"But we had to," she said.

"Why?" Sally asked.

"Because Robert called us."

"He told us what was going on," her husband said.

"I see we were right to come," she said, looking at the reinforcements on the other side.

"Why did Robert call you?" Sally asked.

"You should ask such a question," Mrs. Zilman said. "And your parents right there."

"Now, dear," her husband said.

"I don't know what you mean," Sally said.

The Zilmans hovered beside the woodstove. Mrs. Zilman took off her clear plastic rain hat and shook it and the drops sizzled on top of the stove and steam rose and the bad smell of warm, wet wool drifted across the room as her skirt began to heat up and smoke and Sally looked at it and thought I hope she catches fire, the damn old bitch.

"What do you mean, her parents right here?" Ervin asked.

"What about it, Sally?" Mrs. Zilman asked.

"I don't know what you're talking about," she said.

"You won't get the farm," she said.

"What?"

"Not all of it, anyway."

"What does she mean?" Margaret asked Ervin, holding his arm.

"The laws of divorce divide things equally in this state," Mrs. Zilman said. "Especially when there are no children."

"What divorce?" Margaret asked.

"What are you talking about?" Sally asked. "You mean Robert said . . . ?" she began to ask.

"He didn't have to say it. We could tell."

"What is this all about?" Ervin asked Sally.

"Did he really talk to you about it?" Sally asked.

"Of course he did. He wanted our advice."

"It's not possible."

"Then what are we doing here at four in the morning and how did we know to come up?"

"Where is Robert?" Sally asked.

"He'll be here," Mrs. Zilman said.

"He will?" her husband asked.

"He couldn't have called you. He just couldn't have," Sally said. "And if he did, he wouldn't have asked you to come up. He just wouldn't have," she said and then thought, Could he have done that? For spite? Would he really have done that? She wasn't sure, then, because things had broken too abruptly, and because she wasn't sure she said to both sets of parents, but especially to the Zilmans, who seemed at this moment far worse than her own, "I would like all of you to leave. This is my house," she said, "mine and Robert's, you see, and I would like all of you to leave right this minute, rain or no rain."

"If it's part Robert's then," Mrs. Zilman said, I'll just wait until he tells me to leave his part."

"You'll leave when I tell you to and I'm telling you now," she said and towered over the spindly woman who weighed, after a lifetime of diets, 105 pounds.

"We won't," she said and stuck her nose up in the air and crossed her arms.

"YOU WILL," Sally yelled and pulled her across the room so hard it took Ervin Neal, that Korean War soldier and veteran of a lifetime of domestic conflict, to stop Sally from absolutely slinging the woman right out the door.

"Hold on, Sally," he said and pulled her loose.

"Let go of me."

"She's crazy," Mrs. Zilman said.

"Don't, Sally," Margaret said.

"I knew it," Mrs. Zilman said. "She's crazy and violent."

"No one's leaving, anyway," Ervin said to Sally, who faced all four of them like a wolverine backed into a corner. "No one can leave because the driveway's blocked."

Sally locked herself in the bathroom and left the parents with each other.

Robert drove as fast as he could and still stay on the driveway. He knew it had gotten so slick that, as on snow, he had to keep moving because once stopped, it would be nearly impossible to get moving again. Up ahead he saw his parents' big Lincoln in a ditch.

The Zilmobile, he thought. Holy shit, what's this all about and he zoomed by it and saw no one and looked back to the road just in time to lock his wheels and slide to a stop behind the Dodge and the camper.

Uh oh. Real trouble now.

He began the longest walk of his life. It took longer and was more difficult than being born. It was worse than walking down the hall alone and into the first-grade class by himself when he was six. It was longer than walking down the hall with everyone else in class on his way to the principal when, in high school, he had thrown a pie at the back of a teacher's head—somehow it was going to be so funny, the dare to do it like a drug, the absolutely sleepless night before, and as the pie left his hand and sailed toward the back of that sixty-five-year-old woman's head in her last year at the school, the pie and the gasp from the students and that old gray-hair full of dandruff flaking onto the shoulders of her dress, day in and day out, did she ever wash her hair, the thrill of the whole stunt suddenly collapsed and if he could have gotten that pie back he would have given anything to do so—longer than that walk to be suspended for three days, the only time in his life he had ever gotten into

trouble in school, and the other guys who put him up to it still laughing, while he sat at home grounded forever, longer than the walk to get married in the Baptist church where that wild Neal girl had come home to, bringing with her that poor boy who must have known nothing, but nothing, about her at all, and he finally came to his house, not knowing what he would find but certain and determined if there was a way and she would still have him, to rescue Sally from this trouble.

"Where's Sally?" he asked.

"Robert," his mother said, and rushed forward, as if to protect him from those Neals. "We came as fast as we could."

"What the hell for?" he asked and pushed by her.

"Robert," his father said, and "Robert," Ervin said and offered his hand, "we're glad you came back," he said, blocking Robert from going through the door, and Robert said, looking down at his offered hand and then at his face, "I'm not talking to you. Get out of my way," he said, and slammed the door in their faces and left them with each other, trapped like litigants in a courtroom, forced to face each other after telling every piece of dirt they knew about the other, like members of a tour group trapped on a ship at sea after falling out with one another so badly they couldn't stand the sight, much less the sound, of the other, no way out and no way in, like that they sat, the wives holding the husbands' hands, each looking as married as could be, a little contest going on to see who could act the better wife in this generation where men were men and women were theirs, and the husbands sullen and tough and not looking across the room, mostly wanting to get home and get some sleep and let life go on as usual, goddamn children, it was her idea to have them, and while Robert searched for Sally the tension just grew, until something had to happen, someone had to talk.

"If, uh, you don't mind," Ervin said, "I'm going to try to get a wrecker out here now and tow us loose and pull your car out of the ditch. If you don't mind."

"Fine. Fine. That'd be fine," the dentist said.

"Someone might come out this time of night, even in this weather, for enough money."

"I'll pay," the doctor said. "Whatever it costs."

"I think the camper's okay. I think we can drive it home."

Robert knocked on the door. Sally did not answer.

"It's me, baby," he said.

They held each other for a long time.

"You didn't tell your parents you wanted to divorce me, did you? You couldn't have."

"Never. I never said a word about it."

"Where have you been?"

"Just messing around. I couldn't stay away, though. I thought I might let things settle down and stay away for a few days, but I couldn't stay away from you, baby. I just couldn't."

"Don't leave me again," she said.

"I won't."

"I want to be alone with you. I want them gone. Can't you do something to get them out of here?"

They went back. He had his arm around her shoulders. She had her arm around his waist.

"We've got to get your cars out of the driveway," he said.

"I've already called a wrecker," her father said. "He's on his way."

"Then let's go meet him and see what can be done," Robert said.

"My shoes are ruined," the dentist said.

"I'll take you back out in the truck after we get the road cleared."

"Be careful with the Lincoln."

"Don't worry."

The wrecker came. Ervin and the driver and Robert worked together and pulled the Lincoln back to the paved road. They pulled the wrecked vehicles apart and started the engines. Except for some of the lights and the grilles and the fenders, they worked fine. The radiators had not been punctured and the steering was all right.

"Can I talk with you a minute, Robert?" his mother asked.

"No."

"But I thought, when you called . . ."

"That was a mistake."

"It wasn't."

"Just forget that happened and get in the truck and let's get out of here."

The Neals rode out to the paved road, sitting on the wheel housings in the truck bed, and the Zilmans rode in the cab.

"Are you really going back to her?" his mother asked.

"Of course. I never left. I don't know what the hell you came up here for, anyway."

"Don't talk to us like that," his father said.

"You're like a bunch of vultures."

"That's enough of that, you hear me," his father said.

"Every chance you get, all the time I've been with her, you've tried to make me feel like shit for marrying her."

"Don't cuss around your mother."

"Shut up," he said.

"We sure made a mistake," his mother said.

"You sure did."

"She's the best thing that ever happened to me. Every minute of my life with her has been better than anything that went on before."

"That's not true and you know it isn't," his mother said.

"You wouldn't have run away and called us if it were true," his father said.

213

"Just forget that, I said."

"You want us to just forget you?" his father asked.

"That's fine with me."

"All right, then," he said.

"Robert," his mother said.

"Just get out of the truck," he told them.

The Zilmans left without saying goodbye to the Neals. The Neals stood an awkwardly long time in front of Robert, waiting for him to speak, or to think of what to say.

"I guess Sally will tell you everything," Ervin said.

"Try not to think badly of us," Margaret said.

"We did our best."

"We love you. Both of you."

"We really do."

"Shake my hand, at least. You'll do that, won't you?" Ervin asked.

"Sure," Robert said.

"We're going, then. Tell Sally we'll call her when we get home."

"Take care of our little girl, now, you hear?" Ervin said.

"I always have."

"We're going, then."

"Go," Robert said.

"We'll call you."

"Around supper."

"You two get some sleep."

"We can make it," Margaret said. "We'll sleep after we get home."

"We're a bunch of tough old buzzards," he said. "We've done without sleep before."

"Bye, now."

"Call us if you need anything. Anything at all," she said, and as soon as they turned to go to their vehicles, Robert climbed back in the truck.

* * *

214

"There is nothing left of me," Sally said. "I have never, never, ever spent such a night."

"Me either."

"You're not going to work tomorrow. I mean, today. Surely you're not."

"Are you?"

"No way. I've got to get some sleep. I just have to."

"But what happened? What happened with your father and how did your mother end up here, I mean she can't even drive and when did my parents arrive? You've got to tell me."

"I can't. I don't want to even remember it."

"I can't wait. I've got to know all about it."

"I'll tell you. Later."

They rested and after they rested, they cleaned up, and bathed in their victory.

"We ran them off. We really did, didn't we?"

"You better believe it," he said. "I told my mother to shut up. I've been wanting to tell her that my whole damn life."

"And I think Daddy's going to leave us alone from now on."

"I hope so. But tell me. Tell me all about it," he said and they put on warm pajamas and got under the covers and held on to each other and she told him. It was the right time for everything to come together, for all to be forgiven, for the celebration of freedom from the humiliations and decadence of the past, for their future to glow in that eerie light that surrounded the departing alien craft as the two good people of earth send the creatures away, for the music's crescendo, the crashing of the waves, it was the right time, no doubt about it, for all of this to come together, but it did not happen.

Like shell-shocked and battle-fatigued soldiers who hear the story of their near death once more, like the mother

reliving the death of her child as she had watched her teeter and then fall from the roof, unable to reach her, like that, it just brought it all back again to Robert, and he turned mean as his exhausted system simply overloaded with the confusion and disappointment, and he said, he even heard himself saying it as if he were not, heard himself saying it while he was thinking that he shouldn't, most definitely shouldn't be saying this, he said, "But all in all, after everything's said and done and we've run them off, I've still got to live with what I know, with being number you-know-what," he said, ashamed the very second the words were out and like the pie sailing through the air, too late now to take them back.

"Oh no, baby, no. Why did you say that?" she asked.

"I don't know. It just came out."

"How could you?"

"I didn't mean it."

"But you did."

"I don't know."

"You are a fool. You really are," she said and turned away. "After all this, after the fight I put up for us, after all this you come back with the ridiculous number business."

"It just came out."

"Oh baby," she said. "I can't stand it. It means it's going to be there forever."

"No it doesn't."

"It does, damn you," she said and got out of bed.

"Hey."

"Hey nothing. You better get that out of your head and I mean now."

"Or what? I mean, is this, like, a threat, or a challenge, or what?"

"It's just good sense, that's all. It's just what's right."

"Look. It's hard to get it all balanced out. It's like, I don't know, it's like you think about something one way for a long

time and then you have to think about it another way and it's hard."

"Don't start that crap again," she said. "It's not my fault if you had some idealized version of me in your mind. I never pretended anything."

"But you did. You pretended it all."

"I never pretended a thing."

"Well, it seemed to me you did."

"You're the one who pretended." She walked to the window. "You're the one who pretended I was something no one ever is. Pure and innocent and fresh off the shelf where I'd been waiting like a little doll for you to come along and pick up. I mean, what shit. Give me a break. Can you believe anyone would be like that? Can you believe yourself? That's what we ought to be talking about. Really. Isn't it? Think about it. What kind of fool were you anyway?"

"You've gone too far now. You just have."

"No. I haven't, because I can see it now and I hate what I see. It's just too much. It's the whole thing again. I see that you thought of me one way, and now that it's not as you thought, I'm a fallen woman, and that's exactly," she said, and thought, dear God how could it be, "that's exactly what my father did to me. It's just too much. That is exactly what happened. After I became a fallen woman in his eyes things were never the same again. He couldn't ever think about me in the same way again."

"It's not the same," he said.

"But it is. This whole night, this whole scene, is like a night from my parents' house," she said and her anger broke into despair. "I can't take it. It's not my fault. Suppose I was coming home from work and I was raped. What then? I mean, tell me. Would that be my fault, too? Would you never be the same with me after that? One minute I'm yours and the next minute I'm not. One minute I'm pure and sweet and

all yours and the next minute I'm not. How could that be? You're just like him. How could I have done this to myself? How could I, how could I, how could I? You're mad at me because you found out something about me you didn't like, something about me that didn't fit with the way you thought women are supposed to be, or wives are supposed to be. That's what happened to him. With me and with Mother. How perverse can you get? I'd just as soon be dead," she said and pointed at him and said, "Please leave me alone for a little while. Please. I am going to bed."

He left the room and quietly closed the door and boiled a pot of water for tea and took a sip and then lay on the couch exhausted and soon they were both asleep, even as the sun came up and the rain stopped, they were both asleep, even as the new day began and their chance with it, Robert and Sally slept, separated now by so much more than merely walls.

Ervin and Margaret parked their banged-up vehicles in the driveway. It was eleven A.M. Twenty-four hours earlier, Margaret had just earned her driver's license. Sixteen hours earlier she had been locked in the bathroom.

"That'll give the neighbors something to talk about," she said, taking his arm and glancing back at the wrecks.

"We'll get them fixed tomorrow," he said.

"Should we get the old car fixed or trade it as is for my new car?" she asked.

"Oh. Well. Let me think about it."

"Take today and tomorrow off," she said and he called in sick. He was sick.

"I'm going to stay on that diet," she said.

"That'd be nice," he said. He was so disoriented and uncertain as to where he actually stood with her and with Angie and with himself, he couldn't think. He was like a man

218

who'd come out of shock therapy, and who'd then had a prefrontal lobotomy thrown in for good measure.

"We might take this tour here," she said and pointed to a brochure.

"Okay."

"Are you rested now?"

"A little."

"Do you want to go to bed?"

"No. Nope. Not at all. I'm awake now. The day's begun. Might as well stay with it."

"Then call her."

"Call who?"

"Angela."

"Not now."

"Now."

"But I've got a headache."

"I'll get you some aspirin."

"Let's just forget about it. Let it go. Let it just fade away. How about it?"

"I want you to call her. I want to hear you tell her it's over."

"I can't."

"Now, Ervin," she said and began to get rough. She squeezed his arm and looked him in the eye.

"Just calm down."

"Hold this phone in your hand," she said and she got the telephone directory and dialed her number.

"She won't be there. She'll be at work."

"After last night I bet she takes off, too."

Angie answered. "Is that you, Ervin? You sound funny. Are you at work?"

"I didn't make it."

"Where in the world have you been?"

Margaret picked up the extension.

"Who's that on the phone? I heard someone," Angie said.

"It's me," Margaret said.

"Who is that, Ervin?"

"It's Margaret."

"It's his wife," Margaret said.

"What's this about?"

"Ervin has something to tell you."

"Why don't you let him talk?" Angie asked.

"Go on."

"Well, Angie, Margaret wanted me to call you . . . you see, I had this wreck. . . ."

"Forget the wreck," Margaret said. "Just tell her."

"Well, we had a real long night up there."

"Where?" Angie asked.

"At Sally's."

"Oh. Is that where you went?"

"And lots of things kind of came to a head, and it seems that we're going to, well, it seems that we've decided to stay together after all."

"What are you trying to do, Ervin Neal?" Angie said. "Why are you calling me with her on the other line and telling me this? Don't you have enough guts to be honest about it and do it on your own?"

"Well . . . "

"You don't, do you? It's all been a big act. And I've been a fool again, believing everything I'm told, just like that crippled business. What a laugh. You want me to tell her that? How about it, Ervin?"

"What?" Margaret asked.

"I don't know that she's talking about."

"Oh yes you do. And another thing. You can't break up with me. I was finished with you last night. I don't need a man like you. I don't need a man who's got something like her around his neck," she said and hung up.

"She's a bitch," Margaret said.

"Are you happy now?"

"I am. You did the right thing."

Ervin walked toward the door.

"Wait a minute. What's she talking about, crippled? What was that?"

"I don't know. She's just making up things."

"Where are you going?"

"Outside. May I?"

"What for?"

"I just want to go out."

"Where are you going?"

"In the yard."

"All right. But don't go far."

"I won't."

He put on his lined jacket and, like an old man being let out the front door of the nursing home for a stroll, walked into the yard and then stood there, not sure what next to do.

He shuffled over to the car. He looked at the damage. He looked at the front of the camper. If he called the insurance company, his rates would go up. Maybe Wart could fix them. Maybe he could get used parts and fix them.

He walked down the drive toward the road.

"Where are you going?" he heard her call from the front door.

"To check the mail," he said and pointed to the box on the post at the end of the drive.

"You know it's not here yet. You know it doesn't get here this early."

"Oh. Yes," he said and started back.

"Stay around the house. Go in the backyard and stay there."

He shuffled in that direction. It sounded like she had said, "Go in the backyard and play there," and he thought, Well, maybe she'll fence it in and let me play back there all by myself someday.

Margaret picked up the phone and dialed Evelyn, the woman from her church who'd been driving her on Sunday morning. She looked out the window while she talked.

"And we're taking a cruise, too."

"You are?"

"Yes. Two whole weeks. No house to clean, no meals to cook, no clothes to wash. I'm so excited."

"But why all of a sudden," Evelyn asked, "after all these years? I've never known you two to even take a trip together."

"Oh, nonsense. We always have. It's just that as of late we've been saving up for something special. And here it is."

"Second honeymoon?"

"Something like that," Margaret said.

Ervin shuffled around the backyard until the sun went behind some clouds and he got cold and he came back and sat with her in front of the television and picked up a magazine and looked at the pictures.

When a person burns up in a fire, he thought, remembering a mystery he had read, the police check to see if there is smoke in the lungs. If there is no smoke, then they know the person was dead before the fire and the fire was set to cover the murder.

Therefore, he thought as he looked at the pictures, if a person was drugged unconscious and then locked in a room and then burned up in a house fire, the smoke would be in the lungs and everything would look right.

When you start a fire, he thought, you need to make it start in just one place, and have some frayed wires or something like no screen in front of the fireplace and a log rolls out onto the carpet and sets the house on fire.

When a fire starts in just one place, it doesn't look as if its been set, especially if there's not much insurance and the person who got burned up was getting along fine, according to everyone, getting along better than ever, getting along so

well, wasn't it a shame for such a thing to happen just when they were doing so well.

But what if the person doesn't burn up all the way and even with the smoke in the lungs the drugs are discovered during the autopsy?

That's a problem, like the problem with hiring someone to kill someone, to shoot them, you have the problem of the killer telling just one person about it and that person gets picked up for something and then squeals to make a deal and then they trace the phone calls all around and even with an alibi and the money in cash and all that, the trail leads back to you.

"Come have lunch," she called.

"I'll be right there."

Sally awoke in bed, just as the sun was setting. She opened her eyes and from where she lay, without raising her head, saw a spectacular giant red sun, bigger than usual, as if while she slept the earth had moved closer to the sun. It was just beginning to set below the tops of the pines, the only thing green in the winter horizon. She lay still. She listened for Robert. She did not hear him and she thought, If he will talk to me, I will talk to him.

After a while longer in bed, she went in the opposite direction from where he lay and washed up. She was hungry and had not eaten, she figured as she scrubbed her face, really, since the night before, so long ago now.

She walked through the living room and Robert was on the couch, reading a catalog. He did not look up and she walked by and opened the refrigerator and tore the duck in half and heated it and because she had cooked it twice now, the skin was extra-crispy. She threw the carcass to the dog and gave the cat a tough, hairy piece of skin she hadn't been able to chew.

She went back into the living room and stopped directly

in front of him and he kept on reading. He was now reading the classified ads from yesterday's newspaper. After ignoring her for a moment, he looked up and then past her and chewed on a fingernail and slumped on the couch sullen, not ready to talk.

She went in the bedroom. He heard her opening and closing drawers. She came through the living room on her way upstairs. The first time she came through she had a pile of his clothes, and then his shoes and the stuff off the top of his dresser and then everything from his side of the closet and finally a pillow and two extra blankets.

She moved him upstairs. The stalemate began.

Part III

The HOSTAGE CRISIS

Thirteen

In Wilmington, on a narrow residential street in a house with wrecked cars in the driveway and backwards doorknobs inside, in the dark of the moon, in the cloudy night, Ervin and Margaret lay down together.

Across town, in the apartment complex with the rusty iron stairways and cracked concrete balconies and wobbly wrought-iron railings, behind the hollow-core door with the hole punched through the inside layer of veneer, Angie and a stranger lay down together.

In the first house, in the shared bedroom, with the door closed and the heat from the two bodies rank as rotten meat in the sun, Ervin's gonads tried to pull loose and run out of the room.

And back across town, in the room built out of metal studs and busted sheetrock with no insulation, and a brown rug stained and worn nearly smooth on the concrete-slab floor, and an orange sofa with tufted upholstery frayed and torn by years of nervous picking and pulling while game shows screamed laughter down the throats of tenants, men and women pale as the flesh-colored walls around them, in this room; on the couch with human legs hanging off one

end and another set of legs slung out to each side, all four legs suddenly pulled up in ecstatic contraction as Angie and the strange young man tore into each other.

Back in the first house, Ervin was frozen solid as a sea of ice, blinded, strangled by the scream he had had to swallow and listening as the great white body of his wife shifted in bed and swam slowly toward him.

Across town again, empty eyes stared down the holes of hollow sockets. "Fucked her eyes clean out of her head," the strange young man thought and bared his teeth in a bony grin while she looked up at the face, bitten and chewed and scarred into the skinless face of a blood-red hockey mask. "Don't wake my daughter," she whispered as the man gurgled like death behind the mask. "I wouldn't want her to know about this," she whispered, and pulled him down again with her eyes closed while the dream of lost loves and perfect, beautiful lives flickered like an old film run far too many times, faded, distant, confused, and spliced together now after each painful break in such a way that nothing was clear anymore, only the memory of what might have been when it had all begun so long ago for this Angela of the sweet and innocent and elusive dream.

And yet, across town, where the other woman refused to give up the same dream of so many years, the comic flight of her husband's madness flapped against her like the wings of a bird as she paused in that long journey across the bed, a distance measured in years of determined, faithful forbearance.

She swam across the bed, undulating beneath all that flesh like a dolphin, sleek and powerful.

Ervin's gonads jerked back and tried to hide from the cold female hand creeping toward them.

"I can't," Ervin mumbled.

"What's that, honey?" she asked.

"I said . . . it's late."

"It's not too late," she said and rolled on top of him. "Oh, honey," she said.

Bamboo under the fingernails was nothing compared to this. The water torture, a drop of water every three seconds on the forehead of the bound prisoner, was nothing compared to this. This death was more like the death of the brittle glass catheter, shoved up oh so slowly, and then shattered. This death was more like the murders going on every day behind the locked doors of pleasant-looking dwellings where each person holds the other prisoner until he finally agrees to talk, finally gives in, but a little too late, arms and legs gone, faces strained beyond recognition. Who is this? Who are you? they ask, suddenly looking up from the table with astonishment and horror at what they have done to one another.

"Oh honey," she said again the next morning as they had breakfast.

"More tomahto juice?" she later asked in a queenly voice.

"Of course, my dear," he said, and sucked it down, making his mouth into a long straw like the proboscis of a mosquito. "But of course," he said and smiled at her with his long, grinning tube of a mouth, while his lips, set like the nostrils on the end of the trunk of an elephant, quivered and rolled back in a juicy, red smile of obscene delight.

After breakfast, Margaret called Sally, who was near the phone staring out the window, so that she answered it almost before the first ring.

"And we're going down to get the new car today," she told her daughter. "And guess what else?"

"I don't know."

"We are going on that cruise. For Valentine's Day."

"That's good."

"We're going to Bermuda." There was talking in the

background. "That was your father. He made a joke about Bermuda shorts."

Ervin squatted in front of the television watching nothing in particular but straining to hear it, nevertheless. It was not exactly the strain of squatting with a sore leg, or the strain of listening with the sound turned down that made his face turn red. It was more likely the difficulty of the problems ahead.

It was difficult, for instance, to throw someone overboard without being seen. It was difficult to claim accidental death from choking when you're caught with your fist down the victim's throat. It was difficult to claim that the steering linkage on a brand-new car had come loose and that somehow all the cotter pins holding all the nuts to the tie rod ends had just let go, at full speed down the Interstate, so that both front wheels suddenly turned sideways.

"I'll call again, soon," Margaret said.

"Don't bother," Sally said.

"Oh I will. It's no bother."

"Good-bye."

"Your father says hello."

"Uh huh," Sally said.

"Tell Robert we love him."

"Good grief, Mother. Just hang up. Go buy your car. Hang up, all right?"

Robert looked from the couch when Sally hung up the phone but she neither looked back at him nor said anything. She just left the room and closed the door.

Fourteen

Life goes on, but it will never be the same again, Robert thought as he faced the second day at home with Sally, neither person talking, neither person leaving, neither person daring so much as to step out of the house. The one still inside might lock the doors. The one left inside might appear at the window, arms loaded with the cherished possessions of his or her half of the marriage, books bought before the marriage, furniture from the family house, heirlooms from the family history, where madness, if it existed, and anger and hatred and betrayal remained buried with the white, shining countenance of the silent ancestors.

It was day two of this private hostage crisis, where no dogs barked, no cats cried, and where the damaged hearts of the hostages themselves beat with the erratic murmurs of sadness.

It was difficult to actually go that long without talking to one another. A few hours was one thing. Two entire days confined together was another. Thoughts of reconciliation and anger surfaced ready to be released. The silence continued. Robert suffered in the privacy of his stubbornness. Sally suffered in the rarefied air of hurt feelings. Finally, at

suppertime, that moment of domestic reckoning even in the households of silence—Will he eat? Will he eat with me? Will we eat together and pay homage to the relationship? Will she cook anything I like? Will she cook anything at all? Will we sit down together in at least a momentary truce?—Robert cracked and started talking.

"I see you're not washing the dishes," he said.

She didn't answer. All around her the pots and pans and dishes were scabrous with dried food.

"Well, I'm not going to wash them," he said.

She found a clean aluminum pot and dumped a can of ravioli into it.

"Where'd you find that?" he asked. "You've been hiding food, haven't you? I looked everywhere for that. It wasn't on the shelf."

She stirred it and lowered the flame.

"What are you doing, keeping it in your room now?"

She stirred the ravioli again. It was easy to let the pasta burn and stick to the bottom if one didn't watch it carefully.

"I don't have to talk either," he said. "I can go back to not talking. You're not proving anything by staying at it longer than me."

He opened the refrigerator. There wasn't much left. It had begun to snow outside. If it snowed much, and it stayed as cold as predicted, it would be impossible to get out of the driveway. The state roads wouldn't be plowed until the snow stopped falling.

"It's snowing, anyway," he said, and took out the last slices of bologna, a jar of mustard and the last Pepsi.

"I hate baloney," he said and rolled up one of the slices and dipped it into the mustard and took a bite. "Beef lips, beef hearts and God only knows what else."

She took the pan off the stove and went into the other room. It was time for the evening news. There was no report

on the two people holding each other hostage in the back-woods of Chatham County.

"You haven't phoned in at work," he said. "You're going to get fired."

Sally blew on a steaming square of ravioli that sat neatly on her spoon. It was nice to get them out of the pot whole. It was neater. It was like a little sandwich one ate with a spoon.

"I wonder why they haven't called for you," he said. She had unplugged the phone.

"See, I mean, you think you're the only one with problems, or something. You're not. Everybody comes from crazy families. I mean, I didn't get it, you know, like you, but it was bad enough."

She set the pot on a book to keep it from burning her. She was wearing shorts. The house was warm. There was plenty of wood inside in the bin.

"People never know what they're getting into. The whole thing reminds me of this man who broke into a meat-packing plant and stole two unmarked boxes of frozen meat. These big white institutional boxes, you know. The owner of the plant said the man was going to be surprised when he thawed them out and opened them up, because he had stolen two boxes of beef assholes."

He looked at her for a reaction. She watched the news.

"See, they use everything from the cow. The lips, the nose, the assholes, everything. I don't know what they use them for, but they do," he said. "Imagine going to jail for stealing assholes. Imagine what your name would be forever after that. You'd never live it down."

She put another whole square in her mouth. It was Chef Boyardee. She had been eating it since she was a child. It was as good as ever.

"One time when I was about twelve we had tongue one

night. My father loved tongue. To him it was a special event. My mother brought it in on a platter. There, sitting right in front of us, was this pink, grainy slab of meat in the shape of a giant tongue. It gagged me something terrible. I couldn't swallow it. It just fluttered around in my mouth as if it were my own tongue I was trying to swallow."

She put the pot on the floor. She went back into the kitchen. She returned with a glass of ice water.

"See, we ate a sit-down meal every night. Every night at six. Terrible tension every night that we wouldn't begin right on the dot. That the food wouldn't be perfect. Everyone had to eat whatever was served. My father told my little sister the night of the tongue, if she threw up she'd have to eat the vomit."

He rolled up another piece of bologna and dipped it into the mustard jar and ate it. It wasn't bad, but it certainly wasn't good, either.

"See, he meant well, but he just didn't know how to go about it. My little sister started crying and had to leave the table. At least she didn't have to eat the tongue."

Sally turned to another channel. The "MacNeil–Lehrer Newshour" was on. Four people were being interviewed about a problem. From the camera work it looked as if these combatants were being interviewed from all over the world, in the country of their own origin, and not, as they were, sitting side by side at the same table in the studio.

"See, parents mean well. They just don't know what they're doing, and they don't know how to say what they know they should say. Some of them try to gag you with a piece of tongue. Others do it in other ways."

She scraped up the tomato sauce from the bottom of the pot. She had eaten the entire fifteen-ounce can. She set it down again and changed channels once more.

"See, I've been thinking. You can't blame them, I guess,

even if they do something horrible to you. You can't blame them because they're your parents and whatever they did, it was part of something that was a part of your family, you know, part of your own craziness, I guess I'm saying. But when other people find out about it, it's bad. It's real bad. It's like someone else's dirt is so much dirtier than your own."

It was snowing hard now. It was predicted to be one of the biggest snows ever. The schools would be closed. Everyone would stay home. In the quiet of a snow you can hear someone calling from far away.

"It's like going in someone else's bathroom, you see," he said, babbling on out of control. "Or in a public restroom. One hair right there on the seat and you want to leave. That's just the way it is, I guess."

She turned off the television. She leaned back in the chair. The tomato sauce was already beginning to stick to the pan. There was a moment in the life of a pot of ravioli, when, if you didn't rush the pan to the sink, you might as well forget it. That moment passed when Sally closed her eyes and turned sideways in the chair and draped her legs over one arm and leaned her head into the corner made by the wingback at the top of the chair.

"See, when you love somebody you can't stand to know anything bad about them. You want them to be perfect. You know they aren't. You know they can't be. But you still want them to be. Don't you see what I'm trying to tell you?" he asked. "Won't you answer me?"

She rolled out of the chair and went to the window. The snow was sticking and building up fast. An inch was on the car and on top of the trash can. A deep snow can make a person homesick, even when that person is already at home.

"You see, you get married. Later, you wonder why you did it. It's hard to figure out. It's hard to remember the way it felt, the way you both were back then. You start one way, at

one place, and end up another way, in another place. So much changes. I guess you have to let it happen. I guess you have to go on."

"Let me tell you something now," she said, very slowly, as if she were controlling how she sounded. That was the first time she'd spoken in those two long days.

"I know you're trying," she said. "But you're still missing. The bad things that happen are bad, but they can be put away. Eventually you learn to treat them like bad dreams, like nightmares when you woke up and saw someone in the room and then later woke up again and nothing was there. Eventually you learn to treat them that way. You're a little scared to go to sleep, but you do.

"I'm going to tell you another story since we're into storytelling these days. I'll tell you this one and see how you like it. And then, if you want, I can tell you some more," she said.

"You see, one time we were getting ready to take a trip. Vacations were more horrible than any other time because we were all trapped in the car together. The days leading up to the vacations were as bad as the trip itself. My mother was always the one who wanted us to go. The mandatory one- or two-week family vacation every summer, just like everyone else was doing, just like all good families did. My father hated them and he'd go around for days before they began with this frozen smile on his face, a kind of grimace, a kind of hateful, vicious mask he would wear that would drive my mother absolutely crazy, so that by the time we finally left, they were both in pieces, and I was there, right in the middle of it all.

"By that time neither would be speaking to the other but we'd still go. You see. We'd still go. We had to go through the motions. If he had to ask directions and she hesitated with the map, I can see her now, trying to get it unfolded and then folded back in the right way, if she hesitated a second while

he was screaming down the road about to take a wrong turn, he'd go mad, and we'd end up going the wrong way which just made the trip even longer.

"One time my mother had taken all she could. We had been on the road for two days. We were going to New England by way of Gettysburg and we stopped in Virginia and stayed in a motel. In the motels back then they had rooms with only one double bed. I slept on a cot. I didn't sleep well because I heard them talking to themselves all night, and thrashing around, pushing each other trying to get the other one to the far side of the bed and they didn't sleep well because the next day was real bad.

"We were riding along. I don't think it was on an Interstate, I don't even remember Interstates back then, anyway, I don't remember what kind of road it was, but we were going the speed limit, sixty-five or whatever it was, and they were fussing and fighting, and suddenly Mother opened the door and tried to jump out. My father screamed at her and grabbed her arm and held her in and yelled for me to help. The car was swerving all over the road and he was trying to get it stopped and keep her in at the same time. I reached over to grab her shoulders and pull her back but she was hanging out of the car and I couldn't reach her.

"I don't remember crying at the time, not until it was over and we had stopped and she had pulled free and run into the woods on the side of the road and Daddy and I were sitting there, in shock, I guess, watching her run up the hill.

"We had to wait a long time. I don't know how long. Then, just like that, she came back and got in the car and we started off again. Just like everything was all right. We didn't turn around. We didn't go home. We didn't go see a doctor or have her locked up or anything like that, or have us all locked up, I guess would have been the right thing. No. We just went on to Gettysburg and walked around looking at everything and I bought a doll in a soldier's uniform and a

237

little cannon made out of brass and iron that was supposed to really shoot if you had gunpowder, and they bought some stuff, and we left, and kept on going, driving all the way to Maine, and stopping here and there at Stuckey's and places like that and buying more stuff, and we just kept on going," she said, "just kept on."

She walked out the door and onto the porch. The dog and the cat slept on a blanket. The cat rested his head on the dog's neck. They both stretched when she came out. The cold air woke her up and she stood there with the snow swirling. Robert watched her out the window. She came back a few minutes later and stood in front of him and put her hands on his shoulders, holding him, but keeping him at arm's length.

"Don't you see? It can't happen again. I can't live another life like the one I just spent so many years trying to get away from. I just can't do it. I just won't."

She walked away. She closed the bedroom door behind her. He turned on the television. It was Friday. The Dukes of Hazzard were on. Daisy was wearing short-shorts and stockings and high heels and her legs were tight and smooth and she was wearing a blouse that just wouldn't stay closed. Bo and Luke were running around acting like fools and Boss Hogg wouldn't let Roscoe have any food.

He watched the show for a few minutes. He turned it off. He hated Daisy and the promise she made with the strut and thrust of her body, the vicious female promise of everything for nothing, the promise that says, "You can have me, all you have to do is want me and hold me and be nice and then you can have me and I'll be just like you always dreamed, I'll be just like you always imagined a woman would be. Perfect, and all yours."

He hated the promise. He hated her for promising what she could not give. He hated himself for falling for it. He hated the trap of making real the unreal.

In the night, he went upstairs to bed. In the quiet of the

snow and the night, he heard his wife in the room below. On a night like that, with the snow and cold outside and the sheltering house empty save the warmth of the two people in distant rooms, on a night like that, they met again.

They decided, lost and wandering in the red rage of anger, to meet again. They decided, lost and wandering in the cold blue of solitary defiance, to meet again. They decided, lost and wandering in the empty air of stubborn hatred, to meet again.

There was a stalemate. The things they feared most had discovered where they lived. Those things moved in. Eviction would be difficult.

After the long and desperate night, at the beginning of day three, these hostages surrendered. No film recorded the act. No trained voice proclaimed the act. One had taken the other hostage and held him for ransom. One had taken the other hostage and held her for ransom. The ransom was for life.

It was, it seemed, they would later remark, a peaceful surrender and such a relief to be together again. But something was missing.

Something had been left behind. Or lost. Something like the innocence that existed before betrayal. Something like a precious object that had been carried every day from childhood and then thrown away in a sudden violent moment of unfamiliar madness, when jealousy and fear and the fresh, raw taste of revenge made their unexpected appearances.

It was, it seemed, going to be difficult to ever be the same again.